The New Political Economy of J.S. Mill

The New Political Economy of Economy of J.S.Mill

Pedro Schwartz

London School of Economics and Political Science

Weidenfeld and Nicolson
5 Winsley Street London W1

ISBN 0 297 99469 7

Printed in Great Britain by Redwood Press Limited, Trowbridge, Wiltshire.

Contents

Preface

This book attempts a systematic exposition of John Stuart Mill's theory of economic and social policy. The main thesis is that Mill's thought on policy is the key to understanding his work as an economist.

Historians of economic thought, when dealing with Mill, often fail to ask the main question: what was he aiming to do? Mill sought to transform the political economy of his masters from what he thought was a narrow science into an instrument for social progress. Once this is clear, everything falls into place. Mill may not have interested himself deeply enough in theoretical questions, though he had a considerable contribution to make in that field. But he did not fear to address himself to the great questions of freedom, equality and human welfare — hence his appeal for the present day.

The idea of writing on Mill came to me twelve years ago, when listening to a series of lectures by Sir Karl Popper on Liberty. I wrote a PhD thesis on the theme and presented it in the University of London in 1964. The revised thesis was published in Spanish in 1968 by Editorial Tecnos of Madrid. The present version is a shortened and revised translation of the Spanish edition, undertaken by Mrs B. Leblanc with my help.

During these years I have incurred a great many obligations. I can acknowledge only a few here. While I was writing my dissertation I received generous assistance from R. Kahn, H.W. Bottle, Jack Robson, Peter Jackson, J.H. Burns, and L.A. Rojo, as will appear from the footnotes. The greatest debt, however, I owe my two supervisors at the London School of Economics, Lord Robbins and Professor Cranston, especially the former. Without their advice and encouragement I would not have completed my work.

Finally, I have to thank Mrs B. Leblanc for making the task of translation a pleasure rather than a chore.

The following reviews have allowed me to quote articles I published with them: *Moneda y Crédito* (Madrid), *Anales de Economia* (Madrid), and *Economica* (London). Also, I have used unpublished or rare sources at the following institutions: the British Library of Political and Economic Science (LSE), the British Museum, the Senate House Library (London), the Bodleian Library, the Middle Temple Library, the Athenaeum Club, and University College Library (London).

London, April 1972

N.B. The figures in brackets after quotations indicate the page of the publication in which the passage quoted appears. Full reference to the source will be found in the list of notes and the bibliography at the end of the book.

What can be in a worse spirit than the remarks [of the *Examiner*] on the Conference at the Soc. of Arts? It is the driest & narrowest of the old political economy, utterly unconscious of the existence of a newer & better.

J.S. Mill to Harriet Taylor in 1854

Chapter 1 Introduction

Posterity has dealt harshly with John Stuart Mill. He was first known to his contemporaries as an infant prodigy, a kind of Benthamic reasoning machine, manufactured by his father, James Mill. Later, in 1842 at the age of thirty-six, he made a name for himself in his own right with the publication of his *System of Logic,* and his reputation was further enhanced by his treatise *Principles of Political Economy* which appeared in 1848. He lived for twenty-five years more, during which his authority as an economist was unrivalled in his own country by any other thinker. In economics particularly, it is possible to talk of a Millian orthodoxy (which, of course, did not encourage progress in economic studies): indeed, the *Principles* was reprinted no fewer than seven times within the author's lifetime, and became *the* text-book for British students of political economy for a quarter of a century, if not longer.

The decline in his reputation does not date from his death in 1873, as we tend to assume today. Seen from the present day's viewpoint it may appear that the most important event affecting economic studies in that period, and one most prejudicial to Mill's reputation, was the publication of Stanley Jevons' *The Theory of Political Economy* in 1871. But this is an optical illusion induced by our knowledge of later developments in economic science; marginalism was not accepted in the English-speaking world in the 1870s, but only after the publication of Marshall's treatise in 1890. In the last third of the nineteenth century economists were not interested in abstract discussions of the theory of value; the centre of the stage was not occupied by the marginalists but by the followers of the German historical school, with their rejection of the abstract approach to social sciences and their inductive, practical concept of economics. Mill's attention to historical and institutional circumstances helped to make his work still read and studied. But the first doubts were even then creeping in as to the value of his political economy, and this was because of the *other* side to his thought, his loyalty to the Ricardian doctrine. The fact is, the abstract nature of Ricardo's system was hard to reconcile with the intellectual currents of the last quarter of the nineteenth century. So it was taken for granted that there could be no internal coherence in a system that sacrificed to new gods without renouncing the old. The opinion began to be held —and has lasted down to our day— that Mill as an economist lacked originality in as much as he followed Ricardo, and lacked consistency in that he had initiated the new historicist and institutionalist trends. Walter Bagehot called him in 1885 'le Secrétaire de la Rédaction' of the classical school, and J.K. Ingram, three years later, found Mill solely of interest for his internal contradictions 'which fitted him in a peculiar degree to prepare and facilitate transitions.'[1] From then on it has been a commonplace to speak of Mill as unoriginal and inconsistent,[2] and these epithets have tended to obscure rather than clarify the significance of his work.

With the somewhat belated acceptance of marginalism his downfall was complete. It is true that Marshall (and in this he was followed by a few other economists)[3] made a balanced estimate of Mill's contribution to political economy. But indirectly, he dealt him a mortal blow by once and for all going beyond the analytical thinking of Ricardo and his school, thus finally relegating Mill to the museum shelf.

This eclipse lasted fifty years, strengthened as it was by a general reaction against the Victorian age, a reaction that reached its climax in the antiliberal atmosphere of the period between the two World Wars.[4] The astounding notion also gained ground that Mill was a cold, austere man, only interested in the more remote aspects of logic and economics, completely different, for example, from his romantic friend, Carlyle.[5]

Things began to change with the reawakening of interest in the Victorians at the close of the Second World War. Mill's importance as a historical figure began to be recognized but there was still a lingering antipathy to him as a person and as a thinker. In 1951 Professor Hayek's publication of Mill's correspondence with Harriet Taylor cast a new light on his personality; a different Mill appeared, sensitive, deeply in love with another man's wife, whom he finally married after long years of platonic adoration. Respecting his stature as an economist, as with that of so many others, the great impulse towards restoring him to favour was supplied by J.A. Schumpeter in his *History of Economic*

Analysis (1954). A revision of Mill's role in the development of economics and of the social sciences in general has now become inevitable.

The difficulty lies in that the accusation of both a lack of originality and a lack of internal consistency, which has become common currency for present day historians of economic doctrines, prevents us from perceiving Mill's true defects and virtues as a political economist.

With regard to his alleged lack of originality, if what is meant is that Mill invented nothing or very little in pure economic analysis (apart, perhaps, from what may be found in his *Essays on Some Unsettled Questions of Political Economy* of 1844), it should be quite clearly stated that on the contrary Mill was an inventive economist. Indeed, as Professor Stigler says in a memorable article, 'in terms of identifiable theories, he was one of the most original economists in the history of the science.' Stigler goes on to list six major contributions of Mill's to the theory of value: non-competing groups, joint products, alternative costs, the economy of the firm, the correct exposition of the law of supply and demand, and also of Say's Law. Moreover, Stigler reminds us of Mill's well-known contribution to the theory of international trade.[6] However this does not solve our problem; perhaps Mill did make numerous analytical discoveries and those who accuse him of a lack of originality are strictly speaking wrong; all the same, the feeling remains that there is some truth in the accusation, above all, if we remember the paralysing effect on progress that Mill's dominance in economics had in his time. Professor Stigler himself suggests an explanation:

> This is a very respectable list of contributions. But it is also a peculiar list: any one of the contributions could be made independently of all the others. Mill was not trying to build a new system but only to add improvements here and there to the Ricardian system.

That explains why demonstrating Mill's originality is not enough to dispel the doubts his economic thought inspires, from the point of view of progress in economics. His analytical discoveries leave the real problem untouched, that of his relations with Ricardian doctrine.

The object of the present book is precisely to describe and evaluate Mill's attempt to transform the Ricardian economic doctrine into a more hopeful and progressive system of thought.[7] It would be unrewarding, to take the second current accusation, to ask whether it was inconsistent of Mill to attempt to build a new political economy on the basis of the Ricardian system. We would very probably reach just as unsatisfactory an answer as in the case of his originality. Might it not be that Mill in the end turned out to be consistent just because of his very fidelity to the Ricardian doctrine? And would we then be completely satisfied with this kind of internal cohesion?

As we shall see in the course of this book, questions as to the originality or coherence of Mill's economic thought are irrelevant and unimportant, distracting attention from the real problem. Of course he was both original and coherent, but the questions that go to the heart of the matter are others. What were Mill's relations to his teachers? What was Mill aiming at with his 'New Political Economy'? Was he successful? And whether he achieved his goal or no, how valuable is his doctrine from the point of view of today's economics and social philosophy? These are the questions that should be asked. After all, a history of doctrines is something more than an evaluation of each separate work, either from a present-day point of view if one is an absolutist, or from the contemporary point of view if one has more sense of history. The historian cannot be content with the role of an editor of the *Economic Journal,* for example, or on the other hand (to . choose a review that Mill read assiduously) the *Journal des Economistes,* examining whether the work submitted to his consideration makes any 'contribution' to the science and attains a certain professional level and coherence. Except from an extreme absolutist viewpoint, Mill clearly attained this level, but we should question further the significance of his economic and social thought in the development of the social sciences.

To study Mill's economic doctrine, the best course is to organize it around his theory of social and economic policy. Economics had acquired the reputation of a cruel science, that showed the nations the road to the acquisition of wealth through hard work and selfishness; in Carlyle's phrase, it was 'the dismal science.' Mill wanted to change it into a doctrine of hope, one that was not merely reformist, as with his masters, but progressive in the widest sense of the word. His efforts at transforming it centred mainly on practical questions, which nevertheless involved important theoretical innovations, as will be seen further on. This attempt at transforming the character of economics must be the centre of any study of Mill's social thought.

Certain themes related to Mill's theory of social and economic policy will not be dealt with directly. Some are themes today held to be vital to policy but which in Mill's time were regarded rather as technical questions that ought to be solved with the greatest possible neutrality to prevent their interfering in more important matters. The most outstanding of these was the question of monetary theory and policy. For Mill, the essential side of economics was the real side, and the problems posed by money were in the last resort undesirable hindrances to clear vision. At all events, there is in Chapter 3 a short discussion of this question, explaining the reasons why it is not studied more substantially.

Similarly, with fiscal questions, we might say that broadly speaking Mill shared the Gladstonian conception of taxation, according to which the fiscal system should aim at impartiality. Where this was not so, fiscal questions will be analysed, such as the tax on increases in pure land rent; and, furthermore, full consideration of the theory of expenditure by the State and public organizations can be found in Chapter 6 on *laissez-faire*.

We shall also avoid those themes that are primarily political or administrative. For thirty-five years of his life Mill worked in the East India House, first as a clerk in the political section of the Examiner's Office, then as an Assistant, and later as an Examiner. In the Company's papers there is no evidence that he uttered any important opinion on economic or social questions, if we except some decisions on educational policy (unlike his father, who had to undertake the reform of the Indian land-holding system in his time). We shall not, therefore, make any systematic study of Mill's opinions on Indian problems. With still greater reason we shall leave aside questions of constitutional or administrative law, unless they touch directly upon the heart of his social-economic doctrine (as is the case, for example, with the system of selecting civil servants).

What this book will in fact deal with, after an account of Mill's economic education and his forsaking of the old political economy for the new, are four broad subjects. First of all, in Chapter 5, we shall examine Mill's attitude to trade unions: at the end of his life Mill declared himself resoundingly in favour of unions, but perhaps this praiseworthy show of goodwill towards the workers proved an encumbrance from a scientific point of view. Then comes a chapter on Mill's position on State intervention in the economy, with an attempt to clarify his complex attitude to the problem of *laissez-faire*. Finally, we shall study those parts of his social and economic doctrine that are most direct examples of the 'new political economy': one chapter on his attitude to socialism and another on his discussion of the future of society.

In short, this book is a study of Mill's thought on the 'social question' and the fundamental remedies applicable to it, and endeavours in this way to supply the necessary elements to form a balanced judgment of John Stuart Mill's contribution to the development of political economy.

> We have been accustomed to believe that political economy, which was left, even by Adam Smith, in a state of great vagueness and uncertainty, had been raised to the rank of a science chiefly by three discoveries: the principle of *population,* the theory of *rent,* and Mr. Ricardo's theory of *foreign commerce.*
>
> John Stuart Mill, in 1825

Chapter 2 The Old Political Economy

In 1812, when his son John Stuart Mill was six years old, James Mill who was suffering from one of his frequent attacks of gout in the arm received a letter from Bentham, urging him to make a will:

> if you will appoint me guardian to Mr. John Stuart Mill, I will, in the event of his father's being disposed of elsewhere, take him to Q.S.P. [Queen Square Place], and there or elsewhere, by whipping or otherwise, do whatsoever may seem most necessary and proper, for teaching him to make all the proper distinctions, such as between the Devil and the Holy Ghost, and how to make Codes and Encyclopaedias, and whatsoever else may be proper to be made, so long as I remain an inhabitant of this vale of tears.

In his reply James Mill soon dropped his tone of banter to express the high hopes that he had set on his son:

> I am not going to die, notwithstanding your zeal to come in for a legacy. However, if I were to die any time before this poor boy is a man, one of the things that would pinch me most sorely, would be, the being obliged to leave his mind unmade to the degree of excellence, of which I hope to make it. But another thing is that the only prospect which would lessen that pain, would be the leaving him in your hands. I therefore take your offer quite seriously, and stipulate, merely that it shall be made as good as possible, and then we may perhaps leave him a successor worthy of both of us.[1]

Thus, under the auspices of a twin deity, was sketched the education 'this poor boy' was going to receive. Its severity is well-known: Greek at three years old, arithmetic soon after; then wide reading in history; at eight years of age, Latin; logic at the age of twelve; studies without games, watched over by an implacable father.

The aim of this hard education was to groom John Stuart Mill to be the leader of the Benthamite group, when his father should have disappeared. We shall not trace the development of the Utilitarian group, nor deal with Mill's education in detail. Since we are interested in Mill's contribution to political economy, we shall concentrate on the period from his thirteenth to his fifteenth year: these two years in the boy's life began with some lessons from his father in economics. After a visit to France, when Mill was fifteen, these were widened to include a study of the Utilitarian system in Bentham's *Traités de législation civile et pénale*. Thus it was that Mill learnt the Ricardian system of analysis and the Benthamite political philosophy, the cornerstones of his social and economic doctrine. Let it only be added that, to his credit, Mill sorely deceived the sectarian hopes put upon him.

The Ricardian Economic Doctrine

The friendship of James Mill and Ricardo had great consequences for the development of political economy. For one thing, Ricardo would not have published his *Principles* (1817) 'but for the entreaty and strong encouragement' of James Mill, as the younger Mill relates.[2] For another, John Stuart Mill, who was nurtured by his father on the doctrine of Ricardo, would surely have been a very different economist, had he reduced himself to a fare of Smith or J.B. Say.

At this point, it might be advisable to turn directly to J.S. Mill's economic education, but even for readers familiar with this period's economic thought it may be in order to give a short summary of Ricardo's economic ideas which may come in useful for later comparison with Mill's.

Ricardo began by studying monetary questions. His first appearance in print was to discuss the causes of the premium on gold in the currency market, coinciding with the publication of the famous *Bullion Report* (1810). His doctrine implied a strict quantitativism that placed all the onus for the explanation of economic phenomena on the real, at the expense of the monetary side.

Towards the end of the same year, 1810, there is evidence that Ricardo already held opinions on other themes of political economy that later were to be the object of his general model, to wit, that land, far from being the productive factor in the economy, was its chief limitation; and that the fall in the profits of capital was due to long-term decreasing returns in agriculture. By 1814, he felt he could say that 'it is the profits of the farmer which regulate the profits of all other trades' (*Works, VI, 103–4*).

At this point, Malthus' pamphlets on land rent appeared. The law of rent is simply that of decreasing returns with discrete increases instead of infinitesimal ones. So far, Ricardo had used the law of decreasing returns in agriculture merely to forecast the course of the profit rate. Now Malthus suggested to him that this law might have some bearing on the rate of land rent: the message fell on fertile ground and within a few days Ricardo wrote his *Essay on the Influence of a Low Price of Corn on the Profits of Stock*.[3]

Growth

His model, as he presented it in this essay, was based on a fundamental simplification: he tacitly assumed that the economy was like a huge farm, limited in area, that produced only one commodity, wheat; the advantage of such a simplification lay in the fact that wheat might be considered both a capital good (as seed and a wages fund) and a consumer good (as food for the community), by which means he eliminated the problems of relative prices which were to face him two years later in his *Principles*. Another assumption of fact was that there were three factors of production: land, capital and labour; and that they belonged to three distributive classes: landowners, who received the rent from the land, capitalists, the profits, and workers, the wages. He also assumed that savings were made by the entrepreneurs alone and that their propensity to save was constant. He added to this two working assumptions, that the technological level remained constant, and that population and capital kept in constant proportion; but both assumptions he relaxed half-way through the essay when he came to the practical deductions, to see how the model would behave when they were treated as variables.[4]

Once all this was assumed, he needed a 'law' for the model to function, and for this purpose he chose the law of decreasing returns in agriculture. This meant that whilst the technological level remained unaltered, the rates of rent increased and that if the number of workers did not increase faster than capital did, the rate of profits would fall.[5] Hence he deduced that the fall in the profit rate could not be arrested except by a fall in the wage rate or by an increase in the productivity on the land. As he took for granted that this latter solution was the more acceptable one, he was led to postulating the necessity of removing the tariff barriers to wheat imports. This would in fact have had the same effect as a technological advance in the cultivation of the land; and he accused the protectionists, when they advocated tariffs against imports of cheap wheat, of behaving in the same way as the 'Luddites' who were destroying their threshing machines. It was plainly a hard-hitting political pamphlet.

Distribution

Then came the attempt to publish a second edition of the *Essay*[6] and Ricardo was faced with the need to revise various assumptions in his model before he could put together his *Principles* (1817). The most momentous change, and one which gave rise to all the others, is announced at the very beginning of the book, in the preface: it is the statement that the most important problem for the political economist is distribution. Ricardo, thus, was no longer content to operate with *rates*, he needed to compare distributive *shares*. As, on the other hand, to increase the realism of his model he decided to discard the assumption that the economy only produced one single commodity, he needed a measure of value, in order to compare distributive shares of varied composition and through time. All this involved a series of changes which we shall now examine.

The Theory of Population

Firstly, there is the determination of the distributive share destined to wage-earners. Ricardo, who so far had acknowledged the Malthusian principle without bringing it into his system, now took it up and modified it. It is important to pause here before going on to study the other changes, for this version of the population principle was of capital importance in John Stuart Mill's economic views, and even in his outlook on the world.

Malthus was by no means the inventor of the principle that goes under his name but he succeeded in formulating it so strikingly and opportunely that it is but fair to attribute to him the paternity, if only adoptive. England was at war with revolutionary France, so that Jacobin or egalitarian opinions were beginning to be unwelcome to the British public. Malthus decided to write an essay to attack the builders of Utopias after the French style.[7] For this purpose he put forward two 'laws', one governing population and the other food production. According to the first, if no natural obstacle prevented the population from growing, it would tend to increase in geometric progression. According to the second law, food production was subject to a maximum growth rate, always lower than that of population; in fact, an arithmetical progression.[8] The result was that population tended to grow to the limit set by food resources, that is, the long-run equilibrium between the two forces was to be found at the point where *per capita* food resources were sufficient to maintain the population without any increase or decrease; in short, at a culturally determined but stable subsistence level.[9] If food resources fell below this level, the 'positive check' of death intervened. If food resources, through the alternation of harvests, rose above this level, the population tended to increase, unless 'preventive checks', chiefly vice, came into operation. In conclusion, societies were either miserable or vicious, or (probably) both.

The acceptance of this doctrine implied denying the possibility of a happy egalitarian society, the Utopia blowing in on the winds from the other side of the English Channel. It was no use trusting in the indefinite progress of man and society, for it made plain that there was an 'absolute impossibility from the fixed laws of our nature, that the pressure of want can ever be completely removed from the lower classes of society.'[10] A redistribution of the wealth in privileged hands was *a fortiori* doomed to fail, for once it was carried out, the population would soon increase, with the poor remaining as before and the rich reduced to the level of the poor.

This population theory was attacked from the first. Certainly, facts have refuted it, and the underlying political ideology is hardly attractive.[11] But we should avoid the common mistake of attributing it to the later Malthus, much less to Ricardo, James Mill and the other Ricardians (who held a different population theory based on Malthus' second essay, with some further corrections).

In 1803 Malthus published the second edition of his Essay.[12] In this, which was composed at the time he was experiencing a chaste and happy engagement, he admitted a new check on population: the postponement of marriage by the male until he could command a situation that would allow him to support a family —a check Malthus designated as 'moral restraint'.[13] As a result, it would be possible to control the growth of population without poverty or vice if the custom of 'moral restraint' were extended to all social classes, although it should be emphasized that Malthus was sceptical as to the likelihood of the working classes widely adopting such a restraint and moreover that he was opposed to any artificial form of birth control.[14] The change from the theory of the first Essay to that of the second edition was not, speaking from a scientific point of view, all to the good, because the empirical content of the latter was smaller: Malthus did not specify the conditions under which a society or social class would adopt 'moral restraint.' At one point, it is true, he spoke of a 'level of misery' below which the poor would refuse to reproduce (a notion anticipating Ricardo's 'customary wage') but he did not define the characteristics that determine such a level. On the other hand, it was far more acceptable from a political point of view.

Ricardo took Malthus' second theory and used it to explain the long-term behaviour of wages in his model. However, he made several interesting modifications on the Malthusian schema. Food production no longer had any direct incidence on breeding. For Ricardo, who held a rather more complex vision of society than Malthus had presented in his treatises on population (where in fact Malthus argued on the basis of two distributive classes, wage-earners and rentiers), the workers lived from capital, the accumulation of which was in turn limited by agricultural productivity. The more accumulation there was, the more the rate of profits dropped and the slower was the increase in the total wage fund.[15] On the other hand, he developed Malthus' idea of a culturally determined subsistence minimum, seeking a way out of the 'Malthusian trap' in a deliberately sought-after rise in the workers' standard of living. In his words:

> The friends of humanity cannot but wish that in all countries the labouring classes should have a taste for comforts and enjoyments, and that they should be stimulated by all legal means in their exertions to procure them. There cannot be a better security against a superabundant population.[16]

It is, furthermore, surmised that Ricardo favoured artificial birth control, on grounds that we shall show later. In short, Ricardo was no *avant la lettre* defender of the Lasallian 'iron law of wages.'

With the law of population incorporated into his model, the lines were laid down on which both the wage rate, which had been left indeterminate in his 1815 *Essay,* and the total wage fund would evolve in the absence of the disturbing forces just noted in the long run *per capita* wages would remain constant, and the total wage fund would grow proportionately to population. These are ideas which we will need in the discussion, later on in the book, of J.S. Mill's recantation of the wages fund.

Value

The second main point in which the earlier *Essay* differs from the *Principles* of 1817 is in the study of the theory of value in the later text. Here Ricardo discarded the over-simplification that only one type of commodity should be produced in his model of the economy and generalized the model for $n-1$ commodities plus money.

If he wished to maintain the same general thesis as in the *Essay* that as wealth progressed the rate of profits tended to fall, the inclusion of different goods raised two interconnected problems regarding prices; one was to find a *measure* of value that would make it possible to compare the total value of the different distributive shares through time; the other, to determine the *causes* of value.

The grail-like search for an invariable measure of value takes up an important part of the book. The problem of value-measurement would have been easy to solve if only the theory as to the cause of value traditionally associated with Ricardo's name had been true; that is, the labour-quantity theory of value. If commodities were exchanged according to the quantity of labour they embodied, whatever commodity that 'embodied' a fixed amount of common labour through time would have been the invariable standard that he needed.[17] But in modern economies, as Ricardo admitted, goods were not produced by labour alone, but also needed capital, and the proportion of capital varied in the production of different goods. Moreover, the duration of the productive process in different commodities might be different in each case. Thus there took place, as he said, 'a curious effect,' today called 'the Ricardo effect,' by which as wages rose the relative prices of industrial goods fell (because their labour costs were relatively lower than those of agricultural products). He had to admit, then, that prices did not only reflect the amount of labour, but also the quantity of capital for, and the time that elapsed in, the production of the various commodities. All this led Ricardo to conclude that the labour-quantity theory of value was inexact, although he considered it a useful approximation to the real theory of relative prices (a 93 per cent approximation, as Professor Stigler has ingeniously remarked) and in consequence he had to admit as well that no real product could perfectly fulfil the role of an invariant measure of value.[18]

International Trade

The third main point of difference was that in the *Principles* Ricardo rounded off the free trade conclusions of the 1815 *Essay* by adding a theory of international trade and a calculation of the welfare brought about by this trade, instead of limiting the argument to the effect free food imports would have on profits. We need not examine in detail Ricardo's great analytical discovery in this field, namely his theorem of comparative costs. Suffice it to say that with its help he explained analytically the doctrine that (as Professor Viner puts it)

> if trade is left free each country *in the long run* tends to specialize in the production of and to export those commodities in whose production it enjoys a comparative advantage in terms of real costs. . .and that such specialization is to the mutual advantage of the countries participating in it.

That is to say: 'it pays to import commodities from abroad whenever they can be obtained in exchange for exports at a smaller real cost than their production at home would entail.'[19]

To this he added another theorem on the distribution of precious metals in the world following the line suggested by David Hume, according to whom the imbalances in payments in a gold standard system corrected themselves automatically.

The Rise and Fall of The Ricardian School

These are just a few of the main ideas which make up Ricardo's economic thought. Others will have to be presented in the course of the argument, but it was thought indispensable for the proper presentation of the argument to speak of at least two which are of overriding importance: Ricardo's model of the economy and his version of the Malthusian population theory.

For these and for other ideas, at the time of his death in 1823, Ricardo was the greatest authority on economics in the United Kingdom, and his doctrine was widely accepted even in circles far removed from the Philosophic Radicals. This was due to the fact that, within the strict framework of a quasi-mathematical model, he had succeeded in incorporating a series of ideas that fitted in with the free-trade, anti-aristocratic attitude of a growing section of those taking part in political activities. It soon emerged, however, that his doctrine not only questioned the expediency of certain State interventions in the economy or certain privileges of the landowning class, but also suggested doubts as to the justice or viability of the whole system of private property and free play of the market: thus took place a gradual alienation of the opinion of economists and the general public. Only after making profound modifications in the Ricardian doctrine could John Stuart Mill render it once more acceptable as orthodox economic thought.

Ricardo's economic thought implied changes in the economic ideas of the period sufficiently important for a new school of political economy to be spoken of, as against that of Adam Smith.[20] In practically every period in the history of economic doctrines, economists have thought that they were witnessing the birth of a 'new political economy.' John Stuart Mill, the subject of our present study, claimed to have inaugurated one of these periods of renewal. Claims to have given a Copernican turn to the discipline are usually of no more interest to the historian than in that they reveal the conflicts between economists living at the same time but belonging to different generations, who at a distance would be roughly classed together under a single denomination. Thus, in the case of Ricardo it might in many ways be misleading to name him as one of the 'classics' if that title is also used for Adam Smith. Ricardo, it is true, began to be interested in economics as a result of reading Smith, and to a great extent remained faithful to Smith's thought. But the fact is that in the *Principles* Ricardo's position is chiefly one critical of Smith. Reading the two works side by side, there is an unmistakable intellectual kinship between them, but it should not blind us to the change of focus and the innumerable critical corrections of the Smithian system that are to be noted in Ricardo's work. This is still clearer if we look at the Ricardians who applied to Smith 'the superior lights of Ricardo' and formed a solid phalanx, a real school, behind their teacher, feeling that they had progressed far beyond the hesitant utterances of Smith. If, with Schumpeter, we interpret the term 'school' narrowly, we cannot really speak of a classical *school*, but we can, referring to a much smaller group, speak of a *Ricardian* school.[21]

The sway of this school did not last long. The illusion of a virtually unanimous rallying of all political economists around Ricardo's doctrine was soon dispelled. James Mill showed acumen when he wrote in the letter telling J.R. McCulloch of Ricardo's death: 'as you and I are his two and only two genuine disciples, his memory must be a bond of connection between us.' After reading Dr. O'Brien, one might even say that in a short time he was the only one left in the Ricardian succession — together with John Stuart Mill. The other well-known economists of the time, such as Senior and Torrens, and the lesser known ones, such as

Longfield and his disciples in Dublin, were not Ricardians; that is, they did not attach too much importance to the restrictions of a supposedly diminishing agricultural productivity, nor did they fear that the capitalist system was to come to a standstill through the long-term fall in the rate of profits, nor believe in the urgency of the Malthusian danger, nor uphold a labour theory of value. In the Political Economy Club itself, formed in 1821 as the outcome of meetings in Ricardo's house, and one of ˅whose founding members was James Mill, the Ricardian doctrine was already being criticized, even rejected, within ten years of the master's death.[22]

Professor Meek has tried to explain this swift collapse as the reaction of orthodox economists to the use that certain writers influential with the working classes made of the labour theory of value. But firstly, references to such authors in the writings of economists of standing were scarce.[23] Secondly, these writers did not draw their inspiration for the doctrine of the worker's right to the whole product from Ricardo, but from Smith, according to whom: 'In that original state of things, which precedes both the appropriation of land and the accumulation of stock, the whole produce of labour belongs to the labourer.' Thirdly, there was no need for anyone to carry Ricardo's ideas to their ultimate consequences for the circles of authoritative economists to conclude of their own accord that his doctrine did not fit in with the view they had of the capitalist society. True, the 1820s were difficult years for the British working classes; the price level fell markedly, and growing concentration in the towns meant a higher mortality rate. But the dynamism of the British economy was evident to the most superficial observer, as was, too, the country's capacity to sustain a growing population and the increasing availability of capital for the country's development. These facts, together with a certain relaxation of the economists' critical attitude as they saw their goals of political reform nearing achievement, are sufficient to explain how the Ricardians' fear of reaching the stationary state, their insistence on the urgency of the Malthusian peril, their defence of the labour-quantity theory of value, and their belief in a fundamental conflict of interests between landowners and the rest of society began to be thought exaggerated.[24]

The sway of Ricardian doctrine over British economic thought was in some way restored with the publication of John Stuart Mill's *Principles* in 1848. From an analytical point of view Mill's treatise followed the pattern of the master, while the doctrinal changes that

Mill introduced made it easier to accept the Ricardian heritage. Thus we may speak of a long Indian summer, which, because of Mill's exceptional authority, lasted until about 1870, almost totally paralysing the development of economic science in Great Britain. This tardy Ricardian renascence has created the erroneous impression of an uninterrupted hegemony from 1817 to 1870, hiding from the historians the eclipse in the thirties and forties. Be that as it may, Jevons' attack and the historicist reaction finally put an end to the Ricardian era.

The Economic Education of John Stuart Mill
Returning to the youth of our author, it was in 1819 that James Mill introduced his son, then thirteen years old, to the science of economics:

> Though Ricardo's great work was already in print, no didactic treatise embodying its doctrines, in a manner fit for learners, had yet appeared. My father, therefore, commenced instructing me in the science by a sort of lectures, which he delivered to me in our walks. He expounded each day a portion of the subject, and I gave him next day a written account of it, which he made me rewrite over and over again until it was clear, precise, and tolerably complete. In this manner I went through the whole extent of the science; and the written outline of it which resulted from my daily *compte rendu*, served him afterwards as notes from which to write his *Elements of Political Economy*. (W.Cl., 23–4)

He had early acquired the custom of going for walks with his father and giving him an account of the previous day's reading while out together. 'From 1810 to the end of 1813', that is to say, from the age of four till he was seven,

> we were living in Newington Green, then an almost rustic neighbourhood. My father's health required considerable and constant exercise, and he walked habitually before breakfast, generally in the green lanes towards Hornsey. In these walks I always accompanied him, and with my earliest recollections of green fields and wild flowers, is mingled that of the account I gave him daily of what I had read the day before. (W.Cl., 5–6)

It must have made a curious sight, the father with his five or six years old son gravely discoursing upon serious reading as they followed country lanes outside London. John Mill never lost his fondness for walking, and he added to it an interest in collecting plants after his stay in France with George Bentham, the nephew of the master, who taught him botany.

We have, then, the good fortune to possess a text (James Mill's *Elements*) which no doubt faithfully reflects John Stuart Mill's first lessons in economics, almost as if we had preserved his own handwritten notes. Let us look at it.

Although not without originality, it was an exaggeratedly Ricardian book, especially, however paradoxical it might appear, in those parts where it departs from the master's teaching. James Mill's innovations on Ricardo can be classified into two groups: those in presentation and those in the substance.

Ricardo's book has customarily been criticized for its lack of system. True, the way the material is organized is not ideal, but it obeys the requirements of the argument. Ricardo goes straight to the heart of his difference with Adam Smith, namely, the value theory. His book is organized, as it were, like a wheel turning on its axle, which we might say is his theory of value; on it he fits the hub, his model of distribution; from this he deduces the theory of taxation and other polemical themes in a series of spoke-like excursions from the centre.

James Mill rejected Ricardo's plan, presumably for two reasons: because it was not suitable for students, and because once the Ricardian message was understood (if not accepted) it became unnecessary for dialectical purposes. Since, after Ricardo, James Mill accepted that the laws of value did not materially affect the economic forces that he considered important, he found it logical to relegate the discussion of value to a subordinate place in his book and had to find a new plan for the material. He took his inspiration for this from Jean Baptiste Say, who was heir to a systematic rather than analytical tradition of exposition. Say's book was divided into three parts as its subtitle indicates: *A Treatise on Political Economy: or the Production, Distribution, and Consumption of Wealth*.[25] James Mill added one more part to the three proposed by Say, for as a good Ricardian he kept distribution, which to him was important, distinct from questions of value and price, which were less so. His manual, therefore, was divided into four chapters (apart from the introduction): the first chapter being on production, the second on distribution, the third on exchange, the fourth on consumption.

With regard to innovations in content, the first thing to strike the reader is his treatment of production: barely five or six pages given to what is the basis of the Ricardian system. If Ricardo's model behaves in the particular manner described above, it is due to one constriction, the limited supply of land, and to one tendency, the growth of population. Both characteristics really ought to be expounded in the part on production, but James Mill left them for his second chapter, where he concentrated everything that affected distribution, zealously applying Ricardo's aphorism: 'To determine the laws which regulate. . .distribution, is the principal problem in Political Economy.' In the first chapter he only speaks of two productive factors, labour and capital (carrying his Ricardianism to the extreme of not mentioning land as an original factor),[26] and two distributive classes, the workers and the capitalists.

As we have said, in the second chapter, on distribution, he introduced the two central elements of Ricardianism: the 'law' of diminishing returns and the 'law' of population. In doing so, he took away their substantive rank and reduced them to an accessory role as principles that govern the three distributive shares: rent, wages and profits. The section on wages was the longest and in it he alluded for the first time to the possibility and expediency of artificial birth control. The theoretical basis for the study of wages was the same as in Ricardo, the wages-fund theory.

In Chapter III ('On Exchange') and especially with regard to the labour-quantity theory of value, James Mill proved more Papist than the Pope. He made the mistake of reducing all capital to accumulated labour without making any allowance for payment of the time element. Ricardo would never have dared to assert that it was proved 'by the clearest evidence, that quantity of labour, in the last resort, determines the proportion in which commodities exchange for one another.'[27] We shall see how, in his last letter, written on the very day on which he fell mortally ill, Ricardo criticized a paper of John Stuart Mill's defending the pure labour-quantity theory of value.

The last part of this chapter dealt with international trade and the exposition naturally revolved on the theorem of comparative costs. James Mill also followed Ricardo in the fact that he expounded as a complement to this theorem the functioning of the gold standard mechanism (sections IV and XIII). We should note the original feature that between the exposition of the real side and the monetary side of international trade, James Mill inserted the whole of his discussion of money. Thus in the reader's mind the functioning of the monetary system is indissolubly linked with the gold standard. Incidentally, in his representation of comparative advantage, in the first edition of his study, James Mill committed a blunder by attributing all the gains of bilateral trade to both countries. He corrected this error in the third edition (1826) on the insistence of his son, who was at that time defining his own explanation of how the gains of international trade were shared out with the aid of the notion of reciprocal demand.[28]

The fourth and last chapter studied consumption. After explaining the distinction between productive and unproductive consumption James Mill went on to present the Law of Markets. It is enough to read the section headings to see that his position was completely orthodox on this point; section II was titled 'That what is annually produced is annually consumed' and section III, 'That Consumption is co-extensive with Production.' The rest of the chapter dealt with public expenditure and revenue in the same way as Ricardo but improving the classification of taxes which in Ricardo's work had been very deficient.

After helping to draft the _Elements_, John Stuart Mill proceeded with his economic studies, at first strictly under his father's direction, later with more independence. At first, he says in his _Autobiography:_ 'I read Ricardo, giving an account daily of what I read, and discussing, in the best manner I could, the collateral points which offered themselves in our progress.' The works of Ricardo he read included the pamphlets on Money, which must have been quite difficult for such a young boy. Then he began to read Adam Smith, 'and in this reading,' says Mill, 'it was one of my father's main objects to make me apply to Smith's more superficial view of political economy, the superior lights of Ricardo, and detect what was fallacious in Smith's arguments, or erroneous in any of his conclusions.' Mill ends by observing that 'such a mode of instruction was excellently calculated to form a thinker.' (W.Cl., 24).

It is difficult to overrate the importance of the _Elements_ in John Stuart Mill's education. However, we would not go so far as W.J. Ashley, when he says in his excellent introduction to the _Variorum_ edition of the _Principles_ in 1909, 'For good or ill, . . .John Mill's economics remained those of his father down to the end of his life.'[29] Ashley had earlier made the• disputable assertion that the entire difference between the father's and the son's political economy consists not in the latter's abandoning 'the abstract science,' but in his placing it in a 'new framework.'

There was more than this. The brevity and bareness of James Mill's book were due not only to a desire to present the elements of the science succinctly for the greater convenience of beginners, but above all to his confidence that the social sciences could be dealt with in the same way as Euclidian geometry, starting out from self-evident axioms and by a chain of syllogisms arriving at conclusions the truth of which did not depend on experience. At least, that is what John Stuart Mill believed his father's method to be, and he was years later to argue against it in some articles, and especially in his *System of Logic.*

Moreover, John Stuart Mill made important modifications in the theories his father had taught him. Often, and it is a remarkable fact, these analytical modifications took the form of a return to Ricardo; at other times they were real innovations. Not to go into unnecessary detail, perhaps the best way is to compare the tables of contents of the two Mills' treatises. John Stuart Mill divided his work into five books: Production, Distribution, Exchange, the Influence of the Progress of Society on Production and Distribution, and finally the Influence of Government. The first three books correspond to the first three chapters of the *Elements*, but in Book I (i.e. production) of the *Principles*, apart from the fact that he restored the schema of three factors, three classes, and three distributive shares, he also included all the material with which James Mill dealt in his chapter on distribution; while in Book II, John Stuart Mill studied the distributive institutions that his father barely mentions.[30] Concerning Chapter IV of James Mill's manual, the one on consumption, it does not correspond to any subdivision in his son's treatise, since in Book IV, John Stuart Mill does not study consumption but expounds the dynamics of the Ricardian model. Lastly, though both the son and the father study in the last part of their works the role of government in the economy (in which arrangement both follow on the lines laid down by Smith and Say), it must be emphasized that it is precisely here that John Stuart Mill made one of his most important contributions: his discussion of *laissez-faire.*

The Influence of Bentham
With this John Stuart Mill's formal education ended. Before leaving for France for a long stay in the home of Bentham's brother, Mill helped his father to correct the proofs of his *History of British India* (1818), a book that he says 'contributed largely to my education, in the best sense of the term.' James Mill's *History* dealt almost as much with Great Britain as with India, and what impressed his son was the continuous expression of 'opinions and modes of judgment of a democratic radicalism then regarded as extreme,' and the severity, 'at that time most unusual,' with which he treated 'the English

Constitution, the English law, and all parties and classes who possessed any considerable influence in the country' (W.Cl., 20–21).

His political education, it might even be said his philosophical education, was not completed until he returned from France, for only then did his father give him Jeremy Bentham's *Traités de Législation Civile et Pénale*[31] to read as a complement to his law studies under John Austin.[32] 'The reading of this book was an epoch in my life; one of the turning points in my mental history,' he wrote in his *Autobiography*. He had been brought up within the Utilitarian system as others are in Christianity. This book meant for him one of those conversions that in other circles mark the beginning of an adolescent's religious obsession:

> When I laid down the last volume of the *Traité*, I had become a different being. The 'principle of utility' understood as Bentham understood it, and applied in the manner in which he applied it through these three volumes, fell exactly into its place as the keystone which held together the detached and fragmentary component parts of my knowledge and beliefs. It gave unity to my conceptions of things. I now had opinions; a creed, a doctrine, a philosophy; in one among the best senses of the word, a religion; the inculcation and diffusion of which could be made the principal outward purpose of a life. (W.Cl., 56).

The *Traités* were not a single work, but a collection of Bentham's essays on the philosophy of law, selected, corrected, ordered, and translated by the citizen of Geneva, Etienne Dumont. With a copy of the first edition at hand, it is easy to discover what fired Mill's enthusiasm.

Bentham's philosophy is revealed almost from the first pages of the *Traités*, in Chapter III of the essay, 'Principes de législation.' Mill recalls:

> What thus impressed me was the chapter in which Bentham passed judgment on the common modes of reasoning in morals and legislation, deduced from phrases like 'law of nature', 'right reason,' 'the moral sense,' 'natural rectitude,' and the like, and characterized them as dogmatism in disguise, imposing its sentiments upon others under cover of sounding expressions which convey no reason for the sentiment, but set up the sentiment as its own reason. (W.Cl., 54).

This idea was to be a constant *motif* in his political and

philosophical thought. The notion that truths could be known independently of observation and experience, he would say later, formed 'the great intellectual support of false doctrines and bad institutions' (W.Cl., 191).

He then singles out as another point that remained graven in his mind, the classification of offences in the second essay in the collection: 'Vue générale d'un Corps complet de Lois.' Mill was struck by the fact that the Utilitarian principle allowed the classification methods of botany and zoology that he had been taught during his stay on the continent to be applied to penal questions.'I felt taken up to an eminence from which I could survey a vast mental domain, and see stretching out into the distance intellectual results beyond all computation' (W.Cl., 55).

Finally, the last pages of the collection filled him with enthusiasm, namely, the last section of the essay on 'De l'influence des Tems et des Lieux en matière de Législation,' a section headed 'Vue prospective.' Bentham argued for moderation in the desire and hope for progress, and against the belief in an unlimited perfectibility of the condition of mankind. The golden age promised by Utopia-builders belongs to the realm of poetry, he affirmed; there will always be evil on earth. Not only will there be accidents, disease and deaths, he went on, but without going beyond the sphere of law, legislation itself will always imply evil, since law is impossible without coercion, however good the final result might be. The happiness obtainable on this earth through the operation of law is, in Bentham's words, limited to

> *the absence of a certain quantity of pain* ['mal'] ; the absence of a part of those pains of different kinds to which human nature is subject. The increase in happiness which would result, is doubtless large enough to excite the zeal of all virtuous men in the course of perfection which is open to us.[33]

Bentham added that it was perfectly within the scope of the human intelligence to understand the conditions and characteristics of this happiness, that it is possible to define the ideal of legislative perfection for all time and all places, though concessions would have to be made at the moment when the reforms were applied to take account of the circumstances in each case. Bentham even ventured to define this ideal in a passage of his essay, a passage that must be quoted in full because it sums up the political doctrine of the early Benthamites.

One may think that laws are at their *maximum* of perfection and men at their *maximum* of happiness, in as far as it depends on laws, when great crimes be unknown except through the laws that forbid them: when in the catalogue of forbidden actions, there be no imaginary crimes[34]: when the rights and duties of different classes of men be so well defined in the Civil Code, that there will be no disputes on points of law: when procedure be so simplified, that controversies which from time to time may arise on points of fact will be terminated without more expenses or delay than are strictly needed: when Courts of Justice, though always open, be rarely busy: when nations, having laid down their weapons and disbanded their armies by mutual treaties and not by mutual weakness, pay only imperceptible taxes: when commerce be so free, that what can be done by several, be not granted exclusively to a few, and that oppressive taxes, prohibitions, and favours do not thwart its natural development: when perfect liberty be granted to such branches of industry as ask for nothing but liberty, and when positive encouragements be granted to those which need them: when through the perfection of Constitutional Law the rights and duties of public officials be so well distributed and the disposition of the people to submission and resistance so well tempered, that the prosperity resulting from the preceding causes will be free from the dangers of revolutions: finally, when the Law, which is the rule of human actions, be concise, intelligible, without ambiguity, and in the hands of everyone (III, 390—2).

These were the words that wrought such a transformation on Mill! This was the 'most impressive picture of human life,' 'the vista of improvement. . .sufficiently large and brilliant to light up my life, as well as to give a definite shape to my aspirations'! (W.Cl., 56—7).

The eventual conversion of this narrow system of ideas, so slavebound to circumstances of time and place, Mill was to effect along two roads: one, by abandoning Bentham's neutrality with regard to the art of achieving personal happiness, and turning to 'the internal culture of the individual'; and the other by his criticism of the historical, untemporal attitude of the master, coming to the conclusion that 'all questions of political institutions are relative, not absolute.' But we are running ahead of the facts. For the moment the heir apparent to the Utilitarian school was ready to fight for the cause.

From the winter of 1821, when I first read Bentham, and especially from the commencement of the *Westminster Review*, I had what might be called an object in life; to be a reformer of the world.

J.S. Mill's *Autobiography*

Chapter 3 Youthful Propagandism

For a time Mill acted as his mentors had hoped he would. From his sixteenth to his twentieth year, and even somewhat later, he was the apostle of Utilitarianism. What happened to him after, at the age of twenty, he underwent what he termed a 'mental crisis', we shall leave for the next chapter. Now we shall describe the economic doctrines he maintained whilst one of the faithful, for such a description may not only serve to suggest intriguing avenues of thought on the kind of theoretical economist Mill might have become, had he remained within the fold, but also to draw a contrast between Mill's original attitude towards Political Economy, and his later more flexible, more humane one.

The subjects that occupied him in this early period (approximately from 1822 to 1826) were roughly the same ones that he was to study throughout his life: the theory of value, the principle of population, trade unions, socialism, the theory of money and crises, the theory and policy of international trade, and two mainly practical questions: colonization and the Poor Laws. The spirit in which he studied some of them was very different from what it was to become in later years, we shall see. On others, there was no fundamental change of attitude. But in many, he showed great promise as an economist.

First Steps

What might be called Mill's first public act was the founding of an informal society of young men to debate questions of politics, philosophy and economics. He gave it a name which he had seen used in a novel: the 'Utilitarian' Society. 'With a boy's fondness for a name and a banner I seized on the word, and for some years called myself and others by it as a sectarian apellation.'[1] It was a debating society of the kind usually formed among university students, and made up to Mill for the lack of contact with young people of his own age, which he would have enjoyed had his father held a better opinion of higher education in England and sent him to Cambridge.

He soon began to publish articles, especially on economics. The first two dealt with the theory of value. Colonel Torrens had criticized those parts of James Mill's *Elements* that upheld a strict labour theory of value. Torrens pointed out that if the wages fund was held to be part of capital, the correct theory should be a capital theory of value. Lord Robbins has described how John Stuart Mill entered the discussion and how Torrens, always a skilful debater, tripped him up with the example of the bottle of wine that increases in value without involving further labour.[2] The Ricardians would insist on taking the argument further than Ricardo's own doctrine allowed, and it was some time before John Stuart Mill really understood this doctrine. In 1825, two years after being routed by Torrens, he followed the easy way out by saying that the question of labour value was merely one of terminology.[3] Only in an essay, written around 1830 though not published until 1844, on profits and interest, did he grasp what Ricardo had meant to say: he there stated that 'into cost of production there enters another element besides labour.'[4] Eventually, in the *Principles*, he expounded the law of supply and demand quite acceptably; one might venture to say, better even than Jevons.

Population
Mill then began to take an active part in the propagation of Malthusian ideas.

Speaking of the band of young Utilitarians he captained, Mill stressed the importance they all assigned to the theory of population.

> Malthus's population principle was quite as much a banner, and point of union among us, as any opinion specially belonging to Bentham. This great doctrine, originally brought forward as an argument against the indefinite improvability of human affairs, we took up with ardent zeal in the contrary sense, as indicating the sole means of realizing that improvability by securing full employment at high wages to the whole labouring population through a voluntary restriction of the increase of their numbers (W.Cl., 88—9).

The theme of population and the dangers of excessive growth of numbers was to engage Mill's attention throughout his life. With the years, it is true, he became more convinced that the population problem as such, that is to say, the pressure of numbers on subsistence, had lost some of its urgency. But the limitation on the number of births that he pressed for in his youth for economic reasons, he urged again in his maturity on moral and aesthetic grounds, to protect women from too frequent childbearing and Nature from too many occupants. The principle reappears time and again at different points in his doctrine, in the distribution theory, in his forecasts of economic development, in his criticism of socialism. He used it to solve problems of diverse kinds: workmen's unemployment, pauperism, low wages, the inferior status of women. It helps to justify different practical measures: birth control, emigration, peasant proprietors, freedom of combination, co-operation. Mill might be called the Malthusian *par excellence.*

This obsession led him to reach some quite justifiable conclusions, as well as others perhaps less admissible, and it might be interesting to examine them. No doubt he was acting under the influence of an unconscious complex of hostility to fatherhood and the family, but, to assess his Malthusian doctrine, such a consideration is less relevant than a scientific criticism of his theories.

From the economic point of view, he perhaps exaggerated the extent to which the scarcity of natural resources constricted the development of population, but it led him to the defence of an important doctrine, namely, that birth control favoured the extension of civilized living standards to all.

On the question of birth control, the Ricardians differed fundamentally from Malthus. The latter opposed every 'unnatural' device, not only on moral grounds but also in the belief that man is lazy by nature; the postponement of marriage was an incentive to save during courtship, whereas an early marriage with the assurance of being able to avoid progeny would remove all incentive to work. The Ricardians were more optimistic in this respect, for they thought that the desire to raise their standard of living was a sufficient motive to lead men to work.

Ricardo never made any public statement on birth control, though he was aware of the problem and even joked about it in private.[5] There are no signs of any discrepancies between him and James Mill on this point, and James Mill was so decidedly in favour of birth control that any reserve on Ricardo's part would have occasioned some mention in their letters. James Mill, for his part, even went so far as to make a veiled allusion to the question in his published writings, in spite of the fact that such allusions were sure to create a scandal, mild though they were.[6] He believed he knew of a method, which he probably communicated to Francis Place, that was both safe and discreet, and at the same time ethically more acceptable than abortion.

However, it needed Francis Place, a man of working class origins and thus less bound by middle class inhibitions, to dare to go into detail. At first, he merely alluded to the problem in his book *Illustrations and Proofs of the Principle of Population* (1822). When he decided to take a stand on the subject, he did so anonymously, but the identity of the man responsible soon transpired, at least in working class circles: he undertook the printing and distribution of three leaflets (which were promptly named 'the diabolical handbills'), advising on methods of contraception, so rudimentary, that they were most probably quite ineffective.[7]

One of the most daring was John Stuart Mill, who with other young men was assigned the task of distributing the handbills round London, as a result of which he was arrested. Few details of the incident are known; only that it took place in the summer of 1823, when Mill was eighteen years of age; and that he was taken with other companions before a magistrate, but without further consequences, no doubt because they were all 'young gentlemen.' Mill never spoke of this incident again in later life, except for two or three veiled references to it, but at his death *The Times* brought the affair up in its obituary article, stirring up considerable scandal thereby.

Not content with helping to circulate the diabolical handbills, Mill wrote a series of articles in which he discussed (anonymously) the economic motives for his neo-Malthusianism. John Wooler, one of the radical journalists connected with James Mill, had expressed in the *Black Dwarf* his rejection of the doctrine contained in the handbills, but printed an article (also anonymous, as was the custom) written by Francis Place, whom he knew personally. Place then suggested to John Stuart Mill that he continue the debate.[8]

The problem that was on their minds was unemployment, so widespread in the post-Napoleonic years. None of the three sought the explanation in monetary factors. Wooler, the editor of the periodical, attributed 'poverty' (a single concept embracing both unemployment and low wages) to the unjust distribution of wealth. The two Ricardians, Place and Mill, applied the principle of population.

Mill concentrated his argument on two points: one, the explanation of unemployment in the light of a crude wages-fund theory; the other, the defence of birth control as against 'moral restraint.' It is worth noting that in a discussion on the effect of the growth of numbers on welfare, Mill refrained from using the Malthusian argument itself, namely, that population tends to increase faster than subsistence. He merely stated 'that if there were fewer men, there would not be any men out of work; and if there were no men out of employment, the men who are in employment could make their terms with the capitalists' (751). Thus he limited his consideration of the question to the short term, without realizing that the remedy he suggested, the limitation of the number of births, was essentially a long term one.[9]

With regard to the second point, Mill asserted that he had 'no belief in the efficacy of Mr. Malthus's moral check, so long as the great mass of the people are so uneducated as they are at present.'[10] He concluded: 'I think it highly desirable that the physical check should be known to the people; and I agree with you [Wooler] that each individual will be the best judge of his own convenience (22).'

About a year later Mill had the opportunity of expressing his views on population problems again, this time applying the Malthusian principle, and for the long term. The occasion was a debate with a group of Owenites who had formed what they called the 'Co-operation Society,' to discuss political and economic subjects.[11]

Owen and his followers attributed the poverty of their century not to the effect of population growth, but to the injustice of the distributive institutions. They proposed that the economy should be reorganized under the guise of a conglomerate of co-operative farms, within which there would not be any private property. In these farms, or 'Parallelograms', the proletariat would enter the age of abundance. The Utilitarians argued against this Utopia by raising the spectre of excessive population, as Malthus had done earlier against Godwin.[12]

Mill made a speech that is interesting in that he there applied the Malthusian theory in a different way from that in his letters to the *Black Dwarf*. We are not referring to the absence of any mention of birth control methods, not so surprising in a public debate. The point lies elsewhere; Mill now formulated the Malthusian principle as a law explaining long-run poverty, instead of short-term unemployment. In the *Black Dwarf*, his problem was to explain the unemployment widespread throughout the country in the years of crises following the wars. In 1825 when the debate with the Co-operation Society took place, the economic situation had changed, for it was a boom year which was to lead to the slump of 1826. Unemployment had decreased;

the phenomenon, for which the only solution was the limitation of the number of births, had solved itself on its own. It was necessary to reformulate for the long term. We are forced to conclude that the Ricardians understood the Malthusian principle so vaguely that it was emptied of all empirical content; that is to say, they seemed to think that it could be used to explain any conceivable social situation.

The central argument of Mill's speech was the law of historically diminishing returns in agriculture. He expressly refused to speak of the relation between capital and population (the central theme in his letters to the *Black Dwarf*) on the pretext that he wished to avoid terminological discussions on the word 'capital'. Unquestionably, he chose diminishing returns as the grounds for debate for tactical considerations, since the solution the Owenites proposed for social ills was the creation of agricultural colonies. He must also have been influenced by the rise in economic activity in Great Britain in 1825,. which made it seem ridiculous to assert that capital resources were insufficient to employ all Englishmen.

Mill summed up for his side at the end of the debate. The objection by the other side that must have been most difficult for him to counter was the doubt cast by Thirlwall on any probability that a habit of 'moral restraint' could be extended to all Englishmen. We have already seen Mill's own scepticism on this point when he wrote to the *Black Dwarf*. He could not now openly recommend artificial means of contraception. He now merely said:

> In this room I will suppose that there are fifty bachelors, and when I look at the numbers around me I cannot suppose that there are fewer. I will venture to say that of these fifty there are at least forty who would willingly marry and are only restrained from doing so by prudential motives.[13]

He wound up by expressing his confidence that progressive enlightenment of the people would lead them to observe the same prudence as those who were listening to him.

Socialism
Socialism is another of Mill's major themes, and one which he approached in the period of his youthful propagandism in a remarkably different way from that of his maturity. It was during a second debate at the Co-operation Society that he expressed his views on the subject,

or more concretely, on Owen's doctrine.

Two draft speeches in Mill's hand have survived. Only the second was actually spoken. Though this second speech is more subtle than the other, no doubt due to Mill's efforts to discuss fairly the points of those who had gone before him in the debate, especially W. Thompson's, they both indicate that his opinions on socialism were still within the narrow orthodoxy of the old political economy.

The central idea of the first draft speech was that the existing distributive scheme was the only one possible. The Owenites held that labour was the only source of wealth; Mill intended to point out that labour needed the assistance of capital, and that capital, though itself the produce of labour, was in fact 'the accumulated produce of the labour of the capitalists themselves or of their ancestors.' He expanded this thought in arguments of the kind which have angered socialists more than once since that time:

> What then is the reason why there is a class of capitalists & a class of labourers? It is because one man has worked harder, or squandered less, or had more skill, or more ingenuity, or a smaller family than another. . .& because he has been permitted at his death, to leave the product of his industry to his children & to those persons whom he holds most dear.

If the right of property, he proceeded, were left untouched after the redistribution proposed by the Owenites, inequality would reappear within a few years... At this point the text breaks off without Mill saying what catastrophes would visit a redistribution coupled with the abolition of private property. In sum, Mill was only willing to concede the barest recognition of the fact that 'the working people being the majority of the whole population, the interests of all other classes are of no importance compared with theirs.'[14]

In the second speech, which Mill did actually deliver, his theme is not the distribution of income, but the viability and efficiency of the Owenite as compared with the competitive system. He fastened on two points: incentive and liberty. On both counts, Mill said, the verdict was decidedly against the Owenite system.

On the first count he asserted that the Owenite system 'prevents the powers of production which the society possesses from being called into full action. . .it affords no sufficient security for the good management of the concern.' On the second count he found that

Owenism was 'in its very nature. . .a system of universal regulation.'
There follows an exposition of the doctrine of freedom, full of typical
Benthamite nuances.

> I am not one of those who set up liberty as an idol to be
> worshipped, and I am even willing to go farther than most people in
> regulating and controlling when there is a special advantage to be
> obtained by regulation and control. I presume however. . .that to be
> controlled, even if it be for our own good, is in itself far from
> pleasant, and that other things being alike it is infinitely better to
> attain a given end by leaving people to themselves than to attain the
> same end by controlling them.

Utopians up to then had erred on the side of too much liberty. 'It
was reserved for the nineteenth century to produce a new set of
benevolent enthusiasts whose daydreams have been dreams of perfect
slavery.'[15]
It remained to be considered whether Owenism was more viable in
the long run, on the supposition of some fundamental change in human
nature; whether people could be educated to love the community
better than themselves. Mill answered the Owenites, as later in life he
would answer Harriet Taylor, that excessive confidence in the power of
education was in fact equivalent to a belief in anarchism. As for
himself, he was rather inclined to base reform on self-love, by making
the interests of the individual accord exactly with those of the
community, a Benthamite proposal of the purest water.
    In later life Mill was to change his opinions on a great many of these
points.

The Westminster Review: Money and Crises
The most important part of his work in these years is contained in
articles mainly published in two radical reviews. One, the *Parliamentary
Review*, was intended to come out yearly, though only two numbers
appeared. The other, the *Westminster Review*, was a quarterly and
much more successful. For some time it was the Benthamites'
mouthpiece, and rivalled the two major established reviews, the Tory
Quarterly and the Whig *Edinburgh*. Mill also wrote extensively for the
daily and weekly press, and kept four important studies unpublished
until 1844, two of which we shall comment on later.
    For the first number of the *Westminster*, he collaborated with his

father on a resounding attack against the *Edinburgh Review* and its claims to be the organ of Reform. Mill went on publishing articles of his own from 1824, the year the review was founded, until 1828, that is, from two years before till two years after his mental crisis.[16] The articles were of course anonymous.

So far we have seen how Mill first tackled problems of value, population, socialism; it is now the turn of monetary theory. In this field he departed from the Ricardian doctrine earlier than elsewhere. In his two first articles on monetary questions, one on Blake and another on Malthus, Mill kept within Ricardian orthodoxy, but towards the end of 1825, with its severe financial crisis, having read the monetary writings of Thomas Tooke, Mill took up new doctrines of monetary theory and policy that were to last him until the end of his life. Here his departure from the Ricardian doctrine was not due to philosophical or political considerations, and it was not in the same direction as in other areas of his thought. Indeed, whereas in the questions of trade unions, socialism or *laissez-faire* Mill, in a greater or lesser degree, breathed new life into the old political economy, in the question of money and employment he changed his analytical stance and moved a step backwards in respect of the orthodox tradition.

To start at the beginning, we may note that, in July 1824 when he was eighteen, he wrote a review of William Blake's pamphlet *Observations on the Effects Produced by the Expenditure of the Government During the Restriction of Cash Payments* (1823). In the period when convertibility was suspended Blake had defended the bullionist view that the depreciation in the foreign exchange rate of the pound had been due to over-issue of currency; he now shifted his attitude, attributing the fall to Government foreign subsidies and war expenditure. Against Blake, Mill repeated and even overstated the Ricardian bullionism. He began by going so far as to assert that the economic crisis after the war adverted to by Blake, 'has hitherto escaped our observation. We neither saw nor heard it, except in the cant of the agriculturists.'[17] As for the fall in the exchange rate, he declared that it was impossible for it to have been caused by the British Government's subsidies to its allies, since he held that deficits in the capital account of the balance of payments were at once and automatically compensated for by correcting movements in the goods account, unless there were an internal depreciation in the currency through excess circulation of money.[18] As for government expenditure and its possible effects on prices, Mill sometimes based his criticism on the Turgot-Smith theorem that saving is expenditure, but at other times on what was to be called the 'Treasury View.' Blake, he said, committed two fallacies in his reasoning:

> First, that of supposing that expenditure, as contradistinguished from saving, can by any possibility constitute an additional source of demand: and secondly, that of conceiving that capital which being borrowed by government becomes a source of demand in its hands, would not have been equally a source of demand in the hands of those from whom it is taken (13).

In his excellent introduction to the Essays on Economics and Society in Mill's *Collected Works*, Lord Robbins sums the question up by saying that we should today be inclined to admit that Blake had overstated his case, but that on the other hand, 'Mill's own view at this time cannot be regarded as free from error.' He concludes that 'as a critique of Blake's general position, his [Mill's] paper is radically inferior to the section devoted to that subject in Matthias Attwood's *Letter to Lord Archibald Hamilton.*'[19]

The youthful Mill's Ricardian orthodoxy in macroeconomic questions is further displayed in the next of his essays to be published in the *Westminster Review*. On the surface it is a criticism of the Tory *Quarterly's* economic doctrines, but in fact, it is a sarcastic attack on Thomas Malthus for venturing to criticize the 'new school of political economy,' namely, the Ricardian school.[20] One of the passages Mill selected for his heaviest fire is that where Malthus attempts to explain why since the crisis in 1816, profits had fallen together with wages, in contradiction to Ricardo's postulate that profits vary inversely to wages. Malthus asserted that profits had fallen because a larger proportion of the national product went to wages, but 'this increased proportion awarded to the labourer . . .takes place without being accompanied with . . .an increased demand for labour or an increase in the value of the same quantity of labour.'[21] Mill could not see, what Malthus was unable to express, that the paradox is solved if we assume that this larger share of wages was awarded from a diminished national income. Malthus's problem was that he did not separate saving from investment; he was unable to explain how an increase in saving might be accompanied by a decrease in the demand for labour. So that when Malthus noted that over-production of some goods had not been accompanied by a shortage of others, as Say's law required, and stated that 'no-one ever heard, as a matter of fact, from competent authority,

that for some years together since the peace there was a marked
deficiency of produce in any one considerable department of industry,'
Mill felt it was enough to ridicule the appeal to some unnamed
'competent authority.'

Shortly afterwards, however, Mill was to show signs of having
departed from the orthodox Ricardian monetary position, and moved
towards an anti-bullionist one. Authors usually misunderstand Mill's
position and praise him for his anti-Ricardianism in monetary matters,
assuming that he moved towards a more 'Keynesian' position, but they
are wrong. Mill, once a metallic standard obtained, recommended a
more passive attitude to monetary phenomena than that held by
Ricardo and his disciples, let alone the Attwoods and other Birmingham
reflationists, the true 'Keynesians' in this plot. In 1826, Mill published
in the annual review, the *Parliamentary Review, Session of 1826*, an
article entitled 'Paper Currency and Commercial Distress' in which the
broad contours of his monetary theory begin to emerge: he there
showed himself to be a forerunner of what would later be termed the
'Banking School,' and an early disciple of Thomas Tooke (1774–1858).

This article bears the impress of the economic crisis that occurred at
the end of 1825. The very first sentence shows a marked change of tone
from that in which he criticized Blake for having asserted the existence
of an economic depression at the end of the wars:

> The opening of Parliament in February, 1826, found the nation still
> in the crisis of one of those commercial revulsions, to which all
> commercial countries are liable, but which, partly from the
> unrivalled magnitude of our commercial transactions, partly from
> vicious legislation, are more frequent and more ruinous in our own
> country than in any other.[22]

This *volte face* on Mill's part is yet another proof that the 'revulsion'
of 1825 was an important factor in forcing British economic opinion to
face the realities of early capitalism. In 1798, Malthus was still able to
speak of cycles as phenomena that only watchful observers would
perceive.[23] By 1830 the situation was very different. The post-war
depression, the controversy in 1819 between supporters of monetary
orthodoxy and those in favour of deliberate reflation; the fever of
speculation in 1825; the legalizing of trade unions in the same year,
followed by a wave of strikes; the 1825–6 slump, with the resulting
epidemic of bankruptcies and labour disputes; these were facts that
opened the eyes of the British, John Stuart Mill among them, to the

real problems and conflicts of interest in a capitalist country.[24]

In this article the most important innovation in theory lies in a point Mill was to maintain throughout his life: the distinction between speculative periods and normal periods. 'The proximate cause of the commercial crisis was speculation.' Against it the Government was powerless. 'The cause of the evil is one which legislation cannot reach —the universal propensity of mankind to over-estimate the chances in their own favour.'[25]

Mill thus attributed the crisis to the working of a non-monetary cause; our account of his thought would be incomplete if we did not add that he expressly denied the efficacy of possible monetary causes. It is true that he always admitted that an inconvertible paper money system was inherently inflationary. But in the case of a convertible paper currency all his fears of dysfunctions in the economy vanished. In his view the monetary supply in a convertible paper currency system was a passive variable: fluctuations in the money supply did not cause fluctuations in prices but followed in their wake. Every deliberate attempt to make the money supply completely independent of the economy's monetary demand was useless in times of rising activity (since bank and commercial credit made the supply infinitely elastic), and dangerous in times of revulsion (since it provoked unjustified failures through lack of liquidity).

What strikes the modern reader as strange is that Mill should hold both that money supply was a passive variable of the amount of trade, hence not causing inflation, and that an inconvertible paper money system led to indefinite price-rises, hence causing inflation. This seems a contradiction but may not be one if Mill's theory of the price level determinants is correctly understood.

For Mill the level of prices was determined at any moment in time by the demand for money, or ultimately by the 'animal spirits' of the business community, if we may use this Keynesian expression; within the limits set by the money supply, that is for Mill, by the 'purchasing power' of the public. Only when this purchasing power artificially widened could money supply have an impact on prices.

Mill defined this purchasing power in very wide terms: it consisted of coins and bank notes held by the public, bank deposits in its name and the credit worthiness of each of its members. Hence, banks did not create new purchasing power when they discounted 'real' bills, because they took from the available credit-worthiness of the public and added to its deposits. Such discounting was, to use an expression of Gurley and Shaw's, creation of 'inside' money, and would not of itself result in a price rise.[26] Banks, however did add to the total purchasing power of the community if they discounted bills beyond what the credit-worthiness of the different members of the public justified; the Government also added to the total purchasing power, i.e., created 'outside' money, by printing notes to finance a deficit.[27] However the external sector did not do likewise when gold came in due to a trade surplus. The creation of such 'outside' money, which could cause an inflation, was hence tightly held in check if the country was on the gold standard.

In the view of the Government and Parliament, the fever of speculation and subsequent crisis in 1825–6 had been due not to psychological causes as Tooke and Mill held, but to monetary causes. In fact, it had been decided to put a stop to the issue of notes for small sums. Mill attacked this decision with a very revealing argument. To begin with, he denied that the increase in issue could cause the speculative fever; it was speculation as an exogenous phenomenon that produced an increase in circulation. Secondly, he affirmed that in any case, the prohibition on issues of notes would have little effect in moments of speculation, as credit and bills of exchange were more than sufficient to cover needs in times of euphoria. Thirdly, he stressed the advantage of a convertible paper currency over a purely metallic currency in a crisis, when a timely issue could prevent many unjustified bankruptcies. The remedy lay in reinforcing the banks' security, in repealing the Corn Laws and Usury Laws, which artificially increased economic fluctuations, and in allowing the money supply to fluctuate, as far as convertibility permitted, in accordance with the needs of traffic.

Hence, it must not be thought that because Mill moved away from Ricardian orthodoxy, he supported an active anti-cyclical policy. Quite the contrary; his hostility to a system of inconvertible paper currency favoured by many reflationists, was an essential part of his monetary thought. As he held money supply to be a passive variable respecting business activity, he could not accept doctrines pressing for a deliberate increase in the quantity of money in order to cure deflation; in his view these doctrines meant nothing more than allowing the Government to swindle part of the community through the 'forced savings' inherent in an inflation. It especially irritated him that such positions should be taken up by people with whom he agreed politically, for he feared that Radicalism would thereby acquire a reputation for financial irresponsibility. This is evidenced in the article he published in 1833 against Thomas Attwood, who had played a prominent part in the struggle for the Reform of Parliament, as the able organizer of the Birmingham Political Union. In the essay titled 'The Currency Juggle,' he made a severe attack on Attwood for tarnishing the good name of the Reformers by advocating a systematic depreciation of the currency, which he considered as a scheme 'for the confiscation of private property.'[28] Mill admits that, for Attwood, 'paper money is not capital, but brings capital into fuller employment... High prices occasion 'increased consumption,' 'increased demand' and thereby give a stimulus to production.' To this Mill's reply is that 'what makes a demand for commodities is commodities and not bits of paper' (190–1).

The most famous article of the whole series on monetary questions is the one titled 'The Influence of Consumption upon Production,' written around 1830 but not published until 1844 with the other *Essays on Some Unsettled Questions of Political Economy*. This work has puzzled many historians.[29] In fact, by asserting that Say's law is not always valid in the short run, and this due to monetary reasons, Mill appeared to be groping towards modern macroeconomic theories; but such an interpretation would not fit in with Mill's membership of the Banking School, or with an assumption underlying all his work, namely, the impossibility of prolonged involuntary unemployment.

In this article Mill started out with a reassertion of his ideas on the alternation of normal and speculative periods. He went as far as to say that 'except during short periods of transition, there is almost always either great briskness of business or great stagnation.' This he attributed to the great complexity of the modern mercantile world which continually gave rise to errors of information and unreasonable hopes and fears.

Mill went on to remark the existence of a school of economists who deduced from these fluctuations the possibility of a general superabundance of production. Orthodox economists had generally rejected this possibility, Mill said, with the argument that 'whoever offers a commodity for sale, desires to obtain a commodity in exchange for it.' This orthodox view did not quite satisfy Mill now, as can be seen in the following reflections (culled from a longer passage):

> This argument is evidently founded on the supposition of a state of barter; and, on that supposition, it is perfectly incontestable... If,

however, we suppose that money is used, these propositions cease to be exactly true... In the case of barter, the selling and the buying are simultaneously confounded in one operation... The effect of the employment of money...is, that it enables this one act of interchange to be divided into two separate acts or operations.

The consequence is that 'the buying and selling being now separated, it may very well occur, that there may be, at some given time, a very general inclination to sell with as little delay as possible, accompanied with an equally general inclination to defer all purchases as long as possible.' In other words,

In extreme cases, money is collected in masses, and hoarded; in the milder cases, people merely defer parting with their money, or coming under any new engagements to part with it. But the result is, that all commodities fall in price, or become unsaleable.[30]

Here was, in Mill's view, the origin of such a widely held belief in the possibility of general overproduction. Naturally, Mill held that the difficulties he was outlining were temporary and in the long run 'the essentials of the doctrine are preserved when it is allowed that there cannot be permanent excess of production, or of accumulation.'

Our Keynesian times could not refrain from hailing this article as an important contribution to economic thought and wondering why Mill did not follow it up with more radical departures from the 'classical' position. However, we should beware of taking it out of context. To say that the existence of money allows psychological factors to affect the economic situation is not the same as to say that the cycle may be controlled by means of deliberate variations in the money supply (and still less by variations in public expenditure). The existence of money, it is true, in Mill's view enabled hoarding to take place and a certain deferment in the sale of commodities; but since money supply was conceived as a passive variable, there was nothing to guarantee that an active monetary policy would restore the sway of Say's Law. Mill was not moving nearer to Malthus, Sismondi and Attwood, when he wrote this essay. Quite the contrary; he was moving still further away from them than the strict Ricardians, and of course, further than the other less crude quantity theorists, such as Say himself.

Confirmation of the fact that Mill held monetary supply to be a passive variable is to be found more clearly than anywhere else in his article 'The Currency Question.' It was published in the *Westminster Review* in June 1844 just after Peel's Law separating the Issue and Discount Departments of the Bank of England. Here Mill clearly sides against this measure and takes up arms in defence of the most distinguished member of the 'Banking School', Thomas Tooke, against the most bellicose member of the 'Currency School', Robert Torrens.[31]

The Currency School followed in the tradition begun by Ricardo of regarding with suspicion the Bank of England's privilege of issuing currency. They held that if the monetary system was not to distort the working of the real side of the economy, it was necessary that a convertible paper money should fluctuate as if the currency were wholly metallic; and this to avoid having the issues follow the needs of the discount department. Logically, the Currency School's attitude should have been to demand a control over credit, but both this school and the Banking School pursued the·will of the wisp of an automatic monetary policy (*pace* Friedman).

The Banking School, on the other hand, considered that once the long-term stability of the monetary standard was guaranteed by convertibility, it was all to the good that the movements of the money supply should be different from those which would take place if the currency were wholly metallic. The demand for means of payment under a system of convertibility was a function solely of the needs of trade (and the requirements of safety in times of depression) and therefore to restrict it artificially could only bring disturbances. Remember how widely Mill defined money supply. The most striking passage in the article on this question is the following:

> It seems not easy to understand how an increased creation of the written evidences of credit called bank notes can, of itself, create an additional demand, or occasion a rise of price. Admitting bank notes to be money (which is, in truth, a mere question of language), what does the person do who issues them, but take so much from the third element of purchasing power, namely credit, and add it to the first element, money in hand —making no addition whatever to the total amount?[32]

Mill's treatment of commercial crises and the notion of general overproduction in the *Principles* (1848) confirms the above interpretation of the 'Essay on Consumption and Production.' In the *Principles* Mill insisted on the importance of the question:

The point is fundamental; any difference of opinion on it involves radically different conceptions of Political Economy, especially in its practical aspect. On the one view, we have only to consider how a sufficient production may be combined with the best possible distribution; but on the other there is a third thing to be considered —how a market can be created for produce, or how production can be limited to the capabilities of the market. Besides; a theory so essentially self-contradictory cannot intrude itself without carrying confusion into the very heart of the subject. . . This error has been, I conceive, fatal to the systems, as systems, of. . .three distinguished economists. . . Malthus, Chalmers, and Sismondi.[33]

A reading of the treatise leaves no room for doubt as to which side Mill was on. He adds a new type of commercial crisis to the one he had studied in 1826: that arising from the contraction of loanable funds due to investment in fixed capital, to capital exports, or to increases in raw material prices.[34] He admits that besides the tendency to hoard in times of crisis, the secular decline in the rate of profits is another fact that may seem to support the theory of general excesses of production.[35] But, in sum, the only measure of monetary policy that really wins his approval is the suspension of Peel's law during the 1847 crisis. The later articles confirm that Mill had argued himself into a blind alley.[36] The generations of British students who were to learn their monetary theory from the *Principles* might have found better teachers in other economists among Mill's contemporaries.

Such a lengthy study of Mill's monetary thought going far beyond the bound of his youth was necessary, not so much to dispose of mistaken interpretations of his theory of money, but rather to underline how peripheral money questions were to his New Political Economy. The currency system could be designed so that it managed itself; and the recommendation of any cure for social evils based on the manipulation of the monetary system could be left to cranks. We shall return to these questions no more.

Foreign Trade

Another major topic dealt with by Mill in this period of youthful propagandism is that of free trade, both in its practical and its theoretical aspects. In 1825, the year he made his sarcastic attack on Malthus, he published an article titled 'The Corn Laws' and thus entered upon one of Ricardo's favourite subjects. In January, 1827, he returned to the attack with another article titled 'The New Corn Law.'

Both appeared in the *Westminster Review*.

The struggle against the Corn Laws in Great Britain can be divided into two periods. The first, from the end of the Napoleonic Wars in 1816 to the Corn Law of 1827, is characterized by the predominance of economists in the discussion. It was a period abounding in theoretical argument, though there were also popular works such as the *Catechism on the Corn Laws* by Perronet Thompson (editor of the *Westminster*), which Mill reviewed with warm praise in his article of 1827, the second of those referred to above. Considering it futile to fight against these laws so long as Parliament remained in the hands of the landowners, the Radicals and the Reformers in general concentrated their forces on achieving a reform of the electoral law. When this was achieved in 1832, the new campaign in favour of free trade in corn did not get going until the middle of 1835, and by then its character was quite changed. In this second period, culminating in the repeal of the Corn Laws in 1846, it was not the economists who directed the struggle, but the leaders of the 'Anti-Corn-Law League.' In G.M. Young's words: 'The case for Free Trade was taken out of their hands by men who had learnt their economics in the counting house, their logic on the platform, and their rhetoric in the pulpit.'[37] It is not true however that in this later period the economists were remiss in supporting a cause which had been their own years before, as Mr Grampp has asserted, in *The Manchester School of Economics* (1960), though they may not have agreed wholeheartedly with the League's methods and its dogmatism.

Mill's 1825 article is written in the confident tones of one who sees his ideas about to be realized. For one thing, he takes the principles that justify his policy for granted. 'One part of the argument,' he says, '. . .we hope and believe that we may safely omit'; and that is the demonstration of 'the beneficial tendency of free trade in general.'[38] Then he tries to split the ranks of those who opposed the measure. He presents the landlord as the sole economic agent with an interest in the protection of agriculture, for the farmer, he says, like all capitalists, only seeks high profits, and (according to Ricardian theory) these are incompatible with high money wages and rents. He even tries to conciliate the landlord, who 'if he has an interest opposed to that of the community, he has also an interest in common with them' (64); for it is to his advantage that food should be cheap and poor rates at a minimum, and moreover the price of wheat would not fall as much as he feared with free imports. In any case, Mill was ready to make the same concessions as Ricardo: that the tariff should be gradually lowered and a moderate levy maintained to compensate agriculture for the special tax burdens it bore.

The tone is rather different in the 1827 article. With the chagrin of sour grapes, he exclaims:

> Let those be disappointed who looked for any thing better: we confess that our hopes were never very sanguine. It would argue little experience of human affairs to expect from monopolists the abandonment of a monopoly; from landlords the voluntary abatement of rent.[39]

And he plunges into a disillusioned analysis of the proposed law and the speech of its defender, Mr Canning, and insists on a conflict of interests between landlords and the rest of the community.

Mill took part in the second stage of the free-trade movement, but this time as a foot-soldier in the ranks. He published the essay on the theory of international trade (see below) and drew up the major part at least of the text of a petition adopted in a free trade meeting in Kensington on 15 June 1841.[40] The names of some of the participants in the meeting show that it is not true that political economists and erstwhile Radicals took no interest in the subject of Corn Laws in the forties. It must be admitted, however, that this did not signify outstanding activity.[41]

For posterity, Mill's most important contribution on questions of international trade is the famous article 'Of the Laws of Interchange Between Nations; and the Distribution of the Gains of Commerce among the Countries of the Commercial World,' which is another of those that he wrote around 1830 but did not publish until 1844.[42]

In this article Mill displays his best qualities as a theoretical economist. He expounds a subject of considerable complexity with great clarity; the tone is scientific, the practical consequences of high interest. Mill's aim was to carry Ricardo's study of foreign trade a stage further, by adding to his demonstration of how it produces a net advantage to the world, an analysis of how this advantage is divided among the trading countries. To summarize his argument in modern terms, Mill assumes in the first place a situation of barter; he shows how within the limits set by the real costs within each country, the advantage of trade will be shared out according to the elasticity and intensity of the reciprocal demands. Then he adds the use of money, showing to his satisfaction that it does not alter that conclusion in any way. The third step is to abandon the assumption of free carriage and show that this cost will not necessarily be divided out in the same proportion as the advantage of trade. Then he goes on to examine the effect of taxes on exports and imports on the commodity terms of trade and the effect of technological advances.[43]

Further he elucidates the valid elements in the popular concern to expand exports, to avoid competition with other countries in foreign markets, and to seek protection against the transitory effects of freeing trade. Also important is his demonstration that the payment of a tribute to a foreign country, such as Ireland's remittances of rents to absentee landlords, worsens the commodity terms of trade of the paying country. It is not to be wondered at that Mill was disgusted with the crude propaganda of the Anti-Corn-Law League!

Finally, though this does not strictly belong to the period under consideration, a mention should be made of that pioneering, though analytically less important, discovery of Mill's in the *Principles*: the 'infant industry' argument —a question too familiar to require detailed elucidation.

Emigration and the Poor Laws

This completes the account of the economic ideas Mill upheld before he began to feel the effects of his mental crisis, except for his early opinions on trade unions, which we shall leave for later discussion, and two points where he did not take a leading role: colonization, and the reform of the Poor Law. In both questions, a change was taking place in economic thought precisely at the time Mill was beginning to achieve his independence of mind, but the change was no work of his.

Though the principle of population appeared to suggest the desirability of emigration to relieve demographic pressure, the Malthusians did not particularly welcome the idea.[44] The attitude of some changed through the influence of E.G. Wakefield. In 1828, while confined in a London prison for kidnapping an heiress, Wakefield managed to publish a number of 'Letters from Sidney,' in which he spoke of the sufferings endured by the colonizers in Australia, owing to the very low density of a squatter population in the new lands. Thus began a movement in favour of 'scientific colonization,' that was taken up first by Torrens, then by other economists and by civil servants, and finally bore fruit in prosperous colonies in New Zealand and Australia. Wakefield's and Torrens's plan was that the Government should force a higher concentration of the colonists by charging a price for the unoccupied lands in which they were going to settle the colonizers. In Wakefield's opinion this would have the further advantage that the newcomers be obliged to work for some time as wage-earners, while Torrens tended to emphasize another aspect, the possibility of using the product from the sale of land to pay the fares of future immigrants.[45] John Stuart Mill was a founder member of the National Colonization Society in 1830. He also wrote various articles in the press in favour of this plan in 1831 and 1834 when the discussion on the subject took place about him.[46] All this was routine work.

One point should be noted, though: here is the first instance of his using the Ricardian concept of the stationary state to modify some practical conclusion of Ricardian economics. Wakefield and Torrens contended that scientific colonization was in the long run justified by the help it gave in fighting depressions, and they interpreted this contention as running counter to Ricardian doctrine. The chief reason Wakefield supported a limitation by the Crown on the sale of lands in the colonies was that such a limitation could increase the productivity of a given social wages-fund by forcing a greater division of labour among the immigrants. He adopted Adam Smith's maxim that 'the division of labour is limited by the extent of the market' in order to refute the Ricardian view, deduced from Say's law, that the wages-fund could never lie idle.[47]

Despite Wakefield's anti-Ricardianism (rightly stressed by Dr Winch), John Stuart Mill argued in the *Principles* that Wakefield's stand (and implicitly Torrens's) did not basically contradict Ricardian theory (though apparently contradicting some noted practical deductions from it); in fact, he affirmed that their stand came down to saying that when the stationary state was approaching, the most profitable field of employment for capital would be where returns in agriculture were highest. But, as Lord Robbins observes, our two authors' concept of the stationary state was different from Mill's; for them, once the stationary state had been reached, savings would continue to be made and would accumulate without being invested unless something drastic was done. Mill's more Ricardian position was that there could be no net savings in that state, since the net rate of profits would be nil, there being no danger of generalized unemployment.[48] However, when Mill came to write his chapter on *Laissez-faire*, he had forgotten about Wakefield's animadversions on Say's law, and based his acceptance of Wakefield's colonization scheme on the idea that colonization had social costs and benefits not reflected by price that made State intervention necessary.

The other question on which Mill wrote various articles for the press and on which he, like other economists, changed his opinions, was the Reform of the Poor Laws. This is an affair which has greatly harmed the reputation of political economists, and Mill's in particular. Two points need clearing up. First, it is often said that the classical economists, John Stuart Mill among them, advocated the abolition of all poor relief. And second, it is also said that because they did not dare to propose such a measure outright, they recommended a system under which relief would be meted out in Poor Houses where life would be regulated with inhumane harshness. How much is true in these accusations and how does Mill emerge from them?

It is true that Malthus in his *First Essay* (1798) criticized poor relief as self-defeating, since it tended to worsen the evil (overpopulation) the effects of which it claimed to remedy. It was much better to make the poor rely only on themselves.[49] Consequently, for some time economists, especially the Ricardians (with the exception of McCulloch), proclaimed that it was much better for the welfare of the poor to abolish the relief completely. However, the findings of the Royal Commission on the Poor Laws in 1834 persuaded economists that the total abolition of relief would not only be politically unfeasible but in the end harmful. There were many paupers (the sick, the very young, the insane, the aged) who could do nothing to better their own lot; here self-reliance was a meaningless concept. For the rest, the 'able-bodied paupers,' 'demoralization' could be avoided, and self-reliance reinforced, if relief were made a disagreeable remedy of the last resort, that is to say, a relief granted on such disciplinary terms as to render the life of the poorest paid labourer enviable by comparison. As John Stuart Mill observed: 'The anti-poor-law doctrine is now almost universally exploded among political economists, though political economy still continues to be most unjustly burthened with the discredit of it.'[50]

There remains the second question, whether the economists were responsible for the severity of the regime imposed in the Poor Houses. The answer is that they were not by act of deed, but they were by act of omission. In their recommendations, the Royal Commission requested separate treatment for the able-bodied paupers and the rest; in fact, the Report concluded that four types of institution were necessary, one for each type of pauper (the very young, the sick, the insane and the able-bodied adult). Since it is true that many of the abuses arose out of the neglect of this counsel, the economists cannot be held directly responsible for them. They are, however, open to criticism that they did not foresee that their system would meet with difficulties in practice, nor were they sufficiently vigilant over the New Poor Law's application. More specifically, their foresight above all failed them in that they did not detail sufficiently the necessary institutional conditions for separating the paupers into four classes; and their vigilance failed in not demanding energetically enough the correction of the abuses that time and chance uncovered. Their overconfidence in the smooth working of the new system may be explained by two factors: one (which did not apply to all of them, especially not to Senior) was their Malthusian convictions; another (typical of the age, for better or worse) was their faith in the virtue of 'self-help'. In brief, they were over-fearful of being carried away by sentimentalism.

Conclusion

When we come to the events that close the period of Mill's allegiance to his masters and open his career as an independent thinker, it may be useful to remember that during the time he kept within the frame of the old political economy, Mill was actively and fruitfully engaged in many fields. He dealt, often with originality, with the most important economic themes of his time. If perhaps he was unable to solve the problems raised by the Ricardian value theory; if he used the population principle as a master key to open all doors; if in monetary theory he pursued a course in the opposite direction from that which is considered acceptable today, it is also true that in all these areas there were achievements to be noted in his favour; at the very least, a clear formulation of the problems, and at his best (as in his defence of neo-Malthusianism or his new formulation of Say's law) a lasting contribution to economic practice or theory. Of all that he wrote at this time, his best work is no doubt that concerning foreign trade, especially the article where he completed Ricardian theory on comparative costs. If one wishes to gauge what Mill the *theorist* might have been capable of as a member of the old school, it is enough to glance through the first four *Essays on Some Unsettled Questions of Political Economy*, where time and again the clarity of presentation enhances the originality of thought. Mill *the political economist* is another matter. Here, as we shall see, the change in a later period will be striking. The strict Malthusian anti-socialist, presenting an all but extreme *laissez-faire* position on money matters, the severe defender of the New Poor Law, putting his faith in free trade and emigration as cures for social ills, is a different man from the one we shall meet after the crisis studied in the next chapter. All those elements were included in the new dispensation, but some in modified forms and all in a very different company.

> I found the fabric of my old and taught opinions giving way
> in many fresh places, and I never allowed it to fall to pieces,
> but was incessantly occupied in weaving it anew.
>
> J.S. Mill, *Autobiography*

Chapter 4 John Stuart Mill's Rebellion

There is a certain ambiguity in Mill's reaction against the education he had received. He himself considered it a vitally important break. It obviously played an important part in his life and thought, and greatly affected his economic doctrine. Yet, one may have to conclude that the break was not far-reaching enough.

As was said in the Introduction, many authors have described Mill as an eclectic thinker. But if we look at his life as a whole, this is untenable. The only time he came near to eclecticism as a philosophical system was in the early stages of his revolt against Benthamism, or when he was disappointed by the failure of philosophic radicalism as an independent political movement.[1] Nor can it be argued that his position was unconsciously eclectic, for this would be to ignore the true reasons why his great natural gifts did not yield all the fruit that might have been expected of them. The generosity with which he examined and even accepted ideas from the most diverse sources could be deceptive. In fact, side by side with a great freedom in the details and in the presentation of his system, we can observe a certain rigidity in his unwavering acceptance of the main tenets of Ricardian and Utilitarian doctrine. His new political economy was based on wider premises than his father's was, and reached conclusions more in tune with his times, but basically it consisted of a series of variations (some very original and interesting) on themes present in Bentham, James Mill and Ricardo. John Stuart Mill could not or would not complete his intellectual emancipation.

The key to this continuing servitude no doubt lies in Mill's psyche. True, his individualist radicalism fitted in with certain major trends of the Victorian era, more particularly in its progress towards democracy. Nevertheless, we cannot help feeling that his fidelity to the broad lines of his teacher's thought was due to a profound imbalance in the

emotional side of his nature. This is evidenced by the fact that he had
scarcely freed himself from dependence on his father than he became
sentimentally enslaved to Harriet Taylor, and on her death, gave the
same allegiance to her daughter. In this Mill showed an unconscious fear
of being left alone, a lack of emotional security, in spite of his desire to
be independent. If many readers have considered the *Autobiography*,
for all its studiedly moderate tone, to be a document full of pathos, it is
because, when all is said, the book is an involuntary description of
Mill's failure in his attempts to free himself from his father's
ascendancy.

The Mental Crisis

Two points should be made about Mill's mental breakdown. The first is
that too much attention has been devoted to the crisis itself and too
little to its lasting effects on Mill's personality after he overcame it:
what needs to be explained is not so much his adolescent
heart-searching, as his quasi-neurotic reactions in his adult years. The
second point is that too much weight has been given to the
psychological aspects of his crisis, and too little to the intellectual ones:
after all, Utilitarianism is a thoroughly unsatisfactory ethical doctrine,
and it is only natural that a generous youth should question it.

The crisis occurred when Mill was twenty, starting with a deeply
depressive state, which must have been very painful to bear. Mill
himself recounts its onset and development in his *Autobiography*, in
words which have become deservedly famous.

> It was in the autumn of 1826. I was in a dull state of nerves, such as
> everybody is occasionally liable to; unsusceptible to enjoyment or
> pleasurable excitement; one of those moods when what is pleasure at
> other times, becomes insipid or indifferent; the state, I should think,
> in which converts to Methodism usually are, when smitten by their
> first 'conviction of sin.' In this frame of mind it occurred to me to
> put the question directly to myself: 'Suppose that all your objects in
> life were realized; that all the changes in institutions and opinions
> which you are looking forward to, could be completely effected at
> this very instant: would this be a great joy and happiness to you?'
> And an irrepressible self-consciousness distinctly answered, 'No!' At
> this my heart sank within me: the whole foundation on which my
> life was constructed fell down. (W.Cl., 113).

There is no need to continue the quotation. One should adjourn to the pages of the *Autobiography* itself, for the passages that follow the above make a deeper impression on each re-reading. The account they give of his depression cannot fail to arouse compassion. To sum up in brief what one can find there, Mill tells how he went on with his usual occupations 'mechanically', despite the state of mind in which he found himself, and explains: 'I had been so drilled in a certain sort of mental exercise, that I could still carry it on when all the spirit had gone out of it' (W.Cl., 118). He found no relief anywhere. He even suffered obsessive anxieties, such as that the day must come when the possible combinations of musical tones would be exhausted and it would be impossible to compose new music. As often happens in such cases, he did not see his trouble as a purely personal problem, but 'I felt that the flaw in my life must be a flaw in life itself' (W.Cl., 123).

Relief did not come until after a curious incident, which has been made much of in the psychoanalytical interpretations of Mill's crisis.

I was reading, accidentally, Marmontel's 'Memoires,' and came to the passage which relates his father's death, the distressed position of the family, and the sudden inspiration by which he, then a mere boy, felt and made them feel that he would be everything to them — would supply the place of all that they had lost. A vivid conception of the scene and its feelings came over me, and I was moved to tears. From this moment my burden grew lighter (W.Cl., 119).

Having thus discovered that he still had feelings, he gradually emerged from the state of depression, he avers, by cultivating them: he read poetry ('push-pin is as good as poetry,' Bentham had said), especially the compositions of Wordsworth. This poet's vision made him aware of the possibility of more than the merely negative happiness of the absence of pain which he had wanted to bestow on Humanity in his neophyte years. He had feared the times when nothing should remain to be done for Humanity. From those poems, he says, 'I seemed to learn what would be the perennial sources of happiness, when all the greater evils of life shall have been removed' (W.Cl., 125).

Mill gave an explanation of his crisis which today cannot be considered adequate. The solace he found in poetry led him to attribute his depression to a characteristic of his education, the lack of any systematic cultivation of the feelings:

The habit of analysis has a tendency to wear away the feelings: . . . all those to whom I looked up, were of opinion that the pleasure of sympathy with human beings, and the feelings which made the good of others, and especially of mankind on a large scale, the object of existence, were the greatest and surest sources of happiness. . . My education, I thought, had failed to create these feelings in sufficient strength to resist the dissolving influence of analysis, while the whole course of my intellectual cultivation had made precocious and premature analysis the inveterate habit of my mind (W.Cl., 116–117).

If this leaves one unsatisfied, the next step is, obviously, to psychoanalyse Mill at a distance, though without much hope of cure! As was said above the danger is two-fold: too great an obsession with the crisis itself, when the really interesting psychological problem is Mill's quasi-neurosis in adult years; and too heavy a reliance on psychological explanations of Mill's changes, when doctrinal reasons were obviously also important.

Professor A.W. Levi, a noted Mill scholar and amateur psychoanalyst, has made a very creditable effort at underlining some incidents in Mill's life in order to throw light on his mental crisis.[2] His first point is that, with an education such as his, Mill's relationship with his father cannot have been good. Read the following words about James Mill, which, despite circumlocutions, are meant to apply only to J.S. Mill.

The element which was chiefly deficient in his moral relation to his children was that of tenderness. . . It is impossible not to feel true pity for a father who did, and strove to do, so much for his children, who would have so valued their affection, yet who must have been constantly feeling that fear of him was drying it up at its source. This was no longer the case later in life, and with his younger children. They loved him tenderly: and if I cannot say so much of myself, I was always loyally devoted to him (W.Cl., 43–44).

In his account of the crisis, there is a still more revealing sentence. He regrets having had no one to turn to then:

My father, to whom it would have been natural to me to have recourse in any practical difficulties, was the last person to whom, in such a case as this, I looked for help. Everything convinced me that he had no knowledge of any such mental state as I was suffering from, and that even if he could be made to understand it, he was not the physician who could heal it (W.Cl., 114–115).

In spite of this gulf between them, Mill admired his father, and came to defend his memory energetically in later years.[3] There was an ambivalence in his feelings towards his father, which must have been fostered by the absence of somebody else to turn to, namely, his mother. For John Stuart Mill, his mother was a nonentity. Striking though it is that no mention of her should be found in the published version of the *Autobiography*, it is even more remarkable that he should evince such coldness towards her in the *Early Draft*, completed by 1854. Professor Levi rightly underlines the passage.

That rarity in England, a really warm hearted mother, would in the first place have made my father a totally different being, & in the second would have made the children grow up loving & being loved. But my mother with the very best intentions, only knew how to pass her life in drudging for them. Whatever she could do for them she did, & they liked her, because she was always kind to them, but to make herself loved, looked up to, or even obeyed, required qualities which she unfortunately did not possess.[4]

In view of all this, Professor Levi has diagnosed a repressed death wish towards his father in the case of John Stuart Mill, a repression one might add, due as much to the *mores* of the time as to Mill's noted ambivalence of feeling towards him. The diagnosis is made very plausible by the adduction of the tears Mill shed, after a long unbearable period of dryness, on reading in Marmontel's *Memoirs* the description of the death of the memorialist's father, not to mention the relief he felt after that. Gertrude Himmelfarb adds other pointers as to the deeply buried cause of Mill's neurosis: thus the fact that on his father's death in 1836, Mill suffered a 'brain fever', which left him with a constant twitching in one eye for the rest of his life; it may perhaps have been due to attempts to suppress a certain relief at the disappearance of his taskmaster.[5]

However, these exercises in psychoanalysis can easily become mesmerizing and make us forget that the problem in need of explanation is Mill's inability to free himself totally from his master's dominance, rather than the remote origins of a somewhat acute crisis of adolescence. Mill himself said as much when he revised the *Early Draft* of the *Autobiography* for posthumous publication: 'In all probability my case was by no means so peculiar as I fancied it, and I doubt not that many others have passed through a similar state.'[6]

At least in our culture (though perhaps not in Margaret Mead's Samoa) adolescents used to go through a crisis of belonging and a crisis of integrity, which were especially acute when their education had been an intensely sectarian one, as Mill's was.

Now, Mill in adult years is another case altogether. Leaving aside for the moment his remarkable fidelity to Utilitarianism and Ricardianism, *quod est demonstrandum* in this book, there remains mainly his relationship to Harriet Taylor. To quote Professor Robson's happy phrase, 'she was not only a father-substitute for him, but a mother-substitute as well.'[7] He exaggerated her greatness as a thinker and as a writer, he paid too much attention to her opinions, sometimes overriding his own convictions a little too easily (as in the case of Socialism); it appears even, from unpublished letters mentioned by Professor Robson in his recent book on Mill, that he was dependent on her for practical matters to an extent verging on the ridiculous. When she died, he put her daughter Helen in her place, who had at least the good taste to suppress the glowing passages about her in the *Autobiography*, before releasing it for publication. It may not be quite as paradoxical as it looks to say that it is a measure of Mill's greatness that he overcame these handicaps to a considerable extent. However, rather than his bid for independence, it is his failure to become independent which should require an explanation.

A Different Ethics

Another point to be made to psychoanalytical enthusiasts is that ideological contents of relationships matter as much as their psychological form; and Mill was right in seeing the Benthamite creed as a narrow one. Two shortcomings of Benthamism are relevant in Mill's case. On the one hand the philosophy of personal conduct which Mill had been taught by Bentham and James Mill is untenable. On the other, the methodology of James Mill was clearly incomplete. The methodological revision carried out by John Mill, mainly in his *Logic*, will be left for further on in this chapter, since it came to fruition some years after the crisis. The ethical questions had a more immediate influence.

Every philosophy implies a way of life, though sometimes the connecting link is more historical than logical. When Mill was an obedient member of the school, Benthamism meant for him a very definitive way of behaving.

I conceive that the description so often given of a Benthamite, as a mere reasoning machine, though extremely inapplicable to most of those who have been designated by that title, was during two or three years of my life not altogether untrue of me (W.Cl., 92).

To go a little deeper, one might say that in the system of Bentham it was difficult to distinguish between the criterion of the social good and the rules of personal ethics. Benthamism was really a legal philosophy, which tended to judge actions by their result, rather than a personal morality, basing judgment on intention and motive. The theory of personal ethics of the orthodox Utilitarian could be reduced to two elements: one was the belief that the good life was the result of a judicious arrangement of man's selfish propensities; the other was that the good man was the active man. One may or may not agree with this doctrine, but it must be conceded that it is extremely unpropitious to the valuing of personal relations and to the cultivation of the feelings.[8]

As a result of his crisis, Mill began to discover these two shortcomings of the Utilitarian moral philosophy. Wishing to transcend selfishness in the ethics of personal relations, he adopted a most unfortunate doctrine for one in his plight, that is, for one needing as a matter of life or death Socrates' strong medicine, 'Know Thyself': it was the 'anti-self-consciousness theory' of Carlyle.

> I never, indeed, wavered in the conviction that happiness is the test of all rules of conduct, and the end of life. But I now thought that this end was to be attained by not making it the direct end. Those only are happy (I thought) who have their minds fixed on some object other than their own happiness. . . Ask yourself whether you are happy, and you cease to be so. The only chance is to treat, not happiness, but some end external to it, as the purpose of life. . . This theory now became the basis of my philosophy of life (W.Cl., 120–1).

Thus it was he wished to avoid a selfish attitude to life, by thinking of things other than his own happiness. That is all very well for a man having overcome his inner tensions. For a man whose neurotic condition grew from his fear of self-knowledge, it was poison.

He now also wished to correct the emphasis of Utilitarian education on the active side of man's character, and deplored the state of neglect in which he found his own 'passive susceptibilities'. This is a curious label for the feelings, which usually are anything but passive, and one cannot escape the impression that Mill was still being a Benthamite in this view of them. Still, there was a clear step forward. After the crisis, he said, 'I, for the first time, gave its proper place, among the prime necessities of human well-being, to the internal culture of the individual.' It is in this context that his new interest in poetry, especially that of Wordsworth, must be placed. Thus the crisis released the romantic element in Mill's personality, though it must be stressed that, in spite of his newfound regard for the cultivation of the affections and the feelings, he never became an anti-rationalist: 'I never turned recreant to intellectual culture. . . but I thought that it had consequences which required to be corrected, by joining other kinds of cultivation with it.' This balanced view of the role of the intellect shows Mill to have kept his bearings even in the midst of anguished revision of previous beliefs. Just as his fear of self-analysis must have caused him harm and prevented his full emotional liberation, his courageous decision to abide by the dictates of reason saved him for intellectual creation.

The Rebellion's High Water Mark

Before coming to Mill's revision of his father's methodology, it will be useful to mention briefly the productions of the years when he turned strongly against Benthamism.

The mental crisis overcome, all the influences of nineteenth century thought 'came streaming in upon him.' While his father lived he avoided an open break. But the signs were there for whoever wished to see.[9] His journey to Paris to follow at close quarters the course of the 1830 revolution yielded a series of articles collected together under the title *The Spirit of the Age* (1831).[10] The title itself suggests the St Simonist point of view from which they were written. Historical relativism is much more marked here than in later works. Mill presents his age as one of transition: he longs for the disappearance of intellectual anarchy and the coming of government by the wise.

Directly against his Utilitarian teachers he only permitted himself to write an anonymous appendix, in 1833, to the book by Edward Bulwer-Lytton *England and the English* where 'along with the favourable, a part also of the unfavourable side of my estimation of Bentham's doctrines, considered as a complete philosophy, was for the first time put into print' (W.Cl., 168). If, as Mill says, only a part of his unfavourable opinion was printed in Lytton's book, then his anti-Benthamism must have been virulent indeed. It is true that his praises are loud in favour of Bentham's philosophy of law, even exaggeratedly so, for he gives him credit for no less than inventing the idea of codifying law. But 'the legislator enjoins or prohibits an action, with very little regard to the general moral excellence or turpitude which it implies; he looks to the consequences to society of the particular kind of action.' Bentham's success as a philosopher of law does not necessarily imply equal success as a moralist.

> It is perhaps fortunate that Mr. Bentham devoted a much larger share of his time and labour to the subject of legislation than to that of morals; for the mode in which he understood and applied the principle of Utility, appears to me far more conducive to the attainment of true and valuable results in the former, than in the latter of these two branches of enquiry.[11]

There is a second appendix in Bulwer-Lytton's book, presenting some observations on James Mill. It is presumably from J.S. Mill's pen, and is a much more considerate piece, though some acid drops may be found in it.[12]

Before his father died, J.S. Mill was offered the *de facto* if not *de iure* editorship of the *Westminster Review*. At first, he says, the *Review* 'did not, as a whole, by any means represent my opinions.'

> My father's co-operation as a writer we all deemed indispensable, and he wrote largely in it until prevented by his last illness. The subjects of his articles, and the strength and decision with which his opinions were expressed in them, made the *Review* at first derive its tone and colouring from him much more than from any of the other writers. I could not exercise editorial control over his articles (W.Cl., 169).

Quite a degree of impatience here with someone he had treated so circumspectly in the second of his appendices to Lytton's book! In 1836 James Mill died, and his son could at last spell out his separation from the rest of the philosophical Radicals. He did so in two articles that particularly scandalized the faithful; 'Bentham' (August, 1838) and 'Coleridge' (March, 1840). The work on Bentham is one of Mill's finest, deploying all his analytical and descriptive powers, all his capacity to see both sides of a question, to grasp the truth in two opposing views and form a balanced judgment of a thinker, like Bentham, so difficult to judge calmly (whether for or against). It is there in the first volume of *Dissertations and Discussions* for anyone to read. On the other hand, Mill exaggerated the importance and value of Coleridge as a political thinker and his article gives the impression of attributing to the Lake poet all the non-Benthamite thoughts and sentiments Mill had been developing since the time of his 'mental crisis' — and perhaps, too, those of Harriet Taylor.

His reaction reached its peak in his correspondence with Auguste Comte, to whom he said in a letter of 8 November 1841 (using typically Comtian terms and some exaggeration) that already in 1828 he had effected 'ma sortie définitive de la section benthamiste de l'école révolutionnaire.'

A Partial Return to Benthamism

However, matters did not rest there. His swing away from Benthamism was not a 'sortie définitive' after all. His writings began to show evidence of a partial return to the fold.

The publication of *A System of Logic* (1843) was the first indication that Mill's separation from Benthamism had been less final than might have appeared; although it was an attempt to apply positivistic inductivism to logical and epistemological questions, it owed more to Bentham and James Mill than to Comte. Then *The Principles of Political Economy* (1848) confirmed that John Stuart Mill had decided not to follow Comte's advice and suspend all writing on economics until the Social Science *à la Comte* was complete. Worthy of note, in as far as it affects his relations with Utilitarianism and his father's educational theory, is J.S. Mill's re-edition in 1869 of *Analysis of the Human Mind*, the book of associationist psychology published by James Mill in 1829. John Mill's return, even if partial and conditional, to Bentham is confirmed in the essay on *Utilitarianism* (1863). In it he (unsuccessfully) attempts to reconcile the maxim of the greatest happiness for the greatest number with his disconformity with the judgments of the masses, especially in questions of aesthetics and the conduct of life. The artifice he uses to obtain a hierarchy of values within Utilitarianism was of Platonic origin; he limited the jury to those who had experienced and appreciated the higher, more spiritual pleasures.

It is characteristic of Mill that on the other side of the scales, as a counter-balance to his philosophic Benthamism, we have to weigh his three posthumous essays on religion (1874), especially 'Utility of Religion' and 'Theism.' In these, a different Mill appears, one who writes passionately of the personality of Jesus, who defends a religion of humanity (that is, a humanist creed that expresses the highest of our ethical convictions), one who does not deny the possible existence of a

God infinitely wise and good though not omnipotent, and even seems to share the hope that He exists. Mill was always *willing* to follow his reasoning to the ultimate consequences, even if it disconcerted his friends and followers, as in this case his essays on religion did. If he did not attain complete intellectual freedom, it was no doubt due to the trammels of his education which he could never quite shake off.

The Methodological Bases of the New Political Economy

The pace of our description must slow down on arriving at the repercussions of Mill's reaction against Utilitarianism on his methodology of economics, for they are of the greatest importance for our understanding of Mill's thought.

In the pages of the *Principles* the clearest symptom of the change that had taken place in Mill is the distinction he draws in economic laws, between laws of production and laws of distribution. For Mill himself, it was his most important innovation, for he considered it the foundation of his new political economy. Mill contrasted two types of laws in the economic field. On the one hand, he said, 'the laws and conditions of the production of wealth partake of the character of physical truths. There is nothing optional or arbitrary in them.' On the other hand, he affirmed that 'it is not so with the Distribution of Wealth. That is a matter of human institution solely. The things once there, mankind, individually or collectively, can do with them as they like.' This distinction, which Mill considered transcendental, has its good and its bad points. For one thing, it allowed Mill to emphasize that the system of competition, private property and inheritance was not a postulate of economic science. But for another, it would seem to indicate that Mill was unaware that production and distribution are but two sides of the same coin and that either both must be considered to be governed by inflexible laws, or both be seen as susceptible of institutional modification.

To arrive at such a distinction, Mill changed his youthful opinions on two points: on the method and on the institutional assumptions of political economy.

James Mill's method, as his son understood it, was to construct the social sciences *more geometrico*; starting out from self-evident premises, and by means of a chain of syllogisms working down to universally valid conclusions.

In 1829, in the middle of all the agitation for parliamentary Reform, James Mill had published for the second time his *Essay on Government,* based, apparently at least, on the *a priori* method. 'At this juncture,' Mill writes in his *Autobiography* (133–6) 'appeared. . .Macaulay's famous attack on my father's Essay on Government.'[13] The youthful Macaulay was arguing for the use of the Baconian method of *a posteriori* induction in political sciences.

> I saw that Macaulay's conception of the logic of politics was erroneous;   . . .that even in physical science his notions of philosophizing might have recognised Kepler, but would have excluded Newton and Laplace.

Yet on the other hand, he said: 'My father's premises were really too narrow, and included but a small number of the general truths, on which, in politics, the important consequences depend'.

Mill was to find the solution in the use of the method of 'the Composition of Forces. . .the most complete example of the logical process I was investigating.' This method that John Mill advocated for political science would combine the *a posteriori* method with the *a priori*; the first, or inductive, would be used to discover laws operating in each case; the second, or deductive, to combine these laws, and, as with a parallelogram of forces, obtain the resultant force.

Thus, in the Essay 'On the Definition and Method of Political Economy'[14] though he reaffirmed that the method of economic science was that of *a priori* deduction starting out from a limited number of assumptions on the nature of men and things, he emphasized that such assumptions were abstractions from reality: thus does

> Political Economy presuppose an arbitrary definition of man, as a being who invariably does that by which he may obtain the greatest amount of necessaries, conveniences, and luxuries, with the smallest quantity of labour and physical self-denial with which they can be obtained in the existing state of knowledge (326).

This hypothetical assumption by which economists transformed the endlessly various being that is man into an abstract figure (the *homo oeconomicus* of the later exegetes) makes the political economist's conclusions, according to Mill, only true in the abstract. That is to say, they would be true without qualification or exceptions 'only in a case which is purely imaginary': 'In proportion as the actual facts recede from the hypothesis, he must allow a corresponding deviation from the strict letter of his conclusion' (p. 326). When in any given case disturbing causes intervene, the *a priori* method is not enough; observation will have to be used to determine the extent of the deviation from the abstract model. It should be noted that for Mill observation is not seen as an attempt to refute the abstract hypothesis, but only to discover in each case whether other disturbing hypotheses or laws are in operation.

It must be admitted that though this ensured that Mill's economic system was more realistic than his father's and more flexible in its application to practical cases, it is also true that it made it less susceptible to refutation, for any case that did not fit in with theory could be attributed to the intervention of some cause either unknown or of unforeseeable intensity, as in fact was the case with the theory of historically diminishing returns in agriculture.

Be that as it may, Mill was now in the position of denying the universality of the hypothetical assumptions on which his father's doctrine was based, such as, among psychological assumptions, the the sovereignty of self-interest; and likewise, among institutional assumptions, perfect competition or private property and inheritance; or the existence of three distributive classes among sociological assumptions.[15] The essence of Ricardian doctrine, namely the two laws of diminishing returns and population (apart from the implicit law of the need of capital for the division of labour) remained intact. But he was to use the model itself more as a working hypothesis, universally valid so long as no disturbing forces existed in reality.

A New Concept of Distribution

Once open in principle to a discussion of the institutional assumptions of the Ricardian doctrine, Mill soon fell under the influence of those who in fact rejected them. Especially to be noted at this point are the Saint-Simonians, a socialist group who caused as much of a stir in France as the Owenites had done in England.

This school, founded by Henri, Comte de Saint-Simon, and transformed into a religious sect by his followers, insisted on the historical relativity of ideas, creeds and institutions; and on the other hand sought to replace the 'anarchical' system of free competition by a centralized organization of the economy. The reason for their influence on Mill was not, as for Marx, to have stressed the dynamic and transforming aspects of capitalism, but their doctrine on distribution.

Mill's first reaction to Saint-Simonism was unfavourable; for example, the doctrine of the school concerning inheritance seemed to him a great heresy.[16] He was, however, impressed by the pamphlet which the young Auguste Comte had written in collaboration with Saint-Simon (*Système de politique positive*). With its perusal began Mill's flirtation with Saint-Simonism so entertainingly told by Mr Pankhurst.[17] Though he never actually joined the Saint-Simonians, he was attracted by their connected view of historical evolution[18] and his eyes were opened 'to the very limited and temporary value of the old political economy, which assumes private property and inheritance as indefeasible facts, and freedom of production and exchange as the *dernier mot* of social improvement' (W.Cl., 141).

Mill's new point of view on distribution soon made its appearance in print in a review of Miss Martineau's *Summary of Political Economy* (1834).[19] Mill there charged the English political economists with attempting to construct 'a permanent fabric out of transitory material,' with taking 'for granted the immutability of arrangements of society':

> They revolve in their eternal circle of landlords, capitalists, and labourers, until they seem to think of the distinction of society into those three classes, as if it were one of God's ordinances, not man's, and as little under human control as the division of day and night (225–7).

This idea, by itself, would be an important contribution to economic science, especially when contrasted with popular economic beliefs of the time. But Mill did more; though he had thus underlined the relativity of the conclusions of economic science, he also stressed the aspirations of economic analysis to universality: he proceeded to say that one should not deduce from the sentences quoted above that the science was of no use: 'though many of its conclusions are only locally true, its method of investigation is applicable universally.' This phrase strikes just the right note in the difficult question of giving their due to both contingent circumstance and abstract analysis.

Unfortunately Mill carried his thought a little further than one could wish: he concluded by asserting that he who knows the political economy of England 'knows that of all nations actual or possible: provided he have sense enough not to expect the same conclusions to issue from varying premises' (226). Here he was being a little overconfident. But despite this degree of overstatement, the advance had been very great.

A further influence should be noted at this point, less well-known than that of the Saint-Simonians, that of Adam Smith, surprising as it may seem. The Saint-Simonians, as we have just seen, had made Mill question the eternal validity of the institutional assumptions (property, inheritance) and the realism of the theory of social classes (the division into landlords, labourers and capitalists) in Ricardo's model, notwithstanding his appreciation of the model's usefulness as an instrument in analysis. The return to Adam Smith meant, on the one hand, that he would wish to apply his new concept of the distributive mechanism and the class system to concrete cases, and on the other, that he would start out from not only economic but also sociological, ethical and philosophical premises. James Mill believed, it appeared, in a purely deductive economic science, constructed geometrically on the basis of a few premises as to the nature of man and world. *The Wealth of Nations* was written with a very different approach. As John Stuart Mill says in the preface to the *Principles* 'the most characteristic quality of that work, and the one in which it most differs from some others which have equalled and even surpassed it as mere expositions of the general principles of the subject, is that it invariably associates the principles with their application.'

Finally, came the influence of Auguste Comte (with whom Mill corresponded in the forties), of less importance than might appear, except to the extent that it opened his eyes to the merits of Adam Smith. The French author insisted that political economy could not be expounded in isolation as a self-sufficient system (in the style of James Mill). He asserted that economic science was only a 'provisional' science, in that it would disappear with the definitive construction of a general sociology (to which he, Auguste Comte, was just putting the finishing touches). Mill, nevertheless, upheld the desirability of continuing to study economics independently, in the traditional way, a fair proof of which lies in his decision to write the *Principles* after all.[20]

In the preface to this treatise, he underlined the fact that Adam Smith never separated 'political economy, properly so called' from 'the philosophy of society'. Mill promised to follow this example, declaring that

for practical purposes, Political Economy is inseparably intertwined with many other branches of social philosophy. Except on matters of mere detail, there are perhaps no practical questions, even among those which approach nearest to the character of purely economical questions, which admit of being decided on economical premises alone (xci).

For all these reasons, in the *Principles of Political Economy* (1848) Mill decided to start off on a fresh footing with his distinction between laws of production and laws of distribution, and he set it at the head of his study of distribution, to justify that his treatment of this part of economics differed from that customarily presented. It is useful to look again at the words in which he expressed it:

> The laws and conditions of the production of wealth, partake of the character of physical truths. There is nothing optional, or arbitrary in them. . . It is not so with the Distribution of Wealth. That is a matter of human institution solely. The things once there, mankind, individually or collectively, can do with them as they like.

However, the conclusion is inescapable: the distinction between the laws of production and distribution was a mistake. Neither were the laws of distribution so flexible, nor those of production so rigid.

As a critic said at the time: 'if production be determined by positive and natural laws, independent of the laws and customs of society, the distribution which affects it, and is part of the same system, must be determined by similar laws.'[21] The argument is conclusive. 'Things once there,' mankind certainly cannot do with them as they like. It might be true if things were produced but once. But the distribution of output at one period influences production in the following period. Mill himself must have sensed that something was wrong with making distribution wholly a matter of arbitrary choice, for to some extent he qualified his opening declaration a few paragraphs later:

> Society [Mill said] can subject the distribution of wealth to whatever rules it thinks best: but what practical results shall flow from the operation of those rules, society cannot choose, but must be content to learn. (*Principles* [1st Ed., 1848] *Coll. Works*, II, 200 and note kk).

(Or, as he put in later editions, the results 'must be discovered, like any other physical or mental truth, by observation and reasoning') (200).

Concerning the laws of production, Mill unquestionably endowed them with excessive rigidity. The laws of production do not have the character to which Mill was alluding when he spoke of their likeness to physical truths (as Mill conceived these). It is an error to posit that the productive activities of mankind will be confined within the law-like regularities existing at any given time; that is to say, it is a mistake to believe that tendencies such as diminishing returns in agriculture, or the speed of technological advance, are regularities that will necessarily obtain in the future as they did in the past. Mill also corrected his initial statement on the nature of the laws of production within a few lines of having uttered it:

> We cannot, indeed, foresee to what extent the modes of production may be altered, or the productiveness of labour increased, by future extensions of our knowledge of the laws of nature, suggesting new processes of industry of which we have at present no conception (*Coll. Works*, II, 199).[22]

No doubt this arose from a mistaken notion of what constitutes a 'universal law', be it natural or economic. A 'law' does not prescribe a single necessary path for action; it rather rules out some courses of action as impossible[23] and imposes on all men's actions the condition of its observance in conjunction with other such laws, if their aims are to be realized (as when illnesses caused by the working of natural laws are fought with remedies based on the operation of other natural laws). Mill felt some awareness of this, but did not press his intuition further. Whereas in the first edition (1848), speaking of the laws of production, he said:

> But howsoever we may succeed in making for ourselves more space within the limits set by the constitution of things, those limits exist; there are ultimate laws, which we did not make, which we cannot alter, and to which we can only conform (199, and b—b),

in the third edition, the last clause was modified in the following way:

> But howsoever we may succeed in making for ourselves more space within the limits set by the constitution of things, we know that there must be limits. We cannot alter the ultimate properties either of matter or mind, but can only employ those properties more or less successfully, to bring about the events in which we are interested (199).

There is no longer such a great difference here from the laws of distribution about which he said a few paragraphs further on (in words we have already quoted) that the practical results 'must be discovered. . . by observation and reasoning' (200).

Mill failed to draw a clear distinction between, universal laws or hypotheses, on the one hand, and economic systems on the other; the former, valid for all times and places, and the latter, making up the aggregate of real or initial conditions under which such laws operate. One can however easily exaggerate this criticism. In actual fact, the treatise in its general lines could be said to be groping towards some such division, though the confusion created by the failure clearly to distinguish laws from systems clouds more than one point. Mill ought to have said that on one side were the 'laws' of the Ricardian doctrine relating to both the value of goods and their production and distribution, and on the other, the institutional realities that could vary profoundly from one system to another, within the constraints set by the consequences of the 'laws'. He did not say it, but what Mill did in the *Principles*, whether he formulated it or not, was to keep the core of Ricardian analysis intact in its general outline, while he transformed its aspect and application by holding that it could operate in various institutional systems, and not solely in the one reflected by the assumptions of the Ricardian model. Methodologically, this is very nearly right.

Intelligence [among the working classes] induces combinations, combination tends to create partnership between employer and employed, and this will lead to those higher forms of co-operation which will alike realize all that has been sought either by the economist or the philanthropist.

Henry Fawcett in 1860

Chapter 5 Trade Unions

Within Mill's lifetime, the position of the trade unions in British society was completely overturned. From being secret societies punishable by law they became an accepted part of the machinery of society.

In the first seventy years of the nineteenth century, the history of British trade unionism may be split into five distinct periods. The first period may be characterized as one of persecution under Common Law reinforced by statutes dating mainly from the time of the French wars and the immediate post-war years. With the repeal of the Combination Laws in 1824–5, a second period begins, centred around the first bout of serious conflict with unionized labour in the nineteenth century. The third stage, coinciding with the beginning of the thirties, might be termed 'Owenite', for the Utopian ideals which moved trade unionists at that point; the fourth lasts from about 1835 to 1848 at the latest, and must be thought of as a time of Chartist predominance; and the fifth, the time when the unions forsook political ideals and grew increasingly professional, culminated in the Trade Union Law of 1875, which in its broad outlines was operative for nearly a century.

During the time when they were outlawed, workers sometimes combined spontaneously to better their working conditions, or resist cuts in wages or employment. What little organization there was took the form of friendly or burial societies, which kept up a lively correspondence with other centres and came to the assistance of outside comrades — for example, offering board and lodging to those travelling in search of work. When they employed their funds to support a strike and thus became too much of a threat to the employers, the latter invoked the law against 'combinations', or more often boycotted the leaders by refusing to employ them.

With the first repeal of the combination laws in 1824, labour relations changed considerably. The country was going through a period of growing prosperity which did not slacken until the crisis of 1826. A wave of wage-claims and strikes swept the country, giving rise in 1825 to an attempt to restore the laws against combination, one year after their repeal. The attempt failed, since the resulting 1825 law, though not as lenient as that of 1824, confirmed the repeal and closed for ever the period of systematic persecution.

The economic crisis in 1826 was accompanied by rearguard skirmishes through which the workers tried to resist wage-cuts. During the depression the unionists' ranks were decimated and trade-union activity was not renewed until 1830; and then it took on a quite different character from the preceding period. Instead of the mushrooming of small workshop unions, there were attempts to build up regional and even national unions. The driving force behind such undertakings was the Utopian conviction of Owenite origin that, since labour was the source of all wealth, a universal compact would allow the productive classes to retain the whole of the national income in their hands. This period of trade unionism stretching from 1829 to 1834 may then with all propriety be called the Owenite period.[1]

From 1837 to 1845 runs what may be called the Chartist period. The whole energy of the working classes was channelled into agitation to achieve the twelve points of the People's Charter. This was then, a primarily political trade unionism that was forever extinguished as far as England was concerned, with the final failure of Chartism 'on 10 April 1848 when the great scare of the national petition march on London proved groundless.

Meanwhile and almost without publicity there had been quietly growing up a different type of unionism which would finally prevail in England until the present day: a craft trade unionism, not directly linked to politics, and seeking the association of all the workers within one branch of production in a national 'amalgamated society.' It was a sober, professional trade unionism that claimed to put foremost the interests of its members. With the legal reforms of 1871–5, whereby the trade unions were not held responsible for the damages and losses caused by their members' strikes, it achieved full recognition.

Mill and Trade Unions

This chapter, unavoidably, is not centred on Mill as much as the rest of the book. Were it not that he 'recanted' the wages fund doctrine, thus sowing confusion in the ranks of political economists, his thoughts on trade unionism would not deserve detailed consideration. Nevertheless, recant he did, thus creating the obligation for the scrupulous historian to whittle his gesture down to size.

There being comparatively so little and so unexplicit from the pen of Mill to go by until we come to the 'recantation,' it is essential to put it into context by bearing in mind the periods of trade union history and the pronouncements of other economists.

The defenders of trade unionism started out by simply opposing anti-combination laws: they viewed the problem from an exclusively constitutional angle, considering the anti-combination laws as an infringement of the workers' rights of association. Naturally freedom to combine, when it came, did not solve all labour problems, but it did allow them to come up to the surface. Some economists, notably McCulloch, Senior and Torrens, made an effort to develop economic thought in the field of wages. But Mill seemed to rest content in these years with the constitutional point of view, and did not seem to be especially interested in examining the effects of legalized union activity. The main reason for this is that he apparently thought that trade unionism was a passing phenomenon, and hoped that occasions for labour conflicts would disappear with the growth of co-operation.

When the time came to write the *Principles of Political Economy* (1848) it should have become obvious to him that unions were more permanent institutions than appeared in the beginning; that, since they posed difficult economic, social, and political problems, they deserved detailed treatment. Mill had enough sympathy for the cause of labour to guarantee that his examination of unionism would not be coloured by the prejudices current at the time among the middle classes. But a mixture of inattention and of rudimentary analysis made his study of combinations in the *Principles* unsatisfactory. The treatise again presented the question of trade unions mainly from the constitutional angle, as one more case of erroneous intervention in the economy by the State. Within this inadequate framework he divided the question into two parts: the problems posed by a single trade union enfolding the whole of the working class, and those arising in the case of sectional unions or combinations. To the first he made a cursory application of the doctrine of the wages fund; to the second, he applied the same doctrine with only slight modifications. On the whole it can be said that the discussion showed no evidence of any great effort to present a connected theoretical and practical study of labour relations.

In his later years there was a moment when it seemed that Mill was going to embark upon a new theoretical venture in the economics of labour: the moment when he abandoned the so called doctrine of the wages fund (or better, the Ricardian theory of wages) with its alleged corollary that all unionist efforts to raise wages were futile. At the very least he could have done much useful work by clarifying this theory, for some of its practical conclusions were not as misguided as is often thought. But since he 'recanted' the wages fund doctrine, surely a wonderful occasion had presented itself for him to carry out a complete re-examination of the theory of wages and trade unionism. Mill did not even make the attempt. After his 'recantation' he considered it enough to declare that it was too soon for a definite solution, and to make a few changes in the text of the *Principles* substituting nothing but a weak bargaining theory for the doctrine he had given up. In fact, his interest was far more drawn towards that other great institutional creation of the working classes: co-operation.

Mill's attempt to build a New Political Economy stemmed from his conviction that the economic doctrines of Ricardo and his father, though essentially valid, failed to yield a ready answer to some practical problems which had become urgent after their time. In some cases, such as that of State intervention or socialism, he succeeded in building a fully thought out doctrine based on original analysis. But in the case of the trade unions he failed to do so. A cause of failure was his preoccupation with the danger of excessive numbers: he thought it more important to warn the working classes of the Malthusian danger, than to debate the exact limits of unionist action. His belief that unions were a transitory phenomenon also contributed: he hoped that co-operation would soon make problems of strikes and combinations obsolete. At the bottom of it all were the shortcomings of his theory of wages: the doctrine of the wages fund, though having much to commend it, was unable to cope with the complications of the labour world. Mill's answer to the problem of unions was a mere juxtaposition of conflicting thoughts, rather than a new synthesis on a higher plane.

The Ricardian Theory of Wages and the Wages Fund

Before examining the evidence for such assertions, a point must be settled. It is important to underline that the doctrine of the wages fund, as the Ricardian theory of wages is usually called, was only one of the contributory elements of Mill's failure. Mill himself is responsible for the fact that any mention of trade unions in connection with the classical economists immediately conjures up the doctrine of the wages fund. The association is dangerously misleading.

More false ideas are entertained on the relation between the wages fund doctrine and trade union policy than on almost any subject of classical political economy. According to the accepted version, the point of this doctrine was to show up the futility of unionism. 'If the teaching of political economy on the subject of wages were true,' said the Reverend W.A. Spooner in *Palgrave's Dictionary* , 'any attempts which the working class might make to gain better terms from their employers by means of trade-unions, or otherwise, were either fore-doomed to failure, or, if successful, did but benefit one particular class or section of the labouring classes at the expense of all the rest.' In Spooner's opinion the Wages fund 'contributed to a great extent to render the doctrines of political economy unpopular with the working classes.'

In fact, the true role of the wages fund doctrine in classical economics was very different, but it is difficult to condense it into one striking phrase which could oust the stereotype once and for all. Taussig and Schumpeter have failed to make much impression in the past, but theirs was the right sort of answer.

Three fundamental ideas have to be kept in mind throughout the discussion. The first is that, strictly speaking, the theory of the wages fund is only one element in a theory of wages. It is a theory of the demand for labour and asserts that such demand is a function of the accumulation of capital; it takes for granted the principles governing the supply of labour. Yet the usual interpretation is to see it as a complete theory of wages, inclusive of the factors governing the supply of labour namely, for most interpreters, the population principle. Henceforth, to avoid confusion, we shall speak of a wages fund *doctrine*, meaning the complete Ricardian theory of wages, demand and supply.

The second is that the wages fund doctrine had little to do with trade unions for the greatest part of its currency, mainly because trade unions did not constitute a problem until some years after Ricardo wrote: it was used by the political economists, particularly by the Ricardians, in their theory of capital (to explain unemployment and deprecate unproductive consumption by the rich) and in their theory of distribution (to drive home the need for checking population growth).

The third is that, even when it came to be applied to combinations, the doctrine left much room for trade union activity. In short, the wages fund doctrine was originally intended as a complete theory of wages, and was not aimed at the trade unions, nor did it imply a sentence of sterility on their activity.

Two versions of the doctrine must be distinguished: one is an explanation of short run wages, the other, long run. In the short run, total demand for labour in a year was supposed to be a function of the wage capital accumulated in the previous year, that is to say, a function of an accumulated stock of variable capital. In the long run, on the other hand, the demand for labour was conceived as a function of the rate of accumulation of total capital, that is to say, a function of the flow of savings.

The rate of wages itself, once the demand, short and long run, was given, was determined in a very simple way. In the short run, labour supply was a given stock of workers, competing for employment. Hence, the short run wage was the result of dividing two stocks, wage capital and number of workers. In the long run, labour supply fluctuated according to the revised version of the Malthusian population theory, that is to say, was a function of the standard of living. It increased as the standard of living rose and diminished as it fell, unless the jump upwards was very large and a new customary standard of living established itself. Hence, the 'natural' or long run rate of wages, was in theory held to be fixed at the point determined by the infinitely elastic supply of labour, that is to say, at the customary standard of living; in practice it was thought to rise by steps, if the flow of accumulation grew at a more rapid rate than the net flow of population.

Let us rehearse these very important points again in a little more detail. In the long run, there was a customary or 'natural' wage rate, at which the working classes were prepared to maintain their numbers. If the wage capital increased, workers would reproduce themselves until the rate returned to its customary level by the increased competition for employment. If the wage capital dimished, the birth rate would fall, until true equilibrium was again restored. Obviously these forces would take time before they worked themselves out fully. Be that as it may, in the long run version, the forces shaping the demand and supply of labour were adequately spelt out: the supply was a function of the customary standard of living; the demand, of the rate of accumulation.

The short run version was often called the 'demand and supply theory' of wages, but to call it a theory is a misnomer. To say that a price is determined by demand and supply is to say very little: the forces shaping the demand and supply schedules must be specified before the discussion can begin. In the short run version no substitute was offered for the customary standard of living and the rate of accumulation, as factors determining the *locus*, or rather the path, of the equilibrium. Both the size of wage capital and the numbers of workers on the market went unexplained; they were simply posited with nothing to determine their size, and hence rigidly impervious to human action. In fact, the short run version was an ill-judged and hasty adaptation of the long term theory, when what was needed was an independent explanation. It froze the long run theory of wages into meaninglessness.

Applications of the Wage Fund Doctrine

The classical economist applied both forms of the theory of wages to important problems of the *theory of capital*. A consideration of these points is not in order here however. Let it only be said that the dependence of labour on the flow of savings in the long run was levelled against the unorthodox idea of Malthus that increased saving could lead to unemployment: in the long run, said the Ricardians, employment could only be increased by sustained accumulation. And, as for the short run version of the doctrine, Ricardo used it in the 'machinery question', stressing that the sinking of variable capital into equipment could harm the interests of wage earners.

Now, in their *theory of distribution* which is the point under study here, Ricardo, James Mill, McCulloch and the other Ricardians used the long run version mainly to set out as strikingly as they could the urgency of the Malthusian danger, stressing that (given a rate of accumulation) the increase of wages was in inverse relation to the rate of population growth. It is true that the long run version when applied to unions in a gold-standard economy implied the futility of union action aimed at shifting distribution permanently in favour of wage-earners; but such a conclusion could be deduced directly from their main distributive models.

It should have been clear to them that the doctrine as they formulated it could only play the role of a long run theory of wages and that in the short run it created more difficulties than it solved. When they turned to trade unions, which posed essentially short run problems, the excessive simplicity of their doctrine led them into mistaken views. This is a pity, for even the short run version, properly overhauled, had in it the seeds of an interesting macro-distribution theory. The haughty words of modern commentarists of the doctrine are less in order than may appear at first sight: after all macro-distribution theory is one of the least brilliant aspects of modern political economy; and, on the other hand, the come-back of incomes policies throughout the world indicates a fear of exaggerated increases in money wages, and seems to suggest that the wages fund theory was not so completely wide of the mark.

Be that as it may, it was only natural that non-specialists in economic questions should advance the crudest versions — thereby bringing about the disrepute in which the wages theory of the Ricardians came to be held. Miss Martineau, for instance, in her 1829 novel *The Turn-Out* had set out to prove that *Patience is the Best Policy* and that 'the inconvenience, distress, and mischief produced' by a 'turn-out' 'are very great';[2] though in 1834 she conceded that 'combinations may avail or not, according to the reasonableness of their object,' reasonable objects being an equalization of wages, unreasonable an increase of them.[3]

Professional economists, on the other hand, were agreed that unions could be of use, especially once the assumptions of homogeneity of labour and perfection of the labour market were abandoned, as we shall shortly see.

A fact which cannot be stressed enough is that many of the staunchest defenders of trade unions believed in the doctrine of the wages fund with as much conviction as the most irreducible of their opponents. This is not only true of political economists, such as McCulloch, Torrens, Fawcett, Cairnes, but also of working class leaders such as Francis Place, and even the bugbear of *The Times*, Professor Beesly. Nor were they unduly shackled by such a belief. *General* increases of wages in the *short* run they might mistakenly reject, when they could have accepted them as possible. But they could and did recognize the possibility of *sectional* rises, whether temporary or permanent, not always at the expense of the rest of the working classes; and especially there were the increases in the remuneration of such workers as received less than the market wage — a service to the community which many economists have felt by itself justifies the existence of unions.

The *cliché* that the doctrine of the wages fund was an untenable theory of wages designed to prove the futility of all trade union action, can now be contrasted with what seems to be a truer picture of the facts. It mainly aimed at pressing home the inopportunity of an excess of unproductive consumption and the urgency of the population problem; as a long run theory, despite its analytical defects, it was right in its conclusion that (unless agreeing to inflation) unions cannot affect the long run share of labour in the national income; and, when applied to union activity in the short run, it was compatible with the acceptance of a wide scope for trade union activity.

The Repeal of the Combination Laws (1824—5)

The combination laws 'which seem to us in the highest degree partial, oppressive and unjust, had their origin in a dark and barbarous period.' With these words McCulloch opened an article in favour of repeal published in 1824.

The spread of the liberal ideology during the eighteenth century had been inclining Parliament progressively to limit the intervention of the State in the economy, so that the working classes lost whatever protection they could formerly obtain from the public authorities, while they were forbidden to defend themselves by combination. The political economists and Benthamite Radicals thought that the liberalization of the labour market had not been carried far enough: if an end had been put to the dictation of wages by the authorities, there remained the anti-combination laws to finish with.

One man is to be credited with bringing to a head the Radical criticism of the combination laws: Francis Place. His perseverance and ability in the defence of trade unions may be grasped in Graham Wallas's biography of him. Here we need only know that in 1824[4] with the help of his ever faithful and hard working friend Joseph Hume, MP, he manipulated Parliament into repealing the Statutory and Common Law restrictions on combinations. The total repeal of 1824 unfortunately coincided with a boom of large proportions.[5] This, as we have said, encouraged wage claims and a wave of strikes followed. After much employer agitation, Parliament passed another Act in 1825, which however did not fundamentally affect the advantages gained by unions in the previous year.

The campaign for repeal was powerfully helped by the essay mentioned above of the economist John Ramsay McCulloch in the *Edinburgh Review* for January 1824. In this article and in the small pamphlet on unions which he published in 1826,[6] McCulloch presented the most complete discussion of trade unions of the first half of the nineteenth century, including John Mill's in the first edition of the *Principles*.

McCulloch distinguished two possible situations in the labour market. when wages are '*below* the *natural* and *proper* rate of wages in the particular branch of industry to which they belong'; and when 'they must be *coincident with that rate, – or above it'*(ER319).In the second case he held that workers could not increase and maintain the wage above equilibrium (as one would say today) by combination, unless they discriminated against their fellow workers by impeding entry – an occurrence which he deplored. In the first case, he was confident the competition among the masters would eventually raise the rate of wages to the 'equilibrium' point, since extraordinary profits would entice outside capitalists to enter the industry and bid up the wage rate. But if the workmen were not allowed to combine 'they would be left entirely dependent on the competition of their masters' (p.319). In the 1824 article he also listed another useful effect of combinations, that of raising wages in trades where a combination of the masters kept them artificially low.

It is important not to read into the actions of the men who secured this repeal motives belonging to another age. The combinations they visualized were not the trade unions of the twentieth century, institutions with a paid permanent staff, with ample strike funds, and considerable powers over employers and fellow workers: but more transient agreements among labourers, on a purely voluntary basis, for particular emergencies. Place, for one, believed that with the repeal of the Combination Laws unions would disappear. In a letter of the year 1825, he said:

> He knows nothing of the working people, who can suppose, that when left at liberty to act for themselves, without being driven into *permanent* associations by the oppression of the laws, they will continue to contribute money for distant and doubtful experiments, for uncertain and precarious benefits. . . If let alone, combinations, excepting now and then and for particular purposes under peculiar circumstances will cease to exist.[7]

Unions must be able to inflict damage on employers by means of strikes, thus much was recognized by the repealers. But they did not see that they must be able to exercise some kind of discipline on their members and on fellow workers if they are to be at all effective. The repeal left unions in the anomalous position of having the right to strike, but not the right to carry out the essential actions for the staging of a strike; thus, picketing, and even notifying the strike to the masters, were at different times construed by the Bench as unlawful threats and coercion. The repealers were not wholly responsible for this anomaly.

Place himself had feared that the omission in the 1825 Act of the express derogation of the Common Law on combinations to be found in the 1824 Act, would leave unions in an exposed position. Still it must be said that their conception of purely voluntary unions was unrealistic.[8] Perhaps the very use of the word 'combinations' rather than 'unions' indicates a preconception that these institutions were ephemeral. While 'combination' was the usual term among the legislators and the writers of the higher classes, it seems that 'unions' was of working class origin.[9]

We shall see that Mill never freed himself completely from the Radical preconception that unions were a passing phenomenon.

The Great Fears of 1834

The year 1825 ended with a very severe economic crisis. Until economic conditions began to improve in 1829 the unionist movement appeared to be dead. The next period of unionism was the Owenite period we have spoken of, in which the workers sought to build up general or class unions.

The interest and the fears of the whole ruling class were quickened. A spate of articles, pamphlets, of writings of all sorts, gushed forth from the presses. Mill wrote several articles which we shall study later but clearly the most important contribution from the point of view of the history of economic thought was Robert Torrens's pamphlet *On Wages and Combinations,* published, it appears, at the very beginning of 1834.[10] On the matter of trade unions it is not as complete as McCulloch's two essays, but it opened a new avenue to the study of wages which had been indicated by Ricardo though neglected by the Ricardians: that wages could increase at the expense of profits. This avenue Mill would follow after he had abandoned the 'supply and demand' or short run theory of the wages fund in 1869, hence our interest in it.

One of Ricardo's main corollaries in the theory of distribution was that 'profits vary inversely with wages'. This dictum should not have been interpreted as a mere pronouncement about relative shares, in other words, as proposing the platitude that in a two-factor economy, if the relative share of one rose, that of the other fell.[11] J.S. Mill's interpretation of it in the *Principles* is more correct: 'instead of saying that profits depend on wages, let us say (what Ricardo really meant) that they depend on the *cost of labour*' (*Coll. Works* II, 413): for, since Ricardo assumes the economy to have entered the state of increasingly diminishing returns in agriculture, an increase in wages, and hence in the demand for agricultural goods, must mean an increase in the marginal cost of producing the national output. Any increase in the wage bill meant a diminution in the productivity of capital, and therefore a fall in the rate of profits.

Torrens however interpreted the dictum in its platitudinous version, as dealing with relative shares in a two-factor model, behaving like two buckets in a well. And so, for all his brave words, did Mill after he recanted the wages fund doctrine.

Torrens started by defining an 'actual' rate of wages in strict accordance with the demand and supply theory of the wages fund. There was a 'maximum' which left the capitalist with the smallest rate of profit 'for the sake of which he will carry on his business' (8); there was a 'minimum', below which labourers would refuse to perpetuate their number without increase or diminution. The 'actual' as distinct from the 'maximum' and 'minimum' rate, was determined by the ratio of the circulating capital of the country to the numbers in the labour market. In the fourth chapter of the pamphlet, however (called 'On the Effects of Combinations for Raising Wages'), the 'actual' wage rate was suddenly assumed to be determined by union bargaining. With no warning Torrens conceded the possibility of trade unions raising that rate to the maximum. One must assume that he believed that the 'supply and demand' theory only obtained in the absence of combinations. Instead he proposed a new 'bargaining' theory based on the dictum 'profits vary inversely with wages'. Rather than understanding it as a shorthand description of the mechanism which depressed profits when wages rose through the fall in the productivity of the land, he took it as a dictum about relative shares, meaning simply that if total wages rise total profits must fall. Wages could thus be directly increased at the expense of profits by union action.

From the analytical point of view, this innovation was hardly an advance. If it avoided the undue rigidity of the 'supply and demand' theory, when applied to the very short run it came perilously close to suggesting that there were no limits to union pressure on profits. After his 'recantation' neither did Mill avoid this danger of granting too much scope for wage increases through union action, and he even admitted the possibility of these increases being consolidated in the long run. Torrens was able to escape this latter pitfall by a further innovation in the Ricardian theory of distribution: the linking of the balance of payments with unionist action.[12]

In this second innovation he had been preceded by Senior's deservedly famous *Lectures on the Cost of Obtaining Money* (1830). Senior had made the very important discovery that differences in the rate of wages of two trading countries were due to the productivity of labour in the export industries.[13]

Torrens was not as precise as Senior. He simply said that 'in a country possessing superiority of manufactures for the foreign markets, wages may be raised within the limits of such superiority' (73). Torrens then proceeded to point out that wage increases could be offset by their repercussions on foreign payments, unless they were accompanied by increases in productivity. It is a pity that no other economist of the time, except Torrens, Senior, and Longfield, should have presented the productivity of labour as worthy to be taken into account.

In sum, even though Torrens adopted an approach to trade union activity based on a vulgar interpretation of the Ricardian dictum 'profits vary inversely with wages', he avoided its dangers by adverting to the effects of wage rises on the balance of payments.

When in later years the idea that wages could increase at the expense of profits was severally adopted, people hostile to trade unions pointed to the effects that such a diminution of profits would have on accumulation, and closed this possible opening for trade unions by asserting that wage rises would boomerang on the working classes by diminishing the future accumulation of the wages fund (we shall refer to this as the 'boomerang' version of the wages fund doctrine). Torrens made no allusion to such a possibility. As for Mill, when he came to abandon the 'demand and supply' theory of the wages fund doctrine and adopted the Torrensian approach to the trade unions, he accepted neither the limitation of international competition, nor that presented by the 'boomerang' theory of wages.

The general alarm reached its peak in 1834. During this year Mill wrote three short articles which give some indication that his position on trade unions was that of a friend of the working classes, even if he did not participate in many of their hopes and beliefs. These three anonymous articles were the sum total of Mill's writings on the unions until the *Principles*, which goes to show that the question did not interest him overmuch.

His first note was on the hostile attitude of the Whig Government and indeed of the Reformed Parliament, towards the working classes. *The Times* had praised the Admiralty for having interfered in favour of the masters in a coopers' strike, and urged the checking of 'the spirit and power of combination' by means of 'some more vigorous and comprehensive legislation' than the 1825 Act.[14]

In one of his 'Notes on the Newspapers' in the *Monthly Repository*,[15] Mill warned that such a change in the laws for the more rigorous 'will be received as neither more or [sic] less than a declaration to the working people.., that the Government is their enemy; that it is determined to *keep them down*; to keep them for ever poor, dependent, and servile, trampled into the earth under the feet of their employers.' Violence and threats from the unionists should be curbed. But workers were quite within their rights when expressing disapprobation towards such of their number 'whom they consider as traitors to their caste' — short of 'personal insult or serious molestation.' Mill concluded that 'any attempt to confine the liberty of combination among workers within narrower limits than these, is systematic tyranny.'

Such a declaration was remarkable for its time and day, since at that moment and for many years to follow, the greater part of the middle classes held a 'conspiracy theory' of unionism.[16] Mill's stand is especially significant when his virtual agreement that 'combinations never in reality keep up the rate of wages' is taken into account. These doubts about the efficacy of trade unions he did not consider an argument for persecuting them. If they cannot raise the wages, 'what then?' he asks. 'The working people are entitled to try: unless they try, how are they ever to learn?'

The lesson of experience would be 'that strikes on the old principle, strikes by cessation of working, are always failures. The doctrine of the Trades' Unions now is, that when they resolve upon a strike, their course must not be to cease working, but to work on their own account.' This is one of the earliest, if not the first, favourable mentions of co-operation in Mill's writings. 'Possessing the necessary funds, the labourers mean to become capitalists, and to make actual trial of the difficulties of a joint management.'

Another question arose because the unions, especially the Grand National Consolidated, used masonic rites and oaths for the initiation of their members. These ceremonies were widely denounced[17] and seized upon by the Government to suppress unionism. Six Dorsetshire labourers were tried for administering an oath 'under a sleeping statute which nobody dreamed of, and which was not known to be applicable to the case' (as Mill put it), and were sentenced to the unexpectedly heavy penalty of seven years' transportation to Botany Bay. The

Ministry, far from commuting the sentence, bundled the men out of the country, defending its decision with two arguments: that the labourers must have known that they were doing wrong, since they performed their ceremonies in secret; and that the recent bloody repression of the trade unions at Lyons was a proof of the danger of letting them wax too strong.[18]

In a second note in the *Monthly Repository*[19] Mill agreed that the oaths were a practice to be deprecated. 'The hardship was in not remitting their sentence, when the trial had given the requisite publicity to the law.' It was preposterous for a member of a parliamentary assembly which was notorious for not abrogating laws immediately after their *raison d'être* had disappeared, to put such a construction as the ministerial spokesman on the union rituals, for they were a mere survival from the very recent times when the unions were prohibited by law.

The events at Lyons, Mill interpreted in a very different light. The repression carried out by the French Government was not the retribution for tolerating the labourers too readily. The government of the neighbouring country, said Mill 'absolutely prohibits *all* combinations among workmen'; it has 'made a law to put down all societies whatever, not licenced by its own police'; it 'has now brought upon the second city in the empire the horrors of a five days' struggle of life and death, by attempting to punish the leaders of a strike, after the strike was terminated.'

> If the government which did this [proceeds Mill in a somewhat rhetorical vein] did not, in the opinion of our Ministers, interfere enough; . . .if our Ministers have taken warning from them; and are resolved not to be guilty of a like error; — why then it is time for every Englishman, who has the means, to provide himself with a musket: for there is no knowing how soon the consequences of such a policy may leave him destitute of any other protection (365).

Mill's central plea is in the spirit of his previous note on the trade unions. The best thing the government could do was to let them alone. 'It was well worth the partial stoppage of two or three branches of trade, to let the experiment be tried fairly, what Unions can do.' Outrages, undue coercion could not be countenanced. But 'there has been much cant about tyrannizing over masters.' The unions, in short, ought to be given the benefit of the doubt.

In his third note,[20] Mill embarked on a diagnosis of the tone the periodical press adopted towards working class movements. The explanation of the hysterical tone of the press towards unionism was, according to Mill, to be found in the fact that the papers were organs of the middle classes. Before the Great Reform Act, the middle and the working classes had one interest in common, that of reducing the power of people of large property. The Reform had extended political power to all people of property, large or small, 'to the exclusion of those who are said to have no property.'

> It is very natural, however [Mill continued], that the working classes, even at this early stage in the development of their collective intellect, should feel that their real position in society depends upon something far deeper than the redress of any grievances (such as the Corn Laws) which the majority of their superiors have in common with them. It depends upon the relation which may be established between them and the people of property generally (436).

The middle class were simply taking the attitude of any ruling class whose power is being challenged. 'When they see a power growing up, which is not wholly under their control, their first impulse always is fear; their second, anger' (437).

In point of fact the Great Reform Act did not install the middle class in power; the pre-eminent position of the great landowners continued for many years. But the important thing is that the middle classes thought that the Reform Act had been the watershed, and hence began to identify themselves increasingly with the traditional ruling classes, not least in their attitude to the working people. Such an attitude was not shared by the group of radicals to which Mill by and large belonged.

The Radical Party and the Working Classes
Mill did not change his opinions on the economic creed of the working classes during the thirties: while he still thought that their efforts to raise the rate of wages by direct pressure would be unavailing (thus allowing a smaller scope for trade unions' action than McCulloch and especially Torrens had), he saw their plight with sympathy and wished them to be given full scope for experiment.

After two years the six labourers had been brought back to England. But the sentence and its swift execution had produced the desired effect: the Grand National Consolidated Trades' Union melted quickly and for a few years unions ceased to trouble the possessing classes.

Trade union activity continued on a local scale only, while labour agitation took a political rather than a unionist form: it was the period of Chartism.

Mill, in an article of 1839 which crowned his campaign to form a Radical Party in Parliament, distinct from the Whigs, and under the leadership of Lord Durham, observed the new political consciousness of the working classes with great interest.[21] As he saw it, the new Radical Party had to be based on the alliance of those who were discontented with the established order of society; one of the difficulties of cementing this alliance was the gulf dividing the middle from the working classes. Even if the working classes were not enfranchised the programme of the Radical leader should contain measures to remedy the practical grievances of the workers. The country, said Mill quoting Wakefield with approval, ought to be governed 'as it would be necessary to govern it, if there were Universal Suffrage and the people were well educated and intelligent' (495).

As regards the economic creed of the working class leaders, he did not wish to dissemble that 'even the very best of these men entertain notions in political economy with which we by no means coincide.' They ascribed low wages to everything but the true cause, the over-competition 'produced by their own excessive numbers.' These were Mill's old ideas quite unchanged. When he turned to the Owenism of the working classes, he again wished all encouragement to be given to their co-operative endeavours: since 'the labourers wish to become their own capitalists,' the law ought to be changed to make this possible for them (497—8).

'The Principles of Political Economy' (1848)

Mill gave very little importance to the subject of cômbinations in the *Principles*. He allotted to it a mere four pages,[22] which is next to nothing in comparison with the fifty-one pages given to the effects of population on wages, the twelve given to co-operation,[23] or the forty-nine to peasant proprietorship. In that short space he defended the constitutional right of workers to combine, and discussed two kinds of combinations: general, comprising the whole of the working classes; and partial, endeavouring to raise the wages of only a section of labourers.

His verdict on the capabilities of the type of union which the people were trying to set up in the thirties, namely general unions, was adverse. Could they successfully raise the wage rate, he said, the attempt should not be punished, but rejoiced at. Unfortunately, such a thing was beyond their capabilities. 'The multitudes who compose the working class are too numerous and too widely scattered to combine at all, much more to combine effectually' (*Coll. Works*, III, 929).

But even though they set up a successful combination they would not be able to attain their goal. For 'if they aimed at obtaining actually higher wages than the rate fixed by demand and supply — the rate which distributes the whole circulating capital of the country among the entire working population — this could only be accomplished by keeping a part of their number permanently out of employment.'[24]

Mill was obviously assuming here that the demand for labour had unit elasticity, hence that the resulting unemployment would be exactly proportional to the increase in the wage rate, and that in the end, the unemployed would bid the wage down to its previous level. Thus he was applying the short run version of the wages fund doctrine in the orthodox way.

It can be seen, then, that the section of the *Principles* dealing with general unions was very unsatisfactory. His analysis of partial unions was better. The exhaustion of the efforts of the Chartists to create a working class political force brought about a decided change in the character of working men's activities. Trade unionist leaders began to concentrate on the formation of craft unions, such as the carpenters' union, or the engineers', or builders', a more feasible endeavour in the conditions of the time; meanwhile the Owenite strand in the working class, which had provided the backbone for the Grand Consolidated, concentrated upon the building of co-operatives — an effort crowned with success after the discovery of the Rochdale Owenites in the years following 1844 that consumer co-operatives seemed to be free of the many drawbacks of producers' associations.

Both movements were to leave a permanent stamp on British life. The trade union movement in Britain, instead of developing into national trade unions distinguished by their political affiliations, as on the continent, became a federation of craft unions. The producers' co-operative was virtually to disappear, in favour of consumer co-operatives.

The short run version of the wages fund doctrine was also applicable to sectional craft combinations: since the total amount going to wages was predetermined, an extraordinary increase for one sector of the working classes had to result in lower wages for the rest. But in the first edition of the *Principles* (1848) Mill sharply deviated from this standard theory, and defended partial combinations as usually harmless from the point of view of the whole working class — an important conclusion, since, as we have said, the sectional kind of trade union was beginning to become generalized in Britain.

A 'partial rise of wages, if not gained at the expense of the remainder of the working class, ought to be regarded as a benefit' [1848] (*Coll. Works*, III, [V, x, 5] 930 and gg and hh). The trouble lay in that according to the received opinion no partial combination could avoid harming the interests of the other workers.

It may appear, however, at first sight, that the high wages of the type-founders (for example) are obtained at the general cost of the labouring class. This high remuneration either causes fewer persons to find employment in the trade, or if not, must lead to the investment of more capital in it, at the expense of other trades.

This is a straightforward application of the doctrine, but Mill rejected the conclusion by distinguishing between the short and long run (as he unfortunately did not do for general wages).

The damage which the outside workers sustained from the success of a partial combination could not become permanent, argued Mill. The ultimate regulator of wages is the customary standard of living.

The habitual earnings of the working classes at large can be affected by nothing but the habitual requirements of the labouring people: these indeed may be altered, but while they remain the same, wages never fall permanently below the standard of these requirements, and cannot long remain above that standard [1848] (931).

Hence partial combinations were instrumental in stemming excessive population growth.

If there had been no combinations in particular trades, and the wages of those trades had never been kept above the universal level, there is no reason whatever to suppose that the universal level would have been at all higher than it now is [1848].

There was also the damage to the consumer, since in this case employers would be able to pass on the wage rise by increasing their prices. But such damage to the interests of the consumer Mill did not think too important: 'cheapness of goods is desirable only when the cause of it is that their productions costs little labour, and not when occasioned by that labour's being ill remunerated' (930). In sum, trade unions could be applauded when they struck for higher wages, for shorter hours, and for limiting the number of apprentices.

There were, however, two points on which Mill fell foul of sectional unions. The first was when they attempted to do away with incentives to harder or better work. 'In many trade unions, it is among the rules that there shall be no task work, or no difference of pay between the most expert workmen and the most unskilful.' Unions which pursued such aims were 'a public nuisance', but whether they should be punished by the law or not, Mill did not feel it safe to decide as yet, at least before deeper consideration and wider experience intervened.

The law should, however, fall on the unions which pursued even legitimate goals 'by threats or violence' (933). 'It is. . .an indispensable condition that the combination should be voluntary.' Mere moral compulsion 'the law ought not to interfere with; it belongs to more enlightened opinion to restrain it, by rectifying the moral sentiments of the people.'

Mill's feelings, therefore, were quite favourable to partial combinations in 1848.

But the third edition of the *Principles* (1852) shows that an important change had taken place in Mill's opinion on this matter. He removed the sentence 'Combinations to keep up wages are therefore not only permissible, but useful, whenever really calculated to have that effect,' [1848] (*Coll. Works,* III, 931 pp), and substituted for it a passage containing the assertion that 'combinations to keep up wages. . .are. . .seldom desirable.' What had happened in the meantime to make him change his mind thus, was an event which made a deep impress on public opinion, the strike of the Amalgamated Society of Engineers to put an end to the use of overtime and piece work.[25]

As will be shown in more detail below, Mill considered that piece work and overtime were fundamentally just institutions, in that people who worked hardest were paid most. He had no notion of the use to which masters sometimes put them, namely to exact more work at the standard pay, and to shorten and lengthen the labour day as suited their needs. Mill, who as we shall see in Chapter 8, thought that the property system was vitiated by the fundamental defect 'that the produce of labour should be apportioned as we now see it, almost in an inverse ratio to the labour' [1852] (207), was bound to react strongly against what he saw as endeavours to put the best workmen on a par with the worst. It was hardly surprising that he should decry

> that almost open disregard of all other objects than high wages and little work for their own small body, which were so deplorably evident in the proceedings and manifestoes of the Amalgamated Society of Engineers during their quarrel with their employers [1852].[26]

Added to this was the increased hope which Mill showed in this very edition, of lifting the whole of the working classes out of their dejected condition, especially through the means of co-operation.

> When the elevation of the character and condition of the entire body has at last become a thing not beyond the reach of rational effort, it is time that the better paid classes of skilled artisans should seek their own advantage in common with, and not by the exclusion of, their fellow-labourers.[27]

So Mill changed the opinion he had held in 1848 approving of sectional wage rises won through partial combinations. It is remarkable that precisely at the time when he was writing his most favourable words on socialism, he was harshest on trade unions. This apparent paradox in fact reveals his growing impatience with provisional solutions, and should warn one against interpreting Mill's severe words on unionism as evidence of lack of sympathy towards the cause of labour.

Indeed, one might say that he showed eagerness to grasp any argument which would allow him despite everything to see unionism in a favourable light. The fifth edition of the *Principles* (1862) contained two new arguments in favour of trade unions, somewhat tending to tilt the balance back from the unfavourable position in which the edition of 1852 had left it.

The first, Mill discovered in an article by his friend and disciple Henry Fawcett, 'Strikes: their Tendencies and Remedies' published in the *Westminster Review* for July 1860. Fawcett's article is well worth reading. His use of the distinction between short run and long run wages, and the possible effect of unions on each, allows him to put the matter much more clearly than Mill. His presentation of the idea that both employers and workmen weighed the inconvenience of a strike against the advantages which might be gained by it, is a step forward in the time when workmen were generally believed to engage upon strikes out of sheer perverseness, and foreshadows later analytical developments such as Professor Hicks's 'concession curve' of the employers and 'resistance curve' of the unions.[28]

What struck Mill especially was Fawcett's insistence that unionized workers had come to study the market as carefully as the masters, and to ask for wage increases when profits were exceptionally high. Fawcett put it thus: 'Strikes exert a tendency to raise the wages of a particular class of workmen when the profits of the particular trade are temporarily raised above the ordinary rate' (10). Such increase in wages Fawcett likened to a partnership of the workers in the business — though a forced one: 'as long as this participation of profits is secured by an actual resort to strikes, the workman is forced upon his master as a partner' (17). Better a voluntary profit sharing than the expense of continuous strikes. Fawcett then embarked upon an exposition of the possibilities of co-operation which was directly inspired (it appears from comparison of the two texts) by Mill's chapter on the 'Futurity of the Working Class,' which we shall look at later.

As a result of reading Fawcett's article, Mill inserted in this fifth edition some reflections tending to show that strikes to share in extraordinary profits are

> a commencement of that regular participation of the labourers in the profits derived from their labour, every tendency to which. . .it is so important to encourage, since to it we have chiefly to look for any radical improvement in the social and economical relations between labour and capital [1862] (933).

Another point analysed at length by Fawcett was that trade unions tended to increase the wages of those labourers who because of ignorance, or due to obstacles to mobility, were receiving less than the market wage: 'strikes,' said Fawcett, 'without increasing the general wage fund of the country. . .exert a tendency to equalise wages in different employments.'[29]

A related point was made by the Secretary of the London Consolidated Society of Bookbinders in a pamphlet called *Trades' Unions and Strikes: their philosophy and intention* (1860), which Mill recommended to his readers also in this fifth edition.[30] The author, T.J. Dunning, insisted that capital had an advantage over labour: that of being able to hold out longer;

and as he who can stand out longest in the bargain will be sure to command his own terms, the workmen combine to put themselves on something like an equality in the bargain for the sale of their labour with their employers. This is the *rationale* of Trade Societies, which is very clearly indicated by Adam Smith in his 'Wealth of Nations' (7).

These suggestions must have led Mill finally to introduce into his analysis the single most important argument for the existence of trade unions: that the market is imperfect, that, due to lack of information, to obstacles to mobility, to the fact that labour is a perishable commodity and labourers have few reserves to enable them to stand out from the market if they do not find the terms convenient, a great number of labourers receive less than the equilibrium rate of wages unless they combine.

I grant that a strike is wrong whenever it is foolish, and it is foolish whenever it attempts to raise wages above that market rate which is rendered possible by the demand and supply.[31] But demand and supply are not physical agencies. . . The market rate is not fixed for him [the labourer] by some self-acting instrument, but is the result of bargaining between human beings − of what Adam Smith calls 'the higgling of the market'. . . What chance would any labourer have, who struck singly for the advance of wages? How could he even know whether the state of the market admitted of a rise?

The conclusion was one with which many economists today would agree:

I do not hesitate to say that associations of labourers, of a nature similar to trade unions, far from being a hindrance to a free market for labour, are the necessary instrumentality of that free market [1862] (932).

Mill still retained some important mental reservations about some aspects of unionism, especially the hostility of the men to piece work (though not to their hostility to compulsory overtime). Thus, in 1861, when he had just read Fawcett's article in the *Westminster Review*, Mill expressly rejected Frederic Harrison's assumption that since he approved of Fawcett's ideas he must also approve of the unionist defence of a fixed labour day and a fixed wage.

A building strike was then in force to resist payment by the hour.
Frederic Harrison, the Comtist, said in a letter to the *Daily News*[32] that
such a system seemed to be just because it apparently left the workers
free to work as long a day as they wished. In point of fact, the
employer, by 'sacking' those who refused to work for as long as he
wished, was able to make 'the day perfectly elastic, variable, and
irregular.' The men were simply 'standing on the defensive, and resisting
a change.'

Having been asked whether he agreed with Harrison, Mill answered:

> I regard payment of a fixed sum per day as essentially demoralising,
> and I disapprove of what the men are doing precisely because, as Mr.
> Harrison says, they are on the conservative side, standing up for the
> existing practice, a practice which is making workmen more and
> more fraudulent in the quality of their labour, just as dealers in that
> of their goods.

To this we should add that Mill saw piece work and payments by the
hour as the best possible system, in a pre-co-operative world, of
proportioning wage to the amount of work.[33]

Mill's attitude to piece work and work by the hour must be counted
as unrealistic. His ignorance of actual industrial conditions made him
blind to the dangers of making labour casual (as for example it has been
for a long time on the London docks), of underpaying the men whose
work is not amenable to payment by the piece (as in surface work in
the mines), or of having continual conflict grow out of the attempt to
exact more than the customary work-load from the average wage.[34]

Payment by the piece may be especially suited to some kinds of
work but it is unrealistic to expect that labour problems will be solved
by a wholesale resort to that system. His exhortations to return to
standards of pride in craftsmanship, or even his defence of a generalized
incentive system to make each individual worker's rewards fit his
deserts, evidence ignorance of modern industrial conditions. The
solution for labour problems more often than not lies in reforming
group attitudes to work, not in exhorting individuals to break the
harmony of their relations with their fellow workers.

Mill's 'Recantation'
Up to now, the interest of the discussion in this chapter, lay in the fact
that it was Mill who held all these opinions, in themselves not very deep
or novel. We now have to consider an incident which is interesting of

itself: what has come to be called Mill's 'recantation' of the wages fund doctrine — the most famous and the least known of the incidents of his intellectual history. The responsibility for the exaggerated importance lent to this 'recantation' and the mistaken notions entertained about it must be attributed principally to Mill.

In 1867, after outrages committed by some trade unionists in Sheffield, the Government decided to entrust the examination of the whole problem of labour relations to a Royal Commission. Mill, then still an MP, was offered a seat but refused for personal reasons.[35]

While the enquiry was being held a number of books on trade unionism appeared. One of them, serialized in the *Fortnightly Review* from May to December 1867 (where Mill is sure to have seen it, if he had not already read the draft copy), was W.T. Thornton's *On Labour*.

Thornton was one of Mill's few friends. He had been Mill's assistant when he was working at India House, and during a nervous breakdown which lasted a year was able to keep his post because his share of work was quietly carried on by Mill. They had apparently disagreed on the American Civil War, for Thornton had taken sides with the South. But on many matters their opinions coincided. It is enough to mention the titles of some of Thornton's books: *Over-population and its Remedies* (1846) and *A Plea for Peasant Proprietors* (1848). About him Mill wrote to Cairnes that he was 'a person I particularly respect and like.' The friendship between the two men was a firm one, and suggests some explanation of why Mill made his review of Thornton's *On Labour* the occasion for his 'recantation'.[36]

Thornton's thesis was that 'competition in a small minority of cases, combination in a great majority' determine the rate of wages (85). To defend this thesis he attacked two main positions in the writings of those with whom he disagreed: the first was the belief that the rate of wages was determined by demand and supply; the second what a few pages above was called the 'boomerang' theory of wages, according to which 'artificial' wage rises would have an adverse effect on accumulation, a theory based on the Ricardian dictum that 'profits vary inversely with wages.'

It should be stressed that when he attacked the first position, that wages were determined by demand and supply, Thornton was not referring specifically to the short run version of the wages fund doctrine but generally to all references, vague or specific, to the operation of a law of supply and demand in labour questions.

Thornton attacked this idea on two counts: he denied that the 'law of supply and demand' was a true law, that is, he denied that demand and supply determined the price of any good or service; then he asserted that in the case of labour the inapplicability of the demand and supply apparatus was even more marked, since labour was a perishable commodity and the labourer had no reserve funds to withstand a long bargaining period.

Thornton's attack on the 'law' of demand and supply is the least acceptable part of his book. To prove the failings of this law he gave various examples of small markets where what today would be called discontinuous demand and supply functions obtained, without one equilibrium price being reached, but prices within limits determined by bargain. The agency which in the end determined the equilibrium was 'competition' said Thornton, and not the law of demand and supply! (59).

Mill in his review of the book put up an excellent defence of the position attacked by Thornton, deservedly noticed by Professor Stigler as exhibiting considerable analytical originality.[37] All the cases presented by Thornton, Mill said, hold in very special circumstances, but 'in any considerable market. . .it is the next thing to impossible that more of a commodity should not be asked for at every reduction of price' (637).[38] His argument amounted to saying that Thornton, by choosing competition as the agency which makes equilibrium determinate, was simply expressing a fundamental assumption of the law.

Thornton need not have attacked the 'law' of demand and supply. His argument was strong enough when he said that the labour market was imperfect because of the perishable character of the commodity 'labour' (74) and the lack of reserves of the working man (77). These points had been anticipated by Beesly[39] (if not by others), and, as was shown above, had been inserted by Mill in the sixth edition of the *Principles*. It is not surprising that in the review Mill should concur with Thornton in holding that

> in that contest of endurance between buyer and seller. . .it is almost needless to say that nothing but a close combination among the employed can give them even a chance of successfully contending against the employers (643).

Thornton's arguments were not, therefore, those which persuaded Mill to abandon the short run version of the wages fund doctrine. In point of fact Thornton had only dealt indirectly with this theory allotting it a mere footnote in *On Labour*.[40]

The formulation of the short run version of the doctrine which Thornton chose for his attack in the footnote was that of Fawcett in the book *The Economic Position of the British Labourer* (1865). This detail is also interesting because, as will be shown later, Mill had expressed his first doubts about the wages fund in a letter to Fawcett on the publication of his book, and perhaps it was Mill who had pointed the passage out to Thornton. The passage Thornton quoted from Fawcett ran:

> The circulating capital of a country is its wage fund. Hence, if we desire to calculate the average money wages received by each labourer, we have simply to divide the amount of capital by the number of the labouring population. It is therefore evident that the average money wages cannot be increased, until either the circulating capital is augmented, or the number of the labouring population is diminished (84).[41]

Thornton asked: 'But is there really any such fund?' To answer this question he started from the basis that 'it can only be an aggregate of smaller funds of the same kind possessed by the several individuals composing the nation.' He did not find any such money funds in existence, 'which the owner must necessarily expend upon labour,' and hence rejected the doctrine.

Apart from the criticism that might be levelled at Thornton for presenting the wages fund in monetary rather than real terms,[42] it must be underlined that he did not quite understand the aggregate nature of the fund — neither in the first edition, nor in the second after Mill had made the point in his review[43]: it was not necessary for each single one of the employers of labour to hold a fund earmarked for wages, but simply that the country as a whole should hold capital for the payment of labour, in the form of a stock of wage-goods.

Mill in his review rejected this argument of Thornton's against the wages fund. The doctrine implied a unit elasticity of the aggregate demand for labour, not of the demand of each individual employer.

> In this doctrine it is by implication affirmed, that the demand for labour not only increases with the cheapness, but increases in exact proportion to it, the same aggregate sum being paid for labour whatever its price may be.

For individual employers, a fall in wages does not necessarily mean
that they will feel able to employ a correspondingly increased amount
of hands.

> Does the employer require more labour, or do fresh employers of
> labour make their appearance, merely because it can be bought
> cheaper? Assuredly, no. . . A fall of wages does not necessarily make
> him expect a larger sale for his commodity, nor, therefore, does it
> necessarily increase his demand for labour (644).

But in the aggregate, the situation may be conceived to be different.
The individual employer may not be led to engage more labour with
every fall in wages, but will find himself with an increased profit due to
his lower labour costs. 'As he will not be willing to leave the balance
unemployed, he will invest in some other manner. . .and on the whole
the wages fund will be paying wages as before.'

That Thornton's arguments were not the actual cause of Mill's
change of mind finally seems to be confirmed by Mill's own words. In
the review Mill said: 'I have quoted the argument in my own way,
which is not exactly Mr. Thornton's; but the reasoning is essentially his,
though, in a part of it, I have only been anticipated by him' in
publishing it. With these words Mill seemed to indicate that he was on
the point of pronouncing the demise of the doctrine when Thornton
published his book.

Three years before the recantation, and one year and a half before
he could have read Thornton's attacks in the *Fortnightly* he had written
to Fawcett (1 January 1866), 'The chapter which. . .I least like [of
Fawcett's book *The Economic Position of the British Labourer*, 1865]
is the one on wages, though it will probably be more praised than any
of the rest.' Fawcett, as can be seen from Thornton's quotation above,
had stated the received opinion in its starkest form. 'I think I could
shew,' proceeded Mill, 'that an increase of wages at the expense of
profits would not be an impracticability on the true principles of
political economy.'[44]

On this occasion, however, we need not be satisfied with vague hints.
We may ascertain from his own words what it was he objected to in the
orthodox doctrine of the wages fund. In his review of Thornton's book,
he described the matter in the following terms:

> There is supposed to be, at any given instant, a sum of wealth, which
> is unconditionally devoted to the payment of wages of labour. This

sum is not regarded as unalterable, for it is augmented by saving, and increases with the progress of wealth; but it is reasoned upon as, at any given moment, a predetermined amount. More than that amount it is assumed that the wages-receiving class cannot possibly divide among them; that amount, and no less, they cannot but obtain. So that, the sum to be divided being fixed, the wages of each depend solely on the divisor, the number of participants (643).

The sting of the theory thus lay for him in the short run rigidity of the wages fund. This suggests that Mill's mind was changed by his doubts about the realism of the Ricardian model when it assumed what Böhm Bawerk would call the 'average period of production' to be one of twelve months, that is to say, that a year separated the capitalists' decision to save a given amount for the wages fund from the time when the same capitalists received their income. It seems that Mill came to think that the only basis for speaking of a rigid wages fund lay in this very artificial assumption of income accruing at yearly intervals. According to the old model (as Mill now saw it), trade union action was doomed to failure because employers just did not have the means of granting an increase: the whole of their means was either sunk in fixed capital, or laid out in raw materials, or accumulated in the wages fund. The employer could not pay the increase out of income for he had not yet received it. As Mill put it, 'When he does receive it, he may lay by a portion to add to his capital, and as such it will become part of next year's wages fund, but has nothing to do with this year's' (644).

Mill rejected this picture as, in his opinion, highly unrealistic. The capitalist, he said, did not advance wages at the beginning of the year, and receive his income at the end; he rather made advances continually and replaced them continually from his returns.[45] The profit of the capitalist 'is made as his transactions go on, and not at Christmas and Midsummer, when he balances his books.' According to Mill's new idea, the whole of what the capitalist possesses at any given moment, 'the whole of the proceeds of his business, after keeping up his machinery, buildings and materials, and feeding his family' is the wages fund, and is 'expended jointly upon himself and his labourers. The less he expends on the one, the more may be expended on the other and *vice versa*' (645).

The consequences for trade union policy Mill thought of the highest importance.

The doctrine hitherto taught by all or most economists (including

myself), which denied it to be possible that trade unions can raise
wages, or which limited their operation in that respect to the
somewhat earlier attainment of a rise which the competition of the
market would have produced without them, — the doctrine is
deprived of its scientific foundation, and must be thrown aside
(646).

All these reflections of Mill's on the period of production were
couched in terms of an individual employer, which made for ambiguity
since the point at issue was the *aggregate* wages fund. Be that as it may,
once he had focused on the single employer to prove that the wages
fund was advanced and replaced continually, Mill should have
proceeded to ask what motivates an employer to hire more or less
labour at any given moment. A new departure could have been made in
the analysis of the demand for labour, in terms of the wage rate
compared with productivity, and with expected sales (that is, the rate
compared with the marginal value product of labour). Unfortunately he
did not proceed at all along that way. He simply shifted the argument
back to the aggregate level. Neither did he make any original suggestion
at this level, since on the demise of the 'demand and supply' theory of
wages, he took refuge in the Ricardian dictum 'profits depend on
wages,' and came to hold a position strikingly similar to that of Torrens
in the 1834 pamphlet *On Wages*. Finally, he threw overboard an
important · part of the classical theory of capital when he separated
wages from accumulation.

With his rejection of the assumption that income was produced in
yearly spurts, Mill came to think that the initiative for determining the
size of the share of labour had passed from the employers to the
unions. 'The price of labour, instead of being determined by the
division of the proceeds between the employer and the labourer,
determines it' (645). According to the wages he has to pay, the
employer will have more or less for his own use.

As we have already seen, the short run theory of the wages fund was
usually presented in two ways: 'demand and supply' and 'boomerang'.
According to the first, which Mill as we have seen rejected, the wages
fund was rigid; according to the second, the fund was not rigid, but
elastic, though with a vengeance, for any extension of it beyond the
employers' wishes would lash back on accumulation and eventually
affect wages.

Clearly, then, the conclusion Mill came to when he rejected the idea
of a rigid fund was nothing new. Differences of opinion lay in what

happened after a general rise had been obtained by union action.

Thornton opposed the 'boomerang' version, for which he had nothing but scorn. He directed his attack against an anonymous article in the October 1867 issue of the *Quarterly Review* which, according to him, said that wages and profits moved 'like two buckets in a well, of which neither can rise without the other's falling.' Thornton somewhat misrepresented the writer's views, but that is beside the point.[46] In reply to the 'boomerang' theory, he asserted that general rises in wages could take place while leaving profits intact, namely by leading to a general rise in prices, the increase being passed on to the consumer.[47] Mill was to reject the idea of a *general* rise in prices as impossible.

Such a thing may happen to some extent in the modern world where the quantity of money can be increased by government *fiat*, and the State is pledged to maintaining full employment. But in Mill's time Britain was on the gold standard: a general rise in prices thus induced could not be permanent. Mill rejected Thornton's assurances that the general rise would be passed on to prices: 'a rise in general wages cannot be compensated to employers by a general rise of prices.' By and large Mill's pronouncement is acceptable, though the assumption behind it that such a general increase, necessarily impermanent because of the gold standard, would leave everything unchanged, is less so.[48]

In later years the argument that Thornton had devised to defend trade union action was, it seems, accepted by both friends and enemies of unionism. One may conjecture from certain of Mill's words that workers were exhorted to strike because any fall in profits could be compensated by a general rise in prices, and, confusingly, also exhorted to refrain from striking because they would lose in higher prices what they had gained in increased wages. 'You must have been struck,' Mill wrote to Cairnes on the 4 October 1872, 'as I have been, by the thoroughly confused and erroneous ideas respecting the relations of wages to prices, which have shown themselves to be almost universal in the discussion about the recent strikes.'[49]

The notion [continued Mill] that a general rise in wages must produce a general rise in prices, is preached universally not only by the newspapers but by the political economists, as a certain and admitted economic truth; and political economy has to bear the responsibility of a self-contradicting absurdity which it is one of the achievements of political economy to have exploded.

In sum, it appears that Thornton's book was rather a pretext for Mill than the cause of his change of mind. Mill wished to proclaim his doubts about the doctrine of the wages fund, and found it convenient to do so on the occasion of the publication of his friend's book. Thornton's main argument in the first edition of *On Labour* had been that demand and supply do not determine the price of anything, much less of labour. Mill clearly rejected Thornton's strictures on the 'law' of demand and supply. His reason for accepting the ability of unions to raise the general rate of labour was not that the law of supply and demand was invalid, but that the *demand* for labour was ill described by speaking of a wages fund replenished at yearly intervals. Thornton had touched on this point in the first edition only in a footnote. In his second edition he was led to include the argument in the text because of the importance it had had in Mill's 'recantation'. But it was clear that he did not understand the import of Mill's doubts on the doctrine; for he insisted on the fact that there were no wages funds in the hands of the several employers, though in his review Mill had shown that this did not affect the possibility of there being an aggregate wages fund. Nor did he mention in this edition Mill's actual reason for giving up the doctrine, to wit, the unreality of the assumption of the Ricardian model that income accrued only at yearly intervals. Finally, he continued to hold that a general rise of wages could be passed on to prices, despite Mill's arguments showing that, in the circumstances of the time, it could only take place at the expense of profits.

In all these discussions as to the possibility of wages rising at the expense of profits, Mill made no allusion to the 'boomerang' effect. This is the main criticism levelled against him by the Scottish economist, James Stirling, the translator of Bastiat. In an essay published in 1870 he deplored Mill's abandonment of the doctrine. He did not so much insist on the idea that wages are determined by 'demand and supply' (though he firmly believed they were). He rather made the point (very telling from the point of view of Ricardian economists, that is, from Mill's own point of view) that Mill's new theory 'rests on the monstrous assumption, that it is possible to take from profits and add to wages, without weakening the effective desire of accumulation.'[50] In other words, Stirling asked how Mill could give up the 'demand and supply' view of the wages fund without admitting that inroads into profits would boomerang to the detriment of workers in the last resort.

Mr. Mill has let himself be swayed by feeling. His generous heart is touched with pity: and he casts about for some scientific warrant for his yearnings. All his sympathies are with the workman struggling with his master; and, recoiling from the stern sentence of futility which in common with other economists, he had once pronounced against the efforts of the Unionists, he modifies his stricter doctrine to save the cause of combination (320– 1).

It is difficult to say what made Mill isolate wages from accumulation, and discount the dangers for accumulation of a general rise in wages. He did consider that the rises could not go above certain limits, as we can read in his review of Thornton's book:

What is true is, that wages might be so high as to leave no profit to the capitalist, or not enough to compensate him for the anxieties and risks of trade; and in that case the labourers would be killing the goose to get at the eggs. And, again, wages might be so low as to diminish the numbers or impair the working powers of the labourers.

However, barring those two extremes he spoke as if the general rise did not entail any peril: 'between two limits just indicated. . .there is an intermediate region within which wages will range higher or lower according to what Adam Smith calls "the higgling of the market" ' (657).

James Mill and Torrens had also shown indifference for the fate of accumulation. Perhaps the explanation lies in the fact that the Ricardians thought the stationary state to be imminent. John Mill, who as we shall see, thought the stationary state could be pleasant if the transition was managed properly, was concerned about the position of the labourer when the end of the progressive state would come, rather than about the ways and means to guarantee the continuance of accumulation.

It is only in the backward countries of the world that increased production is still an important object: in those most advanced, what is economically needed is a better distribution, of which one indispensable means is a stricter restraint on population (*Coll. Works*, III, 755).

The 'boomerang' version may have been vulgar economics at the time, but it certainly looks the most interesting formulation today. To analyse a changing economy by means of the concept of 'period of production' à la Böhm Bawerk, is to engage in static analysis of a fundamentally dynamic process. On the other hand, though neo-classical distribution theory is also static theory, it can easily be turned, and in fact has been turned, into dynamic theory: instead of saying that in equilibrium distribution will be governed by the marginal value-product of each factor, it can be stressed that any other distribution but one governed by marginal productivity can lead the economy astray from the path of warranted growth. In simpler terms, this is just what the holders of the 'boomerang' version meant. They meant to say that a forced increase in wages would induce either a straightforward reduction in employment, or a substitution of capital for labour, hence a fall in the marginal productivity of capital and in the rate of interest, which in its turn would mean less incentive to accumulate and a slower growth of national income. Perhaps Mill's lack of interest in the 'boomerang' version may be explained through his dislike of 'growthmanship'.

The conclusion which Mill reached on the power of unions in the *Fortnightly* article, was that

> There is no law of nature making it inherently impossible for wages to rise to the point of absorbing not only the funds which he [the capitalist] had intended to devote to carrying on of his business, but the whole of what he allows for his private expenses, beyond the necessaries of life (*Coll. Works*, V, 645).

Alfred Marshall, in Appendix J to his *Principles of Economics*, criticized this conclusion of Mill's by saying that he had yielded too much to Thornton's arguments. Apart from the question of whether or not Mill had reached his conclusions unaided by Thornton, Marshall was right: Mill had gone too far. The cause of Mill's overstatement lay in his failure to distinguish between the short and the long run. As Marshall put it, when Mill set the limit to the possible rise of wages at the point where the capitalist would be ruined or impelled to abandon his business, 'he did not make it clear whether this statement refers to immediate or ultimate effects: but in either case it appears untenable.'

> As regards long periods the limit is put too high: for wages could not rise permanently so as to absorb nearly as large a share of the national dividend as is here indicated. And for short periods, it is not put high enough: for a well organised strike at a critical juncture,

may. . .make his [the employer's] gross profits for the time a negative quantity (825).

The doctrine of the wages fund, leaving aside its shortcomings as an analytical tool, reaches a roughly acceptable conclusion when it is applied to the long run: that it is impossible for unions permanently and directly to increase the share of labour in the national income. But it does not hold in the short run when the demand for labour is likely to be inelastic, and hence, vulnerable to union pressure.

When giving up the doctrine, Mill should have gone further in his admission of the effectiveness of unions in the short run, but not so far in the long term. In fact, it may be said that his adoption of the Ricardian dictum that 'profits depend on wages' in place of the wages fund doctrine, entailed, for the long run wages, a change for the worse. In Torrens, the drawbacks of such changes were neutralized by his admission that international competition (in prices, not in the bargaining force of unions) set a limit to union activity. For the writer of the *Quarterly* article, and other 'boomerang' theorists, the notion that profits varied inversely with wages was neutralized by a measure of inconsistency (as when in defiance of their theory they denied the possibility of rises in the short run) and a measure of capitalist prejudice (as when, in line with their theory, they stressed the effects of such rises on accumulation). But Mill conceded a role to none of these correcting influences, so that his final position was less acceptable than that of other economists.

Mill's sympathies were clearly with the unionists, and Stirling was probably right to say that this inclination of heart made Mill bend his convictions further than perfect scientific objectivity would have it (whether or not Stirling's own position regarding trade unions was an acceptable one).

Unions in the Last Edition of the 'Principles'
Mill himself seems to have felt that he had gone a little too far in his 'recantation' article. The last edition of the *Principles* published after the great controversy over the wages fund evidences a somewhat cooler attitude towards the capabilities of trade unions than the *Fortnightly* article. Indeed the modesty of the changes which Mill saw fit to introduce in the 1870 edition is surprising in view of the ringing tone of the 'recantation'. In the preface to the edition he said:

There has been some instructive discussion on the theory of Demand

and Supply, and on the influence of Strikes and Trades Unions on wages, by which additional light has been thrown on these subjects; but the results, in the author's opinion, are not yet ripe for incorporation in a general treatise on Political Economy (*Coll. Works*, II, xciv).

Since he decidedly rejected Thornton's strictures on the 'law of demand and supply', one may safely assume that he was referring mainly to his change of mind on the matter of the wages fund. The changes made in that edition, said Mill, only amounted to 'a few verbal corrections.' In fact, he was exaggerating their unimportance a little; but they were still very small in comparison with what the *Fortnightly* article might have led one to expect.

The central passage on trade unions and the wages fund reads thus in the first six editions.

> If they [the multitudes of workers] could do so [combine effectually], they might doubtless succeed in diminishing the hours of labour, and obtaining the same wages for less work. But if they aimed at obtaining actually higher wages than the rate fixed by demand and supply — the rate which distributes the whole circulating capital of the country among the entire working population — this could only be accomplished by keeping a part of their number permanently out of employment.

In 1871, Mill corrected the passage to read:

> If they could do so, they might doubtless succeed in diminishing the hours of labour, and obtaining the same wages for less work. They would also have a limited power of obtaining, by combination, an increase of general wages at the expense of profits. But the limits of this power are narrow; and were they to attempt to strain it beyond those limits, this could only be accomplished by keeping a part of their number permanently out of employment.[51]

What did his final position amount to? On the theoretical plane the changes he had wrought with his *Fortnightly* article still stood: since the wages fund was not rigid in the short run, there was room for wage increases at the expense of profits. Such an opinion was perfectly consistent with his economic system, since he was a Ricardian and he was not excessively concerned with continued accumulation. On the practical plane, however, he recoiled somewhat from the enthusiastic declarations in the *Fortnightly*; nowhere in the article had he said that 'the limits of the power of unions were narrow.' He perhaps felt that, prompted by his wish to 'strike a great blow for labour' (as Marshall put it) he had exaggerated the practical consequences to be drawn from his change of mind on the small point of the rigidity of the wages fund.

The Euthanasia of Trade Unions

At the end of his life, then, Mill came to think that trade unions could raise the general rate of wages at the expense of profits, between narrow margins, and hence backed legal protection for the unions against liability for damages caused by their action, though one cannot help detecting a note of uneasiness about some of the uses to which such protection might be put.

Most important, however, for understanding his attitude towards unionism is his belief that the existing economic system would be superseded by a co-operative commonwealth. It will be remembered that after reading an essay by Fawcett he introduced the argument in defence of unionism, that by striking for higher wages when the employers enjoyed higher profits, the unions were effecting 'a commencement of that regular participation of the labourers in the profits derived from their labour, every tendency to which. . .it is so important to encourage.'[52]

He took up the same idea in his review of Thornton. He thought that masters would have to give workers a participation in the profits of the firm:

[The] growing inconvenience to them from the opposition of interest between themselves and the workmen should stimulate the conversion of existing business into Industrial Partnerships, in which the whole body of workpeople have a direct interest in the profits of the enterprise; such a transformation would be the true euthanasia of Trades' Unionism, while it would train and prepare at least the superior portion of the working classes for a form of co-operation still more equal and complete.[53]

How far from the truth it is that the economic phenomena of society as at present constituted always arrange themselves spontaneously in the way which is most for the common good or that the interests of all classes are fundamentally the same.

J.S. Mill in 1870[1]

Chapter 6 Laissez-faire

The interpretation of Mill's thought on State intervention which has gained widest currency is that put forward by A.V. Dicey in his 1905 *Lectures on Law and Public Opinion in Nineteenth Century England.* Dicey, who was a strong believer in the undiluted virtues of economic freedom, presented Mill, so to speak, as the villain of his piece. Mill, said Dicey, though educated as a liberal, ushered in an era of Collectivism in legal thought and practice, through the indecisive character of the doctrines he taught. This picture of Mill as an eclectic who opened the sluice-gates to collectivist interventionism does not correspond with the facts.

Two Common Errors in the Interpretation of Mill's Views
A correct interpretation of Mill's thought on State intervention must start by avoiding two related mistakes: one, that Mill was born in an anti-interventionist era, characterized by a growing inhibition of Government, which by the end of Mill's life had reduced the State to proverbial 'night-watchman' duties; two, that Mill was educated as a died-in-the-wool liberal, only to be changed by socialist influence into the eclectic Dicey took him to be. Only when these mistakes have been cleared away, can one proceed to the pages of the *Principles* where Mill discussed *laissez-faire*, and show that the doctrines that puzzled Dicey can be explained as the thought of a mature liberal who took into account the demands of the increasingly urban and industrial society in which he lived.

The first mistake can be quickly disposed of by referring to an article of J. Bartlet Brebner's, which, though falling into the opposite error of seeing Mill, and Bentham, as apostles of interventionism, does however make some very apposite remarks on the character of legislation at the time of Mill's early manhood.[2] A glance at the nineteenth-century Statute Books will show that Dicey was wrong in dating the beginning of State interventionism at about the time of Mill's death. The trend started much earlier, only that, as is usual in these cases, people failed to notice what was happening. 'Individualist' measures of the kind Dicey favoured were not the only ones passed at the time. As Brebner notes, if .the Reform of the Franchise took place in 1832, the first effective Factory Act was dated 1833 (the first one at all was enacted in 1802); in 1842, both Peel's Budget initiating free trade in corn and the Women and Children's Labour in the Mines Act were passed; and, if the final repeal of the Corn Laws took place in 1846, the Ten Hour Act entered the Statute Book in 1847. In fact, the 'liberal' and 'collectivist' strands of legislation were inextricably woven throughout the time of Mill, and the diffusion of Mill's thought certainly ushered in no new 'collectivist' period.[3]

Neither is it true that Mill was unfaithful to any 'liberal' education he had received, as Dicey implied. On the contrary, the evolution of Mill's thought went the other way. Mill did not begin as a dogmatic liberal to end as a figure of transition between liberalism and collectivism. He started with an inclination in favour of State interference, let it wax stronger under Continental influence, then in the forties reacted against interventionism, helped by his contacts with Tocqueville; and finally, by 'incessantly weaving anew the fabric of his old and taught opinions,' was able to combine the claims of an active State with those of liberty into a single edifice of thought.

Bentham and James Mill were not collectivists, but they often felt like the impatient reformers of whom John Mill spoke in *On Representative Government*, 'who at times sigh for a strong hand to compel a recalcitrant people to be better governed'. Bentham especially is not well represented by his *Defence of Usury* (1787) or his *Emancipate Your Colonies* (1793), the texts usually remembered when he is mentioned in connection with State interference. A more typical attitude of his is reflected by the following quotation from 'Defence of a Maximum' (1801):

> I have not, I never had, nor ever shall have, any horror sentimental or anarchical, of the hand of government. I leave it to Adam Smith. . .to talk of invasions of natural liberty (Stark, ed., III, 257—8).

It is not that they wished to suppress liberty, quite the contrary, but rather that they did not see any special dangers for liberty in the concession of additional powers to the central government, whether democratic or not. Halévy maintained that in its essence Utilitarianism was not a liberal creed; it would be better to say that the Utilitarian philosophy had non-liberal elements, which when revealed in the application of this philosophy to practical problems, the Utilitarians decisively rejected, taking a clear stand on the side of liberalism.

Thus under the influence of his teachers the young Mill, though never adopting an illiberal attitude, inclined towards an attitude of confidence in the benefits of centralization: he did not defend enlightened despotism, but simply showed a lack of concern for devising checks to ensure that the new powers granted the central government would not be abused.

Such a centralizing attitude can be clearly seen in Mill's writings during the early thirties. Thus, when he defended the setting up of a Central Authority to supervise the administration of poor relief under the New Poor Law of 1834, he put forward arguments which he would have rejected at a later time in life. Admittedly his insistence on the need for a machinery of inspection and enforcement was nothing very startling, nor was his assertion that administration through a central civil service was more flexible than through magistrates, nor his criticism of the inefficiency of local government (though in this he was a little harsher than he would be after reading Tocqueville); but where he did go too far was in his denial that there was any need for a machinery to hear complaints.[4]

There are other indications of a 'centralizing' disposition in Mill's writings of the early thirties: his criticism of the inefficiency of the Reformed Parliament (elected under the new electoral law of 1832),[5] his tendency to speak of Prussia as 'a country which by the excellence of the details of its institution puts to shame all the constitutional Governments of Europe,'[6] for both of which parallels could be found in the writings of other Benthamites.

The Evolution of Mill's Thought on Laissez-faire

One good result of his Benthamite impatience with the reliance on the spontaneous movements of society, was his initiation of the theory of the defects of the market. In an article of 1832, he applauded a proposal to restrict the work of women and children in factories.[7] The objections to such a proposal, he said, consist of arguments drawn from the non-interference philosophy, and resting on the maxim, that government ought not to prohibit individuals, not under the influence of force and fraud, from binding themselves by any engagement which they may think fit to contract, provided it do not violate the rights of a third party.

Mill declared himself in favour of the principle 'up to a certain point'; but he excepted a large class of cases from its province. The principle, he said, is based on the idea that 'an individual may be presumed a better judge of his own interest than the government, at least as governments are now constituted.' The last clause is typical of his Benthamite belief, against which Mill would later react, that soundly constituted governments could not be oppressive (one could also add that it shows evidence of some Saint-Simonian influence, as far as it concerns the belief that the evolution of History will bring about a juster society). But leaving this aside, what are then the cases in which the rule of non-interference may be suspended? They are cases

in which it would be highly for the advantage of every body, if every body were to act in a certain manner, but which it is not in the interest of any *individual* to adopt the rule for the guidance of his own conduct, unless he has some security that all the others will do so too.

The typical case is stealing; even if no government existed, it would be in the general interest that nobody should steal, 'yet if some abstain voluntarily, that very abstinence enables others to benefit themselves by stealing.'

The point of this neat argument must now be obvious. It is in everybody's interest, he said, that children should spend a healthy childhood and receive a sound education; and also that women should look after the home (though he later withdrew this second opinion).[8] But 'any man whose wife and children work *while others abstain*, gets the advantage of the high wages, both for his own labour and for theirs.' From this Mill concludes that 'if it is beyond the competency of the government to do this [prohibit woman and child labour], it is beyond their competency to do anything.'

Mill was mistaken in thinking that the two cases, the limitation on working hours and the prohibition on stealing, were basically alike. They would be if the working classes had the monopoly of the country's productive capacity (if the rate of its elasticity of substitution for capital were nil). But it is not true in actual fact: if we consider the labour market as a whole, the fact that some workers put in more hours than others does not necessarily appreciably reduce the others' remuneration, nor does it start off the vicious circle of forcing every one to give up the shorter work day. However, the notion that there were cases in which the State had to impose a harmony of individual interests in the economic sphere just as in the penal sphere, was a very suggestive idea that Mill was to develop more fully in the future.

The influence of Continental thought which 'streamed in upon Mill' after his mental breakdown in 1826 (*aet.* 20) reinforced the centralizing tendency he had derived from his first teachers; especially since round 1830 (*aet.* 24) he came under the influence of the Saint-Simonians, who were impatient with the doctrine of *laissez-faire* for two reasons: their historicism and their centralism. *Laissez-faire*, in the opinion of a great number of liberals of the period, was valid for all times and places; the Saint-Simonians, however, held that 'the human mind has a certain order of possible progress,' that 'all questions of political institutions are relative, not absolute, and that different stages of human progress not only *will* have, but *ought* to have, different institutions';[9] hence they dismissed the universalist pretensions of vulgar liberalism. Further, they felt that society fared best under a centralized and paternalist system; they therefore mocked those liberals who (in the words of their paper *Le Producteur*) 'see, in a penal code, the fundamental law of society, and have conceived the notion against all evidence, that people must civilise themselves.'[10]

Due to Saint-Simonian influence Mill was at the time somewhat more hostile to *laissez-faire* than other Benthamites — his correspondence shows that he even came to agree on these points with Carlyle, not to be described as a liberal by any stretch of the imagination. It is revealing that the latter, when commenting on the success of Miss Martineau's *Tales* (which naturally favoured *laissez-faire*) sent to him by Mill, should think that 'the very Saint-Simonians could teach her much.' Mill took up Carlyle's verdict that 'she and her Tales are surely a sign of this Country and Time' in a stronger critical vein.

Your criticism of Miss Martineau is, I think, just: she reduces the *laissez-faire* system to absurdity as far as the *principle* goes, by merely carrying it out to all its consequences. In the meantime that principle like other negative ones[11] has work to do yet, work, namely, of a destroying kind, & I am glad to think that it has strength left to finish that, after which it must soon expire; peace be with its ashes when it does expire, for I doubt much it will reach resurrection.[12]

The Liberalizing Influence of Tocqueville

In sum, Mill's centralizing period left him with two positive acquisitions: a belief that rules are relative to time and place, and the seeds of a theory of the defects of the market. But he had not yet realized the impact that an efficient and powerful administrative machinery can have on freedom. His veering in the direction of *laissez-faire* was yet to come.

At that time, he says in his *Autobiography*

> I was. . .actively engaged in defending important measures, such as the great Poor Law Reform of 1834, against an irrational clamour grounded on the anti-centralization prejudice: and had it not been for the lessons of Tocqueville, I do not know that I might not, like many reformers before me, have been hurried into the excess opposite to that, which, being the one prevalent in my own country, it was generally my business to combat (W.Cl., 164).

Tocqueville met John Stuart Mill during his first visit to England in 1835. Their acquaintance did not grow into an intimate personal friendship like that between Tocqueville and his translator Reeves. But both men came to feel a strong respect for the other as a thinker: when Tocqueville published the *Démocratie en Amérique* he found in Mill, to his delight, a man who understood him better than most; and for Mill reading that book was a turning point in his mental history. The *Démocratie* is one of the formative books for Mill's intellect, with Bentham's *Traités de législation*, Plato's *Dialogues*, and Comte's *Cours de philosophie positive*. But while Bentham and Plato contributed to forming his mind, Comte and Tocqueville rather brought to light thoughts which he already carried in him in embryo.

During his first visit to England Tocqueville held a conversation with Mill on the theme of centralization (when, it seems, Mill had not read the *Démocratie*) which he recorded in his *Carnets de Voyage*. Tocqueville was especially interested in the connection he saw between the democratic spirit and the tendency to concentrate in the State (and within the State, in the central Government) functions which before were left to individuals (or to local government); and from this trend he expected dangers for liberty. Mill agreed that the tendency in England was also towards more centralization; but when Tocqueville asked him whether he feared the consequences of such a tendency, Mill answered, 'No'; he relied, Mill said, on the dislike of general ideas as opposed to piecemeal reform, and on the reluctance to meddle into other people's affairs, which characterized 'l'esprit anglais.' His only fear was that aristocratic power should be destroyed before local government was reformed.

We [the Radicals] attack the present communal and provincial institutions because they are instruments of the aristocracy; when we take away this power from our adversaries, we naturally think of vesting it in the government, since there is nothing ready in the present institutions to inherit this power. But if democracy were *organised* in our communes and counties so that it could govern, I am persuaded that we would leave it quite independent from the central government.[13]

Obviously Mill had not changed his mood yet.

The reactions of the English public to the first part of the *Démocratie* (1835) had been governed by Robert Peel's description of it as an attack on democracy. The first purpose of Mill's review of the book in the *London Review* was to show that Tocqueville was a friend, albeit a critical friend, of democracy. It is clear that Mill, like most of his contemporaries, discovered the importance of local institutions in the United States in Tocqueville's book; and that he was especially struck by Tocqueville's presentation of them as an instrument for the political education of the people. This latter idea made Mill see an old proposal of his in a new light: he renewed his plea, put forward in the *Examiner* in 1833,[14] to cover the country with small sub-parliaments to which the local executives would be responsible.

Mill greeted the publication of the second part of the *Démocratie* (and the English translation of the whole work in 1840) with a long and enthusiastic article in the *Edinburgh Review*, but as befitted an established work, he was somewhat more critical. In this article he now expressly linked municipal government with liberty: a greater measure of local autonomy was a school for citizenship and organizing ability. It also guarded, he said, democracy from a danger to which this form of government was peculiarly prone: that the citizens should allow the

central government to assume more and more control, engross more and more of the business of society; and, on condition of making itself the organ of the general mode of feeling and thinking, should suffer it to relieve mankind from the care of their own interests, and keep them under a kind of tutelage: — trampling meanwhile with considerable recklessness, as often as convenient, upon the rights of individuals, in the name of society and the public good.[15]

In the pages of the *Démocratie*, Mill also found arguments to fortify his defence of the peculiar administrative arrangements set up under the Poor Law in 1834. At that time, however, he had stressed the advantages of a centralized administration — arguing that it guaranteed enforcement of the law, while giving scope for flexibility in the application of it. Quite a different aspect was stressed here, under Tocqueville's influence and in keeping with Mill's new mood of diffidence towards centralized authority. What commended the Poor Law System and made its general conception 'almost theoretically perfect' was the combination of local execution with central instruction and supervision. Thus was born the idea of the 'maximum diffusion of power together with the maximum concentration of information' which was to play such an important role in his later thought.

The Benthamite and Saint-Simonian influence had left in Mill an inclination towards government by the best qualified, by the experts (which emerged in the fifties, in his pleas for a reform of the Civil Service) and Tocquevillian influence did not counteract this inclination; it simply made him think further, and advocate *both* an efficient Civil Service and safeguards against the possible misuse of such a powerful instrument by the majority. In the years which followed his reading of Tocqueville and preceded the composition of the *Principles* (1848) his diffidence towards democracy diminished, but the twin recommendation of an efficient Civil Service and guarantees against the abuse of its powers by the ruling majority remained untouched. Thus only with a knowledge of Mill's evolution is it possible to understand his efforts to find the right blend of State activity and guarantees against over-government.

> I have steered carefully between the two errors, and whether I have
> or have not drawn the line between them exactly in the right place, I
> have at least insisted with equal emphasis upon the evils of both
> sides (*Autobiography*.W.Cl., 164).

The Logic of Economic Policy

In short, the facts do not uphold the common belief that Mill moved away from the presumed liberalism of his masters towards an attitude of interventionism; if there was any change it went in the direction of *laissez-faire*: Mill gradually discovered some authoritarian elements in utilitarianism, and felt the need to find his own answers, liberal, but far from the vulgar dogmatism of his times.

It is this avoidance of dogmatism which makes many believe that Mill was further away from *laissez-faire* than his Utilitarian masters. Whenever Mill's teachers were moved to uphold the *laissez-faire* philosophy, they did it somewhat rigidly, for they stated the rule as if it were an absolute. If the content of his thought was more liberal than his precursors', the form in which he expounded it was less cocksure. John Stuart Mill, like other classical economists of the second generation, saw with increasing clearness that rules such as *laissez-faire* could not be absolute, that they had to be conceived as relative to time and space.

It was easier for his masters to lay down the law than it was for him. In an earlier chapter we have described his father's methodology. James Mill, it appears, believed that it was possible to start off from self-evident premises and deduce universally valid practical conclusions. In J.S. Mill's opinion, this 'geometrical' method could only lead to false conclusions. This raised a problem: on the one hand, he found useful the existence of rules to guide the personal and social conduct of mankind:

> There is still a necessity that some rule, of a nature simple enough to be easily understood and remembered, should not only be laid down for guidance, but universally observed, in order that the various persons concerned may know what they have to expect; the inconvenience of uncertainty on their part being a greater evil than that which may possibly arise, in a minority of cases, from the imperfect adaptation of the rule to those cases (*Logic* [1st edition, 1843] II, 622).

On the other hand, it was clear from Mill's analysis that no rules valid for all cases could possibly be devised;

> By a wise practitioner, therefore, rules of conduct will only be considered as provisional. . . The error is. . .apparent, of those who would deduce the line of conduct proper to particular cases, from supposed universal practical maxims; overlooking the necessity of constantly referring back to the principles of the speculative science, in order to attain even the specific end which the rules have in view (II, 617).

The last clause (which is rather obscure) refers to the fact that the application of a rule always has an effect on ends other than the one pursued. The implication is that, when one takes into account the consequences on other aims of pursuing one given aim, the need to examine the scientific grounds of the rule becomes even more imperative. In consequence 'the complete art [i.e. technique] of any matter, includes a selection of such portions from the science, as is necessary to show on what conditions the effects, which the art aims at producing depend' (II, 619).

These considerations led Mill to a difficult dilemma when writing the chapters on the role of the State in his *Principles*. It would be useful, he must have thought, to coin a rule for the use of politicians, the press, and the voters. But economic science had by no means reached perfection, and less than any others could the problems of economic policy be solved on the basis of their corresponding science alone: Comte had taught him that 'for practical purposes, Political Economy is inseparably intertwined with many other branches of Social Philosophy' (Preface to Mill's *Principles*).

At one point he seemed to incline in favour of proclaiming no rule at all and of following the example of John Austin in his essay on 'Centralization' (1847).[16] As he told Austin in a letter that year:

> I have necessarily thought a good deal about it [the province of Government] lately for the purposes of a practical treatise on Pol. Economy & I have felt the same difficulty which you feel about the *axiomata media* such as *laissez-faire*.[17] I suspect there are none which do not vary with time, place & circumstance. I doubt much if more can be done in a scientific treatment of the question than to point out a certain number of *pro's* and a certain number of *con's* of a more or less general application, & with some attempt at an estimation of the comparative importance of each, leaving the balance to be struck in each particular case as it arises.
>
> (Mill to Austin, 13–IV–1847)

But, as will be seen, he finally decided in favour of proposing a rule, namely that of *laissez-faire*. He obviated the drawbacks of this course of action by appending to the maxim 'selections from the body of the science' to fix the limits of the applicability of the rule.[18] It was a fortunate idea, for to it we owe Mill's pathbreaking analysis of the defects of the market which accompanied the proclamation of the rule of *laissez-faire* in the last chapter of the *Principles*.

The Principles of Political Economy (1848)

Mill's attitude towards rules gives one an inkling that, if Mill did not begin as a dogmatic liberal in his youth, neither did he become one later in life. It is true that, from the very outset of Book V in the *Principles*, Mill rejected the attitude of the collectivists, but neither did he take up that of the dogmatic liberals. Indeed, the rationale of the whole chapter is an attempt to transcend both positions, which were those commonly held in his time.[19]

Mill thus opened Book V by distinguishing between two sides.

On the one hand, impatient reformers, thinking it easier and shorter to get possession of the government than of the intellects and dispositions of the public, are under a constant temptation to stretch the province of the government beyond due bounds.

He also rejected the contrary position.

On the other, mankind have been so much accustomed by their rulers to interference for purposes other than the public good, or under an erroneous conception of what that good requires...that there has grown up a spirit of resistance *in limine* to the interference of government (*Coll. Works*, III, 799).

Mill was therefore confronted with the difficulty of avoiding these two extreme positions without being content to take up one of shallow syncretism.To explain how he achieved this, is one of our main objects in this chapter, for though we wish to free Mill from the taint of dogmatic liberalism, we should not like to see him branded as a mere eclectic.

The Four Categories of State Activity

It was to solve that difficulty that Mill divided State activity into 'necessary' functions and 'optional' interventions; and proceeded further to divide the optional interventions into 'authoritative' and 'non-authoritative'. The first division was aimed against the enemies of State intervention, the second against the centralizers.

As far as the enemies of intervention were concerned, Mill, like Austin, found their slogans (such as that the State should only defend the citizens against force and fraud, or that individuals are the best judges of their own interests in all cases) totally unsatisfactory. If one distinguished two kinds of State activity (he proceeded), those activities which everybody, even the extreme liberals, accepted as 'necessary', and the rest which were controversial or 'optional', it would be seen that the 'necessary' functions were much more numerous than anybody seemed to think; and that they could by no stretch of the imagination be considered to be covered by the slogans of the extreme liberals. For example, the slogan that the State should only protect against force and fraud did not cover the enforcement of those contracts, entered upon with the honest intention of performing them but subsequently found too onerous; or the slogan that the individual is always the best judge of his interests, explain the special protection afforded to infants or lunatics. He concluded that the class of accepted or 'necessary' functions of government could not be limited 'by any universal rule, save the simple and vague one, that it should never be admitted but when the case of expediency is strong' (804).[20]

The demand that a strong case should be made before admitting proposed intervention shows that his rejection of dogmatic *laissez-faire* did not imply that he had fallen into the other extreme. The second distinction, that of 'optional' State interventions into 'authoritative' (coercive interventions) and 'non-authoritative' (public services) was precisely directed against the interventionists; by its means Mill signified that even if the balance of expediency seems to incline in favour of an intervention, an important factor must be attended to: that coercive interventions imply a curtailment of liberty, and should be scrutinized with special attention. For example, said Mill, it was one thing that the State establish schools or universities, and quite another that it should forbid anybody to teach without a government licence (937). Thus coercive interventions had to undergo careful criticism.

This second distinction was quite clear. The value of the division of State activity into 'necessary' and 'optional' functions was more doubtful. Once it had served as a debating point to bring home the insufficiency of the slogans of the extreme liberals, it could have been laid aside. In fact, it seemed to one of Mill's reviewers, N.W. Senior, in the *Edinburgh Review*[21] that the division was inconsistent with Mill's acceptance of the criterion of expediency. 'We agree with him that there is absolutely no limit, no exception, to the doctrine of expediency.' All proposed State activities were either necessary or pernicious, Senior implied. 'As soon as it has been shown that it is expedient that a Government should perform any functions, it must also be its right, and also be its duty to perform them.' The word 'optional' should be dispensed with since it conveyed the idea that in

some cases the State was quite free to act or refrain from acting.
But apparently Mill did not realize the import of Senior's criticism.
In the second edition of the *Principles*(1849), he took Senior's point to
have been merely verbal.

By the term optional it is not meant to imply, that it can ever be a
matter of indifference, or arbitrary choice, whether the government
should or should not take upon itself the functions in question; but
only that the expediency of its exercising them does not amount to
necessity, and is a subject on which diversity of opinion does or may
exist (800, c—c).

The answer was very unsatisfactory, for it meant that the distinction
should be grounded on the same public opinion it was intended to
guide, and thus fell into a vicious circle. It is clear that Mill wanted to
keep the distinction but did not know how to justify it.

The real point at issue between Senior and Mill was that the former
thought that to acknowledge expediency as the touchstone of
legitimate State activity implied that all attempts to frame rules should
be abandoned, and that every case should be decided on its merits:
while we know from the *Logic* that Mill thought rules both useful and
possible even when expediency (or Utility) was accepted as the supreme
criterion.[22] In the present case he had decided that the coining of the
rule of *laissez-faire* was convenient —but only if he could keep it from
mistaken interpretations; and the two distinctions together allowed him
to circumscribe exactly the limits of its application (*laissez-faire*
applying mainly to coercive optional interventions), and hence to keep
his distance from both the extreme liberal and the collectivist schools
of thought. Given this, it was difficult for Mill to give up speaking of
'necessary' and 'optional' interventions.

However, Senior was still right in his criticism of the slender basis on
which the distinction had been made. The other distinction (dividing
optional interventions into 'authoritative' and 'non-authoritative') arose
from an essential difference, the use of coercion; but the one under
consideration Mill merely based upon fickle public opinion. It was not
until 1862, in his article on 'Centralization', that Mill discovered where
the difference lay which he had instinctively sensed between the two
kinds of State activity under discussion: he abandoned the expressions
'necessary' and 'optional' and substituted for them 'legislative' and
'administrative'. The rule of *laissez-faire* did not apply to legislative
activity, as, strictly interpreted, it could hardly overstep its function of

establishing the permanent framework of law and order within which the individuals could exercise their liberty; more vigilance was required with regard to administrative interventions, where the function of supplementing and correcting by direct interference the results of this exercise of liberty, was more open to abuse. For the time being, however, he kept the distinction without sufficiently justifying it.

Necessary Functions of the State

Mill gave a great deal of attention to such functions of the State as were accepted by everybody to be necessary for the continuation of social life,[23] especially in so far as the State was not then carrying out as much as could be expected from it. An interesting point is Mill's insistence that the legal framework should not be looked on as fixed once and for all time. It was not until the 1862 article on 'Centralization' that he was to say in so many words that he expected the body of legislation to grow with advancing civilization. But in the *Principles* it was already clear that Mill did not consider it necessary that Government action should be something fixed and settled. This was because (owing to the confusion still reigning in his mind as to the precise difference between necessary and optional interventions) he there proposed a number of optional interventions which were in fact proposals for legislative action to complete the legal framework. It was also because he discussed many reforms this permanent legal framework was in need of: especially reforms in the laws of inheritance which in England tended to concentrate property; in the laws of partnership, which until they were reformed in 1852 made the establishment of co-operatives difficult; and the laws of insolvency, which Mill considered too lenient to the bankrupt.[24]

Optional Functions of the Government: *Laissez-faire* the General Rule

The interest quickens when Mill turns to the consideration of optional Government interventions, in his chapter 'On the Grounds and Limits of the *Laissez-Faire* or Non-Intervention Principle.' Previous economists had never attempted the treatment of optional interventions in a systematic fashion.[25] 'No subject has been more keenly contested in the present age: the contest, however, has chiefly been carried on round certain select points, with only flying excursions into the rest of the field'; and as for the cases left outside discussion, the contestants had been content to make unwarranted generalizations of the principles applied to the few cases examined with any attention. Mill proposed, not to build a general theory on State intervention, since the question did not 'admit of any universal solution,' but to examine 'in the most general point of view' the advantages and inconveniences of government interference along the whole range of conceivable cases (936–7).

He immediately proceeded to exempt a whole series of government interventions from his rule of *laissez-faire*. It was precisely for this purpose that Mill distinguished between 'authoritative' and 'non-authoritative' optional interventions. The first were much more inconvenient because they 'extend to controlling the free agency of individuals.' But the other kind of activity which he defined as, when

> leaving individuals free to use their own means of pursuing any object of general interest, the government, not meddling with them, but not trusting the object solely to their care, establishes, side by side with their arrangements, an agency of its own for a like purpose (937),

could be treated with less caution. He gave as examples a State system of education, or a Church establishment, both cases where the State favoured institutions of its own choosing, without thereby preventing individuals from pursuing religious or educational ends by whatever means they thought fit. 'It is evident,' Mill concluded, 'that the authoritative form of government intervention has a much more limited sphere of legitimate action than the other.' An increase in the number of non-coercive actions had its drawbacks,[26] but by and large Mill reduced the application of his rule of *laissez-faire* to coercive interventions.

Mill's first reason for wishing to limit the number of coercive interventions of the State is implied by the very distinction between them and State services. Coercion is an evil and ought to be limited to minimum necessity. The evils of coercion in the commercial sphere ought not, in the opinion of Mill, to be confused with those of coercion in the personal sphere, that 'circle around every human being, which no government. . .ought to be permitted to overstep' (938). As outlined in *On Liberty* (1854), personal liberty clearly had the character of a *quasi* categorical imperative, and in consequence its infringement could not (in a civilized country) be said to be balanced by any good. The suspension of commercial liberty was a different matter. It is true, he said in the *Principles*, that restraint *qua* restraint is always an evil; 'unless the conscience of the individual goes freely with the legal restraint, it partakes. . .of the degradation of slavery' (938);

...to be prevented from doing what one is inclined to, or from acting according to one's own judgment of what is desirable, is not only always irksome, but always tends, *pro tanto*, to starve the development of some portion of the bodily or mental faculties, either sensitive or active.

But, in the commercial sphere, these evil consequences of an increase of coercion could result in a balance of good. Hence a restraint could be advocated when its advantages weighed more than its disadvantages; while no such calculation was allowed in the personal sphere.

In sum, in the economic sphere, the painfulness of coercion was a cost of government action; it threw the burden of proof on the defenders of the legal prohibition.

The second reason justifying the rule of *laissez-faire* was the danger which excessive State activity entailed for political freedom.

This is the only one of the reasons Mill gives for preferring private activity, that also affects government services. It is mainly the heaping of coercive administrative powers upon the Government that increases its ability to exert pressure on the citizens; but the share of government activity of whatever description in the total activity of the country could also become a danger if allowed to grow to excess. The strongest warning is to be found in a famous passage in *On Liberty* (1854):

> If the roads, the railways, the banks, the insurance óffices, the great joint-stock companies, the universities, and the public charities, were all of them branches of the government; if, in addition, the municipal corporations and local boards, with all that now devolves on them, became departments of the central administration; if the *employés* of all these different enterprises were appointed and paid by the government, and looked to the government for every rise in life; not all the freedom of the press and popular constitution of the legislature would make this or any other country free otherwise than in name (*Everyman* ed., 165).

In the *Principles* he chose to address this warning particularly to democracies. It had been thought, said Mill, no doubt recalling his father and Bentham, that democracy, as it governs in the interest of the majority, could be trusted with the increase in direct authority and in indirect power of patronage which the growth in the functions of the State implied. But this was far from being the case: augmenting the power of government should always and without exception 'be regarded with unremitting jealousy.'

Perhaps this is even more important in a democracy than in any other form of political society; because where public opinion is sovereign, an individual who is oppressed by the sovereign does not, as in most other states of things, find some other and rival power to which he can appeal for relief, or, at all events, for sympathy (940).

Further, if in a democracy most of the affairs devolve upon the central government, there will be a diversion of 'the intelligence and activity of the country from its principal business, to a wretched competition for the selfish prizes and the petty vanities of office' (944).

Thus a centralizing democracy, instead of making people jealous of freedom, and watchful of centralization, will make them hand over more and more power to the State in hopes of being able to use it to their own advantage. 'In some countries the desire of the people is for not being tyrannized over, but in others it is merely for an equal chance to everybody of tyrannizing' (944).

The third reason in defence of the maxim of *laissez-faire* Mill considered the most important: the noxious effect of an excess of State action on the progress of society and the development of the individual. This argument is mainly relevant to coercive intervention, for, although the absolute volume of State activity matters in this respect also, the possibility of freely competing with the State could become an added stimulus to the citizens.

One of the strongest arguments in Mill's mind for individual activity was that social and individual progress was strongly furthered by wide experiment and the free use of individual talent.[27] It is important to note that Mill was not only referring to the carrying on of ordinary business, but even more so to functions of a public nature.

A people among whom there is no habit of spontaneous action for a collective interest. . .have their faculties only half developed; their education is defective in one of its most important branches (943).

Also, when most business, public and private, is concentrated in government hands, there is the additional danger that a praiseworthy desire for efficiency will concentrate the best ability of the country in the service of the State.

Such a system, more completely than any other, embodies the idea of despotism, by arming with intellectual superiority as an additional weapon, those who have already the legal power (943).

Further, even granting that State agency could be superior in efficiency to individual agency, it

> substitutes its own mode of accomplishing the work, for all the variety of modes which would be tried by a number of equally qualified persons aiming at the same end (942).

Variety of experiment, helped by competition to weed out unfit results, was in Mill's opinion a much greater instrument of progress than a uniform procedure however good.

The last argument in favour of *laissez-faire* was not stressed by Mill with as much force as the argument from progress; but it constituted the ultimate justification for his confidence in private agency: it was the efficiency of the free market as compared to an administrative organisation of the economy. He divided the discussion of this point into two parts: he first adverted to the qualities of the market; then, to the defects of administration.

In the first place, then, Mill defended his belief in the advantages of private enterprise 'in all advanced countries' with two reasons, one based on incentive, and the other based on the limitation of the human brain. The grounds for the truth that the government agency is usually less efficient

> are expressed with tolerable exactness in the popular dictum, that people understand their own business and their own interests better, and care for them more, than the government does, or can be expected to do (941−2).

The other reason has been developed this century by liberals and neo-liberals,[28] under the form that the price system is a good gatherer of the information diffused through society. In Mill's words,

> even if a government were superior in intelligence and knowledge to any single individual in the nation, it must be inferior to all the individuals of the nation taken together (942).

In this respect, it must be remembered that he clearly thought the Saint-Simonian belief in a centralist collectivism quite chimerical.

Thus, Mill's criterion for judging 'optional' actions is based in the last instance on his belief in what Marshall called 'the system of economic freedom'; that is to say on the conviction that, within a framework of laws, there can operate in society a mechanism, which, by and large, makes the contending wishes of individuals compatible; and, given his belief that the best society is that which ensures the fullest satisfaction to the freely expressed wishes of its members, it follows that he felt justified in trusting the solution of many conflicts of interests to the spontaneous operation of this mechanism.

This belief of Mill (and other political economists) has been wrongly criticized in two ways. It has been described as inconsistent with every society's need for a measure of artificially imposed harmonization of interests; as was seen above the two things are, in fact, compatible. The second criticism is that Mill's conception necessarily implies the assertion that the State should reduce itself to providing the framework, because the market can be relied upon to do all the rest perfectly.

In partially trusting to the operation of a spontaneous mechanism Mill was departing from the position of Bentham who saw the idea of a 'level' as one of the 'vague generalities' he detested. Would Bentham have been justified in rejecting Mill's belief in the market as superstitious?[29]

Modern opinion is tempted to agree with Bentham; this is due to the fact that today the classical theory of the market tends to be confused with the later analytical discovery of General Equilibrium and the welfare deductions from this argument. But, as Lord Robbins has noted,[30] John Stuart Mill and the rest of the classical school did not base their championship of the system of economic freedom on the refinements of neo-classical economics: their predilection for the market was based on a more realistic consideration than optimum allocation of resources at equilibrium point. They saw the market in a more dynamic light; as a social mechanism which roughly channelled the conflicting appetites of men, so that these appetites were disciplined in the short run, and harmonized in the long; and as a mechanism with many failings which could only be made good by State interventions.

The other element of the comparative superiority of the market over public administration arose from the defects by which the latter was attained. It must be noted that, as befitted a theoretical work, Mill in the *Principles* concentrated on the deficiencies inherent in centralization rather than on the contingent defects of the machinery of government in England at the time.

The deficiencies inherent in centralization, he said, could be readily understood by bringing to mind the 'principle of the division of labour. Every additional function undertaken by the government, is a fresh occupation imposed upon a body already overcharged with duties' (940).

The low state of public administration in England at the time of Mill has been repeatedly used as an explanation of the reluctance of the classical economists to recommend State intervention. This consideration played its part, but, in view of all the foregoing analysis, its importance should not be exaggerated. Most of the arguments put forward by Mill in favour of *laissez-faire* would equally apply to a country with a better government machinery. It must also be remarked that Mill never used the inefficiency of government in his time as an excuse for resisting intervention *in limine*. As will be seen below, he participated in the Northcote-Trevelyan campaign for the reform of the conditions of entry into the Civil Service; and studied the problems of administrative reform repeatedly in such works as *Considerations On Representative Government* (1865).

These then are the arguments presented by Mill in favour of the maxim of *laissez-faire. Laissez-faire*, in short, should be the general rule. When Miss Marian Bowley, in her book on Senior, called the rule of *laissez-faire* in Mill's thought 'a shadow of a maxim,' she was assimilating the position of Mill to that of Senior. She was right as far as concerns Mill's preoccupation with the relativity of rules to time and place; but she was wrong in not seeing the importance of the maxim for Mill as the guide for action 'nineteen times out of twenty.'

Optional Interventions Based on Erroneous Theories
'Before entering on the general principles of the question': which optional interventions the government should undertake (Mill said in the *Principles*), 'it will be advisable to clear from our path all those cases, in which government interference works ill because grounded on false views of the subject interfered with' (913). Thus did Mill announce his rejection of a series of State interventions for being grounded on 'erroneous theories' (V, x).

The authors who characterize the position of the classical school as one of dogmatic *laissez-faire*, refer precisely to this kind of attitude. As Professor Gunnar Myrdal has put it in his book *The Political Element in the Development of Economic Theory*,

Throughout the past century economists. . .have proceeded to calculate *immediately on the basis of their scientific findings*, the course of action which is economically 'desirable' or 'right', just as they have also opposed certain policies on the grounds that their realisation would decrease the general 'welfare' or imply the 'neglect' (or even 'infringement') of economic laws (3—4).

If this statement were wholly true in the case of Mill, it would be serious. Usually criticisms based on methodology are either idle or pedantic. In the case of economic policy, however, the methodological point that one cannot usually 'prove scientifically' the wrongheadedness of a recommendation is an important one to make. The man who 'proves' a policy to be misguided should be seen in most cases as over-stretching his arguments, and concealing his ethical predilections from himself. Science may be able to prove that a course of action will not be followed by the expected consequences, but not that the course of action is bad, especially if the terms in which it is proposed are not too literally interpreted. Mill undeniably did on occasions commit the error Professor Myrdal criticizes.

To be more precise, criticism against a policy measure can be aimed: at (a) its stated goal, (b) the means it proposes for pursuing this goal, or (c) the indirect effects of these means on other goals of policy. Some of these criticisms may be 'value-free', and hence though proclaimed 'scientific' do not fall under Professor Myrdal's strictures: thus, when it is asserted that the means proposed would defeat the avowed or implicit aim of the measure. In his criticism against policies based on 'erroneous theories', Mill usually started on the right note.

There are some things with which governments ought not to meddle, and other things with which they ought; but whether right or wrong in itself, the interference must work for ill, if government, not understanding the subject it meddles with, meddles to bring about a result which would be mischievous (913).

Nothing could be more reasonable than this statement. Mill is saying that a government should have some knowledge of how society works before it attempts to steer it one way or the other, under penalty that it may defeat its own purposes. The trouble lies in that Mill understood the scope of 'scientific' criticism in matters of policy to be much wider than this, and unconsciously slipped into 'proving scientifically' either that a policy measure was wrong, or that a given measure was to be rejected unconditionally, whatever the aim it was intended to promote — surely two instances of the 'Myrdal sin'.

For example in the case of the Usury Laws, he began by asserting unexceptionably that Laws establishing a maximum interest on loans under a penalty are strictly self-defeating.

> An equivalent for the risk of non-payment and of legal penalties, must be paid by the borrower, over and above the extra interest which would at any rate have been required of him by the general state of the market. The laws which were intended to lower the price paid by him for pecuniary accommodation, end thus in greatly increasing it (923).

This is indisputable.

Unfortunately he went further. Among the policies based on erroneous theories he included the scheme of Adam Smith's that the State should fix the maximum rate of interest a little above the market rate, to stop loans to 'prodigals and projectors': respectable borrowers would get loans at, or just above, the market rate, while, due to the insurance premium, the rate for less respectable people would put them above the legal rate and price them out of the market.

Mill could not say that this scheme was self-defeating. Therefore, he tacitly granted that it could be effective, and proceeded to attack its goal: he argued that such a hard treatment for prodigals and projectors would be unjustified.

Adam Smith had said of the prodigal that 'like him who perverts the revenues of some pious foundation to profane purposes, he pays the wages of idleness with those funds which the frugality of his forefathers had, as it were, consecrated to the maintenance of industry.'[31] Malthus had been able to defend unproductive consumption of other people's savings as a way to avoid the crises of overproduction. Mill could not attack Adam Smith in this way, because his theory of crises was different from Malthus's, so that he had to take another line of argument, and lay it down that 'a person of sane mind, and of the age at which persons are legally competent to conduct their own concerns, must be presumed to be a sufficient guardian of his pecuniary interests' (924). This is not a scientific proposition; it is an ethical value judgment about the rights of the individual; and whether or not Mill thought that ethical propositions could be proved, their proof was certainly not the concern of economic science. Mill was introducing an assumption from another province of thought, about which equally competent economists might well disagree.

As far as projectors are concerned Adam Smith condemned them in the same breath with prodigals (much to the indignation of Bentham who considered himself one of the former).[32] Mill felt he could take a different line of criticism in this case from the one he took in the case of prodigals: he argued that some risking of capital was necessary for technological development (926). This argument is within the pale of economic science, for it simply points out certain consequences of fact which follow from the enforcement of a policy: and it is analogous to the assertion that a policy is self-defeating, since the policy defeats, not its own goal, but another goal until then thought to be quite unrelated to it. Unfortunately his argument has a hidden component: it tacitly lays down that to impede technological development is a bad thing, and hence surreptitiously introduces a valuation into the argument. Mill should have framed his criticism of the measures against prodigals and projectors roughly along the following lines: 'on the assumption that individual freedom and technological progress are desirable goals, Usury Laws are inexpedient.'

One could even go further and question whether it is ever possible to prove 'scientifically' that these laws were inexpedient, even if all parties were agreed that individual freedom and technological progress are desirable goals. If interpreted strictly, both as to the means (a penal law) and as to the goals (the protection of the borrower), it cannot be denied that they are self-defeating, as we have seen. But if interpreted more loosely, as designating all devices to lower the rate of interest, or as aiming at other goals in addition to the protection of borrowers, there might be ways of saving them. Changes could occur in the conditions of society or in the technical knowledge of the professional economists which could make usury laws desirable and workable. In the first place in certain circumstances the old style usury laws could be applied to other ends than those originally intended. In time of war, restriction of credit, which previously had been the undesired effect of laws designed to protect the borrower, might become instead their deliberately sought goal. Thus during the Napoleonic Wars they contributed to the diversion of capital to the prosecution of the war. For while the government was able to borrow at the legal rate, other borrowers, especially in the building industry, saw the insurance premium inflate the rate of interest above their capabilities to pay.[33] Secondly, if new developments of a technical nature presented the government with different means of lowering the rate of interest, the goal of the usury laws could suddenly become attainable, as for example with the discovery of the tool of open market operations. Thirdly, there could be cases of change both in the circumstances and in the technique. Thus, if it were discovered that the lenders in a newly settled agricultural district were in a situation of quasi-monopoly, and also that an increase in the supply of loans is a better means of lowering the rate than a penal edict, there might be a case for the State to enter the market as a lender.

In sum, it is impossible to prove scientifically that a policy is self-defeating in every possible case, unless all parties are in perfect agreement as to the goals, and unless it is also very strictly interpreted. If it is granted that there might be different criteria as to the goals, that a measure taken to achieve one specific end might unexpectedly influence other aspects of social life, or even prove useful for an end other than the intended one, that a self-defeating policy might become effective through changes in the circumstances or state of knowledge of society, then it must be regretted that Mill saw fit to assert that some policies were demonstrably harmful because based on erroneous theory.[34]

Permissible Optional Interventions

With the interventions based on erroneous theories well out of the way, in the next chapter Mill broached the topic of those optional (later to be called administrative) interventions which the State, in his opinion, should feel justified in undertaking to correct the shortcomings in the working of economic freedom (V, xi, 7–16).

He introduced the discussion with a general declaration that '*laissez-faire*. . .should be the general practice: every departure from it, unless required by some great good, is a certain evil' (945). As will be shown below, the rigidity of approach promised by the phrase was belied by his open attitude in the analysis which followed it; not forgetting also that from its jurisdiction were excluded all the service activities of the State.

Service activities of the State included not only such measures as a Church establishment, or State schools, which the State undertook in competition with private activity (and which have been noticed above); but also a most important class of interventions – those carried out to make good the absolute deficiency of private enterprise.

In Default of Private Enterprise

Mill followed Bentham in believing that the shorter the list of *sponte acta* by the citizens, the longer that of State *agenda*. His work at India House had made him aware that in countries 'inured to despotism' or 'which have been conquered and are retained in subjection by a more energetic and more cultivated people,' there might be 'no roads, docks, harbours, canals, works of irrigation, hospitals, schools, colleges, printing-presses, unless the government establishes them.'

He also realized that such interventions, apparently undertaken with the only thought of courageously carrying the white man's burden, tended to perpetuate the situation of superiority of the benefactors. To forestall this danger, he coined the rule that such interventions should tend to make themselves unnecessary.

> In these cases, the mode in which the government can most surely demonstrate the sincerity with which it intends the greatest good of its subjects, is by doing the things which are made incumbent on it by the helplessness of the public, in such a manner as shall tend not to increase and perpetuate, but to correct, that helplessness (970).[35]

Defects of the Market[36]

Turning to the optional interventions of the State in developed countries, Mill classified them in two broad categories: (a) those interventions occasioned by the failure of the assumption that the individual knows his interests and the means to fulfil them better than the government; (b) those occasioned by the uncompensated consequences of the actions of the individual for other persons than himself (today called external effects). This classification, though it serves well enough for the chapter here being analysed, is insufficient if all the State interventions discussed by Mill in the rest of the *Principles* are brought into consideration; therefore we must add a third category of reasons for State intervention, namely (c) certain situations arising out of the indivisibility of the factors of production.

A consideration of the defects of the market would not be complete today if it did not include the difficulties born of the fact that the system of incentives, without which the market cannot function, (under certain institutional conditions, such as the existence of property and inheritance, allowing the accumulation of rewards for efficiency) weights consumer choice in favour of the richest. Mill did not discuss these problems under the heading of optional State interventions, but under that of 'necessary' or 'framework' reforms; for the simple reason that he approached them from the point of view of the redistribution of the ownership of the means of production, not redistribution of income. He tried to solve them with such schemes as a ceiling for inheritance, peasant proprietorship, and co-operation, not with graduated income-tax which he considered inequitable. All these proposals will be dealt with in Chapter 8. It is sufficient here to note that when Mill is described as a defender of *laissez-faire*, it must not be forgotten that he was ready to demand reforms in the institutional framework of the market, and that this doctrine proposing that the market be left basically free while the economic and legal framework in which it operates is reformed, is a very interesting and practical idea even today.

Imperfect Knowledge

Mill presented the diffusion of knowledge by the Government as the typical example of non-coercive optional interventions, that is to say, of services.

> There is another kind of intervention [he said in this chapter on *laissez-faire*] which is not authoritative: when a government, instead of issuing a command and enforcing it by penalties, adopts the course so seldom resorted to by governments, and of which such important use might be made, that of giving advice, and promulgating information (937).

He considered this type of activity so important that he presented it as the main occupation of the central government, apart from that tending to create the legal framework for freedom and equality.

Further, the question of knowledge was intimately linked for him with that of adulteration of wares. 'The proposition that the consumer is a competent judge of the commodity,' proceeded Mill, 'can be admitted only with numerous abatements and exceptions' (947). The case of non-material goods, such as education, is one of these exceptions, and will be dealt with later. As far as material objects produced for his use are concerned, the consumer is in general the best judge, but in brackets Mill adds '(though even this is not true universally)', no doubt an allusion to the then prevalent practice of adulteration of wares.

He said no more about this matter in the *Principles* (1848). But in the posthumous *Chapters on Socialism* (1879) he gave it more attention.

> The laws against commercial frauds are very defective, and their execution still more so. Laws of this description have no chance of

being really enforced unless it is the special duty of some one to enforce them. They are specially in need of a public prosecutor.

During the whole of the nineteenth century the lack of purity of food was a deep grievance of the working classes. Present practice prefers direct legislation, coupled with the obligation of truthful labelling. Dicey (mistakenly) thought that there was no occasion for any State intervention in this matter; in his mind, the maxim *caveat emptor* disposed effectively of the question. Mill thought that an attempt should be made at using the courts with the added help of a public prosecutor.

It is still to be discovered how far it is possible to repress by means of the criminal law a class of misdeeds which are now seldom brought before the tribunals, and to which, when brought, the judicial administration of this country is most unduly lenient.[37]

These words imply that, in the event of the failure of this expedient, he would have accepted experiments in direct intervention.

To return to the *Principles*: individuals, then, may be considered competent judges of material objects for their own use in the majority of cases.

But there are other things, of the worth of which the demand of the market is by no means a test; things. . .the want of which is least felt where the need is greatest. This is peculiarly true of those things which are chiefly useful as tending to raise the character of human beings. The uncultivated cannot be competent judges of cultivation (947).

In consequence, the State should enter the market for education. Other economists (such as J.B. Say) have preferred to speak for State intervention in this field under the heading of external effects, that is to say, have justified intervention because of the interest of everyone that his neighbour should be educated. Both approaches are valid. But Mill's indicates a concern for the moral value of education, directly descended from the attitude of the philosophers of the Enlightenment and reflecting his youthful reading of Plato's dialogues.

The incapacity of consumers to judge this particular commodity prompted Mill to recommend two things. The first was that the State should enter the market for education by offering services in competition with the individuals; with the express direction that it should not be bound to make this activity profitable: the State was justified to offer 'better education and better instruction to the people, than the greatest number of them would spontaneously select.'[38] The second was that apart from this service financed by taxation, there were cases where it had the obligation to impose education coercively: 'it is . . . an allowable exercise of the powers of government, to impose on parents the legal obligation of giving elementary instruction to children' (948–9), an instruction which the State would supply free or almost free of charge. This was far from being the case in England at that time, due mainly to disputes as to the religious instruction children should receive in State schools.

It was important, Mill proceeded, that the State should have no monopoly in education 'either in the lower or in the higher branches.' It 'must exert neither authority nor influence to induce the people to resort to its teachers in preference to others, and must confer no peculiar advantages on those who have been instructed by them.' Such a course would be dangerous for liberty.

> Nor is it to be endured, that a government should, either *de jure* or *de facto*, have a complete control over the education of the whole people. To possess such a control, and actually exert it, is to be a despot. A government which can mould the opinions and sentiments of the people from their youth upwards, can do with them whatever it pleases [1848] (950).

Mill then proceeded to discuss briefly a case which he should have included under 'framework' functions: the protection of the lunatic, the idiot, and the infant with respect to their interests; with a passing comment on the unjust use of the laws of lunacy in England to prevent a man from using his own money in ways which displeased his inheritors.

As a special case of the protection of children from the cruelty of their own families, Mill introduced a topic more related to the present discussion: Factory Laws. 'Freedom of contract, in the case of children, is but another word for freedom of coercion' (952). It will be remembered that, as early as 1834, Mill had declared himself in favour of the regulation of the work of children, including at the time the work of women too. In the *Principles* (1848) he limited his plea to children.

Labouring for too many hours in the day, or on work beyond their strength, should not be permitted to them, for if permitted it may always be compelled... Education also, the best which circumstances admit of their receiving, is not a thing which parents or relatives, from indifference, jealousy, or avarice, should have it in their power to withhold.

He was thus linking the limitation of working hours with the education of children, as did most of those agitating for reform of the factory laws at the time.

In the Factory Acts of the century the regulation of child labour was coupled with that of female labour. By the time he wrote the *Principles* Mill had completely abandoned his early belief that women should be protected in their factory life. Whatever incapacity women showed of judging rightly and independently of their own affairs was due, not to an intrinsic difference from men, but to 'the injustice of their present social position,' under the absolute power of their husbands or fathers.

For improving the condition of women, it should, on the contrary, be an object to give them the readiest access to independent industrial employment, instead of closing, either entirely or partially, that which is already open to them (953).

As the work closed to women was mainly work in the mines, this is a typical instance of Mill's confidence, for many of us excessive, that social problems can be better dealt with by encouraging individuals to be independent than by giving direct protection.

Within this category of ill-informed choices by producers, Mill also included what he called 'contracts in perpetuity', that is to say, 'when an individual attempts to judge irrevocably now, what will be best for his interest at some future and distant time' ([1848] 953, note a–a). The State should either forbid them (when they are but slavery in disguise); or (he added, one may suppose, with marriage in mind) should establish strong guarantees that they are freely entered on, and allow their dissolution before an impartial authority if there are sufficient grounds.

External Effects

The second broad category of occasions for the intervention of the State comprised a number of mechanical defects of the market, whereby the wishes of the individuals become unattainable.

Mill opened the discussion of these cases with the theoretical consideration of an imaginary instance, the diminution of the hours of labour of adult workers. Critics have often been puzzled by Mill's noncommittal attitude to this problem in the *Principles*; the reason is that they have tended to confuse this kind of limitation of the hours of work for all workers, which in 1848 was not yet a part of practical discussion,[39] with the limitation of the work of children and women, which was. Mill is now speaking of general limitation 'for illustration, and without prejudging the particular point' (956). In the article on the 'Employment of Children in Manufactories' (1834) Mill had spoken of the need for State action to enforce compacts freely entered on by individuals. He used the same analytical tool in the *Principles* to show that the compact of adult workers to increase their leisure had to be enforced by law or by opinion having the force of law.

> A workman who refused to work more than ten hours while there were others who worked twelve, would either be not employed at all, or if employed, must submit to lose one-sixth of his wages. . . However beneficial the observance of the regulation might be to the class collectively, the immediate interest of every individual would lie in violating it: and the more numerous those were who adhered to the rule, the more would individuals gain by departing from it ([1848], 957, notes e—e, f—f, g—g).

Apparently the only time when Mill applied this analysis to a question of general working hours, was a few years earlier (1845) at the Political Economy Club, where he asked for a legal enforcement of Sunday rest: were it not enforced, he said, 'it will happen that the minority will impose its will, and that the majority will not be able to act in the sense it considers most profitable.'[40] In this case perhaps, Mill was carried away by his analysis: experience shows that, for example, to close shops by law on Sundays has more disadvantages than could be foreseen; and that where liberty is allowed on this point, competition has not been so cruel to those who close down as one could deduce from Mill's principle.

In his chapter on optional interventions Mill adverted to Colonization twice: once from the same point of view as the discussion of compacts to limit working hours, that is, as a theoretical example of interventions to effect the wishes of individuals; and another from the point of view of the protection of the interests of posterity and of the community, in so far as they are affected by the actions of emigrants.

In fact the two can be reduced to one: intervention of the State to protect the body of colonists from their individual transgressions of the common interests, and to protect posterity from the selfish behaviour of living colonists; in both cases, they are external effects of individuals' activities.

We have already given a rough outline of Wakefield's system. It was to his ideas that Mill referred when he made these observations on what today would be termed external effects of colonization. In the first place, the defraying of the costs of the voyage could not be left to private enterprise. If the capitalists of the colony, pressed by the scarcity of labour, put up the money, they had no guarantee that the new immigrants would be content to stay in their employment instead of squatting on the land. If the cost of the emigration was defrayed by the parishes of the mother country to find employment for their paupers abroad, the parishes would gain by a diminution of the rates, but the resulting emigration would not raise wages (since the emigrants were unemployed and not paid out of the wages fund). Thus only in an exceptional case, as in the Irish emigration by means of remittances from previous emigrants, could colonization be self-supporting.

But emigration was certainly profitable, both for the mother country and the colony, because it shifted labour from less to more productive employment. In the second place, immediate squatting on the land by the new immigrants would mean that the colony would lose the economic and social benefits of the division of labour. Land should therefore not be obtainable until the immigrant had spent some time in working for others. The solution to both difficulties was that the Government should put a price on land: it would thus avoid the dispersion of the colonists, and have funds to defray the cost of further migration.

Also along the same lines, Mill studied the defects of individual decision in the case of Poor Relief; to rely purely on private charity meant to abandon in the hands of individuals not only the fate of the paupers themselves but the interest of the community that there should not be a body of permanent paupers. Moreover, private charity 'always does too much or too little. . . And. . .if the poor are left to individual charity, a vast amount of mendicity is inevitable.' The State should offer relief to all the needy on the principle of less eligibility (that is to say, a relief less attractive than the most poorly paid work). But private charity still had the task left of 'distinguishing between one case of real necessity and another,' he wrote in 1848, adding in 1852: 'Private charity can give more to the more deserving' (962, n. e—e).

Connected with the consequences of the principle of population, Mill allowed two other interventions of a much more controversial nature. One was the forcible separation of husband and wife in the Poor House to avoid, as he said, the creation of a hereditary race of paupers. The other was his assertion that one could argue 'for converting the moral obligation against bringing children into the world who are a burden to the community, into a legal one.' Fortunately, he said, the same result could be attained by placing women on a footing of equality with men; for then the wives would be able to free themselves from the burden of constant pregnancy. Even with this exception, Mill's adhesion to the Malthusian principle led him to some inadmissible conclusions.

It is surprising that a most important type of intervention justified by the consequences for third parties of the actions of individuals should be missing from the *Principles*: namely, health legislation. That Mill's feelings in the matter were in favour of Public intervention cannot be doubted. When Chadwick, a friend of his youth, published his famous Sanitary Report in 1842, opening Englishmen's eyes to the filth in which they lived, Mill commended it with the highest praise in a review article in the *Examiner*.[41] Mill especially noted those parts where Chadwick stressed the social costs of bad sanitation: it killed more people than any war; it resulted in infectious diseases which were a major cause of destitute widowhood and orphanage. Especially important as a partial modification of his thought on what Malthus called 'the positive checks of population', was that he underlined Chadwick's conclusion that population was not diminished by misery and vice, but only kept at a younger and more sickly state. The Report seemed destined 'to make an impression on the public mind more extensive and permanent even than that recently produced by the appalling disclosures of the Children's Employment Commission.' All the review articles of the time were anonymous. Yet the anonymity, added to the silence in the *Principles*, might make one think that he did not wish to be publicly linked with Chadwick, after all a controversial and even hated figure. On the contrary, when Chadwick stood for Parliament in the constituency of Kilmarnock (1868), Mill gave occasion to a national controversy by backing him against another Liberal candidate, and thus splitting the anti-Tory vote: in the letter to Chadwick's election committee he notably said that he 'would consider his [Chadwick's] absence from the next Parliament as a public misfortune'; and, reciting the labours of Chadwick's life, Mill added:

> He has been from the beginning the leading mind of the sanitary movement which has done so much, and will do much more to improve not only the health, but the moral and economical condition of the working population generally, and especially of its more neglected portions (22−VIII−1868).[42]

Another important occasion for State intervention was urged by Mill, not in the chapter under consideration, but in another part of the *Principles* expounding the wages fund theory: it is the granting of compensation to workers displaced by machinery. Mill admitted after Ricardo that the simultaneous sinking of large amounts of capital into new ventures could be temporarily injurious to the whole of the working classes; and secondly that 'improvements which do not diminish employment on the whole, almost always throw some particular class of labourers out of it' (*Col. W.*, II, 99). In the first case, Mill proceeded, if it ever happened (unlikely in a country with much capital, where new ventures could only bear a small proportion to the whole), it would be the duty of the legislature to slow down the pace of investment. In the second, much more frequent case, Mill held that 'there cannot be a more legitimate object of the legislator's care than the interests of those who are thus sacrificed to the gains of their fellow-citizens and posterity.' This is very probably an echo of the effect produced on Mill by the 'Report on the Condition of the Handloom Weavers' (1841).[43]

The last kind of intervention called for by mechanical defects of the market had received a short allusion in the discussion of colonization. He returned to this kind of case in the closing paragraph of the chapter. There were situations 'in which important public services are to be performed, while yet there is no individual specially interested in performing them, nor would any adequate remuneration naturally or spontaneously attend their performance'(III, 968). Mill exemplifies these situations with the instances of 'a voyage of geographical or scientific exploration'; and of such public works as lighthouses and other securities for navigation, where from the circumstances of the case the users could not be made to pay for them.

With these examples, Mill wanted to lead on to the discussion of the endowment of a learned class. This was an old preoccupation with him, the roots of which are to be found in his Saint-Simonian period.

Around 1840 he had said that the idea of a national clerisy was one of the most important contributions of Coleridge to political thought. In the *Principles* he declared that

> the cultivation of speculative knowledge, though one of the most useful of all employments, is a service rendered to the community collectively, not individually, and one consequently for which it is, *prima facie*, reasonable that the community collectively should pay ([1848 footnote] 968, a—a).

To anyone tempted to think that this was personal pleading, it will be enough to say that his employment at India House always kept him beyond care; and that he did not resent having to spend his energy in office work, for he found it relaxing; finally it must be remembered that Mill was all his life very generous with his own money to help other writers (as with Spencer, for example).

Mill, remembering his own case, asserted that much sustained research was compatible with employing part of the day in a remunerative occupation; but he admitted the danger in many cases that the researcher's time should be frittered away in futile employment; hence, State help could do much good. On the other hand, Government help might engender a tribe of sinecurists. His solution to avoid both pitfalls was to couple the help for research with the obligation to teach; for at university level, teaching 'is a help rather than an impediment to the systematic cultivation of the subject itself.' Mill showed more confidence in the industry of University professors than Adam Smith; but then Adam Smith was himself a professor.

Mill's attitude was by no means generally accepted at the time. *The Economist*, for example, not only ridiculed the idea of any State aid to research, but even considered the protection of intellectual property a form of monopoly.[44] By these and similar expressions of opinion, Mill felt obliged in the fifth edition of the *Principles* (1862) to add the following words:

> I have seen with real alarm several recent attempts, in quarters carrying some authority, to impugn the principle of patents altogether; attempts which, if practically successful, would enthrone free stealing under the prostituted name of free trade, and make the men of brains, still more than at present, the needy retainers and dependents of the men of money-bags ([1862] 929, g—g).

And in the sixth edition (1865), he specified: 'It would be a gross immorality in the law to set everybody free to use a person's work without his consent, and without giving him an equivalent' ([1865] 929, h–h).

Indivisibility of Capital

We have dealt so far with the defects of the market that come under the twofold classification of the chapter on *laissez-faire*: imperfect knowledge and external effects. The necessary and sufficient condition for a market to be perfect is a situation of perfect competition. The axiom of perfect competition implies three subordinate axioms: not only perfect knowledge and perfect discriminateness of goods, but also a perfect divisibility of factors. In his classification of the defects of the market, Mill omitted one category: oligopolistic or monopolistic situations arising from the indivisibility of capital; however, Mill dealt with two instances of this latter category, one in the chapter under discussion, growth in the size of firms, and the other in Book I on capital, public utilities. We shall begin with the first instance.

Whenever nineteenth-century *laissez-faire* is discussed one should remember that it was based on the assumption of a world of individual entrepreneurs, and not of corporations as it would be today. In fact companies were in disfavour with the economists and with the general public, because they were associated with the unscrupulous speculations of bankers and railway promoters. Mill saw that the size of the investment necessary for producing some goods made it impossible for individual capitalists to undertake production; there were economies to size. But Mill had little confidence in joint stock management, which he found as 'jobbing, careless, and ineffective' as Government management. The springs of self-interest were missing in the case of both joint stock directors, and public officials: 'their proportional share of the benefits of good management, [is not] equal to the interest they may possibly have in mismanagement' (954). In fact, the institution of joint stock companies has worked out better than the classical economists expected. This was becoming clear in Mill's lifetime. Thus in 1865, Cairnes, Mill's most outstanding disciple, in his comments on the text of the fifth edition of the *Principles*, defended the joint stock principle, pointing out that at least in the case of banks the obligation to publish accounts was a great advantage; he added that the public seemed to be beginning to prefer banks on the joint stock principle over those of the traditional type. Mill accepted this criticism and inserted a paragraph embodying Cairnes's observations in the sixth edition (136–7, g–g).[45] Despite this small amendment, Mill did not modify his general attitude. The reason may be the one Mrs Robinson puts forward to explain Adam Smith's hostility to joint stock companies; that Mill, too, underestimated the loyalty of individuals to the institutions with which they are connected.[46]

But Mill was not afraid to draw the consequences of the advantages of large scale production when it meant the merging of joint stock companies rather than the disappearance of individual entrepreneurs. 'Whatever disadvantages may be supposed to attend on the change from a small to a large system of production, they are not applicable to the change from a large to a still larger' (141). This peaceful acceptance was helped by a conviction he later expressed in his posthumous *Chapters on Socialism*: there he said that when in any branch of production a merger takes place,

> the larger capitalists, either individual or joint-stock, among which the business is divided, are seldom, if ever . . . so few as that competition shall not continue to act between them (*Coll. Works*, V, 750–1).[47]

The case for consolidation was clearest in the case of public utilities, he proceeded to say in Book I of the *Principles*.

> It is obvious, for example, how great an economy of labour would be obtained if London were supplied by a single gas or water company instead of the existing plurality. While there are even as many as two, this implies double establishments of all sorts (141).

There followed a good study of the costs and instability of oligopoly. The main danger of consolidation, Mill recognized, lay in the fact that the single company would not reduce its charges to the public in consistency with its lower costs. 'Even if it did not, the community in the aggregate would still be a gainer: since the shareholders are part of the community.' Its charges would hardly be higher than under competition, since when there are so few competitors, after short price wars to drive the weakest out of the field an agreement is generally reached. In sum, 'it is much better to treat it at once as a public function,' either under direct government management, or by concession to the lowest priced company with government inspection.

Mill's Conclusion to His Study of Optional Interventions

With the above consideration of research and large companies, Mill closed the discussion of the cases when government intervention could be considered justified.

> The preceding heads comprise, to the best of my judgment, the whole of the exceptions to the practical maxim, that the business of society can be best performed by private and voluntary agency (970).

The sweeping character of this final declaration is puzzling. It is matched by the generality of the declaration, quoted above, which opens the study of these exceptions: *'Laissez-Faire . . .* should be the general practice.' This passage- totally fails to describe Mill's real attitude to optional interventions. Firstly, the complete catalogue, as listed above, contained many more cases than those comprised between the two sentences: indeed many instances from other parts of the *Principles* have had to be brought into the argument. Moreover the temper of the discussion is misrepresented by the idea of a closed list of permitted interventions: much of it was in the nature of a theoretical consideration of imaginary cases, tacitly presented as models for an undetermined number of real instances. Thirdly and more important still, it was immediately after the closing declaration that he knew of no more exceptions, that he conceded the wide role for the State in underdeveloped countries examined above.

> It is, however, necessary to add [he said] that the intervention of government cannot always practically stop short at the limit which defines the cases intrinsically suitable for it. In the particular circumstances of a given age or nation, there is scarcely anything really important to the general interest, which it may not be desirable, or even necessary, that the government should take upon itself, not because private individuals cannot effectually perform it, but because they will not (970).

Logically there is no contradiction between a closed list of exceptions to *laissez-faire* and a wide interpretation of the legitimacy of interventions in default of private agency in backward countries, since the strict application of the rule can well be limited to advanced countries. But psychologically, the addition of this new call for State intervention seems to be in the nature of an afterthought. If an explanation may be hazarded for this puzzle, the most likely cause of this psychological inconsequence may have been the speed of composition of the *Principles*;[48] before embarking on the discussion of the exceptions to *laissez-faire*, he may have written both the introductory and concluding sentences, containing the rigid reaffirmation of the rule; but once embarked on the actual discussion, he uncovered an unexpected number of defects of the market, and was carried away by the examination of the analytical aspects of the question. If such was the case it is sad that in the revision he should not have brought the frame of his discussion into line with the contents of it, not so much in the interests of formal harmony, as for averting the danger that hasty readers should think this adherence to the rule of *laissez-faire* more rigid and dogmatic than it really was. Nevertheless, and in spite of the fact that his classification of the defects of the market is not perfect, the analysis of them in the *Principles* compares favourably with that of other economists of the time, and indeed of the present day.[49]

Pamphlet on Water Boards

His discussion of the question of public utilities in the *Principles* was very topical. In January 1851, his opinion as the 'author of a work of the highest authority, on the principles of political economy' was sought on the question of the water supply by The Metropolitan Sanitary Association. This was a private body formed to promote the reform of London's health conditions along the lines laid down by Chadwick,[50] who wished to consolidate under the Board of Health, of which he was one of the Commissioners, the water distribution, drainage, and interment systems of the Metropolis.

Chadwick himself asked Mill to favour the Association with an answer, but must have been somewhat disappointed by Mill's carefully worded letter of 15 February 1851.

Mill began by describing the peculiar economic characteristics of water supply. The *Economist* had wrongly compared it with food supply; 'the policy of depending on individuals for the supply of the markets assumes the existence of competition.' The case of water supply is one in which the conditions of carriage make it impossible for more than a small number of individuals or companies to compete; due to their small numbers, their 'interest prompts them, except during occasional short periods, not to compete but to combine.' Water supply is not analogous to the supply of food, but to 'the making of roads and bridges, the paving, lighting and cleansing of streets'and above all to 'the drainage of towns,' to which (he said, reflecting the ideas of his friend Chadwick) it is naturally connected. 'The principle, therefore, of Government regulation, I conceive to be indisputable.'

Concerning the question of what form of government regulation, Mill considered three possible solutions: one was to consolidate all the water companies under the one company guaranteeing the best service at the lowest price, with strict government supervision; the second was to entrust water supply to the municipal authorities; the last, to a centralized board.

Mill rejected the idea of a concession due to his distrust of joint stock companies. He also rejected the second solution in view of the actual state of the affairs of London. Had there been a London government, he would not have hesitated to choose this solution.

> The jealousy which prevails in this country of any extension of the coercive and compulsory powers of the general government I conceive to be, though not always wisely directed. . . yet, on the whole a most salutary sentiment, and one to which this country owes the chief points of superiority which its Government possesses over those of the Continent.[51]

Until the London Municipal Authority were properly constituted[52] 'the authority to which the work may most fittingly be entrusted is a Commissioner, appointed by the Government, and responsible to Parliament like the Commissioner of the Poor Laws.'

From this correspondence Mill emerged as much more jealous of central government authority than Chadwick's friends. This is confirmed by a letter from Mill to Chadwick some years later, on 28 October 1864: 'About the economical advantage, touched upon in your letter, of a consolidation of railways, you are not likely to find any help in the French economists. They are, nearly all of them, much more hostile to consolidation and to government action than I am; and I am more so than you.'[53]

The 1854 Civil Service Reforms

For all these new functions contemplated by Mill, the government needed an improved machinery. The insufficiencies of civil and military administration, brought to light in the Crimean War, speeded the movement for administrative reform. In 1854 appeared the Northcote-Trevelyan Report, and the reformers won the Government's promise that its recommendations would be implemented; namely, that the system of admission to the civil service should no longer be through political patronage, but by means of competitive examinations.

Mill first learnt of the Northcote-Trevelyan plan (so essentially Benthamite in character) through the daily press. He immediately commented on it in a letter to his wife, who was at the time in the South of France.

> The Civil Service examination plan I am afraid is too good to pass. The report proposing it, by Trevelyan & Northcote (written no doubt by Trevelyan) has been printed in the [Morning] Chronicle — it is as direct uncompromising & to the point, without reservation, as if we had written it (3—III—1854).[54]

Shortly after, Trevelyan wrote to ask him for a few words in support of his plan. Without waiting, as he would have liked, to hear Harriet's opinion, Mill wrote straight off to Trevelyan, putting forward an argument, among others, that he would use in all his comments on this reform: that

> if the examination be so contrived as to be a real test of mental superiority, it is difficult to set limits to the effects which will be produced in raising the character not only of the public service but of Society itself.

Eventually Harriet's reply arrived sharing fully in his enthusiasm. He answered her on 14 March 1854, with the following eulogy of the Government for accepting the Report's conclusions:

> I give the ministers infinite credit for it, that is if they really adopt the whole plan. . .but the least they can do consistently with their speeches, will be such a sacrifice of [the] power of jobbing as hardly any politician who ever lived, ever yet made to the *sense* of right, without any public demand — it stamps them as quite remarkable men for their class & country.

Later, some time after Harriet's return, Trevelyan asked Mill to write a longer article in place of the earlier letter of support he had written in March. This was published in the same year in a symposium of opinions on the civil service entry reform.[55] Mill's paper, dated 22 May 1854, began with the following declaration:

The proposal to select candidates for the Civil Service of Government by a competitive examination appears to me to be one of those great public improvements the adoption of which would form an era in history (92).

Both conservatives and reformers should support the scheme, the former because it vindicated the established order by demonstrating that the ruling classes did not desire to exploit their ascendancy, the latter because within its province the reform accomplished what every true reformer desired: that Government should be in the hands of the most competent.

Added to this was 'the extraordinary stimulus which would be given to mental cultivation in its most important branches' by the competitive examination system, not only directly, but also by the fact that the importance of this cultivation thus received nationwide acknowledgement. Last, but by no means least, was the moral example set by the State, in renouncing a system of preference and patronage in favour of selection based on merit.

In the rest of the paper Mill countered some of the objections commonly raised against the plan, and dwelt for a moment on a very important point: the kind of knowledge that should be demanded from candidates. In the 1854 paper he only referred to the examinations for the lower appointments:

The competition for the inferior posts must be practically limited to the acquirements which are attainable by the persons who seek such employments; but it is by no means a consequence that it should be confined to such things as have a direct connexion with their duties (98).

On this point Mill differed from the opinion Chadwick and others expressed in the same publication. Strictly utilitarian opinions regarding the subjects to be taught were in keeping with the spirit of the time. But for Mill it was important that English society should learn to value mental cultivation for its own sake, and moreover, he believed that practical skills could be better acquired in the actual experience of the work they applied to. This did not mean that the examination should be purely literary: the scheme proposed that it should also be scientific, covering technical subjects (94). What it did mean was that it should be general and not just a substitute for practical experience.

Mill developed these ideas in *Representative Government*.[56] Once the competitive examination system was accepted, it was important to determine what knowledge should be required of the candidates. The tests would have to be such as to ascertain whether the candidate had been well educated (344). It must be remembered that at the time young men went directly into an administrative career without first passing through the University, so that candidates were selected in their youth 'not as having learnt, but in order that they may learn, their profession' (341).

On the whole, the passages dealing with this subject in *Representative Government* written as they were five years after the reform was carried through, reveal a certain feeling of disappointment at the shortcomings manifest in the law's operation.[57] In the system as it was finally set up, candidates for the examination for the higher posts needed to be nominated by a minister, which somewhat impaired the principle. But even in those cases where such a nomination was not required, the general standard of attainment in the country had proved so low that the immediate improvement in the quality of civil servants that Mill had expected when the patronage system was abandoned did not materialize. His tacit conclusion appears to be that only in the long run would the effects of the reform be felt.

The 1862 Article on 'Centralization'

Thus little by little, administrative questions were gaining Mill's attention. With present day knowledge it is easy to see that the growth of administration was the real problem in this matter of the province of government. But at the time, it was far from obvious. As Mr MacDonagh has pointed out,[58] in the beginning even interventionists thought that social evils could be solved once and for all by a single piece of legislation; later it appeared that trained full-time inspectors and even enforcement from the centre were sometimes necessary if the law was to be effective; finally, it was realized that for some problems only the versatile instrument of a permanent administration could achieve results.

Mill had discussed administration (as opposed to law) in earlier works, especially in *Representative Government*; but it can be said that only in his article on 'Centralization' in 1862 did he fully realize its possibilities, limitations, and dangers.[59] The article shows traces of the effect on Mill of the greatest political disillusion he suffered in his life: the overthrow of the legitimate government in France by Napoleon III.

At the outbreak of the 1848 revolution Mill had rushed enthusiastically to Paris and made the acquaintance of Lamartine and other leaders of the young Republic. He also wrote various articles in support of the new *régime*, the sudden emergence of which had been received in England as another example of French instability. In the second and third editions of the *Principles* (1849 and 1852), it is easy to see what hopes Mill had set on the Republic, especially for the socialistic and co-operative experiments tried under it. Imagine then, his anger and confusion when the French so easily accepted the adventurer; especially since the very democratic and socialist opinions which had contributed so greatly to the overthrow of the monarchy were held responsible at the time for the installation of the usurper: 'C'est le Socialisme qui triomphe!' exclaimed Thiers on hearing the news of the *coup d'état*.

Mill's explanation for the total lack of resistance shown to Louis Napoleon was the excessive centralization of the French state, which made democratic habits only skin deep: the citizenry was inured to despotism by the continuous interference of bureaucrats, and bribed into conformity by the hope of a place in the administration.[60] Hence developed a recrudescence in him of the anti-centralizing attitude he had shown after reading Tocqueville in the thirties. In consequence, the article is a study of how to forestall the political dangers of administrative activity in modern states.

One of the French authors reviewed in the article, Dupont-White, Mill's French translator, believed that the advance in civilization brought about an increase in State intervention; and hence considered that an increase in State activity was an index (or even a necessary condition) of continued progress. Mill asserted that this belief was born of a confusion between administration and legislation; 'he does not distinguish, or distinguishes only casually and incidentally, between one mode of State interference and another' (*Edinburgh Review*, CXV, 345). While Mill accepted that progress called for increased legislation, he denied that it called for increased administrative intervention: there is a 'diminished need of State actions as institutions improve' (333); 'all the functions of Government which do not consist in affording legal protection, are in reality greatest when civilization is at the lowest' (348). The development of administration in the twentieth century has shown that Mill was wrong in his predictions; today the problem in this respect is not so much to limit the growth of state activity, but rather to devise means of safeguarding the individual from misuse of new administrative powers.

Mill proceeded to assert that State activity using the instrument of the law was by far the less dangerous of the two. 'Extension of legislation in itself implies no fresh delegation of power to the executive.' New functionaries may have to be created to watch over the application of the law; hence, this mode of intervening 'does, at times, imply some increase of public functionaries and patronage' (345). 'But it is not necessary that these officers should have administrative control' (346). It may be enough to grant them powers to prosecute the persistent offenders before the courts. Again, 'there may. . .be over-legislation, as well as over-administration. A legislature, as well as an executive, may take upon itself how individuals shall carry on their own business for their own profit.' But the conclusion was that measures framed as general laws and enforced through the courts constituted no grave menace to individual liberty.

By implication, the granting of further administrative powers to the government was conceived to be fraught with dangers. Administrative interventions were needed; it was legitimate 'that the State be required to render all such services as, being necessary or important to society, are not of a nature to remunerate any one for their performance' (the list of these interventions has been dealt with on an earlier page). But it was necessary to neutralize the potential danger they implied for individual freedom. In the first place, State interventions should only be resorted to when all else had failed: he praised the English habit of not calling for the help of the State until it became abundantly clear that the public spirit of the citizens was not equal to the task. And secondly, when it was decided that the State should intervene, Mill proposed that as many functions as possible be entrusted to local authorities.

It was on the question of local as against central government that Mill thought Dupont-White's opinions less acceptable. 'Our author is weakest where he attempts to show that a people under a centralized government may be free'; some of the Frenchman's pronouncements

would almost lead us to think of him as one who only cares for protecting the collective body of the nation from great acts of high-handed oppression by the chiefs of the State, against which free discussion and representative institutions really are a considerable security; but thinks nothing of the universal habit of trembling before every petty public officer, which, beyond almost anything that can be named, renders people incapable of liberty (329–30).

Dupont-White dismissed local government because he had noted the incapacity and petty-minded tyranny of municipal institutions in France. Mill argued that these defects could be remedied by making them answerable to the citizens, increasing the size of local government units, and, as an additional guarantee, by having the Central Government inspect and supervise. All this was but a summary of what he had said in Chapter XV of *Representative Government*, titled 'Of Local Representative Bodies.' He ended on the familiar note that the centralization of which he could approve 'is that of knowledge and experience rather than of power' (352).

The essay on 'Centralization' is important in that there all the great themes of Mill's thought on the role of the State in society find their true nature and final formulation. In the first place, the distinction between 'necessary' and 'optional' activities is transformed into 'legislative' and 'administrative'. Secondly, Mill has found a symmetry between the position of the individual, and of local institutions, *vis-à-vis* the State. It allows him to explain the relation between the two problems that absorbed him, that of the province of the State and that of Centralization: both 'the limits which separate the province of the government from that of individual and spontaneous agency' and the province 'of central from local government' must be seen as defences of liberty. And finally the article permits one to lay down exactly the limits of Mill's distrust of public activity. Recommendations for new legislation, such as the Factory Laws, Health Legislation, Regulation of Weights and Measures, Punishment for Food Adulteration, were *prima facie* quite free from suspicion. The idea of necessary State activity extended itself to cover all new legislation which the progress of society might demand: 'inasmuch as all new good which arises in the world must be expected to bring new evil as its accompaniment' (348). But such administrative interventions as came to be needed should be closely scrutinized, and, if possible, entrusted to local institutions.

Mill closed the article congratulating the English for their predisposition to be suspicious of any extension of the power of government. 'Even where no general principle forbids its interference,' he proceeds, 'nothing should be done by it, except what has been clearly proved to be incapable of being done by other means.' The line between the situations where the State should intervene and those where it should not is not clearly marked; but

few Englishmen, we believe, would grudge the government, for a

time, or permanently, the powers necessary to save from injury a
great national interest; and equally few would claim for it the power
of meddling with anything, which could be let alone without
touching the public welfare in any vital part.

Conclusion

From all this discussion Mill's position emerges quite clearly. The
political economists of Mill's time based their attitude to State activity
on the belief that the system of economic freedom could attain with
tolerable efficiency the ends of the good society — on condition that
the State establish the necessary framework of law and order, and not
precluding State intervention to correct particular failings. Mill had
much to add to this bare outline of the *rationale* of a liberal economic
policy: he came to distinguish between two kinds of government
activity on the basis of their form, legislative or administrative; he
advocated a radical and continuous reform of the legal framework to
meet new problems raised by the progress of society; practically
reduced the category of suspicious government actions to those
administrative interventions in which coercive powers were employed;
and finally devised the expedient of entrusting as many of these latter
interventions to local authorities so as to make them as harmless as
possible. The whole could be summed up in a phrase of *On Liberty*:
'the greatest dissemination of power consistent with efficiency; but the
greatest possible centralization of information, and diffusion of it from
the centre.'[6][1]

Considered from Mill's own viewpoint, one of his greatest
achievements was the working out of his doctrine of the role of the
State in society. Perhaps on some questions his social philosophy led
him to offer automatic answers rather than the fruit of reflection, as,
for example, when he proclaimed the rule of *laissez-faire* in more
absolute terms than were warranted by the long list of exceptions that
followed. But in general we can say that he was successful in applying
to this problem of political economy his vision of a society composed
of self-governing individuals, a society in which State activity should
never stifle individual initiative. Mill's interpretation of the maxim
laissez-faire, laissez-passer is perfectly in keeping with his vision of the
future society, as we shall see in Chapter 8.

Mill's doctrine is also important for its influence on the economists
that followed after him. Without Book V of John Stuart Mill's
Principles, it is impossible to conceive of   Cairnes's criticism of the

laissez-faire system, Sidgwick's study of the cases where interventionism was justified, Marshall's suggestion and Pigou's codification of the circumstances under which a discrepancy between the private and social marginal product might be expected. From. Mill stemmed the neo-classical (one might say, the Cambridge) tradition of critical evaluation of the working of the market.

From a twentieth century viewpoint the assessment of Mill's contribution will depend on the social philosophy of the individual, though this does not mean that only the most extreme believers in a market economy may find inspiration in Mill's doctrine.

There is a group of thinkers of considerable importance who defend an economic policy very similar to Mill's in many ways; some of them even proclaim themselves disciples of Mill. This group of economists has been called the 'neo-liberal' school. One of its most important figures is Professor Hayek, who not many years ago published *The Constitution of Liberty* to commemorate the centenary of the publication of Mill's *On Liberty*. This book takes up and expands several of Mill's ideas analysed above, especially the distinction between legislative and administrative State action, and the warning against the dangers of the latter. *The Constitution of Liberty* is an important book, full of interesting suggestions even for those who do not agree with its political message. The definition of Law as the science of Liberty, and the consequent analysis of what the Rule of Law implies are of particular interest. But Professor Hayek is in a sense unfair to Mill when he takes him as a text for his commentary. There are two important differences of nuance between the doctrine of Mill and that of the neo-liberals. In the first place, Mill did not consider that the distribution of the ownership of the means of production in Western societies was just, nor did he have any confidence that the spontaneous movements of the market would in time correct this imbalance; and, though he decidedly opposed any progressive income tax[62] (an attitude faithfully reflected by Professor Hayek), he proposed other remedies, such as a limitation to what any person could inherit, which, in Mill's time especially, were very radical. In the second place, Mill's general attitude respecting liberty was much more flexible than that of the neo-liberals; the latter, as Professor Rojo has noted,[63] take a theological attitude towards freedom, in the sense that, whatever proofs of the failings of the system of economic liberty on given points are presented to them, they always take refuge in the unknown benefits which will accrue at an indeterminate future time if no recourse is had to State intervention;

while Mill on the contrary distinguished between personal and commercial liberty, accepting suspension of the latter when the clear utility of the intervention justified it. As a proof of this flexibility it is enough to remember that he was the first to build a general theory of the defects of the market.

Not all economists are conservatives, whatever Professor Stigler may say, least of all in poor countries: but even for these, much could be profitably learnt from Mill's treatment of the problem of *laissez-faire*. They will probably disagree with the line Mill draws to circumscribe State activity. Like Shonfield they will point out that the widespread belief that in capitalist countries State activity is confined within a very narrow radius is largely a myth, and they will draw attention to the irreversible nature of the spread of administrative action in the modern world. They will emphasize the fact that political and personal liberty in some of the capitalist countries most advanced in socialization does not appear to have been diminished, indeed, quite the contrary. But liberty was not a panacea for all social ills in Mill's view either. It was, however, a social good that should be carefully protected, as there was no guarantee at all that it would grow with the progress of civilization. This seems even more true today than in Mill's time. Only a constant vigilance ensures the survival of freedom in the increasingly organized world in which we live. The great lesson Mill offers us is to remind us that the march towards freedom is reversible.

Temperamentally, Mill was always prepared to go to hell with those whom he regarded as intellectuals rather than to heaven with those whom he regarded as philistines — even if he was not quite sure that the intellectuals were right.

Lord Robbins

Chapter 7 Socialism

Time and again it has been asked whether Mill meant what he said when in a passage of the *Autobiography* he declared himself a socialist. In those lines he compared his opinions in the days of his most extreme Benthamism with those he held at the time of writing the *Principles of Political Economy*. In his youth, he said, he had been at one with 'the old school of political economists' in holding 'property, as now understood, and inheritance', as 'the *dernier mot* of legislation'; in short, he had been a 'democrat, but not the least of a Socialist.' In the late forties, under the influence of his wife he came to hold much more heretical opinions. Harriet and he were much less democrats than before, because they feared power in the hands of an uneducated mass, democracy coming to mean the rule of mediocrity: 'but our ideal of ultimate improvement went far beyond Democracy, and would class us decidedly under the general designation of Socialists' (W.Cl., p.196).

Mill made other remarks on the subject that have likewise aroused discussion; for in response to external events, to new reading, and it may be added, to the opinions of the woman he was to marry, he changed his point of view several times in his life. Moreover, since the evidence for these changes is buried in deceased reviews, or consists of differences between one edition and another of his works, it is not surprising that there should be a great deal of confusion about his thoughts on the matter.

Opinions have differed even more in this case than in the question of *laissez-faire*, some writers nearer to the truth than others, but few really accounting for what seem to be the facts. Some have thought that Mill, towards the end of his life, was groping towards Fabian Socialism. Others, such as Schumpeter and Margaret Cole, have asserted that, though he did not think any of the socialist proposals put forward in his time to be practicable, he admitted the superiority of socialism as an ideal, and conceived it as a goal to be attained by slow reform in the Bernstein fashion. Some people, both socialists and liberals, have presented Mill's opinions on socialism as an example of 'shallow syncretism' (to use Marx's words), as attempting the impossible task of reconciling the Old Political Economy with the new demands of the working classes. One opinion at least may be ruled out of court on the strength of the findings of the previous chapter: the one which affirms that Mill 'was well on his way to State Socialism,' though it was held by no less a person than Leslie Stephen. Finally, another group, of which Lord Robbins is the most conspicuous, has contended that, all things weighed, Mill gave less ground to socialism than is generally believed, and that in the end he upheld the superiority of the system of private property and competition.[1]

There is great danger that a discussion such as this falls into a mere dispute about words and their meaning. It would be sterile to debate what socialism and liberalism are in essence, and whether Mill's opinions may be included under one or the other of such abstract definitions. The problem must be seen in its historical context. Judging by our findings so far in the present study, there can be no doubt that Mill was a liberal. But we should understand the interpretation attached to the word in his time. In 1887, Lord Acton wrote in a letter: 'The Revolution, or as we say, Liberalism.'[2] Perhaps this facet of Mill's thought is better described as 'radical', which would indicate the type of nonconformist individualism he upheld. Can he also be said to have been a socialist? Towards the end of his life, Mill was an ardent supporter of co-operativism as were many socialists at the time. Does this therefore justify including him 'under the general designation of socialist'? In this chapter we shall try to offer an answer to this question, and if our analysis is true, we shall see that Mill was much less of a socialist than is generally thought.

Socialism in the Time of Mill

The history of socialist thought during Mill's lifetime falls into two broad periods. The first reaches until around the year 1848. In England it is the period of Owenism, with its repeated attempts at transforming society through Universal Trades Unions and Utopian Agricultural Parallelograms (Owen's quadrilateral settlements). On the Continent it is the period of French socialism, of the 'duodecimo editions of the New Jerusalem' (as Marx and Engels derisively called the Utopian socialists' plans). Owenism had been more fleeting, and had gone quietly into chrysalis with the spread of Chartism, only to reappear transformed into the sturdier if less colourful form of co-operativism. [3] French socialism had a more exciting life: it seemed about to prevail with the 1848 Revolution, but received its death blow in the Paris street fighting in June of that year.

For some fifteen years the gap remained unfilled, both in England and in the rest of Europe. The lull was broken by Ferdinand Lasalle in the early sixties, and a new socialism was born, that of the *Communist Manifesto* (though this pamphlet passed unnoticed in its day), of the Internationals, of Marx and Engels, and Bakunin, a socialism totally different from that which had preceded 1848. The spontaneous associations, the piecemeal experiments of the Owenites, Fourierists and Cabetists, had disappeared from England and France, and now existed only in North America. In Europe socialism became a movement of class struggle; its aim was to conquer the State and establish the supremacy of the proletariat, not stopping short of a revolution if necessary. The change was so great that the names famous before 1848 — Louis Blanc, Cabet, Fourier — were almost forgotten in the sixties. [4]

Mill gave almost exclusive attention to the thinkers of the first period, and was not really aware of the profound transformation wrought on socialist thought by the Germans. His doctrine is not to be read in the light of socialism today, or of the International, but always bearing in mind the features of Utopian socialism.

Pre-1848 socialism was far from being homogeneous; like socialism today, it flowed in different, even independent streams of thought. But despite this, it is still possible to say that the socialism of the first period constituted a distinct mode of thinking, with certain features common to all its branches.

In the first place it stemmed from the Enlightenment, maintaining and even exaggerating the optimism of Enlightened thought, with its combination of belief in the omnipotence of Reason, and a faith in the goodness of Nature (human or physical).

The second distinguishing characteristic of these early socialists consisted in their pacifist millenarism. [5] They had an absolute confidence that the evil of society could be utterly destroyed, and a total certainty that their schemes were the ones which could effect the regeneration of society. But it must be noticed that they were not revolutionaries. Their unbounded optimism, allied to their belief that man was essentially rational, led them to expect a sudden conversion of

the world to their views if they were but once put in practice. Hence
most pre-Marxian socialists expected all things for all men from a
piecemeal application of their principles and shunned attempts to
establish their schemes by compulsion.[6]

The third characteristic of these socialists was their enmity to the
system of competition. It would be wrong to believe that they fastened
their criticism exclusively onto private property. Some of them did not
even want to abolish it. Competition was for them the real cause of the
waste and poverty prevalent in society. It was competition which
fostered the 'anarchy' of existing society, and competition again which
occasioned the conflicts between classes and countries. In the classical
formulation of a very able book, *L'organisation du travail* (1839) by
Louis Blanc, competition between labourers reduced wages, between
capitalists provoked crisis, between nations caused wars.

Their concrete proposals for the future society differed widely,
depending mainly on which of the ingredients, natural harmony or
rationalism, had more weight in their thought (and whether they
believed the Golden Age lay in the past or in the future). Some went so
far in their confidence that the 'natural' society was the good society
that they deprecated all State interventions in social affairs: thus the
anarchist Hodgskin who during his many years on the staff of *The
Economist* was a staunch defender of absolute *laissez-faire*. Others
believed that society, to be perfect, had to be planned and directed
from the centre: thus the Saint-Simonians, who proposed the
establishment of a hierarchical and theocratic organization where
production would be controlled, and distributive shares awarded by the
central authority.

It is within such a framework that we must interpret Mill's
pronouncements on socialism. The most obvious instance of the need
for this historical approach is his use of the words 'communism' and
'socialism'. Examining his chapter on Property in the first three editions
of the *Principles* it is clear Mill used these words differently from the
way they are used today. For Mill the distinction between
'communism' and 'socialism' lay in the fact that the communists
insisted on absolute equality of remuneration, whereas the socialists
admitted inequality of distribution, and even some measure of private
property. The role of the State (let alone the preference for revolution
or gradualism) had nothing to do with the distinction between the two
forms: the 'communists' he principally studied were the Owenites, who
wanted to organize society into a federation of independent communes;

while among the 'socialists' he included both those who wanted a strong central authority, like the Saint-Simonians, and (in a later edition) those again who wanted a loose federation of communities, like the Fourierists.

'The Principles of Political Economy' First Edition, 1848

Mill's youthful attacks on Owenism have been described in an earlier chapter. The *Principles* was the first treatise of political economy to give serious attention to socialism, and include a general and systematic discussion of it.[7] The innovation in theory that enabled Mill to take this step has already been mentioned: namely, the distinction between laws of production and laws of distribution. As we said earlier, this distinction was defective and in the last count unacceptable, but it had the advantage of making a deeper study of socialism possible, for socialism can only be considered seriously when the belief that there is only one possible scheme of distribution has been abandoned. That is why Mill presented this distinction precisely at the beginning of Book II of the *Principles*, a book in which he attempted to compare the system of competition and private property with the proposals of the Utopian socialists.

One of the defects in the said distinction, however, did affect his presentation of socialism: the excessive freedom granted in principle to Society for the choice of a distributive system (though this admission of freedom was immediately followed by the assertion that an ill-advised choice could have disagreeable consequences) means that Mill's exposition is excessively polarized. On the one side, he started off with complete freedom of choice in the election of a distributive system, only to add, on the other side, the disagreeable consequences of certain schemes. He began by supposing

> a community unhampered by any previous possessions; a body of colonists, occupying for the first time an uninhabited country; bringing nothing with them but what belonged to them in common, and having a clear field for the adoption of the institutions and policy which they judged most expedient ([1848] *Coll. Works* II, 201 [II, i, 2]),

and then he proceeded to inquire whether it would be advisable for them to choose a socialist system, by examining what consequences such an adoption would have for their welfare. Now no social group first chooses its distributive institutions arbitrarily, and then abandons or modifies them if their consequences are too disagreeable to bear. Societies find themselves with a distributive scheme in working order (whatever its drawbacks) and their members may decide to attempt a modification of its defects if they are too heavy to bear.

Hence a logical arrangement of the analysis of socialism would be to start by looking at the distributive arrangements existing at the time; then present socialist criticisms of the system of private property and competition; then examine the remedies proposed by the socialists: and finally criticize these remedies, and propose alternative ones. This was the order Mill followed in the posthumous *Chapters on Socialism*.

But in the *Principles* the matter was not arranged in this way. After supposing the existence of his body of Robinson Crusoes, who had to weigh the relative merits of the different possible distributive schemes in the abstract, he was naturally led to engage on a juristic discussion of the right of property, of little interest or relevance in a book of political economy; he then examined the proposals of the socialists; but extraordinary though it may seem, competition as such was not discussed in the first edition of the *Principles* at all, and barely mentioned in the second. The arrangement of the posthumous *Chapters* was undoubtedly superior.

Even from the point of view of the discussion of early socialism, the first edition of the *Principles* was published prematurely. The wave of socialism had been mounting ever since the Saint-Simonian squall, but it was not to break for the first time until a few months after the publication of the treatise, during the French revolution of 1848. Mill's discussion of Socialism in the first edition reflects the relative quiet of the time before 1848; though most of the ideas of pre-Marxian socialism had been published long before, he only examined Owenism and Saint-Simonism, in a comparatively short space, and in a markedly detached manner.

Thus Mill turned his attention first to the study of Owenism or 'communism'. He did not think it to be strictly impracticable. There is no example, he said, of Owenism having been tried on a national scale;[8] a loose federation of communities, self-sufficient enough to allow them to exclude foreign competition, and disciplined enough to keep a strict check on population, would afford the majority a better living than that which they get in countries where population is unchecked. This was not an enthusiastic verdict. The implications were that it was unlikely that population would be controlled in an Owenite commune, that Owenite communities would prove to be less efficient than competitive societies if they had to compete in the international market, and that the condition of the minorities of richer people would deteriorate under Owenism. It is precisely these topics — population, efficiency, and the fate of minorities — which he proceeded to discuss.

On the subject of population, it is clear from a remark further on in the chapter,[9] that Mill thought that population was less likely to be controlled in an Owenite community than under the existing system. Secondly, Mill elaborated the comparison of efficiency between the two systems, by examining the problem of incentive under Owenism. On this other count

> the objection ordinarily made..., that each person would be incessantly occupied in evading his fair share of the work, is, I think, in general considerably overstated ([1848] *Coll. Works*, III, 975–6 [II, i, 3]).

There follows a discussion of the kind of incentives which play a role in social life, especially interesting because, according to Mill's own definition of Economic Science a few years back, economics only took into account the desire for wealth.[10] Mill points out that such institutions as the army do not rely on pecuniary incentives: in this case it is 'the sense of honour and the fear of shame' which prompt people to do their duty — failing which there can be a resort to disciplinary action. Indeed

> mankind are capable of a far greater amount of public spirit than the present age is accustomed to suppose possible ([1848] *Coll. Works*, vol. III, p.976).

A society relying on public spirit and discipline, however (he proceeded, as he would not in the third edition), could not expect its members to perform more than routine duties:

> if the question were that of taking a great deal of personal trouble to produce a very small and unconspicuous public benefit, the love of ease would preponderate ([1848], *ibid.*)

The Owenites might argue that in the existing type of society workers have less incentive to work efficiently than they would have in the Owenite society as described by Mill. Mill answers that superintendence, the hope of gaining promotion or permanence of employment, and the system of piecework, partially remedy the position in a competitive organization. But where workers in a competitive system have no incentive to perform more than the customary work-load, Mill concedes that the situation could be bettered under Owenism.[11]

After thus considering the problem of efficiency under Owenism from the point of view of incentive to work, Mill turned to the problem of efficiency posed by the sharing out of the work among the members of the community. The arguments he adduced were not quite based on the efficiency of resource allocation, for that function of the price system had not yet been explicitly formulated, but what he clearly stated was that, once the price system is removed, it becomes impossible to compare one kind of work with another. The goal of equality, said Mill, is strictly unattainable.

> The produce might be divided equally, but how could the labour? There are many kinds of work, and by what standard are they to be measured one against the other? ([1848] *Coll. Works*, III, 977).

The logic of the situation drives Owenites to ask that everybody should take every kind of work in turns. But, said Mill, the benefits of the division of labour would be lost. (He could have specified a little more and have said that it is the benefits of specialization which are lost.)[12] Under the competitive system, 'these things do adjust themselves with some, though but a distant, approach to fairness' ([1848] *ibid*). The discoverer of the theory of non-competing groups did not forget that

> this self-adjusting machinery does not touch some of the grossest of the existing inequalities of remuneration, and in particular the unjust advantages possessed by almost the commonest mental over almost the hardest and most disagreeable bodily labour ([1848] *ibid)*.

He hopes, however, that education would put down some of the barriers.

The final argument against Owenism concerns the fate of minorities within the communes, and is in substance an expression of fear for liberty under Owenism. As the betterment of the condition of the people under this system depends on a restriction of population, and hence the same degree of welfare can be obtained in a competitive system by limiting the population, whatever the minority in a competitive system would have over and above the mean standard of welfare, should be counted as an advantage of the property system.

It is an abuse of the principle of equality to demand that no individual be permitted to be better off than the rest, when his being so makes none of the others worse off than they otherwise would be ([1848] *Coll. Works*, I, 980).

The advantages of merely obtaining the necessaries of life should not be exaggerated. Once obtained, happiness lies in 'higher' things. If the variety of characters and pursuits disappeared, life would become one monotonous routine.

The perfection of social arrangements would be to secure to all persons complete independence and freedom of action, subject to no restriction but that of not doing injury to others: but the scheme which we are considering abrogates this freedom entirely, and places every action of every member of the community under command (*Coll. Works*, III, 978).

Turning to Saint-Simonism, Mill conceded to it higher intellectual merit but less feasibility than Owenism. Nothing was to be said against it on the grounds of incentive, for in the Saint-Simonian organization the produce would be divided unequally according to the services rendered by the individual to the community. The difficulties arose with the method of assessing these services. In Mill's opinion, the essential flaw which doomed Saint-Simonism from the start was the nature and extent of the powers vested in the central authority. According to the Saint-Simonians, the authority must decide on the function of each member, must grade the importance of each occupation, and reward the member according to the value of his work and his merit in carrying it out. Such a degree of centralization, said Mill, is not feasible, because it assumes in the directing authority much more knowledge than human nature can attain, and in the citizenry more abject obedience than it is possible to expect from civilized men. In practice, supposing the experiment to be carried out in a European community, and under conditions like those of the Paraguay missions under the Jesuits, the heads of the association would feel the need gradually to increase the weight of their authority, because the ordinary members would find themselves questioning the division of the produce at every step. 'A fixed rule, like that of equality, might be acquiesced in, and so might chance, or an external necessity', but not the arbitrary will of the government.

To suppose that one or a few human beings, howsoever selected, could, by whatever machinery of subordinate agency, be qualified to adapt each person's work to his capacity, and proportion each person's remuneration to his merits — . . .or that any use which they could make of this power would give general satisfaction, or would be submitted to without the aid of force — is a supposition almost too chimerical to be reasoned against ([1848] *Coll. Works*, III, 982 [II, i, 4]).

The conclusion from his study of socialist doctrines in the first edition was, for Mill, that the balance clearly inclined in favour of the competitive system.

There has never been imagined any mode of distributing the produce of industry, so well adapted to the requirements of human nature on a whole, as that of letting the share of each individual (not in a state of bodily or mental incapacity) depend in the main on that individual's own energies and exertions, and on such furtherance as may be obtained from the voluntary good offices of others ([1848] *Coll. Works*, III, 982 note a—a [II, i, 5]).

Although in Mill's opinion, the existing system was by no means perfect, he believed that

it is not the subversion of the system of individual property that should be aimed at; but the improvement of it, and the participation of every member of the community in its benefits. The principle of private property has never yet had a fair trial in any country; and less so, perhaps, in this country than in some others.[13]

Mill and the 1848 Revolution

Even while the first edition was being printed, the July Monarchy fell and a Provisional Government took the reins in France. At first the English reacted complacently to the sight of the French constitution toppling before the assault of the Parisian people, while the 'matchless constitution' was so easily resisting the Chartists.[14] When the French workers rose in June 1848 against the Provisional Government, complacency gave way to virulent anti-socialism; but Mill's attitude never wavered from a strong partisanship of the new Republic.

His first reactions to the news from Paris are known from a letter he wrote to a Mr Chapman 'hardly yet out of breath from reading or thinking about it.' His feelings were of trepidation at the idea of how much was at stake on the success of the new Republic; he feared that the situation in Italy would lead to a war: he worried lest the French Government should have labour troubles.

> Communism has now for the first time a deep root, and has spread widely in France, and a large part of the effective republican strength is more or less imbued with it. The Provisional Government is obliged to coquet with this, and to virtually promise work and good wages to the whole labouring class: how are they to keep their promise, and what will be the consequences of not keeping it? (Mill to Chapman, 29 February 1848).[15]

Since Mill had no great confidence in the ability of any government to increase wages and to maintain full employment at the same time, he was afraid that the French authorities would come into conflict with the working class, as indeed came to pass over the *Ateliers nationaux*. But it should not be thought that it was the influence of the socialists in the new Republic which worried him. To Mrs Austin (who was much more fearful of, and was soon to prove very hostile to, the new regime), he wrote that, in his opinion, what the Provisional Government would do in the matter of wages and labour would be for the good. There will be a great deal of experimental legislation, he said,

> some of it not very prudent, but there cannot be a better place to try such experiments in than France. I suppose that regulation of industry in behalf of the labourers must go through its various phases of abortive experiment, just as regulation of industry in behalf of the capitalist has done, before it is abandoned, or its proper limits ascertained (Mill to Sarah Austin, 7 March 1848).[16]

What depressed him about the incidents which took place on the forcible closure of the *Ateliers nationaux* in 1848, was not the revolt of the workers of Paris in itself, but rather the change of spirit it had caused in many Frenchmen. 'It is wretched,' he told J.P. Nichol on 30 September 1848, 'to see the cause of *legitimate* Socialism thrown so far back by the spirit of reaction against that most unhappy outbreak at Paris in June.' But he still saw reason for hope at seeing so many men among the Provisional Government and its supporters, 'who have sincerely every noble feeling and purpose with respect to mankind, which one thought was confined to perhaps a dozen people in Europe.'[17]

On seeing the attitude of the English grow hostile Mill formed the design of answering the attacks against the French Republic. The result

was an article in the *Westminster Review*, 'the French Revolution of
1848 and its Assailants', especially directed against an inept pamphlet
of Lord Brougham's.[18] The article contained an interesting discussion
of socialism.

The presentation of anti-property doctrines does not follow the
order of the *Principles*, but that of the *Posthumous Chapters*, the aim
being to make as strong a case for socialism as possible, so that the
reader should be impressed with its *prima facie* plausibility. Mill begins:

> No rational person will maintain it to be abstractedly just, that a
> small minority of mankind should be born to the enjoyment of all
> the external advantages which life can give, without earning them by
> any merit or acquiring them by any exertion of their own, while the
> immense majority are condemned, from their birth, to a life of
> never-ending, never-intermitting toil, requited by a bare, and in
> general precarious, subsistence (34).

This apparently unjust situation, continues Mill, may be defended by
an appeal to expediency: to oblige those who produced and
accumulated riches to share them with those (perhaps unlucky ones)
who did not, may be deemed to be a greater injustice. The socialists,
unlike the levellers of old, accept this argument. They have no intention
of confiscating the property of the capitalists. They wish to achieve
socialism through the peaceful building up of co-operation, until the
capitalist will have no other alternative but to lend his capital to the
associations. The Provisional Government had been put in power
greatly through the help of the Paris workers: it was only natural that
an amount of public money should be allocated to socialist or
co-operative experiments, even if the only result were to prove
conclusively to the workers that co-operation was unworkable.

Further, Mill says, there is no necessary connection between socialist
beliefs and the clash of June 1848 between the workers and the Gardes
Nationaux: 'it was from no inherent tendency in the principles or
teaching of the Socialist chiefs, that this insurrection broke out' (37).[19]
The barricades were due to the unfortunate accident that the
Revolution of February had brought socialism into an apparent
position of power; any retreat from it was bound to provoke
disturbances.

Two major themes of Mill's discussion of socialism are summed up in
this article: one, that only that socialism is interesting which wants to

establish itself through piecemeal experiment: the other, that socialism is not of necessity revolutionary.

Despite his sympathetic presentation, however, Mill again concludes that socialist proposals are impracticable: but for the first time (as he was to do in the second edition of the *Principles*) he offsets this judgment by asserting that perhaps a better humanity will make it possible in the future; and (as he had done in the first edition) he admitted the justice of many of the socialist criticisms of the system of private property, and called for the reform of the property system. The co-operative scheme is not feasible in the present state of education at least. But in a 'world governed by public spirit, without needing the vulgar incentives of individual interest' (38) socialism or co-operativism may be feasible as it is not now. And the rejection of socialist methods imposes the obligation to attain the same ends by a modification of the system of private property.

> We hold with Bentham, that equality, though not the sole end, is one of the ends of good social arrangements; and that a system of institutions which does not make the scale turn in favour of equality, whenever this can be done without impairing the security of the property which is the product and reward of personal exertion, is essentially a bad government (38).

How different his attitude was from that of other economists: Senior, for example, viewed socialism with undisguised scorn and alarm.

> Even plunder or confiscation is less fatal to abstinence, than what is called socialism or communism. . . The socialist nation, unless it is to starve, must be divided into slaves and slavedrivers.[20]

'The Principles', Second Edition (1849) The Influence of Harriet

Another person reacted to 1848 with even greater enthusiasm than Mill: Harriet Taylor. While Mill (in not very good health) was correcting the text for the new edition, Harriet (also ill) had had to leave for the South of France. Of the letters they wrote to each other, only a few of Mill's have survived.[21] Reading them it seems that under the impact of the French Revolution she travelled further in the direction of socialism than Mill ever did, and caused him to show a little more indulgence towards collectivist thought than it was his own inclination to do.

The extant letters mainly touch on the themes of monotony under 'communism' (as Mill called the Owenite system), and the worth of the system of Fourier (which Mill was to discuss for the first time in this second edition he was preparing).

We have already studied a passage in the first edition of the *Principles* where it was asserted that even if Owenite communities turned out to be able to survive, they would have the twin disadvantages of monotony and regimentation. Harriet now objected to it. In his letter of 19 February 1849, Mill reminded her that in the first edition one sentence, underlining that bodily comfort once obtained, it was usually taken for granted, had been 'inserted on your proposition & very nearly in your own words'. The phrase read as follows in the *Principles* of 1848:

> The necessaries of life, when they have always been secure for the whole of life, are scarcely more a subject of consciousness or a source of happiness than the elements ([1848] *Coll. Works*, III, 978, note f–f [II, i, 3]).

Harriet not only objected to this statement, but just as 'strongly & totally' to the rest of the argument, which was to the effect that under communism the personal position of people would be unaffected by their exertions, so that labour would lose its main attraction; and that identity of education would destroy the variety of ideas and characters.

There was nothing wrong with her changing her opinions thus, he said, yet he would have to see whether his had changed or not; 'by thinking sufficiently I should probably come to think the same – as is almost always the case, I believe *always* when we think long enough' (*Coll. Works*, vol. III, p. 1027 ap. G). Obviously Mill's progress along the road to socialism was slow compared with Harriet's, but his wish to agree with her was great. In consequence, despite his reluctance to let the argument go, he greatly toned down the passage in the second edition: the reflection on the necessaries of life disappeared altogether; substituted for it was the assertion that the attainment of necessaries by all under 'communism' meant that 'there would be an end to all anxiety concerning the means of subsistence; and this would be much gained for human happiness'; but, he continued, the same could be achieved in a system of private property (alluding, perhaps, to the limitation of population growth), with the advantage that 'the individual system. . .is compatible with a far greater degree of personal liberty'.[22]

From what Mill writes, one can surmise that Harriet also objected to the following sentence on tedium and lack of incentive under Owenism, in the first edition:

I believe that the majority would not exert themselves for anything beyond this [i.e. beyond attaining the condition of operatives in a well regulated manufactory], and that unless they did, nobody else would; and that on this basis human life would settle itself into one invariable round ([1848] *Coll. Works*, III, 980, note n).

Mill tells Harriet that to delete it would be to imply that the two previous pages of argument were false. However, the second edition did not contain the incriminating statement.[23]

Yet one should not think that by making these changes Mill was only obeying his wish to give way to his friend's opinion. It is true that he told Harriet that he would not print the objections to communism she dissented from,

even if there were no other reason than the certainty I feel that I never should long continue of an opinion different from yours on a subject which you have fully considered.[24]

But there was one thought which may have helped him to give way to Harriet's opinion. As he told her on 21 February 1849:

I saw on consideration that the objection to Communism on the ground of its making life a kind of dead level might admit of being weakened, (though I believe it never could be taken away) consistently with the principle of Communism, though the Communistic plans now before the public could not do it (*Coll. Works*, III, 1028).

Finally another consideration must have led him to make light of any excessive concessions to Harriet: he considered the assertions put forward in this edition were merely provisional, since they could be corrected at a later date by a more deeply meditated work on socialism. For some time around 1849, Mill had the definite intention of publishing a separate book on socialism (a project which was only to be incompletely realized towards the end of his life). The idea seems to have been born during the correction of the proofs for the second edition, when Harriet asked him to strike out the passage quoted a few lines above.

Then again if the sentence 'the majority would not exert themselves for anything beyond this & unless they did nobody else would &c' is not tenable, then all the two or three pages of argument which precede & of which this is but a summary, are false, & there is nothing to be said against Communism at all — one would only have to turn round & advocate it — which if done would be better in a separate treatise & would be a great objection to publishing a 2d edit. until *after* such a treatise.[25]

But when the time came to prepare the third edition, he decided against a separate treatise, and instead rewrote the chapter completely.

In fact, he came to have some cause for regret that he had ever included a reflection about tedium under 'communism' for it was interpreted as that he was in favour of keeping the people hungry. An anonymous writer in the *London Leader* (a working class weekly) remarked that at first, co-operation had been considered too bad; now it was presented as being too good.

The harmony and competence likely to result are felt, or assumed to be so overwhelming, that a surfeit of enjoyment is dreaded. That recent work on Political Economy, which was the first to admit the feasibility of associative views, yet foreshadowed the inanity and monotony which must supervene when the spur of animal want was conquered and withdrawn.[26]

Mill answered on 1 August 1850 that in his opinion, on the contrary,

the drudgery to which hunger, and the fear of hunger, condemn the great mass of mankind, is the chief cause which makes their lives inane and monotonous.

But the rich could also be bored, and were so usually, because 'they do not cultivate and follow opinions and preferences or tastes of their own' and bend overmuch to other people's opinions.

Now this is the bondage I am afraid of in the co-operative communities... No order of society can in my estimation be desirable unless grounded on the maxim, that no man or woman is accountable to others for any conduct by which others are not injured or damaged,[27]

he concluded, with a thought around which he was to build his *Essay on Liberty*.

He thus came to concentrate all the arguments against the Owenite communities into a single one: the fear for freedom. Though his severity against 'communism' was somewhat relaxed,[28] he still refused to accept it as a practical solution for the problems of society.

In the second edition there was one great innovation in the sections devoted to the study of 'socialism' (i.e. collectivist systems admitting of inequality of distribution): while Saint-Simonism was considered in the same terms as in 1848, a completely new section was added: the discussion of Fourierism.

Mill found in Fourierism a system which in some degree combined the advantages of Owenism (its decentralization and its capacity of being tried in a piecemeal fashion) and those of Saint-Simonism (rewards in proportion to the services of each to the community). Thus on the ground of incentive it was much more acceptable. 'This system does not contemplate the abolition of private property, nor even of inheritance'. On the contrary, said Mill, according to the Fourierist distributive scheme, after the subsistence of all members is assured,

> the remainder of the produce is shared in certain proportions . . . among the three elements, Labour, Capital, and Talent ([1849] *Coll. Works*, III, 982 [II, i, 5]).

(Schumpeter irreverently remarked that Fourier assigned to capital a greater portion than actually goes to it under capitalism).[29] The remuneration of labour would vary according to the grade of the labourer's skill. Incomes would not have to be spent in common: families would only have to live in apartment blocks, by which the costs of running the dwellings of the community would fall, and also the expenses of retailing the goods consumed by the households would diminish.[30]

Another proposal of the Fourierists, one to solve the problem of incentive in the *Phalanstères*, Mill did not judge so kindly. Fourierists thought that they could render all kinds of labour attractive, simply by playing on men's passions; they derived this confidence from the fact that people undertake the heaviest labours for their pleasure: thus as children loved dirt, Fourier apportioned to them the removal of the garbage.[31] Mill remarked that the essence of fatiguing amusements is that 'they are pursued freely and may be discontinued at pleasure'.

Taken as a whole, however, the discussion of incentive under Fourierism leaves it in possession of the field as compared with other collectivist schemes, especially on the supposition that humanity will progress.

With every advance in education and improvement, their system tends to become less impracticable, and the very attempt to make it succeed would cultivate in those making the attempt, many of the virtues which it requires ([1849] *Coll. Works*, III, 985).

Despite the superiority of Fourierism over other schemes in the matter of incentive, Mill did not think it to be practicable, for the same reasons that Saint-Simonism was not: the difficulty of establishing a planned system of distribution once the market is dispensed with, and the impossibility of running the whole economy from the centre. It is true that the Fourierists wanted to transform society in a piecemeal fashion, by progressively covering the country with phalansteries. But,

> when we remember that the communities themselves are to be constituent units of an organised whole, (otherwise competition would rage as actively between rival communities as it now does between individual merchants or manufacturers,) and that nothing less would be requisite for the complete success of the scheme, than the organisation from a single centre, of the industry of a nation, and even of the world;

it is clear that the system of private property will prevail for a considerable time to come ([1849] *Coll. Works*, III, 985).

As for the grading of the rewards by the votes of the community (in the Saint-Simonian scheme, the duty of the central authority), unless the members of the phalansteries had qualities of forbearance and humility not generally found in the men of the present time, the system

> would engender jealousies and disappointments destructive of the internal harmony on which the whole working of the system avowedly depends ([1849] *ibid*).

Mill, however, does not press this argument as hard as he did against the Saint-Simonians, perhaps because he thought that grading by votes was much more feasible than by the central authority, but more likely because he had the inclination to treat Fourierism a little more kindly than the logic of his arguments warranted.

Hence, the problem is why Mill treated the system of Fourier, who after all was an unredeemed madman, with so much forbearance. How could Mill pay so much attention to the thought of a man who explained the difference between the movements of the planets and the comets by the fact that the latter had souls? Or who predicted that children would be so well educated in the phalansteries, that they would not only be able to write with both hands, but even play the organ with their toes?

At the time of the second edition he must have thought the ridiculous side of Fourier's thought less important than some years before, since in 1833 he had written to Carlyle:

> One or two [of the Saint-Simonians],. . . .have become disciples of Fourier, a sort of Robert Owen who is to accomplish all things by means of co-operation & of rendering *labour agreeable*, & under whose system man is to acquire absolute power of the laws of physical nature; among other happy results, the sea is to be changed into lemonade.[32]

On 31 March 1849 (too late to make any further corrections in the second edition), he wrote to Harriet that he had been reading the latest book by the most conspicuous of the disciples of Fourier, Victor Considérant. 'Many of the details *are* & *all* appear, passablement ridicules'.[33]

In his letters to Harriet also, he seemed less confident than in the *Principles* (1849) that the progress of man would make the Fourierist system more practicable. Mill did not fall into what Sir Isaiah Berlin has called 'The Community of Saints Fallacy'; though he did not actually argue that it is precisely 'good' people who tend to disagree most violently about morality and politics, he pointed out to Harriet that she overestimated the ease of educating people to be as unselfish as the success of collectivist schemes demanded. To develop people's good intentions is not enough; it is necessary

> to prevent self-flattery, vanity, irritability & all that family of vices from warping their moral judgments as those of the very cleverest people are almost always warped now.[34]

Ten days later in another letter he applied this thought to Fourierism. The root of the whole Fourierist system, from which its validity derives, is the assumption that people 'will always in a phalanstère like what is best'. In Fourierist writings, he misses a call for 'an education of the moral *sense*. . .a feeling that one *ought* to do, & wish for, what is for the greatest good of all concerned'. Owen, he points out, at least did not exclude such an education, even if he did not expressly recommend it.[35]

A further problem has now appeared, not only must one explain Mill's excessive kindness to Fourierism both in the *Principles* and in the letters (for even in his letters to Harriet he was not severe enough), but also the discrepancy between his private thoughts as expressed in the letters, and his public declarations in the treatise. As for this second question, it is tempting to lay all the blame on his subservience to Harriet's opinions; but one should not forget Mill's own personal wish to treat socialism more leniently in the second edition, and his tendency to lean over backwards in favour of socialist schemes in reaction to ignorant criticism.

The answer to the original problem of why Mill paid any attention at all to Fourierism, may be a little more conjectural. In the first place an explanation could be drawn from the structure of Mill's discussion of socialist schemes in the *Principles*: Fourierism, *as described by Mill*, neatly fitted an empty space in his argument; it combined the advantages of both Owenism and Saint-Simonism without their disadvantages; Mill must have felt he had found a system which would give further plausibility to the socialist case. In the second place, there is evidence that Mill was struck by the freedom of Fourierist opinions on the position of women in society: 'Fourrier [sic] if I may judge by Considérant is perfectly right about women both as to equality & marriage', he told Harriet. But Mill had read Fourier in the bowdlerized presentation of Considérant. 'I suspect that Fourier himself went farther than his disciple thinks prudent in the directness of his recommendations' (App. G, 1028). Mill must have more than confirmed this suspicion when he turned to Fourier's own works later in life. But despite his own heroic chastity he was not to be excessively shocked by Fourier's extravagant proposals of minute regulation to make relations between the sexes happier:[36] in the *Posthumous Chapters* he was content to warn his readers that they should judge Fourier's recommendations on the organization of society independently of his recommendations on marriage.[37] In 1849, he concluded to Harriet that the Fourierists' attitude to the position of women in society

> strengthens one exceedingly in one's wish to proner the Fourierists [sic] besides that their scheme of Association seems to be much nearer to being practicable at present than Communism.

At this point another element needs to be examined: Mill's

invocation of the future. Though he quite definitely rejected Fourierism, some doubt could arise from his distinction between its possibilities at a present and at a future time. This question is especially important in view of Schumpeter's assertion that Mill was a Reformist socialist, hoping that Socialism would become practicable with the progress of humanity. Apparently Mill expected Fourierism to become more feasible with such progress.

The question is complicated because Mill, when discussing socialist systems, used the future in two ways. In the first place, starting from the idea (implicit in the second edition and explicit in the third) that his arguments could not be conclusive for or against until corroborated by experiment, he suspended judgment until such a time when experiment would have been carried out.

> We are as yet too ignorant either of what individual agency in its best form, or Socialism in its best form can accomplish, to be qualified to decide which of the two will be the ultimate form of human society ([1849] *Coll. Works*, III, 986−7 [II, i, 6]).

In the second place, he used it in a somewhat different sense, more favourable to socialism than the previous one. An example of this use is the following sentence:

> With every advance in education and improvement, their [the Fourierists'] system tends to become less impracticable . . . ([1849] *Coll. Works*, III, 985 [II, i, 5]).

This means quite a different thing. Here Mill does not suspend judgment, he asserts that the progress of human nature (i.e. the diminishing selfishness of men) will make Fourierism more practicable. This use of the future has led many to interpret Mill's attitude to be that he thought socialism to be fitted for a better type of man, to be superior as a goal to the system of private property, and in fact, the system towards which history was moving.

This interpretation does not seem to be tenable, though Mill's pronouncements are ambiguous. If his words are read with care, it will be seen that he said no more than that the progress of humanity would remove some of the difficulties of socialism, but he never said all. Even if there were progress and some of the difficulties disappeared, it was by no means sure that socialism would be chosen, for 'we are as yet too ignorant. . .to decide which of the two will be the ultimate form of human society'.

That the above is the correct interpretation is strongly suggested by one of Mill's letters to Harriet. It seems that again his inclination to give in to his wife made him be kinder in public than in private. During the revision Harriet had objected to a phrase which never came to be printed. According to Professor Hayek[39] it was to have been inserted just before the sentence quoted above, which runs 'We are as yet too ignorant. . .' It read:

> It is probable that this will finally depend upon considerations not to be measured by the coarse standard which in the present state of human improvement is the only one which can be applied to it (Mill to Harriet 19 February 1849, *Coll. Works*, III, 1027 and note 8).

In another letter written when the book was in the press, Mill made a comment which may be assumed to refer to this deletion. He told her he did not mean to allude to any mysterious change in human nature. He explained that in his opinion many people at the time were necessarily cut off from sympathy with the multitudes; it was impossible to know if a moment would come when the minority would be able to sympathize with the mass, and 'how far the social feelings might then supply the place of that large share of solitariness & individuality which they cannot now dispense with'. On the other hand, once the more obvious and coarse obstacles to communism

> have ceased or greatly diminished, those which are less obvious & coarse will then step forward into an importance. . .which does not now practically belong to them (Mill to Harriet Taylor, 25 March 1849, *Coll. Works*, III, 1030).

Unfortunately, Mill's thoughts were not so clear in the treatise as in the letters, and many people made the mistake of believing that he meant that with the progress of man, socialism was sure to arrive.

In sum, the second edition, despite all the changes noted, still stated 'the difficulties of socialism . . . so strongly, that the tone was on the whole that of opposition to it,' to use Mill's own words when describing the first edition. The chapter concluded with the familiar idea that

> in the present stage of human improvement at least, it is not (I conceive) the subversion of the system of individual property that should be aimed at, but the improvement of it, and the participation of every member of the community in its benefits ([1849] *Coll. Works*, III, 986—7 [II; i, 6]).

The Third Edition of 'The Principles' (1852)

In the three years following the 1848 Revolution, Mill gave much time to reading socialist books, and to meditating, and discussing with Harriet, the problems posed by property and socialism.

That this was so is indicated by the complete rearrangement of the discussion of property in the third edition of his treatise, though there are other proofs of his interest; the main one being a review of a book (Newman's *Political Economy*), where, due to the author's flippancy about socialism, he bent over backwards in favour of socialist ideas, showing himself less temperate in their defence than in the passages he was writing for the new edition.[40]

The most notable difference from previous editions lies in the changed tone of the chapter. In the third edition, it contained none of the severe words of the first, none of the definitely adverse judgments of the second. The whole discussion acquired the character of the observations of a friend rather than the strictures of a critic, however open-minded. The chapter was again divided into two parts: 'communism' and 'socialism'. It was the first which underwent the greatest amount of change.

To begin with Owenism then, Mill first reversed the argument based on population growth: in the 1848 and 1849 editions, Mill had seemed sceptical about the capacity of Owenite communes to stave off over-population; in 1852 he declared that

> the Communistic scheme, instead of being peculiarly open to the objection drawn from the danger of over-population, has the recommendation of tending in an especial degree to the prevention of that evil ([1852], *Coll. Works*, II, 206 [II, i, 3]).

The reason was that it afforded the individual especial motives for restraint: equality of income insured that every member of the community would immediately feel the effects of an excessive increase in population; public opinion would hence be strongly set against the offenders.[41]

Secondly, the discussion of incentive under Owenism was also importantly changed. In the previous editions Mill had conceded that in a 'communist' society the public spirit of the individuals and the pressure of public opinion could conceivably force every member to perform the customary work-load; but had added that since this work-load would be determined by the majority, it would be extremely small ([1849] *Coll. Works*, III, 976 [II, i, 3]). Similarly, he had also conceded that in a competitive society many people worked for a fixed

salary and had no interest in increasing their exertions: but had
countered this by noting that as many were subject to the spur of
self-interest ([1849] *Coll. Works*, III, 979–80). In the third edition the
whole aspect of this argument underwent change. Though he still
admitted that the customary work-load would be set low by the
majority, he noted that the members of a commune would be
well-educated, and hence could be expected to discharge their task as
well as salaried officers (civil servants) in England.

> Undoubtedly, as a general rule, remuneration fixed by salaries does
> not in any class of functionaries produce the maximum of zeal: and
> this is as much as can be reasonably alleged against Communistic
> labour ([1852] *Coll. Works*, II, 205).

He went further. 'Mankind are capable of a far greater amount of
public spirit than the present age is accustomed to suppose possible,'[42]
he repeated in 1852, as in 1848 and 1849; but there followed no
qualification in terms of a small common work-load. The very reverse
argument followed: public opinion would tend, not so much to enforce
a common standard, but to incite communists to emulation. 'A contest,
who can do most for the common good, is not the kind of competition
which Socialists repudiate' ([1852] *Coll. Works*, II, 205). The
conclusion to the argument on incentive was that the question must be
left open.

> To what extent, therefore, the energy of labour would be diminished
> by Communism, or whether in the long run it would be diminished
> at all, must be considered for the present an undecided question.

Thirdly, in the matter of the apportionment of labour, similar
difficulties were pointed out as in the other editions. But some weight
was taken from them in 1852 by two reflections: in the first place, Mill
expressed the hope that human intelligence would find the means to
overcome the difficulty of apportioning labour to aptitude by
conscious plan; in the second place he noted that

> the worst and most unjust arrangement which could be made of
> these points, under a system aiming at equality, would be so far
> short of the inequality and injustice with which labour (not to speak
> of remuneration) is now apportioned, as to be scarcely worth
> counting in the comparison ([1852] *Coll. Works*, II, 207).

All these changes in the argument could not but lead to a different conclusion on the value of communist proposals.

> If the choice were to be made between Communism with all its chances, and the present state of society with all its sufferings and injustices; if the institution of private property necessarily carried with it as a consequence, that the produce of labour should be apportioned as we now see it, almost in an inverse ratio to the labour. . .; if this or Communism, were the alternative, all the difficulties, great or small, of Communism would be as dust in the balance (*ibid*).

These are strong words; they imply a greatly increased sympathy towards Owenite proposals, and a growing impatience with the existing state of society. However Mill qualified them immediately, as he had failed to do in the review of Newman's *Political Economy*, so that in the end the balance was still slightly tilted against communist systems. In the first place Mill warned the reader not to compare the system of private property as it is, with ideal communism: 'the principle of private property has never yet had a fair trial in any country; and less so, perhaps, in this country than is some others'.[43] There followed an allusion to the definition of property as based on 'the guarantee to the individuals of the fruits of their own labour and abstinence', implying that a property system built along these lines would be much more acceptable than the existing one ([1852] *Coll. Works*, II, 208 [II, i, 3]). He asked the reader to compare ideal socialism with the system of property as he would amend it, when it would include the two conditions without which communism itself would not work: restraint of population and universal education.

The second qualification was the fear which Mill felt for liberty in an Owenite society: the treatment of this argument is basically the same as in the other editions, though again the tone is softer. Of course, said Mill, this difficulty of communism, like all the others, is 'vastly exaggerated'. . . 'The restraints of Communism would be freedom in comparison with the present condition of the majority of the human race.'[44] Yet, he added: 'the question is, whether there would be any asylum left for individuality of character.' And the conclusion, though worded in a very lenient manner was still adverse: 'it is yet to be ascertained', he said, 'whether the Communist scheme would be favourable to' liberty.

In the treatment of 'socialism' the changes introduced were much smaller. Mill added a few reflections on the fact that co-operation in France, which started on the principle of equal sharing was turning to payment by the piece: the communist principle of distribution is only adapted to a 'much higher moral condition of humanity'; under existing conditions, the 'socialist' system of incentives is much more practicable. As far as Saint-Simonism is concerned, the 1852 edition reproduced the reflections of the previous ones almost word by word.[45] The discussion of Fourierism was also reproduced without changes, with one[46] notable exception: to wit, that the whole final part of the discussion was removed, leaving only one argument against the Fourierists standing: that the essence of amusement lies in the fact that it can be discontinued at pleasure, and giving up the most important argument against the Fourierists: that directing the whole economy from a single centre was impracticable (the reason being perhaps that Mill had heard of the attempts of Fourierists at establishing isolated phalansteries in North America, with no hint of centralized direction). In consequence the discussion of the sytem of Fourier concluded differently: instead of declaring Fourierism not feasible in existing circumstances, Mill on the contrary called for its being tried in practice: for, he said now, the Fourierist and other socialist schemes 'are all capable of being tried on a moderate scale, and at no risk either personal or pecuniary, to any except those who try them' ([1852] *Coll. Works*, II, 213–4).

It is far from easy to reach a definite opinion about Mill's attitude to anti-property schemes in the 1852 edition. There is little doubt that his point of view was markedly more sympathetic; many arguments levelled against socialism in previous editions were waived. But in the final resort none of the schemes of reform proposed by the socialists was adopted by Mill.

Only one obscurity remains: Mill was again led by his desire to treat socialism fairly, to suspend his judgment until some further time. The position was similar in all fundamental respects to that of the second edition. Both uses of the future are there in 1852. The first use, the suspension of judgment until experiment has been carried out, was expressed a little more clearly.

> It would be extremely rash to pronounce it [Fourierism] incapable of success, or unfitted to realize a great part of the hopes founded on it by its partisans. With regard to this, as to all other varieties of Socialism, the thing to be desired, and to which they have a just claim, is opportunity of trial. . . It is for experience to determine how far or how soon any one or more of the possible systems of

community of property will be fitted to substitute itself for the 'organisation of industry' based on private ownership of land and capital ([1852] *Coll. Works*, II, 213−4 [II, i, 4]).

The second use of the future on the other hand (the expectation that the progress of humanity will make socialism more practicable), was expressed in a way which has caused the maximum possible confusion. In the preface to this edition one can read:

> The chapter on Property has been almost entirely re-written. I was far from intending that the statement which it contained, of the objections to the best known Socialist schemes, should be understood as a condemnation of Socialism, regarded as an ultimate result of human progress ([1852] *Coll. Works*, II, xciii [Preface]).

It was primarily on the basis of this assertion that Schumpeter proposed his idea that Mill understood socialism as the goal of social evolution, to be achieved by gradual reform.[47] The changes of the third edition, he said, 'really amount to *explicit* recognition of socialism as the Ultimate Goal'. But Schumpeter's idea must be rejected: on the next page of his preface, Mill declares the goal of social evolution to be

> to fit mankind by cultivation, for a state of society combining the greatest personal freedom with that just distribution of the fruits of labour, which the present laws of property do not profess to aim at.

There was no assurance, he continued, that this goal would take the form of a socialist organization.

> Whether, when this state of mental and moral cultivation shall be attained, individual property in some form (though in a form very remote from the present) or community of ownership in the instruments of production and a regulated division of the produce, will afford the circumstances most favourable to happiness, and best calculated to bring human nature to its greatest perfection, is a question which must be left, as it safely may, to the people of that time to decide.

In conclusion the danger lies in exaggerating the pro-socialism of the third edition rather than in underestimating it, especially if one remembers that in it he went out of his way to defend competition, as we shall see. He ended the chapter being able to affirm:

the political economist, for a considerable time to come, will be chiefly concerned with the conditions of existence and progress belonging to a society founded on private property and individual competition ([1852] *Coll. Works*, II, 214 [II, i, 4]).

He did not dismiss the socialist proposals completely: he rather suspended judgment on their worth, asked for an 'opportunity of trial' for them, and left it for future generations to decide (with better human material at their disposal) whether they were superior to a reformed system of private property. Lord Robbins is right in calling this 'a plea for an open mind'.[48]

Mill's Socialist Sympathies Cool Down; Changes in the 'Autobiography'
With the death of his wife and the disappearance of the Utopian socialists from the European scene, Mill's attitude to socialism became somewhat more detached.

In 1854, when his wife was still alive Mill had written a great part of his *Autobiography*, and she had read the draft and corrected it. In 1861 Mill reread this Early Draft and made some further changes;[49] the differences between the description of their socialist feelings in the draft of 1854, and in the final form of 1861 give an indication of the evolution which was taking place in Mill's ideas.

Only two changes need be noted here. Both the First Draft and the final version contained the passage

> The social problem of the future we considered to be, how to unite the greatest individual liberty of action with an equal ownership of all in the raw material of the globe & an equal participation of all in the benefits of combined labour (*Early Draft*, 173, W.Cl., 196).

But the final version added:

> We had not the presumption to suppose that we could already foresee, by what precise form of institutions these objects could most effectually be attained, or at how near or how distant a period they would become practicable.

The second important addition followed the assertion that men were capable of showing much more public spirit than could normally be observed, and that in modern life the calls upon the disinterested collaboration of citizens were far fewer than 'in the smaller commonwealths of antiquity'. The final draft added:

These considerations did not make us overlook the folly of premature attempts to dispense with the inducements of private interest in social affairs.[50]

The importance of the additions could well be minimized by presenting them as mere clarifications by Mill in 1861 of what he and Harriet had written in 1854. Yet the reluctance which Mill must have felt to touch a text approved of by his wife, makes all changes however small much more significant than they may appear at first sight. And the further evidence of a changed attitude to be found in the posthumous *Chapters on Socialism*, confirms the belief that the corrections of the First Draft of the Autobiography indicate a cooling down of Mill's socialist sympathies.

The Posthumous 'Chapters on Socialism'
In his last years, specifically in 1869, Mill finally undertook the book on socialism which he had been intending to write since 1849. But death interrupted his task. The chapters he was able to complete were published by his step-daughter in the *Fortnightly Review* for 1879.[51] They are of the greatest import for anyone interested in the history of Mill's opinions — for they afford evidence of a decided cooling off of Mill's socialist sympathies. They must also attract the curiosity of the general historian — as showing the small importance and little sympathy granted to the new State socialism of German origin by at least one keen student of collectivist thought.

Mill totally changed the arrangement of his material. Abandoning the discussion of the right of property which opened his study of socialism in the *Principles*, he followed the order of his 1851 article on Newman: examination of the attacks on competition by the socialists first, defence of competition next, analysis of alternative socialist proposals to follow. He did not live to complete the chapter on the reforms of the system of property.

His principal motive for studying socialism at such length, Mill said in the introduction, was that there seemed to be no reason for the working classes to stop short of economic equality when they would have achieved political equality; and as the realization of the second goal was near, the discussion of the first had become urgent.

The first chapter, dealing with the socialist attack on the competitive system, exhibits Mill's fairness at its best. It is a thought-provoking presentation of the socialist case against the society of the time.

A socialist might concede perhaps, said Mill, that the incentives of private property have allowed humanity to progress to its present state. But how great is the poverty that still exists, the socialist might note.

> What proportion of the population, in the most civilised countries of Europe, enjoy in their own persons anything worth naming of the benefits of property?

The retort could be that the riches of the capitalists give the workers their daily bread:

> but. . .their daily bread is all that they have; and that often in insufficient quantity; almost always of inferior quality; and with no assurance of continuing to have it at all,

he said, making one of the few allusions in his works to economic crises as a problem of policy for the effect they have on the welfare of the labouring classes (713).[52] There is one argument in favour of the present state of affairs which would be unanswerable: since a tolerable life for human beings can only be the result of labour and abstinence, a society would be considered just where 'every one who was willing to undergo a fair share of this labour and abstinence could attain a fair share of the fruits'. But in the existing society, 'the reward, instead of being proportioned to the labour and abstinence of the individuals, is almost in an inverse ratio to it' (714). The most powerful of all circumstances determining a man's situation is birth, then accident, then opportunity; often success goes not to virtue, but to sycophancy, hardheartedness, cheating. In sum, the existing form of society has permitted great poverty, and in a way almost totally unconnected with desert.

The arguments against competition were also presented in their strongest form. After long quotations from Louis Blanc's *L'organisation du travail*,[53] and books by Considérant, the disciple of Fourier, and by Robert Owen, Mill sums up the socialist arguments against competition thus. Blanc holds, in the first place, that the uncertain future which confronts the workers makes it highly unlikely that they will control the number of their children. There is secondly the moral argument that competition constitutes a system of private war where

> hardly any one can gain except by the loss or disappointment of one or of many others. In a well-constituted community every one

would be a gainer by every other person's successful exertions (715–6).

Then, proceeds Mill, competition is presented by Blanc as the origin of the low wages of the labourers, and the bankruptcies of the capitalists; both evils increase with the progress of wealth and population. Competition enables large capitalists (holds Blanc, expressing views later echoed by Marx)

to undersell all other producers, to absorb the whole of the operations of industry into their own sphere, to drive from the market all employers of labour except themselves, and to convert the labourers into a kind of slaves or serfs, dependent on them for the means of support, and compelled to accept these on such terms as they choose to offer.

Due to this increasing concentration of capital and the consequent progressive wretchedness of the working classes, 'society. . .is travelling onward. . .towards a new feudality, that of the greatest capitalists' (716).

Finally the socialists pointed out the widespread adulteration of goods and other unfair practices in retail trades. As is known from the above chapter on *laissez-faire* this was a very real grievance in the nineteenth century.

When in the second of his Chapters Mill turned to criticizing what he conceived to be the exaggerations of the socialists it became noticeable how much cooler his appreciation of socialism had become since 1852: 'Though much of their allegations is unanswerable, not a little is the result of errors in political economy.'

Mill hastened to make it clear that by speaking of these errors he did not mean

the rejection of any practical rules of policy which have been laid down by political economists, I mean ignorance of economic facts, and of the causes by which the economic phenomena of society as it is, are actually determined (727).

He began by denying the existing of a '*baisse continue des salaires*'. The facts do not warrant such an assertion, except when chosen unfairly. He then proceeded to point out that the socialists were mistaken when they affirmed that their own system was the only solution for the problem of population. It is a matter of congratulation that the leading socialists should have recognized that not only the existing society, but also a socialist community, would have to contend with this difficulty. But when claiming it to be insoluble except under socialism, the socialists were committing the same error 'which was first committed by Malthus and his followers, that of supposing that because population has a greater power of increase than subsistence, its pressure upon subsistence must be always growing more severe'.

It is possible for such a pressure to diminish in the course of time.

> Experience shows that in the existing state of society the pressure of population on subsistence, which is the principal cause of low wages, though a great, is not an increasing evil (728—9).

On the contrary, the situation seems to be getting better. These opinions are a far cry from those of his youth.

In the third place, Mill remarked, 'Socialists. . .have a very imperfect and one-sided notion of the operation of competition'. To the socialist argument that competition tends to concentrate capital (and hence place it in a position of superiority regarding labour), Mill answered that such a concentration could only happen where technological conditions created a situation of increasing returns to scale; in his words,

> where, as in the case of railways, the only competition possible is between two or three great companies, the operation being on too vast a scale to be within the reach of individual capitalists.

His exaggerated confidence that concentration would not go too far is well known.

> When this change is effected, the larger capitalists. . . among which the business is divided, are seldom, if ever, in any considerable branch of commerce, so few as that competition shall not continue to act between them (730—1).

Mill accepted that competition, though it tended to lower prices, was not the best security for quality. He felt sure that the law could be strengthened against abuses of the retailers; and greeted the appearance of the Co-operative stores, in which he saw a very probable remedy for this social sore, and a remedy compatible with all kinds of social organization.

The final point of the socialist case which Mill wanted to correct, was the false idea entertained by socialists and trade unionists on the share of capital in the national income. Mill (as he did in the *Principles*) distinguished, within the ordinary rate of interest, the interest paid as a remuneration of abstinence, the compensation for risk, and finally the 'wages of superintendence'; on all these points Mill assumed that the returns to the capitalists were compensations for services to the economy.

No doubt if he is very successful in business these wages of his are extremely liberal, and quite out of proportion to what the same skill and industry would command if offered for hire. But, on the other hand, he runs a worse risk than that of being out of employment; that of doing the work without earning anything by it.[54]

Further, the redistribution of the amount made in profits by the capitalists among the workers, would mean dispensing with the services of the former, without adding much to wages per head;

were the whole of it added to the share of the labourers it would make a less addition to that share than would be made by any important invention in machinery, or by the suppression of unnecessary distributors and other 'parasites of industry' (735).

In conclusion, Mill found that the socialist case against the existing system was somewhat exaggerated.

The present system is not, as many Socialists believe, hurrying us all into a state of general indigence and slavery from which only Socialism can save us (736).

After defending the competitive system Mill proceeded to attack the theories of the socialists directly. It is here that the markedly changed tone of his discussion may be noticed best. He started by distinguishing sharply between two kinds of socialists. The first kind are

those whose plans for a new order of society, in which private property and individual competition are to be superseded and other motives to action substituted, are on the scale of a village community or township, and would be applied to an entire country by the multiplication of such self-acting units.

By considering the second kind Mill showed that he was aware of the existence of a socialism quite different from the 'duodecimo editions of the New Jerusalem' to which he had up to then given his undivided attention.

The other class, who are more a product of the Continent than of Great Britain and may be called the revolutionary Socialists, propose to themselves a much bolder stroke. Their scheme is the management of the whole productive resources of the country by one central authority, the general government. And with this view some of them avow as their purpose that the working classes, or somebody in their behalf, should take possession of all the property of the country, and administer it for the general benefit (737).

For Mill, one of the most important arguments in favour of the form of socialism he had studied in his previous works was that it 'can be brought into operation progressively, and can prove its capacities by trial'. It is arguable that he thus missed the Messianic element in much of Utopian socialism, mistaking its expectation of total triumph through the example of a few, for an experimental attitude. Be that as it may, it went against the grain of his careful intellectual nature ever to contemplate a jump into the unknown as the solution of social problems, also his keen sense of justice and of respect for the individual made him wary of measures which would result in the confiscation of property or even in the taking of human life.

It must be acknowledged that those who would play this game on the strength of their own private opinion, unconfirmed as yet by any experimental verification — who would forcibly deprive all who have now a comfortable physical existence of their only present means of preserving it, and would brave the frightful bloodshed and misery that would ensue if the attempt was resisted — must have a serene confidence in their own wisdom on the one hand and a recklessness of other people's sufferings on the other, which Robespierre and St. Just, hitherto the typical instances of those united attributes, scarcely came up to.

At the time of the Great Reform Bill, when it seemed that only revolution would curb the opposition of the House of Lords, Mill, like the rest of the philosophical radicals, was in some sympathy with those who wished to take up arms in favour of political reform. It appears, by what he told Sterling in a letter, that he was even resigned to the possible extension of the revolution from the political to the social field.[55] But Dr Hamburger, in his book on James Mill, has shown how the philosophical radicals' pro-revolutionary sympathy was mainly a stratagem to force the hand of the Whig government, though a risky one. A phrase in this letter has been construed by Mr Packe as indicating that at the time the young Mill was in a phase of revolutionary fervour, that he was 'an uncompromising intellectual red'. The passage does not justify such an interpretation. On the contrary he appears to be telling his friend that he would like the revolution to spare a few conservative thinkers.[56] At no point in his life did Mill favour revolution except in situations where he thought that the only issue was force: that was how he defended 1848 against Brougham. What his position was with respect to the Commune of Paris in 1871 is not known for sure. The available evidence seems to indicate that he deplored the excesses of the revolutionary party; but he was by no means unsympathetic to many of its demands; and was deeply shocked by the savage repression carried out by the government of Versailles.[57] All this indicates an open mind as regards revolutions in certain difficult situations, but certainly not a predilection for them.

In the *Posthumous Chapters*, his judgment of the revolutionary socialists was adverse. He thought that they would encounter in an acute form the difficulty of all socialist systems attempting to centralize the economy.

> Apart from all considerations of injustice to the present possessors, the very idea of conducting the whole industry of a country by direction from a single centre is so obviously chimerical, that nobody ventures to propose any mode in which it should be done (748).

The result of such an attempt could only be chaos. But some of the revolutionists would welcome chaos if it pulled down the society they abhorred, 'for if appearances can be trusted the animating principle of too many of the revolutionary Socialists is hate. . .' These are very harsh words, and Mill must have realized they were so, for to judge by the structure of the phrase, he seems to have had second thoughts, and appended the following words to those just quoted:

> . . .a very excusable hatred of existing evils, which would vent itself by putting an end to the present system at all costs even to those who suffer by it, in the hope that out of the chaos would arise a better Kosmos, and the impatience of desperation respecting any more gradual improvement.

Mill warned that chaos would be the very worst situation in which to rebuild society, and reminded the revolutionists of Hobbes's description of the state of war of all against all as a description of what could happen. Whatever the situation of the most unfortunate members of society, nothing excused pulling down everybody to their level.

Mill's acquaintance with the new socialism born after the fiasco of 1848 was superficial. The new school was built around the thought of the German socialists, Marx, Engels, and Lasalle, and of the Russian anarchist Bakunin. It seems that Mill had heard and read something about these new socialists. In a letter to Georges Brandes of 4 March 1872, he gave his Danish correspondent an opinion on the First International. He distinguished between the English and the Continental members of the association.

> The English members, some of whose leaders I am personally acquainted with, in general seem to be reasonable men, seeking practical amelioration in the condition of the labourers, capable of appreciating the obstacles, & with little hatred towards the classes whose domination they want to bring to an end.

The Continental socialists, on the other hand, much more accustomed to relying on the government for the redress of grievances, think that they have but to conquer political power to reach their goals;

> & not only the French socialists, who are perhaps more moderate than many others, but even more so those of Belgium, Germany, & even Switzerland, under the apparent direction of some Russian theoreticians, think that one only has to expropriate everybody, & pull down all existing governments, without worrying, for the moment, about what one will have to put in their place.[58]

Obviously Mill did not know them well enough to untangle Marxist from Bakuninist. Moreover, it is known for a fact that Mill had not read any of the books of the Germans who so transformed the socialist movement. The Belgian writer Lavelèye, when he visited Mill in 1873, spoke to him 'about the German socialists. He did not ignore their names, but he had not studied their books. He urged me to make them known . . .'[59]

The socialism Mill was prepared to consider and recommend for experiment was precisely of the sort which Marx and Engels had treated so harshly in the *Communist Manifesto*. The distance between the world of Mill and the world of Marx was very great. This, together with Marx's obscurity (the first English translation of *Capital* appeared in 1886) may perhaps help to explain the fact that Mill, living in the same town as Marx, and though their ways crossed, should have paid so little attention to the thought of the German socialist.[60]

The discussion of the non-revolutionary socialists is divided along the familiar lines of 'communism' on the one hand, and 'socialism' on the other. The difficulties which Mill foresees for 'communism' are familiar. First are the drawbacks on the score of incentive. Then come the difficulties arising from the apportionment of work among the members. An attempt to make everyone take turns at all kinds of work will cause the advantages of the division of labour and specialization to be lost; and especially the attempt to make the authority grant exceptions to the rule on the grounds of hardship will give rise to disputes. (Mill perhaps drew on American experience to point at discord as the main enemy of all piecemeal socialist establishments.) After listing other possible causes of discord, he indicated a drawback of the greatest importance for his way of thought; even if disputes were avoided it would be at the price of a greater evil: 'a delusive unanimity produced by the prostration of all individual opinions and wishes before the decree of the majority' (745). Mill feared that room for the spontaneous development of human nature (in his opinion an essential condition of progress) would not exist under communism.

> In Communist associations private life would be brought in a most unexampled degree within the dominion of public authority, and there would be less scope for the development of individual character and individual preferences than has hitherto existed among the full citizens of any state belonging to the progressive branches of the human family (746).

There is no doubt that Mill's tone in the *Posthumous Chapters* when speaking of the 'communist' system was much less indulgent than that of the third edition of the *Principles*, if only because in the *Chapters* there was no deferment of the decision to a time when humanity will have progressed further.

As in the *Principles* Mill turned eagerly to Fourierism because it forestalled the arguments about incentive which so damaged the Owenite cause. And one feels again that the Fourierism Mill described was more an image tailored to fit his argument, than the actual scheme proposed by Fourier. In the treatise Mill had given no indication of the *passablement ridicules* proposals of the French thinker. In the *Chapters* he was barely more explicit. A mere footnote told his readers that in the writings of Fourier 'he will find unmistakable proofs of genius, mixed, however, with the wildest and most unscientific fancies

respecting the physical world'. Also in the same footnote, despite his
initial sympathy with Fourier's feminism, he warned that the opinions
of Fourier on the economic organization of society, should be
considered independently of his 'peculiar opinions' on marriage (748
note).

Mill concluded his examination of the anti-property doctrines with
the words,

> an entire renovation of the social fabric, such as is contemplated by
> Socialism, establishing the economic constitution of society upon an
> entirely new basis, other than that of private property and
> competition. . .is not available as a present resource. . . For a long
> period to come the principle of individual property will be in
> possession of the field (749–50).

The verdict then was negative. But the fairness of the discussion
clearly revealed that in Mill's opinion socialism deserved careful
consideration; one distinguished reader, the young Marshall, even felt
that his 'tendency to socialism. . .was fortified. . .by Mill's essays in the
Fortnightly Review'.[61]

Mill and Socialism

Thus Mill at the end of his life had travelled a long way from the
position he had taken at the debate of the Co-operation Society in his
early youth (described in Chapter 3). The change in his attitude may be
said to have started from the time he came into contact with the
Saint-Simonians and began to have doubts about the universality of the
distributive model proposed by the elder generation of political
economists.

The chapter on Property in the *Principles* was based precisely on this
new awareness of the provisionality of the distributive scheme of any
society, expressed in the distinction between the laws of production
and of distribution. The chapter changed from one edition to the next,
but the fundamental attitude of wishing to believe in socialism in one
form or another, though not feeling able to overcome his doubts (as
Lord Robbins puts it), remained throughout. 'In the first edition the
difficulties of socialism were stated so strongly, that the tone was on
the whole that of opposition to it'; there Mill found Owenism
practicable under certain very strict conditions, but undesirable for its
curtailment of personal freedom; Saint-Simonism he deemed not to be
feasible because it posited the direction of the whole economy from a

single centre. The second edition, following hard upon the revolution of 1848, showed more warmth towards collectivism, especially in the form proposed by Fourier; but in the end the verdict was again adverse, Fourierism being rejected for the same reason as Saint-Simonism: that it involved excessive centralization. In 1852 'most of what had been written on the subject in the first edition was cancelled, & replaced by arguments & reflections of a decidedly socialistic tendency' (as Mill put it in his first draft of the *Autobiography*).[62] Many strictures against the practicability of Owenism were relented (though fears for liberty under it persisted); the excessive centralism of the Fourierist scheme was passed over in silence, and judgment was suspended until the results of piecemeal experiments in socialism were available. However, at no point in the various editions was there a full acceptance of socialist schemes. Thus we are forced to conclude that too much importance has been given to the sentence where Mill classifies himself and his wife 'under the general designation of Socialists'. Mill wrote it when his wife, whose socialist leanings were stronger than his, was still alive. It referred to his sentiments at a certain moment, namely, when he was correcting the *Principles* for the third edition in 1852, rather than to his own beliefs in the second half of his life.[63]

From this peak of enthusiasm Mill descended to a more sceptical stance. The posthumous *Chapters on Socialism* reveal a considerably cooler attitude than that of the third edition of the *Principles*. Mill presented the socialist attacks on the competitive system fully and fairly; he admitted the lack of incentive for many among the working population, the unfair grading of work and rewards by the effect of the existence of non-competing groups, the lowered quality of consumption goods through the competition of retailers; but he concluded that on the whole the attacks of the collectivists were exaggerated. As for the concrete proposals of the socialists, Mill reached the same negative answer as in the *Principles*, though he worded it here a little more decidedly; he rejected Owenism, Saint-Simonism, and Fourierism as either impracticable, or if practicable, undesirable. The whole discussion gave an impression of greater detachment than the previous ones, due not so much to actual changes in argument as to a different and more critical tone.

Mill's rejection of the schemes he examined, whether Utopian or revolutionary, is final and we should not be misled by the fact that he was fair and open-minded to the point of indulgence. This was in part due to his inexcusable subservience to his wife's opinions, and in part it was also a natural reaction against the general opinion of his contemporaries, typified in Macaulay's lament that the working classes ignored 'the reasons which irrefragably proved this inequality [of the rich and the poor] to be necessary to the well being of all classes'; or Louis Reybaud's shocked question in his essay on Mill:

> To speak in the same breath of that monstrosity called *Communism* and a social order, no doubt imperfect and susceptible of many ameliorations, but viable at least and proved by the experience of centuries, is this worthy of a thoughtful man, of a serious spirit, of an economist?[64]

Neither can it be forgotten that he was the first economist to study socialism at such length and in such a thorough and systematic fashion. But he found two insuperable obstacles for his acceptance of any of the collectivist schemes (apart from his detestation of gratuitous violence): his belief in the relative efficiency of competition, and his fears for liberty in a socialist commonwealth.

Therefore the assertion that Mill was a socialist must be rejected. But it would be wrong to conclude that his thought involved a complete acceptance of the social organization of his time. Mill put forward proposals for important reforms in the competitive system, chiefly in his chapter 'On the Probable Futurity of the Labouring Classes' which we shall study next. As Lord Robbins said recently,

> in that chapter, it is clear that Mill's utopia is not nearly so much in the duo-decimo editions of the new Jerusalem. . .but in the development of workmen's co-operatives. . . In the last analysis, that is to say, Mill's socialism proves to be much more like non-revolutionary syndicalism than anything which would be called socialism at the present day.[65]

> The grand, leading principle, towards which every argument unfolded in these pages directly converges, is the absolute and essential importance of human development in its richest diversity.
>
> Wilhelm von Humboldt as quoted by Mill

Chapter 8 The Future of Society

Mill's chief aim when he wrote *The Principles of Political Economy, with some of their applications to social philosophy* was to help build a better society. Though he also wished to correct the theoretical defects in the economic treatises of the time and incorporate the latest analytical refinements into one comprehensive study of political economy, his main concern was with the practical applications of scientific principles. He made this clear in the very subtitle of his work. And foremost among the practical questions he considered was that of Equality.

The economic revolution of the eighteenth and nineteenth centuries brought about a change in the egalitarian tradition. Up to then it had been of a levelling character, and had exerted little influence on the societies of the time, whose organization was solidly hierarchical. The people, except for occasional explosions of wrath in the form of peasant *jacqueries*, seemed to rest content within systems of political, social, and economic inequality. Some philosophers let their imagination dwell in *Utopia*, where echoes could be heard of Sparta and the Roman republic. Only when equality was demanded in the name of Christian principles, as during the Puritan revolution in England, was there danger for the established order.

One might say that a system of social equality is only workable in an affluent society. In any case, the growth of the productive powers in some European societies meant, among other things, that the establishment of a large degree of equality was a practicable possibility. This brought about a two-fold change in egalitarianism. Firstly, from being a levelling attitude, it by and large became an 'uplifting' creed, to use a Victorian word; or, in the more modern expression of T.H. Marshall's, a movement for the 'extension of citizenship'. And secondly, it lost some of the glamour and coherence which lofty ideals have when they exist only in the minds of philosophers.

In sum, when the task is not to level all classes to the situation of the lowest, but to open up for everyone the opportunities of civilization, the measures to be taken cannot be simple. Such is the setting for Mill's discussion of equality: he was no leveller, and hence was conscious of some of the difficulties which could arise in an egalitarian system.

Here enters a third contestant in the discussion, beside the leveller and the modern egalitarian, to wit, the enlightened conservative. The latter wishes to preserve a way of life for himself and those of his class and tends to make concessions to egalitarianism only in as far as they prove to be a case of *plus ça change, plus c'est la même chose*. As usual, Mill has been thought to be an eclectic on the question of equality, standing midway between the leveller and the conservative. An attentive examination of his writings, however, shows Mill to have been an egalitarian, yet one who was looking forwards to a kind of equality different from the mechanical 'soak the rich' brand. Mill himself relates how his contemporaries made that mistake to their peril. Recalling the bitterness of the campaign against him when he sought re-election to Parliament, he noted that 'all persons of Tory feelings were far more embittered against me individually than on the previous occasion. . . As I had shown in my political writings that I was aware of the weak points in democratic opinions, some Conservatives, it seems, had not been without hopes of finding me an opponent of democracy' (W.Cl., 262).

Enlightened conservatives tend to defend their position by speaking of a conflict between liberty and equality. That they did so in the nineteenth century may be seen from the extensive references in the opening pages of Tawney's *Equality*. Since Mill cared so much for Liberty, it might be thought that he too grounded his fears of equality on the same bases as the conservatives — not so. Obviously, he disliked uniformity as much as any man and warned of the risk that, in a democracy, public opinion might trammel the right of individuals to live as they wished. Nevertheless, there is a positive way of understanding equality which need not conflict with individual freedom. For the conservative, all egalitarianism is negative, more often than not tainted with envy — remember Hayek's diatribe against distributive justice in the *Constitution of Liberty*. For the modern egalitarian, equality is not so much a matter of justice as a question of opening up the opportunities of modern civilization to the great mass of the people. This may mean coercing some people, or taking power, economic and political, away from them, because their privileges are a cause of the subjection or darkness suffered by the majority. But fundamentally it means not taking away from the few or sharing among the many the spoils of class war. It means creating the conditions for the many to obtain for themselves the opportunities of civilized life. The modern egalitarian should identify himself with the prophet giving the widow her cruse, not with the dishonest steward of the parable.

Thus Mill certainly feared the advance of equality because under certain conditions it might foster a regime of unfreedom. He had other fears, however, which have nothing in common with those from which the enlightened conservative professes to suffer. He feared not only the oppression of the few by the many, but the corruption of the many into a state of uniform stupor. He feared that the Malthusian danger, democratic demagoguery, the vulgarity of the middle classes, would divert the progress towards democracy in the direction of the ant-heap, instead of the free, equal, self-governing society he wished for.

The difference between his position and that of the conservatives was clearer for Mill than it is for us. In the nineteenth century, the enlightened Tory was a paternalist, while the radical egalitarian was a believer in the independence, self-government and personal responsibility of the lower, and indeed all, classes. Today the matter is less clear, since many egalitarians, if not most, believe in the protection of the working classes and the poor through a comprehensive system of social benefits and social security, which to a nineteenth century radical would have looked paternalistic. Thus apparently, the twentieth century egalitarian has sided with the paternalistic Tory against the self-help radical. In a way this is true and is but another example of that most useful of social mechanisms, the convergence of opposing ideologies in practical action. But there is one thing the conservative, enlightened or not, knows by instinct: the higher classes must rule. And hence a link subsists between the nineteenth and the twentieth century radical: both think real equality does not exist as long as the political and economic power of society lies out of the hands of the working class. The question of who rules is crucial for both: the differences between Mill and today's radical lies in their divergent opinion on how best to fit the majority for power and how to guard against their abusing it. Mill in this, as in many other things, followed Plato and believed the citizen must be able to govern himself before governing others, while today many believe it illusory to expect the poor, the ignorant, and the oppressed to raise themselves from their degraded state by their bootstraps, so to speak.

Whatever his differences of opinion with the radical of today, it is clear that Mill considered himself anything but a conservative. In the opening pages of the chapter on 'The Probable Futurity of the Labouring Classes', the main object of our analysis in the remainder of this book, Mill drew a contrast between two rival theories of the good society which underlined the difference of his outlook from that of the conservative. One of the theories was that of Disraeli and Carlyle, at bottom a plea for thé return to a feudal society, where the rich would act '*in loco parentis* to the poor, guiding and restraining them like children'. The other was his own theory of self-dependence.

The idea of drawing this contrast did not occur to Mill at the time of writing the *Principles*, but some years before.[1] In 1844 he offered to write an article on the labour question for the editor of the *Edinburgh Review*, MacVey Napier. He wanted to attack a general attitude at the time tending

> to rivet firmly in the minds of the labouring people the persuasion that it is the business of others to take care of their condition, without any self control on their own part; − & that whatever is possessed by other people, more than they possess, is a wrong to them, or at least a kind of stewardship, of which an account is to be rendered to them.[2]

This letter, whose tone, it is true, is much less socialistic than the corresponding passages in the *Principles* written three years later, is interesting because it shows that the contrast between the two theories fitted in with Mill's basic beliefs: his belief in the Malthusian doctrine, leading him to reject any scheme not based on fostering workers' self-control, and his belief in the powers of education, making him underline the moral effects of the practice of self-government. Napier accepted the idea. In the resulting article Mill attacked the Young England group headed by Disraeli.

> The apostles of the new theory. . .cannot mean that the working classes should combine the liberty of action of independent citizens, with the immunities of slaves. There are but two modes of social existence for human beings; they must be left to the natural consequences of their mistakes in life; or society must guard against the mistakes, by prevention or punishment.[3]

The dichotomy sounds overly sharp to those of us who under the influence of socialism believe society should actively promote the individual's right to develop all his faculties fully. But it led Mill to draw up clearly the basic principle of social policy that he advocated: that the only hope for lasting improvement lay in making workers and other subject classes increasingly responsible for their own lives and for defending their own interests, as full citizens, free from the interference of their 'betters'.

In the *Principles* the presentation of the idea lost some of its severity. Mill started by attacking the paternalist stance, throwing doubt on the idea that the social system to which those conservatives desired to return had ever existed in reality. A class in a position of preponderance can be expected to betray its trust and use its power mainly for its own ends, he said. Even if the ideal did exist in the past, a return to a feudal system was impossible. 'The poor have come out of leading strings, and cannot any longer be governed or treated like children.'

The working class had decided to take the responsibility for their destiny in their own hands. 'Modern nations will have to learn the lesson, that the well-being of a people must exist by means of the justice and self-government, the δικαιοσύνη and σωφροσύνη of the individual citizens' (*Coll. Works*, III, 763 [IV, vii, 2]).

Two things have to be said about this vision of society. Firstly, it is very different from the kind of society sought after by those we have called enlightened conservatives. Mill truly believes that political, social, and economic equality is the state to be aimed at in the reform of the society of his time. Hence political, economic and social power must change hands.

Secondly and on the other hand, in it Mill warns that unless the people's independence is strengthened, their sense of responsibility cultivated, their intelligence increased, the society which could result might be a mass society, even if a formally free one. Hence equality will be illusory or inhuman, unless the majority have made themselves fit for power.

For the purpose of understanding the real character of the good society for Mill, neither hierarchical nor regimented, which must be both free and self-governing in all spheres of activity, instead of 'the egalitarian society', we shall call it 'the co-operative society'.

The present chapter thus tries to present the positive proposals of Mill's social philosophy. It has two objects. In the first place, it makes a systematic presentation of Mill's doctrine on the 'egalitarian', or 'co-operative society', as we have called it. This doctrine so pervades his

writings that though it is mainly to be found in the *Principles*, in other
works there are reflections on the free development of the individual
(in *On Liberty*), the equality of the sexes (in *The Subjection of
Women*), the protection of minorities (in *Representative Government*),
which may not be studied in full here, but which will have to be kept in
mind during the exposition.

In the second place, it attempts to evaluate Mill's vision of the future
society by trying to answer two questions. One regards the intellectual
integrity and capacity of the creator of this vision, the other its value as
a guide for action. Just as it is unfair in the matter of socialism to speak
of a 'shallow syncretism', since Mill, in the final count, came down in
support for one of the sides of the argument, here it may be possible to
prove it false that he tried to reconcile the irreconcilable. Can a guiding
principle be found which holds together Mill's vision of an egalitarian
and self-governing society as a viable intellectual construction?

The second query is as to the realism of Mill's proposals. Was what
he proposed feasible? Did he get to the bottom of the social question,
or was it no more than an illusory palliative? Though the world of
today is in many respects different from that Mill knew, by and large
the social problems which he examined in his writings still seem as
important now as they did at the time. It will scarcely be surprising if in
matters of detail his discussion appears outdated, but do his proposals
for the solution of those problems when broadly interpreted still
deserve attention? Does his conception of the good society point in the
right direction, or must it, in the light of later experience, be considered
as showing a path that leads nowhere?

The Reform of the Property System

It is best to start the description of Mill's ideas on how to achieve
equality in a modern society with two preliminary points: his proposals
for the reform of the institution of property in general and for the
reform of land tenure.

'It is not the subversion of the system of individual property which
should be aimed at; but the improvement of it, and the participation of
every member of the community in its benefits,' said Mill in conclusion
to his study of socialism in the first edition of the *Principles* (1848). In
other words, he held that property was the origin of unjustifiable
inequalities, but such effects were not necessary or inevitable, because
the institution was susceptible of reform. This is the prevailing idea in
his analysis of property.

Mill began by countering the extended idea that private property was a sacred natural right, which had existed since the dawn of social life, unchanged and unchangeable. Many allusions to that idea are found scattered in the pages where he discussed property, but the *locus* of his reflections on the matter is the beginning of Book II, on Distribution. One reads there that private property, as an institution, did not owe its origin to any of those considerations of utility, which plead (so strongly, he said in the first edition) for the maintenance of it when established (*Coll. Works*, II, 201, [II, i, 2]). The preservation of the peace was the original object of civil government, he proceeded, and this peace was maintained by protecting possession of 'even what was not the fruit of personal exertion'. In short, the origin of property was irrelevant to a discussion of its utility as an institution in the present time. In fact, 'the laws of property have never yet conformed to the principles on which the justification of private property rests' (*Coll. Works*, III, 986 [II, i, 6]).

The justification of private ownership alluded to in the last quotation was the traditional 'labour theory of property'. 'The foundation...is the right of producers to what they themselves have produced' (*Coll. Works*, II, 215, [II, ii, 1]). The classic formulation of this principle was made by Locke in his *Second Treatise of Civil Government* (1690). Locke admitted the Natural Law idea, which seemingly conflicted with the idea of private property in material things, that the earth had been given to all mankind in common. Property could nevertheless exist, he contended, because a man had a right to himself.

> The labour of his body and the work of his hands, we may say, are properly his. Whatsoever he removes out of the state that nature hath provided and left in, he hath mixed his labour with, and joined to it something that is his own, and thereby makes it his property.[4]

Locke's definition, however, was incomplete. As it stood it gave ammunition to the opponents of the competitive system; many socialists attacked property precisely on the basis of the right of the workman to the produce of his labour; they pointed to the fact that a great part of the produce of labour was paid to non-labourers under the form of profits and rents.

When Mill went to debate the Owenite system at the Co-operation Society in 1825, he was confronted with precisely such an argument.

The manuscript of his intended speech records the answer which he wished to give these socialists: that they did not understand the role played by savings in a modern economy, and did not see that (except in the most primitive communities, if at all) labour could not create value unless aided by capital. 'Wealth is indeed the produce of labour,' he said, 'but not of unassisted labour.' On this point, he held the same position in the *Principles*.[5]

The Lockian principle was thus reformulated by Mill as justifying not only the property of things produced, but also the property of things saved from the produce of earlier labour. Many socialists, however, could accept this reformulation and still be able to make a very strong rejoinder. Thus the Owenites put forward that, since capital was nothing but accumulated labour, it ought to belong to the labouring classes, at some point it must have been stolen from its rightful owner. Mill intended to answer them in a way which he was to repudiate later in life: 'the capital is the produce of labour, sure enough, but of what labour? They are [sic] the accumulated product of the labour of the capitalists themselves, or their ancestors'.[6]

Four reasons make it impossible to trace accumulated fortunes wholly back to labour, begging for a revision of the labour theory of private property.[7] One is the element of luck, connections, all the unlaboured-for components of the situation of an individual (and of a great part of his personal ability, too, that which he owes to his education, his family); the second is the snowball effect of large fortunes, the advantage which having money means for making more money; these two were not underlined by the socialists of the nineteenth century, and apparently passed unnoticed by Mill. The third and the fourth loomed large in the shaping of Mill's opinions on property. They were: the fact that one cannot assume, as a matter of course, that the right to the produce of one's labour includes the right to receive property by inheritance or bequest; and the fact that natural resources whose ownership contributes to the existence of so many fortunes, cannot by any stretch of the imagination be included in the produce of labour and saving.

For the young Mill these two difficulties did not exist, but for the Mill of the *Principles* they demanded a re-examination of the right of property. It is instructive to contrast at this point the attitudes of Mill and the French politician and publicist Thiers. In 1848, the latter published a book called *De la propriété*, where he defended the property system as it existed in France (admittedly much more equitable than the English system of the time) exclusively on the basis of the right of the individual to the produce of his labour – including, with less logical rigour than could be desired, both inheritance and the ownership of natural resources under such a justification.

Thiers thought it enough to say that 'property is not complete unless it is transmissible by gift or inheritance', and reinforced his pronouncement with the assertion that 'the new and greater inequalities which result from it [inheritance], are absolutely necessary, and compose one of the more fruitful and beautiful harmonies in human society' (58). Mill on the contrary wished to reform the whole institution of inheritance. He distinguished between the changes to be made in the transmission of property when the dead owner had omitted to make a will, and when he had made one.

If one has a right to own the produce of one's labour and abstinence, it is clear that one should be able to dispose of it in the manner one prefers, thought Mill. 'The right of each to his own faculties, to what he can produce by them, and to whatever he can get for them in a fair market,' was not the whole of the right of property: this right also included the 'right to give this to another person if he chooses, and the right of that other to receive and enjoy it.' But when a person neglected to make a will, he could not be said to have given his property: 'the right of inheritance, as distinguished from bequest' did not form part of the right of property ([1848] *Coll. Works*, II, 218 [II, ii, 3]).

Bentham, in his *Supply without Burden: or Escheat vice Taxation* (1795) had attacked the general assumption that collateral relations had a right to inherit the property of a person who had died intestate. Mill went further. He not only denied the right of a collateral relation to inherit *ab intestato* (excepting cases of hardship, when a small pension was in order), he even asserted that children could not expect the whole of the property of the intestate parents to devolve upon them, but only such portions as would under the existing system go to second or natural sons. Parents who wished their children to be better off could resort to a will. 'The surplus, if any. . .[the State] may rightfully appropriate to the general purposes of the community' (*Coll. Works*, II, 222–3).

If Mill had wished to restrict his reforms of the right of property to such as would make property conform to its justifying principle, he would have left the right of bequest well alone. But in his opinion, many of the evils of the society of his time were born of the excessive concentration of fortunes, and one of the obvious causes of such concentration was the transmission of property by testament. He decided that a reform was needed here too. The Utilitarian part of his thought came into play at this point.[8]

In his essay on *Utilitarianism* (1863) Mill admitted that the principles of justice and expediency could clash with one another or at least appear to do so, and that people found it 'difficult to see, in Justice, only a particular kind or branch of general utility, and think that its superior binding force requires a totally different origin' (Everyman edition, 39). Mill thought he could resolve this difficulty. In the ultimate resort Justice was reducible to Utility.

> Justice is a name for certain moral requirements, which, regarded collectively, stand higher in the scale of social utility, and are therefore of more paramount obligation, than any others: though particular cases may occur in which some other social duty is so important, as to overrule any one of the general maxims of justice (Everyman, 59).

He was in effect drawing a distinction between short run expediency, which can be calculated for each case, and long run expediency, which is embodied in rules, the result of a long test of experience.[9] In consequence, the fact that an institution had given rise to rights which were to be respected as of justice, did not exempt it from examination by the test of expediency and from reform when necessary.

These thoughts were present in embryo in the *Principles*. 'Property is only a means to an end, not itself the end. Like all other proprietary rights, and even in a greater degree than most, the power of bequest is liable to conflict with objects still more important.'[10]

Two existing institutions Mill felt to be especially obnoxious: entail and endowments. In the case of the first he weighed the incentive of the idea of setting up a family establishment against the drawbacks of tying down a property, and found entails wanting. He reached the same negative conclusion in the case of endowments, as when a testator, 'in founding a place of education (for instance). . .dictates, for ever, what doctrines shall be taught', for it was 'impossible that any one should know what doctrines will be fit to be taught after he has been dead for centuries' (*Coll. Works*, II, 223 [II, ii, 4]).[11]

Mill went further, and considering that it was not enough to abolish entail and endowment, he observed that it was an established usage of legislation to regulate and curtail the power of bequest; as for example in countries like France under the influence of the Roman Law, a *legitima portio* was reserved for the immediate relatives of the deceased. Mill did not think the Roman system a good one from all points of view. There was a clash of expediency in the matter of bequest: on the one hand the possibility of disposing freely of one's property was an incentive to industry, while on the other, excessive inequalities of fortune not born of industry or frugality produced the evils pointed out by the socialists. Mill solved the contradiction by saying that he would 'prefer to restrict, not what any one might bequeath, but what any one should be permitted to acquire, by bequest or inheritance' (*Coll. Works*, II, 225 [II, ii, 4]). In other words, he proposed that a maximum be established for what a person could receive in this way.[12] The benefits which Mill expected from his scheme were very great: 'wealth which could no longer be employed in over-enriching a few, would either be devoted to objects of public usefulness, or if bestowed on individuals, would be distributed among a larger number' ([1848] *Coll. Works*, II, 226).[13]

A. Bain relates:

> what I remember most vividly of his talk pending the publication of the work, was his anticipating a tremendous outcry about his doctrines on Property. He frequently spoke of his proposals as to Inheritance and Bequest, which, if carried out, would pull down all large fortunes in two generations. To his surprise, however, this part of the book made no sensation at all.[14]

Bain tentatively proffers an explanation: 'Probably the people thought it the dream of a future too distant to affect the living; or else that the views were too wild and revolutionary to be entertained'.

The Ownership of Land

The labour theory of property also affected the ownership of natural resources. The problem was faced by Locke, but his solution is not satisfactory. Once it was admitted that man could appropriate as much land as he mixed with his labour, was it permissible that he should appropriate more than he could personally use, asked Locke. The right to engross the produce of the earth to let it rot, he answered, was not included in the right of property.

But since gold and silver, being little useful to the life of man in proportion to food, raiment, and carriage, has its value only from the consent of men, . . .it is plain that men have agreed to a disproportionate and unequal possession of the earth, they having, by tacit and voluntary consent, found out a way how a man may fairly possess more land than he himself can use the product of, by receiving in exchange of the overplus gold and silver which may be hoarded without injury to any one, these metals not spoiling or decaying in the hands of the possessor.[15]

Thiers did not pay much attention to the problem. When he did examine the matter, he achieved a justification by introducing arguments logically unrelated to the labour theory of property: he exaggerated the fact that without labour natural resources are useless; or introduced considerations of expediency, such as the effects of land nationalization on productivity; or the fact that the fixing of rents through any mechanism but that of the market would be a source of quarrels; or the utility of a class of rich people for society.[16] We do not mean to say that considerations of expediency should not enter an argument on the right of property: but that when a general principle clashes with general expediency (whatever this may mean), either the practical difficulty should be shown to be temporary, or the principle should be modified. The latter is what many liberals coming after Thiers have done: they have widened the basis of the right of property, and have come to consider it not so much as a reward for labour, but rather as a remedy for scarcity; thus justifying the private property of natural resources on the reflection that the system allows scarce resources to be allocated with the least wastage.

Mill did not take the path of Thiers or that of modern liberals. He remained well within the theory which justified property exclusively on the basis of labour.

The essential principle of property being to assure all persons what they have produced by their labour and accumulated by their abstinence, this principle cannot apply to what is not the produce of labour, the raw material of the earth (*Coll. Works*, II, 227 [II, ii, 5]).

To use the distinction which he later expounded in *Utilitarianism* between justice and expediency, Mill was in fact saying that property in land could not be considered a 'right' as of justice, but simply a useful expedient to be preserved only if the direct results of it appeared to be immediately conducive to the general welfare.

When the 'sacredness of property' is talked of, it should always be remembered, that this sacredness does not belong in the same degree to landed property. No man made the land. It is the original inheritance of the whole species ([1848] *Coll. Works*, II, 230 [II, ii, 6]).

In the third edition [1852] when the radicalism of his outlook reached its peak, he went on: 'Its appropriation is wholly a question of general expediency. When private property in land is not expedient, it is unjust.'

In the case of land, the reasons which led Mill to propose a modification of the existing institutions were not purely derived from a strict application of the definition of property. A great deal was due to the special position of land in the economic doctrine of Ricardo. For the Ricardians, rent was received by a distinct class of society: the landlords. Their interests were opposed to those of the rest of the community. Further, they earned their share in the income of society through no effort of their own. As Mill put it, 'they grow richer, as it were in their sleep, without working, risking, or economizing' (*Coll. Works*, III, 819–20 [V, ii, 5]).

Mill did not derive a land policy merely from these notions. He took his analysis a little further by developing a suggestion of Ricardo's. Ricardo had insisted that by rent he meant only 'that portion of the produce of the earth, which is paid to the landlord for the use of the original and indestructible powers of the soil', which should be distinguished from the portion 'paid for the use of the capital which had been employed in ameliorating the quality of the land, and in erecting such buildings as were necessary to secure and preserve the produce' (Sraffa, I, 67).

Mill's animadversions regarded only the income engrossed by the landlords by their ownership of the 'original and indestructible powers of the land', not the income derived from the capital investment in agriculture. Indeed, he thought that 'though land is not the produce of industry, most of its valuable qualities are so' (*Coll. Works*, II, 227 [II, ii, 5]).

Mill's policy with respect to land was twofold. In the first place, he thought he could distinguish within rent the part which was due to capital improvements from that due to the external effects of social changes, such as the growth of towns or especially the growth in demand for food, and proposed devices to tax this unearned increase in the incomes of the landlords.

Secondly, he recommended that the improver of the land be ensured of its ownership. In agriculture 'the labour and outlay are immediate, the benefit is spread over many years, perhaps over all future time'. Therefore, if a holder 'undertakes such improvements, he must have a long period before him in which to profit by them: and he cannot continue always to have a long time before him, unless his tenure is perpetual' ([1848] *Coll. Works*, II, 227 [II, ii, 5]).

Such a policy applied in point of fact only to peasants because Mill asserted (with some injustice) that the great landlord was not generally an improver. In England, he said, the firstborn, who inherited the land, rarely had capital to invest, for the pecuniary resources of the estate had usually been apportioned to the younger brothers. The Irish landlord was worse in that he usually left on the land nothing but a pittance of potatoes for its cultivators. Consequently, he asserted in the third place, the State had the right to expropriate land with due compensation when under its direction the agricultural productivity could be expected to increase. That is the logical justification of the proposals made by Mill late in life for the buying up of land by the State and for the establishing of peasant proprietors and agricultural co-operatives on it.

Peasant Proprietors
Mill allotted an inordinate amount of space to the discussion of this last point, the small peasant property. The main reason for the importance he lent to the introduction of this system of land tenure was the fact that he saw it as the only solution for the Irish problem.

During the two years in which he wrote the treatise, Mill occupied himself for a considerable period of time in a journalistic campaign in the *Morning Chronicle* for the establishment of peasant properties in Ireland.[17] The full extent of the calamity caused by the potato plague had become clear in 1846. The government, reluctantly at first, with the urgency of despair later, set up a programme of direct relief, and proposed, as a long term measure, the extension of the English Poor Law system to the neighbouring island. Mill thought the application of the Poor Laws would only worsen the long term prospects of the Irish. The cause of the catastrophe, for him, had been the total lack of control of the Irish peasantry not only over their numbers, but over their situation as a whole; which lack of control in its turn was the result of the system of land-holding prevalent in Ireland.

Many of the ideas expressed in the articles were incorporated into the *Principles*, but in his treatise, Mill appeared to be in two minds about the question of peasant property, especially after the third edition.

In the first part of the work he gave what on the whole was a favourable verdict on the institution in question. When discussing 'Production on a Large and a Small Scale' in the first book, he asserted that diffused ownership was preferable because it resulted in a larger gross product. Also in the first half of the work he extolled the beneficial effects of peasant property as a distributive arrangement, with regard to the industry, the education, the self-control, and in general the moral and social situation of the peasantry (*Principles* [II, vii]).

But when, at the end of this work, he turned to the examination of the Futurity of the Working Classes, his verdict was different. At that point, he had suggested in 1848 that 'a people who have once adopted the large system of production, either in manufactures or in agriculture, are not likely to recede from it; and when population is kept in due proportion to the means of support, it is not desirable that they should.' In 1852, however he felt able to add:

Something better should be aimed at as the goal of industrial improvement, than to disperse mankind over the earth in single families, each ruled internally, as families now are, by a patriarchal despot, and having scarcely any community of interest, or necessary mental communion, with other human beings ([1852] *Coll. Works*, III, 768 [IV, vii, 4]).

The reason for this sharp change of opinion was the possibility, which to all appearances suddenly dawned on Mill, of combining the productive advantages of large scale enterprise with the moral and social benefits of diffused ownership by means of partnerships and of co-operatives.

The civilizing and improving influences of association, and the efficiency and economy of production on a large scale, may be obtained without dividing the producers into two parties with hostile interests and feelings... The relation of masters and workpeople will be gradually superseded by partnership in one of two forms: temporarily and in some cases, association of the labourers with the capitalist; in other cases, and finally in all, association of labourers among themselves (769).

Thus, despite the importance Mill lent it, the system of peasant property turned out to be for him merely a local or temporary remedy, to be superseded by partnership and co-operation.

The Future Society

However, the type of individualistic and egalitarian society that Mill was trying to defend by means of these criticisms of the property system, and even more, the co-operative social organization he hinted at, at the end of his analysis of land distribution in the 1852 edition, involved rather more than a new definition of the right of property. Mill had to show that conditions necessary for his ideal to be realized were materializing in society; that if due precautions were taken and the relevant reforms carried out, the spontaneous movement of the economy and society as a whole would tend in the desired direction; it was necessary to define the 'laws' which in his opinion governed the progress of society, and which properly modified would lead to the goal he desired. Once these historical trends were defined, he could determine the guiding principle and nature of the new society.

These 'laws' are to be found in the Book he inserted in his treatise between Book III 'Exchange' and Book V 'On the Influence of Government'. This Book IV is titled 'Influence of the Progress of Society on Production and Distribution'. It was a remarkable, if not very happy innovation of Mill's. He opened Book IV with the following remark:

> The three preceding Parts include as detailed a view as the limits of this Treatise permit, of what, by a happy generalisation of a mathematical phrase, has been called the Statics of the subject. . . All this, however, has only put us in possession of the economical laws of a stationary and unchanging society.

Book IV would consider 'the economical condition of mankind as liable to change. . . Thereby adding a theory of motion to our theory of equilibrium − the Dynamics of political economy to the Statics' ([1848] *Coll. Works*, III, 705 [IV, i, 1]).

Such a division, however, did not play as important a role in Mill's economic thought as he leads one to think, since the economic theory presented in the first three books of the treatise was fundamentally dynamic and not static as Mill affirmed.

If attention is paid to Mill's own words at the beginning of Book IV, one of the most important influences on him at this point was that of Comte. Mill attributed the general idea of devoting a book in his treatise to the future evolution of society to Comte's insistence on the need for a dynamic analysis to supplement the statics which usually formed the principal object of social speculation. But in fact the distinction between statics and dynamics did not correspond to the matter of the treatise. *The Principles* was built around the Ricardian model, which Baumol has called 'the magnificent dynamics'. The dynamic laws of the economy shown at work in the said Book IV, had been presented and fully explained in Book I, chapters x to xiii dealing with the laws of increase in Population, Capital, and Land. The reason which led Mill to separate the statement of these laws from the description of their consequences does not lie in the distinction between 'statics' and 'dynamics', but in the peculiar position of value in his economic system.

We have already seen how, though Ricardo opened his *Principles of Political Economy and Taxation* (1817) with a discussion of value, he was really advocating the demotion of the analysis of value from its place of pre-eminence in economic theory. The point of Ricardo's discussion was to show that value, rather than being the determinant of the economic system, was determined by cost of production, that is to say, by the laws of the increase of population, of the accumulation of capital, and of historically diminishing returns on the land. Faithful to this view, John Stuart Mill devoted Book I to Production; Book II to Distribution, and only in the opening chapters of Book III on Exchange did he come to a discussion of value. It was impossible for him to explain the matter of Book IV (which, in fact, was a mere corollary of the laws of production expounded in the first book) until he had dealt with value; because Book IV dealt not only with the future evolution of numbers, physical capital and physical productivity on the land, as deducible from the three laws, but also the future path of prices, wages, interest, and rents, for the determination of which he needed the concept of value and the notion of a medium of exchange.

So that it was not the use he made of the idea of 'dynamics' so much as the demands of his concept of value that led Mill to separate all considerations of the future of society from the rest of the book. Though that might be open to criticism from the analytical point of view, it had the political advantage of stressing the importance Mill gave to his plans for the reform of society.[18]

Mill's conception of the Future Society was not of Comtian, but rather of mixed Ricardian and Saint-Simonian origin. From Ricardian economics Mill took the idea of a secular fall in the rate of profits, and that of the proximity of the stationary state (both of which Ricardo viewed with foreboding). Then, under the effect of Saint-Simonism he transformed the Ricardian conception and admitted the possibility of making this stationary state a happy one for humanity.

For Mill, as for Ricardo, the rate of profits was ultimately determined by the productivity of labour-and-capital on marginal land. Further, Mill held that technological advance was not great enough to offset diminishing returns of the land. Hence he considered that with increasing accumulation and the consequent increasing application of wage capital to the land, the rate of profits would fall until it reached a point where net accumulation stopped.

> When a country has long possessed a large production, and a large net income to make savings from, . . . it is one of the characteristics of such a country, that the rate of profit is habitually within, as it were, a hand's breadth of the minimum, and the country therefore on the very verge of the stationary state (*Coll. Works*, III, 738 [IV, iv, 4]).[19]

Countries such as Great Britain and Holland were in this situation, though not the United States, due to its reserves of virgin land. Only the waste of capital, through over-trading or speculation, or the effects of improvements in production, or the possibility of importing cheap commodities, or the overflow of capital to the colonies, prevented the stationary state from setting in.

Adam Smith had depicted a stationary state as 'dull', and a regressive one as 'melancholy': only in a progressive state, he thought, could the condition of the people be cheerful and hearty (Cannan, I, 83). This assertion originated in Adam Smith's belief (from which Malthus drew inspiration) that once capital accumulation ceased, nothing would stop the people from breeding themselves into a state of mere subsistence. After Malthus's second edition of his *Essay on Population*, the inevitability of poverty in a stationary state ceased to be one of the corollaries of political economy. Still 'the tone and tendency' of the speculations of political economists went, as Mill put it, 'completely to identify all that is economically desirable with the progressive state, and with that alone.' Mill felt that he could completely invert the accepted doctrine. The stationary state could be happy, the progressive was disagreeable.

His hopes for a happy stationary state were principally based on the confidence that the growth in numbers could be checked.

> The doctrine that, to however distant a time incessant struggling may put off our doom, the progress of society must 'end in shallows and in miseries', far from being, as many people still believe, a wicked invention of Mr. Malthus...can only be successfully combated on his principles (*Coll. Works*, III, 753 [IV, vi, 1]).

If the growth of population were stopped while there was still time, the final stages of progressive accumulation would result in even higher wages, and the stationary state (when both accumulation and the growth in numbers would come to a stop) would make the high living standard of the working classes their permanent condition.

Further, the stationary state in Mill's opinion 'would be, on the whole, a very considerable improvement on our present condition.' Mill's reasons for this belief were various, some apparent in the pages of his treatise, others buried in his past. His dislike for the narrow tastes and pursuits of most of his contemporaries was one he avowed.

> I confess I am not charmed with the ideal of life held out by those who think that the normal state of human beings is that of struggling to get on; that the trampling, crushing, elbowing, and treading on each other's heels, which form the existing type of social life, are the most desirable lot of human kind, or anything but the disagreeable symptoms of one of the phases of industrial progress (*Coll. Works*, III, 754 [IV, vi, 2]).

In more primitive times the stimulus which kept the energies of mankind in employment was war: in this time it was money getting: but he still thought that 'the best state for human nature is that in which, while no one is poor, no one desires to be richer, nor has any reason to fear being thrust back, by the efforts of others to push themselves forward'.[20] Economic growth was only important 'in the backward countries of the world'. In the most advanced countries, 'what is economically needed is a better distribution, of which an indispensable means is a stricter restraint on population' ([1848] *Coll. Works*, III, 755). Added to his dislike of the pervasive adoration of money was his expectancy that the stationary state would not mean the end of technological innovation. Not only would there 'be as much scope as ever for all kinds of mental culture, and moral and social progress.'

Even the industrial arts might be as earnestly and as successfully cultivated, with this sole difference, that instead of serving no purpose but the increase of wealth, industrial improvements would produce their legitimate effect, that of abridging labour (*Coll. Works*, III, 756).

Such a social state would be considered today to be very far from stationary. Mill was able to hold that consoling conception of the stationary state because he defined economic activity as the creation of material wealth only, that is, of output susceptible of accumulation, and hence considered that leisure was not an economic good at all.[21]

The most important factor did not show on the surface of the argument, a factor which accounts for the enthusiasm which Mill showed for his new conception: the mark left on his thought by the Saint-Simonian doctrine. Mill's argument as expounded above makes use of Saint-Simonian categories, such as the idea of a military age when the principal occupation of men was war, and of a mercantile age mainly interested in the accumulation of money. On a deeper level, it seems impossible to admit that the purely economic concept of the stationary state (even if combined with a hope that population would be checked) could sustain by itself the ideal of a good society which Mill was attempting to erect on it. Other concepts, of Saint-Simonian descent, must have played a part, such as the idea of progress,[22] and, perhaps unbeknown to Mill himself, the idea that time would stop and humanity would reach a New Jerusalem.

Once he had laid down the basis for his analysis, Mill could proceed to the matter of his famous chapter 'On the Probable Futurity of the Labouring Classes'.

Social Equality and Political Safeguards

The first manuscript draft of the *Principles* did not contain this crucial chapter. Mill says in his *Autobiography* that Harriet Taylor 'pointed out the need of such a chapter, and the extreme imperfection of the book without it' (W. Cl., 208). In that case Harriet made a most opportune suggestion, for the chapter is the centre-piece of Mill's New Political Economy.[23]

From the literary point of view it is a failure: it begins strongly with a denunciation of the paternalist view of society, discussed above in connection with Mill's egalitarianism, but tapers off with page after page of minute detail (accumulated through the various editions) of

French and English co-operative ventures. Were it not for the imbalance in its arrangement, the chapter with its conception of a society incorporating the best features of the property system and eliminating all that did not contribute to the extension of citizenship would be one of Mill's best works. As it stands, it is still impressive. J.E. Cairnes summed up the contemporary impression by drawing a contrast between 'the dreariness of the outlook' of the earlier political economists, and the new vision of Mill. 'The celebrated chapter on "The Future of the Industrial Classes". . . it is no exaggeration to say, places a gulf between Mill and all who preceded him, and opens an entirely new vista to economic speculation'.[24]

Assertions that Mill though not a leveller was an egalitarian need to be substantiated with concrete examples: they can be found in the chapter so praised by Cairnes. In that chapter Mill proposed safeguards to counteract tendencies in an egalitarian society towards uniformity, but he also commented adversely on a whole series of inequalities.

He wished to see every man and woman accede to full citizenship, that is to say, become just and self-governing individuals: just, in that they enjoyed exclusively what was due to them for their own exertions and abilities, self-governing in that they freely participated in the political and economic decisions affecting their lives.

The first passage to be noted is not present in the first edition of the *Principles* but was added by Mill in the third [1852]. In it Mill expresses strong disagreement with the class divisions of his time.

When I speak, either in this place or elsewhere, of the 'labouring classes', or of labourers as a 'class', I use those phrases in compliance with custom, and as descriptive of an existing, but by no means necessary or permanent, state of social relations. I do not recognise as either just or salutary, a state of society in which there is any 'class' which is not labouring; any human beings, exempt from bearing their share of the necessary labours of human life, except those unable to labour, or who have fairly earned rest by previous toil ([1852] *Coll. Works*, III, 758 [IV, vii, 1]).

This passage has an old-fashioned ring today. It should be understood in its context. The *rentiers* were a conspicuous feature of the society of his time. Yet he worded the passage so as to give it a wider scope than mere inveighing against the idle rich. He spoke out to disclaim the permanence of class divisions and widened his enquiry from a discussion of the hopes of labour to a discussion of the future of the whole of society, rich and poor, indeed of the whole of humanity.

He thus gave expression to what was implicit in previous editions: that, despite the title of the chapter, he by no means wished to restrict himself to labour questions. Indeed, one of the first topics to which he turned his attention was another kind of inequality which particularly incensed him: the differences made between men and women.

It was within the logic of the Utilitarian position to consider that innate differences were either nonexistent or unimportant. The psychology of the Utilitarians stemmed directly from Helvétius, who insisted on the primordial importance of environment for the formation of character, so that Mill was predisposed to assume that whatever differences could be noticed between men and women at the time were purely the produce of social forces. When he was still a very young man, he, with other young Utilitarians, criticized·James Mill's *Essay on Government* (1824) for maintaining 'that women may consistently with good government, be excluded from the suffrage, because their interest is the same with that of men' (*Autobiography*, W.Cl., 87).

Naturally his acquaintance with Harriet contributed to his feminism. In his *Autobiography* Mill insists that he did not take up the cause of female emancipation under the influence of the woman who was to be his wife; indeed we have seen that he had held these opinions before he met her. But, he adds, 'what is true is, that until I knew her, the opinion was in my mind, little more than an abstract principle,' and this opinion was strengthened not only by the influence of Harriet's ideas on the need to develop one's potentialities to the utmost despite the pressures of society, but mainly by the direct contact with a woman of whose moral and intellectual qualities Mill had such a high opinion.[25]

From then on, Mill found a solid ally in his friend for the battle in favour of feminine emancipation.[26] His first great blow for the cause was in the *Principles*. The gist of his reflections there was that from the purely economic point of view he considered the subjection of women to be pernicious for society, because the dedication of one half of humanity to the reproductive function could only give a strong incentive to inordinate population growth; in the chapter under consideration, he insisted that population growth could not be checked until women were offered alternative occupations if they wished to follow them (*Coll. Works*, III, 765 [IV, vii, 3]).

He carried on the battle to the political field. One of the measures which he mooted in Parliament was that of extending the suffrage to women. His amendment to Disraeli's 1867 Reform Bill in which he did so was expected to receive no more 'than a few stray votes'. He strongly defended it with a temperate speech which brought Bright on to his side, among others. When 'the votes recorded in favour of the motion amounted to 73 — made up by pairs and tellers to above 80, the surprise was general, and the encouragement great' (*Autobiography*, 258).

After he left Parliament, Mill wrote his great manifesto on the question, *The Subjection of Women* (1869). At the time the book caused scandal: witness the words of James Fitzjames Stephen on reading the essay:

> There is something — I hardly know what to call it; indecent is too strong a word, but I may say unpleasant in the direction of indecorum — in prolonged and minute discussions about the relations between men and woman, and the characteristics of women as such.[27]

Today it is the soberness of the argument which strikes one, relying on considerations of expediency rather than on abstract declarations of right, though naturally the moral argument is present in the background lending urgency and power to the discussion. That much of what Mill asserts should seem today natural and uncontroversial is a measure of the success of the feminists of all ages, including Mill: for, though the emancipation of women was as Mill put it, 'in the direction of the best tendencies of the age,' it is far from impossible for such sociological tendencies to be thwarted by deliberate policy.

Thus, with Mill's help, the women's suffrage movement made a strong beginning. Had he not died so early, there is little doubt that votes for women would not have been so long in coming.

Lastly, another great cause defended by Mill throughout his life was that of the total freedom of the slaves. The omission of a discussion of slavery in the chapter under consideration is significant: it is as if Mill had wanted to settle the question by implication, as too obvious to bear discussion when the main topic was the self-government of English wage-earners.

He had adverted to the question of slavery in Book II, on Distribution, as one of the forms of apportioning the ownership of the means of production, restricting himself to the economic aspect of the question. The slave system could be more profitable to the masters than that of hired labour 'so long as slave countries are underpeopled in proportion to their cultivable land' ([1852] *Coll. Works*, II, 246 [II, v, 2]). As for example, in the West Indies, where in his opinion the compensation to slave owners in 1833 did not perhaps offset their loss (249). In other situations, free labour being so much more productive, the owners would gain with the change. In any case, Mill's treatment of the question implied that it was not to be decided on these grounds: 'more needs not be said here on a cause so completely judged and decided as that of slavery' (250).

The abolition of slavery was one of the great achievements of the nineteenth century. Though the freeing of the slaves in the British colonies was obtained in 1833, the battle was by no means totally won.[28] England's mood began to change in the late forties, a reversal which was complete when during the War of Secession virtually the whole of the higher classes sided with the South.[29] Mill never wavered from the course which the Utilitarians had taken during the controversy with the planters in the early thirties, but his attitude was the exception rather than the rule. In 1849, Thomas Carlyle, when considering the effects of the end of slavery in the West Indies, was moved to deprecate the 'rosepink sentimentalism' which had emancipated the slaves, and to advocate the reintroduction of the whip to force the negroes, 'sitting yonder with their beautiful muzzles up to their ears in pumpkin,' back to work.

This was the occasion for Mill to express himself more clearly than in the *Principles*. He answered the ranting of his friend of old with great passion.[30] He opposed the 'gospel of leisure' to Carlyle's 'gospel of work' and maintained 'that human beings *cannot* rise to the finer attributes of their nature compatibly with a life filled with labour.' It was the tendency of 'the progress of science and the increasing ascendancy of justice and good sense' to reduce 'the exhausting, stiffening, stupefying toil of many kinds of agricultural and manufacturing labourers' (28). Carlyle had derided the anxiety of the age to abolish pain. Mill gladly accepted the accusation, indeed asserted that the age was not humane enough: 'can any worthier object of endeavour be pointed out than that of diminishing pain?' (30). His greatest worry was the effect of Carlyle's piece in the United States. Here he showed the first indication of his feelings in the coming great contest of America:

At this crisis of American slavery, when the decisive conflict between right and iniquity seems about to commence, your contributor [he said addressing the editor of the review] steps in, and flings this missile, loaded with the weight of his reputation, into the abolitionist camp (31).

The aim of diminishing pain he had learnt from Bentham and his father, but 'the gospel of leisure' was his own contribution to Utilitarian social philosophy – it indicates in one striking phrase one of the traits of the good society as he conceived it.

The Civil War began. The Northerners seized the British ship *Trent* and brought the two countries to the brink of war. Mill held his peace until the Union's reparations had soothed Britain's ruffled feelings. He then wrote an article 'The Contest in America', in which he came out strongly in support of the North.[31]

He expressed the same opinions in private. His letters of the time are full of the American War. There are numerous letters to Americans deploring the attitude of the British press and governing classes, many of which were published in the American press. He expressed his happiness at Lincoln's anti-slavery proclamation; he was even more cheered by the siding with the North of the British working classes, and especially admired the fact that the agitation should begin in the areas hardest hit by the 'cotton famine'; he deplored the *Alabama* incident; tried to convince Thornton to change sides.[32] Finally he induced Cairnes to make a book of a proposed article about the war (and reviewed it with high praise); almost every letter to Cairnes at that time has an allusion to the war in America.[33]

Years later, when he sat in Parliament, he resoundingly showed his concern for an equal and fair treatment of all individuals, whatever their race, in the affair of the Governor of Jamaica, Edward John Eyre. Mill took the leading part in prosecuting the Governor and his associates for murder during the repression of a revolt in the island of Jamaica: the details of the case will be found in his *Autobiography*. The only point which needs be stressed now is that his role in that affair was one of the main causes of his unpopularity in his last years.

The evidence for Mill's egalitarianism is thus overwhelming. Yet the picture would not be complete if his fears of a mechanical equality were not taken into account: he defended the equality of free citizens not the uniformity of sheep. This fear inspired in him certain reserves concerning the political power gradually being bestowed on the working classes in the last twenty five years of his life. In the chapter of the *Principles* we are now considering he evaded the issue:

The political consequences of the increasing power and importance of the operative classes, and of the growing ascendancy of numbers, which, even [in England and] under the present institutions, is rapidly giving to the will of the majority at least a negative voice in the acts of government, are too wide a subject to be discussed in this place. [34]

But the importance of the question was too great to be left at that, and we must fill in the missing details from other sources where his position is more clearly stated.

For Mill, the people could intervene in government in two equally important ways, through municipal and through national institutions.

In the chapter on *laissez-faire* above, we have seen how great a role a well organized system of local government played in his thought; he expected from it deep educational effects on the mass of the people, a lightening of the task of Parliament, an increase in administrative efficiency without the drawbacks of centralization; and he proposed for its constitution the purely democratic system devised by Bentham. One might say that for Mill municipal government was a *pendant* of co-operation, offering the same opportunities for self-government in the administrative field, as the other in the economic.

In the national field Mill was less fully in favour of unchecked democracy, for in common with many of his contemporaries he feared universal suffrage within the context of a largely uncultivated population. He thus separated himself from orthodox Benthamism and Radicalism (one of whose characteristics was 'an almost unbounded confidence' in the efficacy of representative government) on the question of suffrage, as he did on that of the ballot. The ballot he opposed in his last years, through the confidence he felt that an open vote strengthened the sense of responsibility of the citizens. And as for extending the right to vote, though he accepted universal suffrage, he proposed that its concession should be hedged by important safeguards.

There were two dangers in democracy, he noted in *On Representative Government*:

danger of a low grade of intelligence in the representative body, and in the popular opinion which controls it; and danger of class legislation on the part of the numerical majority, these being composed of the same class. [35]

To counter the first danger and correct 'the natural tendency of representative government, as of modern civilisation. . .towards collective mediocrity' (265) he proposed the device of plural voting. Yet it is very important to stress that he defended the introduction of such a system only when universal suffrage for men and women was instituted. Also, it was not property-owners who were to have a weighted vote, but those having attained a certain level of education. The remedy for the second danger, the way to ensure that 'minorities should be adequately represented', was a plan named after its inventor, a certain Mr Hare: a form of proportional representation with the possibility for the voters to pick people from different lists (so called *panachement*) so that especially distinguished men of national reputation, whose supporters were scattered all over the country rather than concentrated in one constituency, could be elected to Parliament and defend 'opinions and interests which the ascendant public opinion views with disfavour' (268). Further details of these proposals can be found in the pages of *On Representative Government*, where Mill gave them passionate support, but it may be fair to sum them up as the expression of Mill's dislike for the party system.

Once again, there can be no doubt that he was impressed by the popular backing obtained by Louis Napoleon in the plebiscite after his *coup d'état*. In the field of ideas, the influence of three thinkers can be noted: Tocqueville, James Mill, and through the latter, Plato. J.S. Mill himself notes in his *Autobiography* (W.Cl., 162) that the reading of Tocqueville's writings, while confirming him in the appreciation of representative government, made him aware 'of the specific dangers which beset democracy, considered as the government of the numerical majority.' The other two influences must be traced below the surface. As respects James Mill, Dr Hamburger has pointed out in his study of the Radical party, that the former thought all partial interests to be 'sinister' and hence was no lover of party. To this must be added the influence of Plato, inextricably linked with that of James Mill, for

> there is no author to whom my father thought himself more indebted for his own mental culture, than Plato, or whom he more frequently recommended to young students (W.Cl., 18).

Plato, who was the *maître à penser* of many nineteenth century liberals, has, after the revision of Crossman and Popper, a bad reputation today. To think that Mill believed in government by a small *élite*, because he was influenced by Plato in these questions is to simplify matters overmuch. Mill sought, as far as possible, not a republic governed by philosophers, but one composed of philosophers. This was very far from being the case in early Victorian England! It is easy to recommend universal suffrage without qualms after a century or more of experience and with the prospect of seeing the right to vote exercised by a much better educated people. After all it must be remembered that Marx thought that the granting of universal suffrage in England would be a revolutionary measure, making proletarian rebellion unnecessary.

Further, it cannot be over-emphasized that the core of Mill's social philosophy was an ethical view of human problems. He believed the new society to be impossible until a fundamental change had occurred in the moral constitution of individual men and women. This is what led him to question, as no truly orthodox Benthamite would have done, the efficacy of institutional reforms. Thus for example he wrote in a letter of January 1850:

> At present I expect very little from any plans which aim at improving even the economical state of the people by purely economical or political means. We have come, I think, to a period, when progress even of a political kind is coming to a halt, by reason of the low intellectual and moral state of all classes, and of the rich as much as of the poorer classes only. Great improvements in education. . .is the only thing to which I should look for permanent good.[36]

This letter may reflect some of the listlessness of the *temps mort* which preceded Disraeli's Parliamentary Reform of 1867. But even when his faith in political and economic reforms revived, the reliance on a change in the moral disposition of the people, one might even say, a change in human nature, was still of the essence of Mill's hopes for the future. In this, as was noted above, he showed himself close to the Platonic tradition which believes that man must learn to govern himself before governing others. It explains why he was so meticulous as to the means to be adopted to obtain the better society, means which should not 'demoralize' the people, but rather strengthen their independence.

All these remarks should not be interpreted as the unconditional defence of a historian for his favourite author but as an attempt to place Mill's thought within the context of the time and in the line of the political tradition to which he belonged. In his time and within that tradition, Mill was far from being a Tory, or even a 'philosophical conservative'. Mill himself righted his contemporaries on this point. His record in Parliament, he claimed, showed that it was quite wrong to take him as an opponent of democracy merely because he 'was able to see the Conservative side of the question.' When his criticisms led him to propose the establishment of proportional representation, hardly any conservative supported him. Similarly they misunderstood his approval of plural voting:

> it was forgotten that I had made it an express condition that the privilege of a plurality of votes should be annexed to education, not to property, and even so, had approved of it only on the supposition of universal suffrage. How utterly inadmissible such plural voting would be under the suffrage given by the present Reform Act [Disraeli's], is proved. . .by the very small weight which the working classes are found to possess in elections even under the law which gives no more votes to any one elector than to any other.[37]

Rather than bring him to book under the head of egalitarianism, where he was in a stronger position than most of his contemporaries, it would be better to criticize him for his lack of understanding of a party system, or his confidence that intellectual education was a guarantee of good sense.

The Organization of Labour: Co-operation

Having dealt with the political aspects of the kind of society Mill advocated, we must proceed to see how he applied the principles of justice and self-government to that part of men's lives which they spend at work. In 1848 it was still too early to think that co-operation, that is to say, the ownership of the means of production by those who used them in their work, would be a practicable proposition: the French Republic had not been installed, under which most of the earliest experiments in co-operation were carried out; the law in England made it almost impossible for associations to recover the funds defalcated by dishonest officials. It was therefore partnership rather than co-operation which Mill advocated in the first edition.

The wage relationship symbolized for Mill all that was undesirable in the condition of the working class. He could not believe that given an improvement in intelligence and in the arrangements of society, the labouring classes would be content 'with the condition of working for wages as their ultimate state.' In a new country, such as Australia or the United States, there was hope that the labourers could themselves one day become employers: but in an old society (the more so since the Stationary State was imminent) they would have to be labourers for ever.

> To work at the bidding and for the profit of another, without any interest in the work — the price of their labour being adjusted by hostile competition, one side demanding as much and the other paying as little as possible — is not, even when wages are high, a satisfactory state for human beings of educated intelligence, who have ceased to think themselves naturally inferior to those whom they serve.[38]

Thus, the first reason then for Mill's dislike of the wage relationship was that it perpetuated a situation of master and servant in the labour world. The second — also alluded to in the passage above — was that it created a clash of interests between employer and employed, and it inflamed the hostility among the classes.[39] The third and most important, was that it had a demoralizing effect on the working classes. It induced labourers to work as little as possible for as high a wage as they could get, and thus eroded their professional standards.

Mill's dislike of the 'cash-nexus' did not evidence a wish to return to a feudal society, as it did with Carlyle.[40] He advocated its disappearance, not because it made for an impersonal society, but because it tended to perpetuate the division of the possessing from the non-possessing; and because by demoralizing workers, it made their progress more difficult. In 1848, the solution lay in Partnership. This would be a means

> to obtain the efficiency and economy of production on a large scale, without dividing the producers into two parties with hostile interests, employers and employed, the many who do the work being mere servants under the command of the one who supplies the funds, and having no interest of their own in the enterprise except to fulfil their contract and earn their wages ([1848] *Coll. Works*, III, 769 [IV, vii, 4]).

Such a form of participation would give an interest in the enterprise to 'every one who contributes to the work, whether by labour or by pecuniary resources' (III, 1007).

In his article on the Christian Socialists of 1848, Dr John Saville has described the vogue for co-operative ideas among the middle classes in the fifties, encouraged by the experiments in production co-operatives carried out in the early days of the second Republic in France.[41] Mill caught the co-operativist infection and never recovered. In the 1852 edition, he inserted in the latter part of his chapter, a whole new section on co-operation. Partnership was better than the fragmentation of property, but co-operation better than both.

> The form of association [he said] . . .which, if mankind [continue] to improve, must be expected in the end to predominate, is not that which can exist between a capitalist as chief, and workpeople without a voice in the management, but the association of the labourers themselves on terms of equality, collectively owning the capital with which they carry on their operations, and working under managers elected and removable by themselves ([1852] *Coll. Works*, III, 775 [IV, vii, 6]).

The goal to be pursued, proclaimed Mill in a classic definition of the co-operative ideal,

> should be not solely to place human beings in a condition in which they will be able to do without one another, but to enable them to work with or for one another in relations not involving dependence (III, 768 [IV, vii, 4]).

The change in Mill's opinion, from deprecating the co-operative ideas of the Owenites, to advocating co-operation as the solution for the greatest social problems of the age, apparently amounted to a complete *volte-face*. It must be remembered, however, that the main drawback to the Owenite associations was their total rejection of competition; they pretended to enforce complete equality of work and remuneration among the members, thus renouncing the benefits of the division of labour and of differential incentives. The new associations born in France under the Republic had soon abandoned the system of giving 'equal wages whether the work done was more or less' and 'after allowing to everyone a fixed minimum, sufficient for subsistence' apportioned 'all further remuneration according to the work done: most of them even dividing the profits at the end of the year, in the same proportion as the earnings' (*Coll. Works*, III, 782–3 [IV, vii, 6]).

Another reason for scepticism on co-operation disappeared in 1852. In his review of Help's *Claims of Labour* (1845)[42] Mill referred to groups of workers following the advice of a pamphlet of the Society for the Diffusion of Useful Knowledge, to 'make themselves capitalists', 'by bringing their small means into a common fund, by forming a numerous partnership or joint stock'; though the experiment would have been most useful, proceeds Mill, 'it was found that the defects of the law of partnership. . .presented difficulties rendering it impracticable to give this experiment a fair trial' (385). He urged Parliament to change the law. This was not done until 1852, owing to the efforts of the Christian Socialists, as Dr Saville has shown. Mill helped with his declarations before the 'Select Committee on Investments for the Savings of the Middle and Working Classes' (1850) (*Coll. Works*, V). In a letter to Professor Rau of 7 July, 1852, he explained what those defects were.

> Much could not be done while the law of partnership remained what it was up to a few days ago. According to that absurd law, the managing members of an association, being the joint owners of its funds, could not steal or embezzle what was partly their own, and could not be made criminally responsible for any malversation.

In that letter, however, and despite the change in the law, Mill showed himself sceptical about the possibility that these associations should come into existence in England in the near future; but 'in France the success of the associations has been remarkable, and holds out the brightest prospects for the emancipation of the working classes.'[43]

The success of the Rochdale pioneers completed his conversion to the new form of association. In 1862 Mill inserted in the *Principles* a detailed account of the fortunes of this co-operative. However, he did not approve uncritically of all the decisions of the English co-operators. In a speech to the London Society for Promoting Co-operation,[44] he deplored the recent decision of the Rochdale society to restrict full membership to those who had subscribed capital.

> It is not genuine Co-operation where any of the producers are excluded from the profits. So long as this is the case, nothing more is effected than to take a few working people out of their own class and transform them into employers of labour.

The aim of Co-operation should not be 'to benefit a few, but to elevate the whole of the working class.' He staked great hopes on the new movement. The masses of the people, he said, were in a degraded state, 'only fit to be receivers of wages.' The spread of co-operation must effect a moral revolution, transforming the dishonest, the idle, the intemperate, the spendthrift, into different men; and affecting even the capitalists themselves, who

> will be ashamed to be the only persons who do not take their share in the useful work of the world, and will be willing to invest their capital in co-operative societies, receiving a fair interest for its use. This is the millennium towards which we should strive.

He summed up: 'I. . .feel assured that co-operation will ultimately regenerate the masses of this country, and through them society itself.'

It is important to underline that his doctrine was not the same as that of the Christian Socialists. Dr Saville has described the blend of inflammatory language with conservative ideology of most Christian Socialists; they tried to steal the thunder from Chartism by rejecting the principle of competition and seeking to restore a paternal-filial relationship with the leaders of society, especially between the aristocracy and the people. However with the co-operative social organization Mill advocated, he wished neither to eliminate competition nor consolidate class differences.

On the question of paternalism enough has been said in previous pages. The point of competition must be stressed. Mill himself drew attention repeatedly to the fact that his idea of co-operation was different from that of most of the socialists of his time. He wanted competition within the co-operatives, so that reward should be commensurate to the contribution of each, and competition among co-operatives, so that the public be protected from inefficiency. In the third edition of the *Principles* [1852], where he introduced the discussion of co-operation into his treatise, he closed the chapter On the Probable Futurity of the Labouring Classes with a new section containing a defence of competition; he 'endeavoured [one could read in the Preface]. . .to disconnect the co-operative cause from the exaggerated or altogether mistaken declamations against competition, so largely indulged in by its supporters.' In the new section he stated:

> I agree, then, with the Socialist writers in their conception of the form which industrial operations tend to assume in the advance of improvement. . . But while I agree and sympathise with Socialists in this practical portion of their aims, I utterly dissent from the most conspicuous and vehement part of their teaching, their declamations against competition. . . They forget that wherever competition is not, monopoly is; and that monopoly, in all its forms, is the taxation

of the industrious for the support of indolence, if not of rapacity ([1852] *Coll. Works*, III, 794 [IV, vii, 7]).

Many existing social evils (he proceeded) which are laid at the door of competition, are due to other causes, such as over-population. And those evils which competition undoubtedly causes, such as jealousy and hostility, are a worthwhile price to pay for the benefits it confers. 'Competition may not be the best conceivable stimulus, but it is at present a necessary one, and no one can foresee the time when it will not be indispensable to progress' (III, 795). As the attack on competition was the central element of the socialist case against the existing economic order, such an addition as that of the section on competition just after the new defence of co-operation, can only be interpreted in the sense that Mill wished to underline the differences between his own brand of co-operation and that of the socialists (Christian or otherwise).

In a letter which Mill wrote to Harriet in 1854 there is a direct reference to the Christian socialists. He expresses his surprise that a group of socialists should make no objection to this section on competition when asking permission to reprint the chapter on Futurity in pamphlet form. 'I did not expect the Xtian Socialists would wish to circulate the chapter as it is in the 3rd edit. since it stands up for Competition against their one-eyed attacks & denunciations of it'.[45]

On the other hand, this declaration perhaps enables us to understand the significance of the phrase 'under the general denomination of socialists' we quoted at the beginning of Chapter 7. The phrase was in all likelihood written two years after the third edition had been published, that is to say, in 1854.[46] What Mill specifically wished to indicate then, one may surmise, was that he and his wife agreed with the socialists on the value of co-operatives, but could not go along with them in their criticism of competition.

The belief that co-operation is imperfect without competition is central to Mill's social doctrine. Mill, by attempting to combine competition and co-operation, endeavoured to transform the property system, without subverting it, to such an extent that it should retain its good qualities while acquiring some of the more desirable traits of 'socialism', namely, a greater equality among, and fairness towards, individuals.

Public Activity in Mill's Last Years
Mill's public life in his last years gives us the opportunity of observing

how he defended in practice the doctrines he had advanced in theory in the works we have just analysed. The completion of *A System of Logic* (1843) had brought to a close the first stage of Mill's active participation in the political life of the country.[47] During the next twenty-two years he was mainly occupied in composing speculative works; in fact, that was his sole occupation on leaving India House. His 'tranquil and retired existence as a writer of books', however, did not prevent him from taking part in the polemical debates of the day, such as when he took up the defence of the East India Company before its extinction or championed the North in the American Civil War. The authority he enjoyed as author of the *Logic*ʾ and above all, of the *Principles*, assured him of a hearing and his influence was much greater than as a leader of the little band of philosophic Radicals in the twenties.

In 1865, by standing as a candidate for a seat in the constituency of Westminster, Mill began the second stage of active participation in politics. Even a short review of Mill's activity as a parliamentarian shows that he went against the grain of received opinion. 'Mill never conservatized', as Dicey said.[48]

To begin with, the conditions under which he agreed to present his candidacy were quite unprecedented. He refused to canvass for votes, nor incur any expenses. If he were elected, he said, he would not concern himself with local questions. Only a few days before the election was he persuaded to expound his ideas in two speeches, in which he let it be known what points he would defend in Parliament, particularly the concession of votes for women. Mill relates how the comment was overheard that 'the Almighty himself would have no chance of being elected on such a programme' (*Autobiography*, W.Cl., 240): nevertheless, he was returned.

In Parliament his main concern, though he may not have been fully aware of it, was to avoid acting as a party man. It is true that he admired Gladstone and would not have chosen any other leader to follow. During the latter part of Gladstone's government, he faithfully supported the liberal position — it was Mill who gave the Tories the *sobriquet* of 'the stupid party', adding, moreover, that he did not mean that all the Tories were stupid, but that all the stupid were conservatives. There is, however, a very revealing phrase in his description of his electoral campaign; he says that he 'did not choose to stand as the mere organ of a party' (*Autobiography*, W.Cl., 237). In the House of Commons he acted on the idea that 'when anything was likely to be as well done, or sufficiently well done, by other people, there was no necessity for me to meddle with it.' He came to regret his over-specialization in unpopular causes, for when his position in the House was secure, he says, 'I confined myself, as I have since thought too much, to occasions on which my services seemed specially needed, and abstained more than enough from speaking on the great party questions' (*Autobiography*, W.Cl., 245). This neglect of party issues, this desire to serve only the public interest and not any sectional or class interest, had been as we noted above, typical of James Mill and the philosophic Radicals of the twenties. J.S. Mill took up the same position again: he was the Platonic philosopher who defended unpopular truths in the popular Parliament.

One of his main themes was Ireland. His first vote in the Commons was in support of a motion put forward by an Irish member, and his second speech was attacking the Government's intention to prolong the suspension of *Habeas Corpus* in Ireland, 'denouncing, on this occasion, the English mode of governing Ireland.' It was not exactly the most propitious moment for such a speech, for public opinion was alarmed by the terrorism of the Fenians. His intervention met with such hostility that Mill kept silence during some time. In the three Parliamentary sessions during which he was a Member, Mill attacked the Irish problem a number of times, giving proof of a true understanding of the desires of the peasantry in that island which Professor Black has so justly praised. Ireland wanted to obtain the 'disestablishment' of the Church of England and 'tenant rights'. The second point, that is, the agricultural worker's security of tenure, indemnification for improvements, and rent reviews, was the one that met with most difficulties and Mill returned to the subject again and again. As a summary of his ideas he published a pamphlet, *England and Ireland* (1868), the leading features of which were

> on the one hand, an argument to show the undesirableness, for Ireland as well as for England, of separation between the countries, and on the other, a proposal for settling the land question by giving to the existing tenants a permanent tenure, at a fixed rent, to be assessed after due inquiry by the State (*Autobiography*, W.Cl., 249).

Such an infraction of property rights was unacceptable to both landowners and English public opinion alike. Mill continues: 'The pamphlet was not popular, except in Ireland, as I did not expect it to be.' But his own extremism made the measure Gladstone proposed in the next Parliament seem moderate by comparison, and it was accepted, though hindsight makes it clear that nothing less than what Mill proposed could have solved the problem. Mill's services to the Irish cause did not end there. In his *Autobiography* there is an allusion to the fact that Mill helped to obtain a pardon for the Fenians in 1867; but a more complete account is to be found in Mr Packe's biography. It is easy to understand Mill's popularity in Ireland.

Another important issue Mill debated in the Commons was electoral reform. His participation had three main objectives: to enlarge the working class vote, to extend it to women, and to introduce the plural vote. 'With regard to the working classes,' Mill says describing his first steps in Parliament, 'the chief topic of my speech on Mr Gladstone's Reform Bill was the assertion of their claims to the suffrage' (245). Gladstone's government fell, and Disraeli presented in his turn a proposed law to extend the suffrage. Mill put forward two amendments: one on personal or proportional representation, and the other, votes for women. Both questions we have touched on earlier. Here we need only stress his special relationship with the London working classes, on occasions even literally acting as their spokesman. The *Autobiography* recounts the most important moments, from the time during his electoral campaign when he won the applause of a working-class gathering by frankly admitting that he had written that English workmen were generally liars, to his defence of the right of assembly in speakers' corner in Hyde Park. Nor should we forget that those were precisely the years in which the issue of trade unions was being debated and which for Mill culminated in his recantation of the wages fund doctrine which we have studied in an earlier chapter.

Finally, attention should be drawn to a whole set of initiatives taken to protect the rights of the individual in the face of public authorities. The one that caused most commotion and contributed most to his failure to win re-election was the affair of Governor Eyre. He also played an important part in defeating the plan to allow extradition of political refugees. As a counterweight, there is his defence of capital punishment, which reminds us of Mill's view that the individual's rights were inseparable from a strict interpretation of his responsibilities.

These are only a few of the hundred and forty odd times Mill intervened during his three sessions as a member of Parliament; they would seem to support the view that Mill did not follow a middle course, an easy eclecticism among the popular trends of the day, but that he kept within a strict code of ideas that shocked his contemporaries, one of radical or egalitarian individualism. It was not for nothing that he was under attack from the great conservative and liberal press, right up to the end of his days and even on the occasion of his death, for having shown himself 'in the trials of public life, intemperate and passionate.'[49]

Losing his seat in a year of Liberal victory, Mill returned to private life with relief, but he was now a political figure who could not entirely escape public activity. In 1869 he was offered the Presidency of the Land Tenure Reform Association. Mill drew up the Association's programme and statement of aims, which, indeed, were very Millian. The objective was to achieve the following reforms: abolition of all impediments to the transmission of landed property, including entails; the taxation of the unearned increments in rent from land; the use of public lands to set up agricultural co-operatives and peasant proprietors and to build workers' dwellings; preservation of the commons; and the concession of powers to the State for the conservancy of properties possessing special interest or beauty. Only perhaps the mention of workers' dwellings is one not usually encountered in Mill's works. When we think that he even contemplated the possibility of nationalizing the land (with compensation), we can see that Mill's radicalism had lost none of its vigour with the passing of the years.[50]

Conclusion

At the beginning of this chapter two queries were made. The first was whether a unifying principle could be found in Mill's work, which made his vision of the future society a viable intellectual construction. There can be no doubt that the unifying principle is there. We have seen how he proposed to reform the property system by removing two of its characteristics incompatible with a justification of the system on the basis of personal effort: entail and inheritance. Next, it has been shown how he transformed the Ricardian conception of the stationary state into a potentially happy one, where men cease to accumulate material wealth and devote themselves to the cultivation of their higher faculties; and finally, how he formulated the ideal of a society based on justice and individuals' self-government. All this responds to a unitary vision resulting from an individualistic social philosophy based on equality and responsibility. The same vision directs the application of these principles, presented in the chapter On the Probable Futurity of the Labouring Classes and later writings: the refusal to accept class divisions, the protest against the subjection of women, the total repudiation of slavery, the extension of the franchise to the working classes (with the safeguards of a proportional electoral system, *panachement* and plural voting for the educated), the transformation of the economic system, especially through an extension of co-operation. Indeed, co-operation fitted in perfectly with his whole doctrine of how to achieve the good society. From the moral point of view, since the establishment of a co-operative was usually the result of the unaided efforts of its members, it strengthened the qualities of self-reliance and foresight of the individuals involved, the running of it taught them the virtues of self-government, and of a freely accepted discipline and collaboration, together with the habit of continued and regular work. From the point of view of justice, each received, better than in any other system, the due reward for his abilities and exertions. From the economic angle, the advantages of large-scale enterprises were combined with the incentives of diffused property. From the social and political viewpoint, co-operation broke down the barriers between capitalists and workers, increased the intelligent participation of all in communal affairs, and transformed the citizenry so deeply that the ideals of democracy could be effectually realized without the possible drawbacks of popular government. His defence of co-operation was the keystone of his moral, economic, social and political opinions, crowning and sustaining the whole. Mill, in sum, wanted to see the establishment of a society of free, equal and responsible individuals.

The second query we posed is harder to answer. It comes down to whether Mill's vision was a realistic one, viable in practice. Time has given a part of the answer. The stationary state, happy or unhappy, that Mill foresaw has not arrived nor does it show any signs of arriving. And this reveals a basic defect in the Millian system, an incapacity to understand the dynamism of the capitalist system, which for better or for worse has turned out very different from what Mill expected. In the words of the originator of another great dynamic system of thought, 'what earlier century had even a presentiment that such productive forces slumbered in the lap of social labour?' What Marx, the other disciple of Ricardo, thus revealed in the *Communist Party Manifesto*, the growth potential, the capacity for transforming the world that capitalism carried within it, went unguessed at by Mill.[51]

Another unrealistic element in Mill's thought is his conception of social conflict. It is not necessary to believe that 'the history of all hitherto existing society is the history of class struggles,' in order to uphold the superiority of Marx's view of society in this respect, over

Mill's. The belief, rooted in philosophic radicalism, that an adequate institutional framework could guarantee a government motivated only by the public interest, that the existence of parties, particularly if based on class interests, was in some way a corruption of the ideal system, led Mill to overestimate the possibilities of reconciling social antagonisms.[52]

This fundamental apoliticism (which underlay the political attitudes Mill adopted and gave them their extremist character, that of refusing to 'play the game') contributed to Mill's confidence in the co-operative system and its power to transform society. Marx underlined the apolitical nature of the upper classes' co-operative convictions. He too believed that co-operativism would be the economic form of society once capitalism had disappeared. That is why he insisted with characteristic violence on the difference between his kind of co-operativism and that so much in vogue at the time. In the *Address and Provisional Rules of the Working Men's International Association* (1864) we can read:

> The experience of the period from 1848 to 1864 has proved beyond doubt that, however excellent in principle and however useful in practice, co-operative labour, if kept within the narrow circle of the casual efforts of private workmen, will never be able to arrest the growth in geometrical progression of monopoly, to free the masses, nor even to perceptibly lighten the burden of their miseries.

The upper classes' interest in co-operation is deceptive, he adds.

> It is perhaps for this very reason that plausible noblemen, philanthropic middle class spouters, and even keen political economists, have all at once turned nauseously complimentary to the very co-operative labour system they had vainly tried to nip in the bud by deriding it as the utopia of the dreamer, or stigmatising it as the sacrilege of the socialist.

Applied to Mill these words would be unjust, but at bottom Marx was right when he asserted in conclusion that what these people he attacked had lost sight of was that 'to conquer political power has therefore become the great duty of the working class.' That is to say, either co-operation should be carried out nationally, dislodging the owners of the means of production from their positions of power, or it would fail irremediably.[53]

Granting these criticisms of Mill's hopes that a co-operative social organization could be gradually and peacefully substituted for the capitalist system there remains the particularly attractive and topical proposal of combining co-operation with free competition. The only instance in the world today is that of Yugoslavia, without any imitators among those countries qualified for such a step through having first effected the necessary political revolution.[54] Doctrinally speaking however, there have been and still are many men who would support the setting up of a co-operative social organization (among them we should have to count Marx, though he would have preferred planning to market mechanisms). There are many today who are dissatisfied with the incomplete democracy existing in the advanced countries, where a people bent upon their private affairs abandon the direction of society both in its political and its economic aspects to the ruling few. Particularly interesting in this respect is Mr Bottomore's essay *Elites and Society* (1964). Mr Bottomore quotes Alfred Marshall as a forerunner of the position he defends. The ideal of a classless society, he argues (139) can be found in Marshall's short essay, 'The Future of the Working Class' (1873).

Marshall's argument is that the increase of leisure in modern society offers an opportunity for the disappearance of the difference between the workman and the gentleman; the machine will do away with the brutalizing influence of mere physical drudgery: if the scope of education is drastically extended, the new leisured classes can be integrated into cultured society.[55]

Marshall invoked Mill's chapter 'On the Probable Futurity of the Labouring Classes' as his guiding light at the beginning of the Essay, and, indeed, devised a similar title for it, but he was further away from Mill (and Mr Bottomore) than such an invocation might lead one to expect. Marshall was advocating a wide increase in education so that the leisure which was coming for the working classes be put to its best use. Mill and Mr Bottomore also proclaimed the gospel of leisure in a classless society. But they go further, where Marshall perhaps would not have followed them: they advocate steps for the creation of a self-governing society, where the important political and economic decisions would be taken, not only in the last resort, but in their day to day management, by the self-governing citizens in active co-operation.

We might ask if this is not over optimistic. As Mr Edmund Wilson expressed it in a postcript to his book *To the Finland Station* (1940):

What we now know invariably happens when the poor and illiterate people of a modern industrial society first master advanced techniques and improve their standard of living, is that they tend to exhibit ambitions and tastes which Karl Marx would have regarded as bourgeois.[56]

Experience seems to show that the great majority of people wish to escape the responsibilities of power, and the need for taking important decisions; they feel however uneasily that they have no time for social matters and are pre-eminently interested in their personal life and the life of their own small group rather than in the affairs of the community.

Such an attitude is one which Mill hoped to see disappear especially under its form of money-making, for it was incompatible with the effective implementation of his co-operative ideals, and with a higher employment of the human faculties. Whether Mill's hopes sprang from an over-intellectualized view of human nature, or whether they truly indicate a viable path for the transformation of society, is one of the great social questions of the present, as it was of the, nineteenth century.

We are not at liberty to play chess games, or exercise ourselves upon subtleties that lead nowhere. It is well for the young to enjoy the mere pleasure of action, physical or intellectual. But the time presses; the responsibility on us is heavy.

Alfred Marshall

Chapter 9 Conclusion: Where Mill Failed and Where He Succeeded

In the Introduction queries were raised as to the value of Mill's work as an economist. Under question were his philosophical position in relation to that of his father and Bentham; and granting, as one must, his consistency and originality as an economist, the success and significance of his endeavour to frame a new political economy, different from that of Ricardo. Now that the most important points in his theory of economic and social policy have been examined it is possible to venture some reply to those queries.

Concerning his general philosophic position in relation to his two mentors, the inescapable conclusion is that he did not manage to gain sufficient independence from their teaching. He was indelibly marked by the education he had received. On a conscious level, John Stuart Mill tried to reshape Bentham's and James Mill's doctrines and face them objectively. He had no compunction in alienating the Benthamites or the Radicals through his connections with other schools of thought. But in spite of the painful experience of his mental crisis there never took place in him that emancipation on the deeper levels of his personality which would have enabled him to carry out this work of intellectual revision. The mental crisis was followed by a period of estrangement from the Utilitarian school, but in his mature years Mill returned to the beliefs of his youth, though now endowed with an intellectual and emotional equipment that his father and Bentham had lacked.

Let us turn to his contribution as an economist. His attitude to Ricardo is of paramount importance here, as curiously enough, is that towards Harriet Taylor. In questions of economics, Mill tried both to maintain Ricardo's theoretical schema, and modify its practical conclusions. This meant that he patched up the theory where it showed the passage of time, and changed the practical import of the theoretical model by making different assumptions from those of Ricardo and giving entrance in the economic argument to political and ethical considerations. This work of conservation in the analytical field, and modification in the practical, is a peculiarity of John Stuart Mill's, and I do not think it has been attempted by any of the dominant figures of the science. It is therefore worth looking at a little more closely.

Hugh Dalton thought he could explain Mill's failure to produce a new theory of wages by Mill's respect for 'the wrong opinions of dead men,' and by the fact that at sixty-three 'he was past constructive mental work'.[1] The truth of the matter may be a little more complicated than that.

The psychological explanations that account fully for his fundamental fidelity to Benthamism are less adequate to explain the persistence of Ricardian analysis in his doctrine; indeed, not even in *Essays on Some Unsettled Questions of Political Economy*, when his reaction against his father and Bentham's thought was at its most extreme, does he show any sign of departing very far from theoretical Ricardianism.

One should rather look at his conception of science than at his subservience towards his father, to understand why he thought that the Ricardian analytical fabric could be left to stand virtually intact and that it was worth while to employ his great analytical faculties in correcting the defects of Ricardian analysis. Today, scientific advance is usually described not inductively, but in terms of hypothesis and *refutation*; hence a conservative attitude is held to be the worst enemy of progress. In an inductivist age, and for a positivist philosopher, as in the last count Mill was, the situation was very different: progress came not through refutation of hypotheses, but through accumulation of factual knowledge. Mill had learnt in Comte that the history of science could be divided into three periods: the first was an era of mythical explanations; the second metaphysical; the third an age of construction. Thus, once humanity was purged of its prejudices, science could grow steadily by accumulation, each scientist adding a storey to the edifice initiated by his predecessors. Comte (and sometimes even Mill) believed that a time would come when the roof would be reached, the house completed and truth attained. It has been observed that Mill, who was very modest for himself, made high claims for the attainments of his century. The idea that the theories of gifted economists like Ricardo could need a fundamental revision was alien to his idea of the cumulative growth of science. In 1873, in a conversation to which we shall return below, Mill felt able to tell Laveleye: 'the investigations of pure economics are almost completed,'[2] an echo of that notorious earlier statement, so derided by Jevons, in the first edition of the *Principles*: 'Happily, there is nothing in the laws of Value which remains for the present or any future writer to clear up; the theory of the subject is complete' (III, i, 1).

Comte also influenced Mill in another direction. He did not manage to persuade him to abandon all endeavours to frame an economic doctrine independently of a general sociology, but he strengthened his desire to add to the study of economic questions 'some of their applications to social philosophy.' On this point also the Comtian seed fell on fertile ground. Adam Smith had attempted something of the sort, under the influence of the natural law tradition, seventy years before. But above all (and here psychology steps in once more) Mill was influenced by another person very important in his emotional life — Harriet Taylor. Throughout this book we have come across instances of her sometimes regrettable influence, and now we shall consider its general character. Mill says in his *Autobiography*,

> What was abstract and purely scientific was generally mine; the properly human element came from her: in all that concerned the application of philosophy to the exigencies of human society and progress, I was her pupil, alike in boldness of speculation and cautiousness of practical judgment (W.Cl., 210).

Thus his wife was one of the forces that impelled him to stress the practical side, the institutional framework and political consequences, of economics. We have noted how he stressed her contribution to the crucial distinction between laws of production and laws of distribution. Though he surely exaggerated her part in inventing the distinction, she must have made some contribution on this point, perhaps by hailing as a discovery what she had heard him say *en passant*. Whether exact on all details or not, the well known passage in the *Autobiography* where he speaks about her role in the composition of the *Principles*, does show that at least she reinforced his interest in applied economics.

> The purely scientific part of the Political Economy I did not learn from her; but it was chiefly her influence that gave to the book that

general tone by which it is distinguished from all previous expositions of Political Economy that had any pretension to being scientific, and which has made it so useful in conciliating minds which those previous expositions had repelled. This tone consisted chiefly in making the proper distinction between the laws of the Production of Wealth. . .and the modes of its Distribution (W.Cl., 208–9).

A last factor, particularly relevant in the case of an economist, must be taken into account: Mill was no mathematician, either by training or, which is more important, by inclination. Due to this fact, he resisted the trend towards the formalization of economic knowledge (the same happened to him in logic). This is of great moment, not only because generally speaking economics have proved to be peculiarly well adapted to mathematical treatment, but because at that concrete juncture in the development of economic science, a mathematical presentation was well apt to show the points where the Ricardian model should be conceived as a particular case, and those where it could be generalized, a task at which the young Marshall was working in those years for his own use. Mill cut himself off from this evolution, however. On 5 December 1871, he wrote to Cairnes:

I have not seen Mr. Jevons' book, but as far as I can judge from such notices of it as have reached me, I do not expect that I shall think favourably of it. He is a man of some ability, but he seems to me to have a mania for encumbering questions with useless complications, and with a notation implying the existence of greater precision in the data than the questions admit of. His speculations on Logic, like those of Boole and De Morgan, and some of those of Hamilton, are infected in an extraordinary degree with this vice. It is one predominantly at variance with the wants of the time, which demand that scientific deductions should be made as simple and as easily intelligible as they can be made without ceasing to be scientific.[3]

Such a resistance to applying an exact treatment to matters which at first sight could not bear it, can perhaps be explained by the fact that Mill had witnessed two or three failures in this field: Bentham's felicific calculus, Ricardo's strong cases and numerical examples, and Malthus's unhappy use of arithmetical and geometrical progressions in his theory of Population; they conceivably gave rise to the repugnance Mill felt for all such 'chess games'.

His lack of interest in questions of pure analysis was strongest in his last years. In the 1873 conversation with Lavelèye, after the sentence quoted earlier, Mill proceeded to tell his Belgian correspondent where he thought economists should turn their attention when pure analysis had been almost completed:

> We ought to betake our investigations to that region, so vast and so little explored, of the relations of ethics, and especially of law, with economics.[4]

Yet already in 1852 he was writing to Professor Rau:

> I confess that I regard the purely abstract investigations of political economy (beyond those elementary ones which are necessary for the correction of mischievous prejudices), as of very minor importance compared with the great practical questions which the progress of democracy and the spread of Socialist opinions are pressing on, and for which both the governing and the governed classes are very far from being in a fit state of preparation.[5]

Having discussed Mill's relations to his teachers and analysed his aims as an economic thinker, we still have two points on which to conclude: how far were his endeavours successful and what do they signify in the history of economic doctrine.

His 'new political economy' concentrated on four themes: trade unions, *laissez-faire*, socialism, and the future society. We can now attempt to weigh up his achievement in each one.

Mill failed in the matter of trade unions, but the explanation usually given for his failure must be rejected; it is not true that Mill shut the eyes of his reason to follow the promptings of his heart. He failed first because, like many other radicals of his time, he did not think the problem important; in his early years, all his attention was focused on the control of population, and in his later years all his hopes were banked on co-operation, whose triumph would make the trade unions obsolete. Secondly, he failed because in the years of his recantation of the wages fund theory he showed that lack of the urge to theorize that we have discussed above.

In the matter of trade unions Mill was not misled by partiality, he failed by default.

On the question of State intervention, by contrast, he was successful both theoretically and practically. Not only was he able to incorporate ideas from the most different quarters (such as the Utilitarian demand for State efficiency and the Tocquevillian fear of centralization) and take into account new social developments (such as the growth of public administration and the spread of democracy), but more, he did so by inventing a new tool for the theory of economic policy, a systematic conception of the defects of the market mechanism. Though the needs of the present day demand important modifications in Mill's doctrine, it must be considered an achievement of the highest order, and, hence, a triumph for his 'new political economy'.

Even more perhaps than in the case of *laissez-faire*, historical changes have made Mill's discussion of socialism incomplete. The brand of socialism which he thought could be dismissed in a few lines, revolutionary State socialism, has become the most important manifestation of the creed. With regard to Utopian socialism, Mill was primarily interested in its individualistic aspects, though the understanding he showed toward these doctrines must be valued as·a convincing proof of his openness of mind and willingness to listen to opinions coming from the most diverse of sources.

Finally, his conception of the Future Society in the opinion of some shows a Utopian character and a misunderstanding of the true nature of capitalism which diminish its usefulness as a guide for action. Nevertheless, the ideal of a society of equal, free and just individuals, politically and economically self-governing, is very far from outdated, as is shown by the widespread resentment of the bureaucratic character of modern industrial society.

From the point of view of the history of economic analysis, Mill may not have attained the very first rank, but he certainly has a right to a prominent place. The refusal to formalize economic science and concentrate his energies on theoretical investigations is no doubt to be regretted, especially considering his proved analytical gifts. By refusing to take part in the criticism of Ricardian analysis, Mill remained a disciple of Ricardo, but he certainly was the most outstanding. Mill crowns an era in economic thought.

However, it would be a mistake to judge Mill's significance only by his contribution to analysis. From the point of view of the history of economic doctrines in the wider sense, Mill cannot be overlooked. His aim, and one in which he was largely successful, was to restore Adam Smith's concept of a broad political economy, which instead of confining itself within the limits of a narrow professionalism would use economic knowledge to interpret and change society. The liberal tradition is at present undergoing a searching reappraisal, but as long as economists concern themselves with the problems of freedom and the role of the individual in an industrial society, something will be learnt from John Stuart Mill.

Appendix 1 Some Opinions of Mill as an Economist

This Appendix is an extended footnote to an assertion made in Chapter 1. It was noted there that the twin accusations of unoriginality and inconsistency levelled against Mill's economic thought became the by-word of economists, especially but not exclusively outside Britain. Some of the evidence for this assertion is marshalled below.

Thus, though Bagehot and Ingram were among the first to attack Mill on those counts (see Chapter 1, note 1), it was mainly abroad that the stereotype was created. Superficial knowledge of English political economy undoubtedly contributed. N.K. Bunge, Professor of Political Economy at St Petersburg University, in 'J. Stuart Mill envisagé comme économiste', *Esquisses de littérature politico-économique* (1898, though the essay was first published in 1868), thought Mill to have been fundamentally inconsistent. For the American R.T. Ely, in *The Past and Present of Political Economy* (1884), Mill as an economist was a 'trimmer' (p.42). Maurice Block, in *Les progrès de la science économique depuis Adam Smith* (1890), did not think that Mill shone as an economist. J. Rambaud, in his *Histoire des doctrines économiques* (1889), quoted Block's opinion with approval. Luigi Cossa, in *Introduzione allo studio dell'Economia Politica* (3rd ed, 1892) concurred in the opinion that Mill was inconsistent (p.349). Finally, Charles Gide's treatment in *A History of Economic Doctrines* (1915), by C. Gide and C. Rist, was sympathetic but not very illuminating.

I unfortunately do not know German, but it is likely that criticism in that country should have been as harsh as elsewhere, it being the home of the historical school. Marx, though, as Bela Balassa has shown, he was unfair to Mill, excluded him from the category of the vulgar apologists.

Worthy of separate mention is E. Cannan's book, *Theories of Production and Distribution* (1898), which, though unduly severe upon Mill and the whole of the classical school, has the merit of inaugurating the tradition of writing the history of economic doctrines from the point of view of pure analysis, which has been continued by F. Knight, J.A. Schumpeter, and Mark Blaug, among others.

The *cliché* is still current among living writers. To cite only two: Mr R.K. Lekachman, in his *A History of Economic Ideas* (1959), feels that he can say: 'Mill's position could scarcely strike anyone in the 1950's as consistent. Its humanitarianism was crippled by a view of the market directly opposed to it. The drive toward equality foundered on the rock of competition. Mill's concrete solutions were Utopian. However, if to be modern is to be torn between alternative goods and to be aware of some of life's complexities, Mill was a modern' (p.197). Another is Professor E. Roll who shows sympathy to Mill, but unfortunately repeats the usual commonplaces about him. See his *History of Economic Thought* (3rd ed, 1954), where after saying that Mill 'was not original as an economist', he asserts that 'his significance lies precisely in the fact that he was able to make eclecticism in theory and compromise in politics into something like a generally accepted system of impressive quality' (p.354). Professor Roll concludes: 'Mill's search for a compromise in the field of economic theory was less successful than in the field of social philosophy and public policy. It left far too many logical inconsistencies to serve as an adequate complement to the philosophy of compromise and steady reform' (366).

The more acceptable opinions of Marshall, Ashley, and Edgeworth have been noted in Chapter One, as have the efforts of Professor Hayek, Schumpeter, and Professor Stigler to rehabilitate Mill. These points need not be rehearsed here. It remains only to say that, surprisingly, there is no systematic study of Mill's theory of social and economic policy. On this point only three works can be mentioned. The first is that of Leo Rogin. His approach is better than most. By taking as a starting point for the interpretation of the history of economic doctrines 'the hypothesis that new systems first emerge in the guise of arguments in the context of social reform', he was able to give its due to the policy side of Mill's economics. One need not agree with Rogin's theory as an explanation of the growth of the whole of economics, to see that it fitted the case of John Mill tolerably well. Still, his treatment of Mill is not deep and systematic enough. (See L. Rogin, *The Meaning and Validity of Economic Theory* (1950), esp. xiii and 280–331.) The second work is Lord Robbins's *The Theory of Economic Policy in English Classical Political Economy* (1953). As the title indicates, it deals with the whole of the classical school and does not, therefore, make an exhaustive study of Mill. However, the paragraphs on Mill, and especially the study of Mill's attitude to socialism, form an inestimable guide to anyone approaching the subject for the first time. Last, is the interesting work of the late A.L. Harris, *Economics and Social Reform* (1958), who, though he started out from different premises, reached conclusions on Mill very like mine.

Appendix 2 The Diabolical Handbills

In the issue of Sunday, 11 September 1825, the editor of the *Trades' News-paper and Mechanics' Weekly Journal* asked indignantly:

> Was it the author of the 'Illustrations and Proofs', who employed certain young gentlemen (only think of employing *young* gentlemen on such a mission) to hand about at market time among the wives and daughters of mechanics and tradesmen, copies of one or other of the productions aforesaid, and which young gentlemen were, for their pains, dragged by an indignant crowd before a Magistrate, and held to bail, (though by some well understood manoeuvring, never brought to trial) for their misdemeanour?[1]

The author of the 'Illustrations and Proofs' was none other than Francis Place. The productions alluded to are apparently the diabolical handbills. And one of the young gentlemen was no doubt J.S. Mill.

The events to which the journal referred had occurred several years earlier. It is impossible to determine the date exactly, but it was most likely in the summer of 1823, when Mill was seventeen years old.[2] Nor is it known for certain who wrote the handbills,[3] though Place was responsible for their printing and distribution. J.S. Mill's arrest is known through some disclosures made immediately after his death, disclosures which we shall deal with later. The texts of the diabolical handbills are the following (the originals are to be found in vol. 61 of the Place Papers, *British Museum*, on the pages corresponding to August, 1825):

**TO THE
MARRIED OF BOTH SEXES
OF THE
WORKING PEOPLE**

This paper is addressed to the reasonable and considerate among you, the most numerous and most useful class of society.

It is not intended to produce vice and debauchery, but to destroy vice, and put an end to debauchery.

It is a great truth, often told and never denied, that when there are too many working people in any trade or manufacture, they are worse paid than they ought to be paid, and are compelled to work more hours than they ought to work.

When the number of working people in any trade or manufacture, has for some years been too great, wages are reduced very low, and the working people become little better than slaves.

When wages have thus been reduced to a very small sum, working people can no longer maintain their children as all good and respectable people wish to maintain their children, but are compelled to neglect them; − to send them to different employments; − to Mills and Manufactories, at a very early age.

The misery of these poor children cannot be described, and need not be described to you who witness them and deplore them every day of your lives.

Many indeed among you are compelled for a bare subsistence to labour incessantly from the moment you rise in the morning to the moment you lie down again at night, without even the hope of ever being better off.

The sickness of yourselves and your children, the privation and pain and premature death of those you love but cannot cherish as you wish, need only be alluded to. You know all these evils too well.

And, what, you will ask is the remedy?

How are we to avoid these miseries?

The answer is short and plain: the means are easy. Do as other people do, to avoid having more children than they wish to have, and can easily maintain.

What is done by other people is this. A piece of soft sponge is tied by a bobbin or penny ribbon, and inserted just before the sexual intercourse takes place, and is withdrawn again as soon as it has taken place. Many tie a piece of sponge to each end of the ribbon, and they take care not to use the same sponge again until it has been washed.

If the sponge be large enough, that is as large as a green walnut, or a small apple, it will prevent conception, and thus, without diminishing the pleasures of married life, or doing the least injury to the health of the most delicate woman, both the woman and her husband will be saved from all the miseries which having too many children produces.

By limiting the number of children, the wages both of children and of grown up persons will rise; the hours of working will be no more than they ought to be; you will have some time for recreation, some means of enjoying yourselves rationally, some means as well as some time for your own and your children's moral and religious instruction.

At present every respectable mother trembles for the fate of her daughters as they grow up. Debauchery is always feared. This fear makes many good mothers unhappy. The evil when it comes makes them miserable.

And why is there so much debauchery? Why such sad consequences?

Why? But, because many young men, who fear the consequences which a large family produces, turn to debauchery, and destroy their own happiness as well as the happiness of the unfortunate girls with whom they connect themselves.

Other young men, whose moral and religious feelings deter them from this vicious course, marry early and produce large families, which they are utterly unable to maintain. These are the causes of the wretchedness which afflicts you.

But when it has become the custom here as elsewhere, to limit the number of children, so that none need have more than they wish to have, no man will fear to take a wife, all will be married while young — debauchery will diminish — while good morals, and religious duties will be promoted.

You cannot fail to see that this address is intended solely for your good. It is quite impossible that those who address you can receive any benefit from it, beyond the satisfaction which every benevolent person, every true christian, must feel, at seeing you comfortable, healthy, and happy.'

TO THE
MARRIED OF BOTH SEXES

In the present state of society, a great number of persons are compelled to make an appearance, and to live in a stile, which consumes all their incomes, leaving nothing, or next to nothing, as a provision for their children. To such persons a great number of children, is a never failing source of discomfort and apprehension; of a state of bodily, mental, and pecuniary vexation and suffering, from which there is no escape. This state of things pervades, to a very great extent, that respectable class of society called genteel. To those whose incomes depend on some particular exertion, which cannot be remitted, these distressing circumstances are from various causes, greatly increased. To those who constitute the great mass of the community, whose daily bread is alone procured by daily labour, a large family is almost always the cause of ruin, both of parents and children; reducing the parents to cheerless, hopeless and irremediable poverty; depriving the children of those physical, moral, and mental helps which are necessary to enable them to live in comfort, and turning them out at an early age to prey upon the world, or to become the world's prey.

For these general reasons, cognizable by every body, it is of the greatest possible importance that màrried people should be informed of the methods used to prevent such tremendous evils.

If methods can be pointed out by which all the enjoyments of married life may be partaken of without the apprehension of TOO LARGE *a family*, and all its bitter consequences, he surely who points them out, must be a benefactor of mankind. Such at any rate are the motives which govern the writer of this address.

The means of prevention are simple, harmless, and might, but for false delicacy, have been communicated generally. They have long been practised in several parts of the Continent, and experience has proved, that the greatest possible benefits have resulted; the people in those parts, being in all respects better off, better instructed, more cheerful, and more independent, than those in other parts, where the practices have not prevailed to a sufficient extent.

The methods are two, of which the one to be first mentioned seems most likely to succeed in this country as it depends upon the female. It has been successfully resorted to by some of our most eminent physicians, and is confidently recommended by first rate Accoucheurs, in cases where pregnancy has been found injurious to the health of delicate women. It consists in a piece of sponge, about an inch square, being placed in the vagina previous to coition, and afterwards withdrawn by means of a double twisted thread, or bobbin, attached to it. No injurious consequences can in any way result from its use, neither does it diminish the enjoyment of either party. The sponge should, as a matter of preference, be used rather damp, and when convenient a little warm. It is almost superfluous to add, that there may be more pieces than one, and that they should be washed after being used.

The other method resorted to, when from carelessness or other causes the sponge is not at hand, is for the husband to withdraw, previous to emission, so that none of the semen may enter the vagina of his wife. But a little practice and care in the use of the sponge will render all other precautions unnecessary.'

TO
THE MARRIED OF BOTH SEXES
IN
GENTEEL LIFE.

Among the many sufferings of married women, as mothers, there are two cases which command the utmost sympathy and commiseration.

The first arises from constitutional peculiarities, or weaknesses.

The second from mal-conformation of the bones of the Pelvis.

Besides these two cases, there is a third case applicable to both sexes: namely, the consequences of having more children than the income of the parents enables them to maintain and educate in a desirable manner.

The first named case produces miscarriages, and brings on a state of existence scarcely endurable. It has caused thousands of respectable women to linger on in pain and apprehension, till at length, death has put an end to their almost inconceivable sufferings.

The second case is always attended with immediate risk of life. Pregnancy never terminates without intense suffering, seldom without the death of the child, frequently with the death of the mother, and sometimes with the death of both mother and child.

The third case is by far the most common and the most open to general observation. In the middle ranks, the most virtuous and praiseworthy efforts are perpetually made to keep up the respectability of the family; but a continual increase of children gradually yet certainly renders every effort to prevent degradation unavailing, it paralizes by rendering hopeless all exertion, and the family sinks into poverty and despair. Thus is engendered and perpetuated a hideous mass of misery.

The knowledge of what awaits them deters vast numbers of young men from marrying and causes them to spend the best portion of their lives in a state of debauchery, utterly incompatible with the honourable and honest feelings which should be the characteristic of young men. The treachery, duplicity, and hypocrisy, they use towards their friends and the unfortunate victims of their seductions, while they devote a large number of females to the most dreadful of all states which human beings can endure extinguishes in them to a very great extent, all manly, upright notions; and qualifies them to as great an extent, for the commission of acts which but for these vile practices they would abhor, and thus to an enormous extent is the whole community injured.

Marriage in early life, is the only truly happy state, and if the evil consequences of too large a family did not deter them, all men would marry while young, and thus would many lamentable evils be removed from society.

A simple, effectual, and safe means of accomplishing these desirable results has long been known, and to a considerable extent practised in some places. But until lately has been but little known in this country. Accoucheurs of the first respectability and surgeons of great eminence have in some peculiar cases recommended it. Within the last two years, a more extensive knowledge of the process has prevailed and its practice has been more extensively adopted. It is now made public for the benefit of every body. A piece of soft sponge about the size of a small ball attached to a very narrow ribbon, and slightly moistened (when convenient) is introduced previous to sexual intercourse, and is afterwards withdrawn, and thus by an easy, simple, cleanly and not indelicate method, no ways injurious to health, not only may much unhappiness and many miseries be prevented, but benefits to an incalculable amount be conferred on society.'

The affair became the indirect occasion for a discussion in the pages of the *Black Dwarf*, studied in the text of Chapter 3. Wooler, the editor of the periodical, had his attention drawn to the handbills by a certain Mrs Fildes of Manchester, a midwife by profession, who in some indignation sent him a few copies of the leaflets.[4] In the following number there appeared a leading article attacking the principle of population, in the next a reply presumably by Place, and then (27 November 1823) the first of the Mill articles listed in the Bibliography.[5]

Though the echo of the leaflets in public controversy was thus small, there must have been a great deal of gossip about it at the time. The proof of this is that the satiric poet Thomas Moore published anonymously in *The Times* of 21 February 1826 an 'Ode to the Goddess Ceres' which contained the following stanza:

There are two Mr. M—'s, too, whom those that like reading
Through all that's unreadable, call very clever;
And, whereas M— Senior makes war on *good* breeding
M— Junior makes war on all breeding whatever!

And on 3 November of the same year Moore returned to the attack with an amusing 'Ode to the Sublime Porte' in which he made fun of the *Westminster Review*, attributing to the young Mr M a fictitious article entitled 'Hints to Breeders'.

No more was heard of the matter until 1832, when John Roebuck, a Canadian friend of Mill's and his companion in the London Debating Society, was a candidate for the parliamentary seat of Bath. A lawyer named Abraham Hayward, a socialite who was later chosen by *The Times* to write Mill's obituary, said of Roebuck that he had taken part in the distribution of the handbills. Hayward knew Mill and Roebuck through having debated on the side opposing them in the above-mentioned Debating Society. This occasioned a small incident between Hayward and Roebuck which did not get to the public ear.

Although it is not directly related with the matter we are considering, it should be observed that in January 1838, Hayward took offence at some remarks that appeared in the *Westminster Review* naming him and Disraeli, among others, as deserters to their class, who did 'the base work of the aristocracy, fighting for them, writing for them, joking for them, blackguardizing for them, and . . .lying for them.' Mill answered his protest saying that though he was the proprietor of the review, he had neither written nor edited these statements, and he considered they were not meant to apply to any one individually but to a class. 'I am going to have to fight a duel on your account,' he joked in a letter to John Robertson, who had written the incriminating lines.[6]

In 1845 Hayward was made Queen's Counsel by the Lord Chancellor and was immediately put forward for the Bench in one of the Inns of Court, the Inner Temple. Roebuck blackballed his nomination, thus frustrating Hayward's ambition, and the latter placed an appeal. It is known that Hayward had a letter printed and circulated and that Thomas Falconer, Roebuck's brother-in-law and for a time co-editor with Mill on the *Westminster*, replied with a *Note upon a Paper circulated by Abraham Hayward, Esq. of the Inner Temple, one of Her Majesty's Counsel* (dated 14 July 1845, British Museum Library, reference no. 8052.1. 4). In Falconer's *Note*, among other things we may read:

Mr. Hayward. . . says:- (I only cite part of the passages for they tell what ought to have been suppressed in justice to a third party [Mill?], and mention facts not at all needed to be told for Mr.

Hayward's defence) – 'In the early days of the London Debating Society (1826–1830) it was attended by a set of young men who possessed the most ultra doctrines on all subjects. Among *their* schemes for the amelioration of society was one described in a pamphlet, called, I think, 'What is Love.' – It was generally believed at the time that two or three of the set had got into a scrape by throwing the pamphlet down the areas of houses.' – 'Mr. Roebuck, to all outward seeming, agreed with them in their leading and characteristic doctrines, and it is not surprising that occasionally he had the credit of countenancing one which he repudiates.'

Mr. Roebuck came to England in August 1824, and the scrape referred to occurred about two years before. The scrape, if it had been proper to mention it, might have been noticed by Mr. Hayward, without any attempt to identify any one of the parties. The then very young and enthusiastic political economists who fell into it, knew little of the opinion of the world or the nature of the fault which they committed; they were at the time entitled to pardon, and every generous person who was personally acquainted with them in 1823, must have felt it to have been a duty to have been silent on the subject, or if mentioned by others, to ask that their honourable career might cover a youthful fault.

The matter did not rest there. In 1848 the appeal was heard, which gave rise to various publications,[7] but above all, to the official *Report on the Proceedings before the Judges, as Visitors of the Inns of Court, in the Appeal of A. Hayward, Esq., Q.C.* (London, 1848).[8] In this report a Statement (B) is appended to Hayward's reprinted petition. The first paragraph reads:

In the early days of the London Debating Club (1826–1830) it was attended by a set of young men who professed the most ultra doctrines on all subjects. Among their schemes for the amelioration of society was one described in a pamphlet (called, I think, *What is love?*) generally attributed to a man of some note in his day, and of unimpeachable character in private life [Francis Place?]. The gentleman most eager in the promotion of it was and is very generally esteemed, society having agreed to forgive him his boyish theories on this rather delicate subject [J.S. Mill?]. It was believed at the time that two or three of the set had got into a scrape by throwing the pamphlet down the areas of houses, but I never heard the precise nature of the scrape till long : afterwards. Moore's verses alluding to the scheme (see 'Ode to the Goddess Ceres', and 'Ode to the Sublime Porte') had made it a common topic of jocularity. As Mr. Roebuck was the constant associate in public of its most prominent supporters, and to all outward seeming agreed with them in their leading and characteristic doctrines, it is not surprising that occasionally he had the credit of countenancing one which he repudiates.

This statement, dated 19 June 1845, appears to be the original to which Falconer was referring in *Note upon a Paper*. Both in Falconer's *Note* and in Hayward's statement some dubious points are to be found. Falconer speaks of 1822 and Hayward of *What is Love?*, whereas the date seems to have been 1823 and the text in question the 'diabolical handbills'. Furthermore, *What is Love?* was written by R. Carlile, the political agitator, and not Place, who seems to be the object of Hayward's allusion.

According to N.E. Himes in 'J.S. Mill's attitude towards Neo-Malthusianism', after his articles in the *Black Dwarf*, Mill always observed the strictest prudence on birth control questions. Himes notes the following incident. In 1870 a public discussion was held between Charles Bradlaugh and the Rev. David King on Bradlaugh's *Elements of Social Science*. Bradlaugh asserted that Mill had publicly approved of his book, which was in favour of birth control. When the debate was over, King asked Mill if this were true and in reply Mill merely said that he had not publicly approved the book and it was not likely he should ever do so.

However, there are signs that in private Mill still favoured artificial birth control. Himes relates how in 1868 a certain Haslam of Dublin had sent Mill a pamphlet called *The Marriage Problem* which openly discussed the limitation of progeny. Mill wrote to him as follows:

19 February 1868.

I thank you for your pamphlet. Nothing can be more important than the question to which it relates, nor more laudable than the purpose it has in view. About the expediency of putting it into circulation, the morality of the matter lies wholly between married people themselves, & that such facts as those which the pamphlet communicates ought to be made known to them by their medical advisers. But we are very far from that point at present, & in the meantime everyone must act according to his own judgement of what is prudent & right.

Mill died on 9 May, 1873. The next day *The Times* published an obituary, soon recognized as the work of Hayward, where the following words could be read:

> He must have been a boy in years when a foolish scheme for carrying out the Malthusian Principle brought him under the lash of the satirist. In Moore's *Ode to the Goddess Ceres* we find. . .

and Hayward proceeds to quote the stanza we have given above about the two Mills' attitude to 'breeding'. The obituary ends:

> Of late years Mill has not come before the world with advantage. When he appeared in public it was to advocate the fanciful rights of women, or to propound some impracticable reform or revolutionary change in the laws relating to the land; but, with all his errors and paradoxes, he will be long remembered as a thinker and reasoner who has largely contributed to the intellectual progress of the age.

The next day, 11 May, was a Sunday and the Rev. Stopford Augustus Brooke preached a sermon praising Mill and criticizing *The Times* obituary. Hayward immediately replied with a letter which he attempted to have published in *The Times* and on failing, printed and circulated it as a pamphlet. I am reprinting it here in its entirety, as it was believed lost.[9]

JOHN STUART MILL

Wagner
'Ich hab' öfters rühmen hören,
Ein Komödiant könnt ein Pfarrer lehren'

Faust
'Ja, wenn der Pfarrer ein Komödiant ist;
Wie das denn wohl zu Zeiten kommen mag.'

May 12, 1873.

Reverend Sir,

I am informed that your morning Sermon of yesterday was principally devoted to the laudation and exaltation of John Stuart Mill, and that you took occasion to denounce the Notice of 'so great a man' in the *Times* of Saturday last [May 10] as disgraceful to the country he adorned. Now I challenge you to specify a sentence or remark in that Notice (hastily written as it was) which is inaccurate, illiberal, or unjust, and I question the fairness or propriety of your denouncing the writer before a fashionable audience, mostly composed of your own female admirers, because his honest estimate of a public character falls below (what others may think) your most mistaken and exaggerated one.

To decide the question raised by yourself and others, we must turn to Mill's life and opinions, which have thus become as legitimate topics of inquiry as those of Hume or Rousseau. In the first place, then, he was a sceptic of no common order. He was the apostle of the philosophy of unbelief, the philosophy which leads straight to materialism. There is no reference to this in the Notice, and far be it from me to endeavour to raise a prejudice against him on this account; but his scepticism certainly forms one reason among many why his praises should not have been exceptionally and ostentatiously heralded from the pulpit by one of the Queen's chaplains — it not being the custom to play Bossuet in this fashion in this country.

Take next the moral aspect of his opinions. It is said in the Notice that, when a boy in years (he was past 20), he fell under the lash of the satirist by a foolish scheme for carrying out the Malthusian principle. This is a studiously mild statement: the fact being that he also fell under the notice of the police by circulating copies of 'Every Woman's Book or What is Love?' and flinging down the areas of houses, for the edification of the maid-servants, printed papers or broadsheets containing practical directions for sexual intercourse without adding to the population. Nor was this a repented error of his youth. It was the persistent error of his mature years; and not long since he was still making converts to the same theory — a theory wholly disconnecting sexual intercourse from sentiment or love; in fact, brutalising it. And this from a great teacher of morals, whose surpassing merits are impressed on ladies by one of the most popular and eloquent of metropolitan preachers!

Great thinkers are not prone to run into error from personal motives or impulses. When Mill fell in love with the lady (a married woman) who afterwards became his wife, he wrote a succession of papers in the *Examiner* against marriage as a lasting tie, and in favour of unlimited liberty of divorce.

You perhaps agree in his doctrine of property in land; but you will hardly approve of his absurd and impracticable scheme for confiscating any increased value to the profit of the community.

There is no necessity for dwelling on his extension of sympathy with Messrs. Bradlaugh and Odger, nor his various other crotchets, which, I think, fully justified me in saying that he was often wrong-headed if always kindhearted. He latterly did an infinity of mischief by lending mischievous people the authority of his name.

Religion, sexual intercourse, marriage, property, − here are matters forming the very foundation of society. Can intellectual greatness coexist with confirmed error touching each? Or, assuming its existence, ought it to be deified from the pulpit, or by the press, without reference to its employment or its tendencies?

As to the main element of greatness − originality, I deny that he was original in the proper sense of the term, *i.e.*, that he produced anything both true and new. He advanced knowledge by systematising it, and by clearing the way for its reception; but he added little or nothing to the common stock. To class him with Locke, Bentham, Adam Smith, or Malthus, is preposterous.

Your very obedient Servant,
THE WRITER OF 'JOHN STUART MILL' IN 'THE TIMES'.

To the Rev. Stopford Augustus Brooke.

Such a broadside instantly drew answering fire. W.D. Christie, an old family friend, published *J.S. Mill and Mr. Abraham Hayward, Q.C.; a Reply about Mill to a Letter to the Rev. Stopford Brooke, privately circulated and actually published. By −, C.B. 1873*. Christie's reply rightly set the record straight on certain points, such as that the incident occurred in 1823, that what Mill distributed was not *What is Love?* and that the series of articles on divorce in the *Examiner* was pure invention, .and he expressed indignation at the insinuation contained in the reference to Mrs Taylor. This publication is of easier access which makes it unnecessary to reprint it here, even in part. G.J. Holyoake also published a reply to Hayward, titled *J.S. Mill as some of the Working Classes Knew Him. . .An answer to a letter circulated by "The author of the article in 'The Times' on Mr. Mill's death"* (London, 1873). It appears that the whole exchange caused considerable scandal, to the point that Gladstone withdrew from the committee set up to erect a monument to Mill.[10]

Notes

Chapter 1   Introduction

1   W. Bagehot, *The Postulates of English Political Economy* (1885), 30. J.K. Ingram, *A History of Political Economy* (1888), 150.

2   See Appendix I.

3   Thus W.J. Ashley ('Introduction' to the 9th edition of Mill's *Principles* [1909]) and F.Y. Edgeworth (article on Mill in *Palgrave's Dictionary*).

4   The batch of papers bought by the London Library of Political and Economic Science (the nucleus of the *Mill-Taylor Collection* at the London School of Economics) was acquired from Messrs Trout and Co. for £25 in March, 1922. Another batch was auctioned in August 1926 and it seems to have fetched £22.50. (Information from Mr Allen, formerly Keeper of Manuscripts in the said Library).

5   Carlyle said of Mill's *Autobiography:* 'I have never read a more uninteresting book, nor I should say a sillier, by a man of sense, integrity, and seriousness of mind... It is wholly the life of a logic-chopping engine, little more of human in it than if it had been done by a thing of mechanized iron. Autobiography of a steam engine, perhaps, you may sometimes read it. As a mournful psychical curiosity, but in no other point of view, can it interest anybody.' J.A. Froude, *Thomas Carlyle. A History of His Life in London, 1834-1881* (1884), II, 420. Reference seen in B. Willey, *Nineteenth Century Studies* (1949), 152.

6   G.J. Stigler, 'The Nature and Role of Originality in Scientific Progress,' in *Essays in the History of Economics* (1965), 6-11. S. Hollander, in 'The Role of Fixed Technical Coefficients in the Evolution of the Wages-Fund Controversy,' *Oxford Economic Papers*, NS, XX, 3 (Nov, 1968), shows that Mill was aware 'of the "substitution effects" generated by relative price changes in the case of the consumer.' This is another analytical discovery, to be added to Stigler's list.

7   As may be seen from the quotation on the title page, the
        expression 'New political economy' is Mill's own. It appears in a
        letter written by Mill to his wife (Yale University Collection of
        J.S. Mill's Letters, 7/Feb/54, f.2 v. transcription by Professor J.
        Robson). The occasion was the attack of the *Examiner* on a
        decision of the Society of Arts to convene a conference between
        the striking Preston cotton-spinners and their masters.
        Especially galling for Mill must have been the dismissal by the
        Examiner of the limitation of the hours of labour and the
        participation of labourers in profits as an example of 'the plea
        of a poor, vapid, silly humanity to check and retard society in
        its natural growth'. (28 January 1854, p. 51, and 4 February
        1854, p. 68).

Chapter 2   The Old Political Economy

1   J. Bentham to James Mill from Queen Square Place, Saturday
        25 July 1812, in the Introduction, to *The Letters of John Stuart
        Mill*, edited by H.S.R. Elliot (1910), xv-xvi. James Mill to J.
        Bentham, 28 July 1812, in Alexander Bain, *James Mill, a
        Biography* (1882), 119-120.

2   J.S. Mill, *Autobiography*, World Classics, 23.

3   See P. Sraffa ed., *Works*, IV, 4-5.

4   Whereas Ricardo never attempted to formulate a functional
        relationship for technology, he did so for population in the
        Principles of 1817. In the *Essay on the influence of a Low Price
        of Corn on the Profits of Stock*, of 1815, his wage theory was
        still Smithian. *Works*, IV, 23.

5   The text in this passage is expressed throughout in terms of
        rates in order to avoid the difficulties noted by Professor Blaug
        with respect to the determinateness or not of the distributive
        shares. Cf. M. Blaug, *Economic Theory in Retrospect* (2nd ed,
        1968), 81, n. 2 and 104-106. Professor Blaug's other book on
        the Ricardian School, *Ricardian Economics* (1958), is essential
        reading for any study of the period.

6   But cf. P. Sraffa, *Works*, IV, 8.

7   Malthus' pamphlet, usually called the 'First Essay on
        Population' to distinguish it from later editions of the same

where his doctrinal position had varied, was actually entitled: *An Essay on the Principle of Population as it Affects the Future Improvement of Society, with Remarks on the Speculation of Mr. Godwin, M. Condorcet, and other Writers* (1798). The first essay on population was anonymous.

8   In the second edition of his Essay Malthus seemed to wish to suggest a law of diminishing returns instead of this arithmetic progression. Cf. G.J. Stigler, 'The Ricardian Theory of Value and Distribution' in *Essays*, 166.

9   Cf. Stigler, *Essays*, 164.

10   T.R. Malthus, *First Essay*, Table of Contents (ch. V, iii).

11   Stigler remarks, *Essays,* 169, that this theory is none the less one of the most important in the history of social doctrines. Cf. G.F. McCleary, *The Malthusian Population Theory* (1953) *passim* and esp. 171.

12   In 1803 Malthus published under his own name: *An Essay on the Principle of Population or a View of its Past and Present Effects on Human Happiness with an Inquiry into our Prospects Respecting the Future Removal or Mitigation of the Evils which it Occasions.* The very title shows the shift in position.

13   In the First Essay the possibility of postponing marriage was also mentioned. However, this possibility figured as normally accompanied by vice, instead of as a solution compatible with a happy and virtuous life. In the second edition see esp. IV, i [1803], 487.

14   See p. 27 below.

15   Since in the *Principles* Ricardo had introduced the wages fund theory, he could relate the aggregate share of wages to *per capita* wages, as he had not done in the *Essay*.

16   This passage dates from the second edition of the *Principles* (1819). The paragraphs on this subject in the first edition had been criticized by an anti-Malthusian, George Ensor. See Sraffa in *Works*, I, 100, n. 1. Cf. Stigler, *Essays*, 164. The most serious, though not formalized, discussion of this problem at that time is to be found in T.R. Malthus, *Principles of Political Economy*

(1820) IV, ii: 'Of the causes which principally affect the habits of the working classes.'

17 It was necessary to assume further that the disutility of common work was the same for the different individuals and constant through time and that the various kinds of work could be reduced to common work: two doubtful assumptions.

18 G.J. Stigler, 'Ricardo and the 93 Per Cent Labor Theory of Value' in *Essays*, 326-342. See also, for the invariable measure of value, the comments of P. Sraffa in *Works*, I, xl-xlix.

19 See J. Viner, *Studies,* 104-6, for some precedents of this discovery and 438-40 for the passages quoted. Also L. Robbins, *Robert Torrens and the Evolution of Classical Economics* (1958) 18-24.

20 Malthus, for example, in an article in 1824 on McCulloch's contribution to the *Encyclopaedia Britannica*, spoke of a 'new' school of political economy, contrasting it with the tradition of Adam Smith. See [T.R. Malthus], Art. I, *Quarterly Review*, XXX, 60 (January, 1824), 297-334. (Attribution by *Wellesly Index*). J.S. Mill, in his turn, wrote a severe criticism of Malthus, thus confirming the impression of the school's coherence. See 'The *Quarterly Review* on Political Economy' in *Westminster Review* (1825) reprinted in *Collected Works,* IV, 23-43.

21 Cf. Schumpeter, *History*, 470. See also R.L. Meek, *Economics and Ideology*, (1967) 51-5.

22 See the diaries of J.L. Mallet, Secretary of the Club, on the session of 13 January 1831 and that of 15 April in the same year, in Political Economy Club, *Proceedings*, VI (London, 1921), 223-5.

23 Cf. however James Mill to Lord Brougham, 3 September 1832, in A. Bain, *James Mill*, (1882), 364. For Meek's somewhat exaggerated opinion on the importance of 'Ricardian Socialists' as they are usually called, see his *Economics and Ideology*, 66-73.

24 See Mallet's diaries, entry for 15 April 1831.

25 The title of the English translation of 1821.

26   Indeed, in his chapter on rent Ricardo claimed to show that rent was not the cause, but the effect of price — 'getting rid of rent', as he said in one of his letters. With James Mill's reduction of the factors of production to two, receiving rent for land appeared even less justified than in Ricardo's treatise.

27   Thus concludes section II of Chapter III in the first edition of the *Elements* (1821). See Ricardo's letter of 5 September 1823, in which he criticized John Stuart Mill for defending the mistaken opinions put forward by his father in the *Elements*.

28   See J.S. Mill, *Autobiography*, W. Cl., 101-3.

29   W.J. Ashley, Introduction to the *Principles*, viii.

30   These changes in the book on distribution spring from a return to Ricardo, but also from J.S. Mill's innovation in distinguishing between laws of production and those of distribution, which we shall see in the next chapter.

31   The edition J.S. Mill used was the French one of 1802. He says in his *Autobiography* (W.C1., 56) that 'the Traité de Législation wound up with what was to me a most impressive picture of human life. . .' This is a clear reference to the second section of the fifth chapter of the essay 'De l'Influence des Tems et des Lieux en matière de Législation.' In the second edition (1820), Dumont did not end with this essay, but with the 'Vue Générale d'un Corps complet de Lois,' a much less stirring essay than the one Mill alludes to.

32   John Austin and his wife, Sarah Austin, invited John Mill to stay with them for a period in 1822, precisely when Mill says he was studying Roman Law under Austin. See Michael St John Packe, *The Life of John Stuart Mill* (1954), 51. Professor Robson in *The Improvement of Mankind* (1968), 6, underlines the importance of Austin's teaching in Mill's 'conversion' to Benthamism.

33   Translated from the 1st edition of the *Traités* (1802), III, 392.

34   Bentham was thus referring to actions in his opinion wrongly classified as crimes, those which 'according to the principle of utlity' are not 'harmful to the community,' that is to say, harmful 'to one or many of the individuals composing it'. See for example *Traités* (2nd ed., 1820), III, 246 and 211.

Chapter 3   Youthful Propagandism

1   J.S. Mill, *Autobiography* (W.C1.) 67. Cf. M. Mack, *Bentham* (1962), 338.

2   Cf. Robbins, *Torrens*, Chap. III, par. 7, especially 70-71. J.S. Mill maintained his interest in the question, perhaps particularly due to the fact that his father was preparing a new edition of the *Elements*; he sent an essay to Ricardo, who also found fault with his theory of value. See Ricardo's letter of 5 September 1823, *Works* IX, 285-7.

3   [J.S. Mill], 'The *Quarterly Review* on Political Economy,' *Westminster Review*, III (January 1825), reprinted in *Collected Works*, IV. In this case, the young Mill's attitude is disingenuous especially considering the importance he and his father had assigned to the theory of value.

4   J.S. Mill, 'On Profits and Interest,' fourth of the *Essays on Some Unsettled Questions of Political Economy* (1844), *Collected Works*, IV, 297. For the date of composition, see the textual editor's note, *ibid*, 230.

5   Ricardo, *Works*, VIII, 71 and 80-1.

6   See G.F. McCleary, *The Malthusian Population Theory* (1953), 85.

7   It is not known whether Place wrote them or whether he only organized their printing and distribution. For the whole question see Appendix II, especially n. App. II, 3.

8   Cf. Place Coll., vol. 68, ff 115-117. The articles by Mill are to be found in vols. XI and XII of the *Black Dwarf.*

9   The argument is very rudimentary: a number of people are unemployed, therefore the solution lies in decreasing the number of new arrivals on the labour market. Mill offered no explanation of how there could be unemployment when according to the wages fund theory a diminution of wages should have meant an increase in employment in inverse proportion. *Bk Dw.*, XI, 22 (27 Nov. 1823), 748ff.

10   *Bk. Dw.*, XII, 1 (7 Jan 1824), 21ff. Place was still more sceptical regarding moral restraint; see Field, 'Early Propagandist Movement,' *Essays on Population* (1931), 111.

11   Cf. *Autobiography* (W.C1.), 104-6.

12   Curiously enough, Owen is said to have brought from France the idea for the procedure later popularized in the 'diabolical handbills.' Cf. Appendix II. He certainly was aware of possible population problems in a 'non-capitalist' society.

13   See J.S. Mill, 'Two Speeches on Population,' in *Journal of Adult Education*, IV, 1 (October 1929), 59.

14   J.S. Mill, 'Intended Speech at the Co-operation Society, never delivered,' 1825 MS: Connecticut College for Women. I owe the knowledge of this speech to the kindness of Professor J. Robson, whose typescript copy I am using.

15   Mill's 'Closing Speech on the Co-operative System' has been published under the wrong title. See the bibliography under Mill's manuscripts. I have used Professor Robson's typescript copy of the original MS.

16   From 1834 to 1840, when he believed in the possible success of a Radical Party distinct from the Whigs, Mill edited the *Westminster*, and was even for some time its owner. Cf. J. Hamburger, *Intellectuals in Politics* (1965), 168.

17   Reprinted in *Collected Works*, IV. The quotation is on p. 3.

18   On this point it seems the truth is divided between Blake and the young Mill, for neither can the compensatory movements in the goods account be so swift as Mill postulated, nor can remittances have a permanent affect on the exchange rate without a continuous injection of liquidity in the home market.

19   Lord Robbins's introduction to the *Collected Works*, IV, xiv-xv. See also Ricardo, *Works*, IV, 323-56.

20   [J.S. Mill,] 'Art. IX. The Quarterly Review', *Westminster Review* (January 1825). Reprinted in *Coll. Works*, IV. The quotation is on page 25.

21   That is to say, without increase in the number of hours of work or in wages per hour.

22   Mill, *Coll. Works*, IV, 73.

23   [T. Malthus], *An Essay on the Principle of Population* (1798)
      Chapter II.

24   See *Coll. Works*, IV, 74.

25   Cf. B.A. Corry, *Money, Saving, and Investment in English
      Economics* (1962), 104-5, who rightly notes the presumption of
      Mill's concluding remarks.

26   John G. Gurley and Edward S. Shaw, *Money in a Theory of
      Finance* (1960), 72-75.

27   Cf. F.W. Fetter, *The Development of British Monetary
      Orthodoxy 1797-1875* (1965), 192.

28   [J.S. Mill], 'The Currency Juggle,' *Tait's Edinburgh Magazine*
      (January, 1833). Reprinted in *Coll. Works*, IV. The quotation is
      on p. 184.

29   B. Corry, *Money, Saving, and Investment*, 105-6. Robbins,
      introduction to *Coll. Works*, IV, x-xi.

30   *Coll. Works*, IV, 276-7. The concept of hoarding may have been
      suggested to Mill by the famous 'hoards' of the 'Banking
      School.' Cf. Robbins, *Torrens*, 131 ff.

31   *Westminster Review* (June 1844). Reprinted in *Coll. Works*, IV.
      For Torrens's part in the controversy, see Robbins, *Torrens*,
      94-5, 326-8, and in general, chapters IV and V of Robbins's
      book.

32   *Coll. Works*, IV, 354.

33   *Coll. Works*, III, 575-6 [III, xiv, 4].

34   See *Principles, Coll. Works*, III, 540-4 [III, xii, 3].

35   *Principles, Coll. Works*, III, 575 [III, xiv, 4].

36   Cf. Robbins, Introduction to *Coll. Works*, IV, xx-xxi.

37   G.M. Young, *Victorian England, Portrait of an Age* (1953), 10.

38   *Westminster Review* (April 1825). Reprinted in *Coll. Works*, IV.
      The quotation is on page 47.

39   *Westminster Review* (January 1827). Reprinted in *Coll. Works*,
        IV, 141-159. The passage quoted is on page 143.

40   See *Coll. Works* V, Appendix B, 761-3, esp. the textual editor's
        note. Although Mill gave the petition as his in his bibliography,
        to my mind it includes phrases by other organizers; for example,
        the allusion to the Bible's condemnation of hoarders of wheat is
        uncharacteristic of Mill and was used by the Reverend Doctor
        Vaughan in his speech.

41   The chairman of the meeting was a Mr Prescott, probably W.G.
        Prescott (1800-1865), of the firm of Grote, Prescott & Co., one
        of the three founding members of the Utilitarian Society
        presided over by the young Mill [cf. *Autobiography* (W.C1.)
        101; and J.S. Mill to Mr and Mrs George Grote, 14 November
        1822, *Coll. Works*, XII, 15, n. 6]. The announcement also says
        that the presence was expected of a Mr Senior, probably the
        economist, and Charles Villiers, MP, Mill's erstwhile collaborator
        in the attempt to form a Radical Party. It must have been
        Charles Villiers (or perhaps Joseph Hume, the friend of Francis
        Place) who presented the petition in Parliament (both appear in
        Hansard as having presented petitions for London districts in
        the days following the Kensington meeting).

42   This is the first essay in J.S. Mill, *Essays on Some Unsettled
        Questions of Political Economy* (1844). It is reprinted in *Coll.
        Works*, IV, 232-61. Note the occasion for publishing the Essays,
        mentioned in the Preface *(Coll. Works*, IV, 231). Cf. also
        Robbins, *Torrens*, 33 and 225. In this early period of his life the
        policy aspects of free trade occupied him in three articles. In
        1826, he wrote on 'The Silk Trade,' *Coll. Works*, IV, 125-139.
        In 1828, in the last number of the *Parliamentary Review*, he
        published 'Intercourse Between the United States and the
        British Colonies in the West Indies,' and 'Trade with India.'

43   The adjustment mechanisms are more complete in this essay
        than in the *Principles*, for they include changes in money
        incomes. Cf. J. Viner, *Studies*, 300-1.

44   See D.N. Winch, 'Classical Economics and the case for
        Colonisation,' *Economica*, NS, XXX, 120 (November 1963).

45   Robbins, *Torrens*, 171-3.

46   See the articles in the bibliography under 27 Feb 1831, 20 July
      1834, 23 October 1834; 29 January 1837; 22 February 1837. He
      was not, however, a member of the other two societies, the 'South
      Australian Land Company' (1831) and the 'South Australian
      Association' (1834).

47   E.G. Wakefield, *England and America* (1833), II, 103 ff. Quoted
      by D.N. Winch, 'Classical Economics and the Case for
      Colonisation', *Economica*, NS XXX, 120 (November 1963),
      391. Torrens, also, justified colonization by appealing to the
      possibility of savings not finding a field of employment because
      of the secular fall in the rate of profits and unfavourable
      movements in the rates of exchange of those countries with
      relatively larger investments.

48   Robbins, *Torrens*, 247-8. J.S. Mill, *Principles*, in *Coll. Works*,
      III, 735-6 [IV, iv, 2].

49   One of Malthus's recommendations in *An Essay on the Principle
      of Population* has escaped notice: he proposed the
      establishment of poor-houses, though under very severe
      conditions of life and with work made compulsory; they would
      be open to anyone who needed assistance, of whatever
      nationality he might be.

50   [J.S. Mill], 'Notes on Newspapers, 23rd July. Lord
      Brougham's Speech on the Poor Law Amendment Bill,'
      Monthly Repository, NS VIII (1834), 597.

Chapter 4 John Stuart Mill's Rebellion

1   Cf. Joseph Hamburger, *Intellectuals in Politics. John Stuart Mill
      and the Philosophic Radicals* (1965), 270-1.

2   A.W. Levi, 'The Mental Crisis of John Stuart Mill,' *The
      Psychoanalytic Review*, XXXII (January 1945), 86-101.

3   Cf. 'Letter to the Editor,' *Edinburgh Review*, LXXIX (1844),
      267-71.

4   *The Early Draft of John Stuart Mill's Autobiography*, ed. J.
      Stillinger (1961), 184.

5   G. Himmelfarb, ed., in J.S. Mill, *Essays on Politics and Culture* (1962), xix-xx.

6   Cf. *Early Draft*, 11.

7   J.M. Robson, *The Improvement of Mankind. The Social and Political Thought of John Stuart Mill*, (1968), 62.

8   Professor Robson's book was of great help to me in formulating these matters, though he expresses kindlier feelings towards Benthamism than I do.

9   In Henry Cole's diary, an entry dated November 23 1831 reads: 'With Utilitarians, said he [Mill], he was a Mystic — with Mystics a Utilitarian, with Logicians a sentimentalist & with the latter a Logician.' See Anna J. Mill, 'Some Notes on Mill's Early Friendship with Henry Cole,' in *The Mill News Letter*, IV, 2 (Spring, 1969), p.6.

10   [J.S. Mill], 'The Spirit of the Age,' a series of articles published in the *Examiner* from 6 January to 29 May 1831, and republished under Mill's name, with an introduction by F.A. von Hayek in 1942.

11   [J.S. Mill]: 'Appendix (B). Remarks on Bentham's Philosophy,' in E.L. Bulwer, *England and the English* (London 1833), 328 and 324.

12   [J.S. Mill?]: 'Appendix (C). A Few Observations on Mr. Mill,' *ibid*, 345-55. I attribute this appendix to J.S. Mill, though nobody else seems to do so, because of the similarity in style to the former one and because it seems unlikely that Bulwer would ask anyone else to undertake it. Despite a less critical tone than in the one about Bentham, a close reading brings to light the main points of difference between father and son. James Mill is criticized for not properly appreciating the differences in aptitudes and character in different people, and also because 'he saddens the Present by a reference to the Past — he does not console it by an alluring anticipation of the Future: — he rather discontents us with vice than kindles our enthusiasm for virtue.' (355).

13   J.S. Mill, *Autobiography* (W.C1.) 133-6. Bain disagreed with J.S.

Mill's harsh judgement of his father's essay: 'His father knew as much history as any man of his time... But in such a very synoptical article, the citation of historical instances would have been impossible.' A. Bain, *James Mill*, 232-3. I think Mr Hamburger comes nearer the truth than Bain, and certainly nearer than J.S. Mill, in his interpretation of the essay as not so much a theoretical treatise, in spite of its style and way of reasoning, but more a political pamphlet against the British Constitution of that time. See Hamburger, *Intellectuals in Politics*, 36.

14   Fifth of the *Essays on Some Unsettled Questions*. Also *Coll. Works*, IV, 309-339.

15   Cf. G.C. Archibald, 'The State of Economic Science,' in *British Journal for the Philosophy of Science*, X, 37 (May 1959). On pages 64-5 assumptions used by economists are classified into four types: (a) assumptions as to motivations, such as the maximization of profits or of utility; (b) empirical assumptions as to the existence and stability of functional relationships; (c) *coeteris paribus* assumptions; (d) contextual or institutional assumptions. Assumptions examined and modified by Mill are of the (a) and (d) types.

16   Mill to D'Eichthal, 15 May 1829, in *Coll. Works*, XII, 34.

17   R.K.P. Pankhurst, *The St. Simonians, Mill and Carlyle. A Preface to Modern Thought* (London 1957), especially chapter II, titled 'The Wooing of J.S. Mill.'

18   See *The Spirit of the Age*, particularly the introduction of Hayek, xvii-xix.

19   A [J.S. Mill], 'Miss Martineau's Summary of Political Economy,' in *Monthly Repository* (May 1834). Also *Coll. Works*, IV, 223-8, source of the quotation in the text. There is an earlier mention of the distinction in the works of a British economist: see N.W. Senior, *An Introductory Lecture on Political Economy* (London 1827), 8.

20   See W.J. Ashley's Introduction to the *Principles* (1909), xii-xx.

21   [Thomas Hodgskin], 'Literature. The Principles of Political Economy,' *The Economist*, 27 May 1848, 603-4. Source of the

attribution, E. Halévy, *Thomas Hodgskin, 1789-1869* (Paris, 1903), 184.

J.K. Ingram notes that Lord Lauderdale had shown at the beginning of the nineteenth century that the nature of distribution in a community reacts on production. See Ingram, *History of Political Economy* (1888), 151.

For his part, Marx criticized the distinction several times in his writings, both in the manuscripts collected by Kautsky under the title *The History of the Theories of Surplus Value* and in the manuscript titled 'General Introduction to the criticism of Political Economy.'

22   Indeed we cannot. But Mill should have remembered these words when revising Chapter XII of the first book of the *Principles*, 'Of the Law of Increase of Production from the Land,' and he would have avoided speaking of a law of historically diminishing returns in agriculture, held in suspension by the counteracting force of technological advance. In any case, this saving clause made any refutation of his hypothesis quite impossible.

23   See K.R. Popper, *The Logic of Scientific Discovery* (1959), Sect. 15.

Chapter 5   Trade Unions

1   Cf. Beatrice and Sidney Webb, *History of Trade Unionism*, 157 ff.

2   [Harriet Martineau], *The Turn-Out: or, Patience the Best Policy* (London, 1829), 60.

3   [Harriet Martineau], *A Manchester Strike* (1832), 135 and 31. It would be another 33 years before Mill mentioned trades unions' contribution to the perfection of the market. Miss Martineau perhaps drew this idea from McCulloch's *Essay* (1826).

4   See also Francis Place, 'Narrative of the Proceedings to Procure the Repeal of the Laws against Combinations of Workmen. . . 1810-1825.' British Museum, Add. Mss., 27.798.

5   As is normal in times of labour shortage, the men became
         belligerent. Moreover, in the words of Place, *loc. cit.*, 'all
         expected a great and sudden rise in wages, when the
         Combination Laws should be repealed.' He added
         characteristically: 'not one of them had any idea whatever of
         the connection between wages and population' (f. 22).

6   The wave of strikes which followed the total repeal of 1824,
         prompted McCulloch to insist on the need for punishing
         obstruction and intimidation by trade unionists. See J.R. McC.
         [John Ramsay McCulloch], *An Essay on the Circumstances
         which Determine the Rate of Wages, and the Condition of the
         Labouring Classes,* Edinburgh (1826), 188. This pamphlet was a
         revised version of his 'Combination Laws — Restraints on
         Emigration.' *Edinburgh Rev.,* XXXIX (January 1824) to which
         quotations in the text refer.

7   F. Place to Sir Francis Burdett, 25 July 1825, in 'Narrative of
         the Proceedings', ff. 57-8.

8   Unions, if they are to subsist, must maintain a permanent
         organization, collect funds regularly, communicate decisions to
         their members, by means of pickets if need be, and exclude
         those blacklegs brought in only for the purpose of breaking a
         strike, who in ordinary times could not be competitors in that
         labour market.

9   Francis Place, in a short note appended to an article on unions
         by a W. Longson which he was sending to Mill, said: 'Longson
         has been engaged among the weavers in organizing what they
         call unions, that is, associations in the towns and villiages [sic],
         gradually to increase their wages.' This was around the month of
         September, 1824. 'Francis Place Collection,' vol. 68, f. 105 [d],
         British Museum, Department of Printed Books. Mr Peter
         Jackson kindly showed me this passage.

10   For the date of Torrens's pamphlet, see the anonymous *The
         Strike, or a Dialogue between Andrew Plowman and John
         Treadle* (London 1834), 3 and 5.

11   If we bear in mind that the Ricardian model contained a third
         factor, land, and a third distributive share, rent (which have
         been excluded from the above exposition for the sake of
         simplicity) it ceases to be true that whenever the share of labour

increases, that of profits must diminish, for it may be rent that diminishes. Cf. Blaug, *Economic Theory in Retrospect* (2nd ed.) 106.

12   This relationship between international trade and trade union activity was not an innovation simply in the sense that Torrens thus added something to the Ricardian system, but in the sense that he modified it, since Ricardo had stated that money wages did not affect prices (either on the home or on the international market). Ricardo was right for the long run, but trade union activity mainly pursues short-run objectives. Cf. Robbins, *Robert Torrens and the Evolution of Classical Economics*, 296.

13   Senior's is the most interesting performance in the theory of wages — until Cairnes's *Leading Principles* (1874) in the chapter on International Trade (not on the Wages Fund). As Professor Viner puts it in his *Studies in the Theory of International Trade* (1937), Cairnes 'reached the correct conclusion that while the general level of wages and foreign trade were intimately connected, the connection was not one of simple cause and effect operating in a single direction, but of joint dependence on "the productiveness of industry" as a whole and on the demands for different commodities. He left vague, however, the precise nature of the interrelationships between productivities, wage levels, and international specialization' (457). Senior's linking of wages and productiveness was lost on his contemporaries and one might say even on himself.

14   *The Times*, 15 March 1834, p. 5, 1st. leader.

15   [J.S. Mill], 'Notes on the Newspapers. 15 March. The Trades' Unions,' in *Monthly Repository*, NS, VIII (1834), 246-8.

16   Even in the sixties the trade unions had to be defended from accusations that they were 'secret,' 'irresponsible' and 'coercive.' See T.J. Dunning, *Trades' Unions and Strikes* (1860), 7-17.

17   See, for example, *Character, Object, and Effects of Trades' Unions: with some Remarks on the Law Concerning Them,* (London, 1834), which gives a detailed description of the rituals, and asserts them to be so fearful that 'a London Journeyman, who entered a Union during the past year. . . was literally deprived of reason, and died in the agonies of raving madness' (66).

18   *The Times*, 19 April 1834, p. 3, cols. 4-5.

19   A. [J.S. Mill], 'Notes on the Newspapers. 19 April. Government
        by brute force,' in *Monthly Repository*, NS, VIII (1834), 364-8.

20   A. [J.S. Mill], 'Notes on the Newspapers. 1 May. The Press and
        the Trades' Unions' in *Monthly Repository*, NS, VIII (1834),
        435-7.

21   [J.S. Mill], 'Reorganisation of   the   Reform   Party,'   in
        Westminster Review, XXXII, 2 (April 1839), 475-508.

22   He also alluded to trade unions in the chapter on 'Of the
        Differences of Wages in Different Employments', *Principles, Coll.
        Works*, II [II, xiv, 6], 396-398, on the ground that unions could
        create artificial differences in wages.

23   Co-operation received twelve pages in the 1848 edition, but
        twenty-five in the 1862 edition, for example, while the space
        allotted to unions only grew to six and a half in this edition.

24   [1848] *Coll. Works*, III [V, x, 5], 930 and *dd*.

25   Cf. S. and B. Webb, *History*, 216, note 2.

26   *Coll. Works*, III, 931. Beesly defended the Engineers against Mill
        in the *Westminster Review*, October, 1861, 531-2. Beesly
        asserted that the engineers had only struck for banning
        systematic overtime and for limiting the hours of work, but not
        for limiting entry. He should have added that they struck for
        the banning of piecework: see the 'Circulars of the Executive
        Council of the Amalgamated Society', in *The Operative*
        (London), 29 November 1851, 173-5.

27   But in 1852 he was still against any legal prohibition of strikes:
        see *Coll. Works*, III, 932.

28   J.R. Hicks, *The Theory of Wages* (2nd ed., 1963), 153 ff. Quota-
        tions in the text are from Fawcett's article in *Westm. Rev.*, NS,
        XVIII (July 1860), 297 ff.

29   *W.R.*, NS, XVII, 10. note 3 above.

30   [1862] *Coll. Works*, III [V, x, 5], 934 footnote.

31   After his 'recantation,' Mill changed this first sentence to read: 'Even assuming that a strike must inevitably fail whenever it attempts to raise wages above that market rate which is fixed by the demand and supply. . .' (932).

32   Frederic Harrison, Letter to the Editor of the *Daily News*, 1 August 1861, p. 3, cols. 4, 5, 6.

33   Mill to Chapman, 4 August 1861, Elliot ed., *Letters*, I, 247-8. 'At the same time,' he continued, 'I think men would be right in standing out for the recognition of a certain length of working day, beyond which the payment per hour should be higher, and that in this way it should be made the interest of the masters not to overwork the men.'

34   Mill seems to have alluded to the possible dangers of the piecework system only twice. The first time was in 1857 when at the suggestion of Harriet Taylor he inserted: 'when the payment per piece is not sufficiently high, that is a just ground of objection'; in a passage likening dislike to piecework to 'a desire to cheat, by not giving work in proportion to pay.' F. Hayek, *John Stuart Mill and Harriet Taylor*, note 35 on pp. 307-8, and *Coll. Works*, III [IV, vii, 6], 783 footnote. The second time was in the posthumous 'Chapters on Socialism' in *Coll. Works*, IV, 743. I was helped greatly with regard to Mill's attitude to piecework by a discussion with Mr W. Wolfe.

35   See Mill to S.H. Walpole, 29 January 1867 in the *Mill-Taylor Collection*, Box of Additional Material (M 452). The following passage is interesting. 'There are others whose presence in the Commission would be, as much as mine, a guarantee to the working classes that justice would be done to their opinions and objects: for instance, Mr. Fawcett who has made it the subject of one of his chief studies [see n 41 of this chapter] who knows the workman's side of the question (we all know the other side) and who is much trusted by them.'

36   See W. Thornton, 'His Career at India House,' in *J.S. Mill, Notices of His Life and Works. . . reprinted from the Examiner* (1873), 22. Also, Bain, *J.S. Mill*, 174. About Thornton taking the side of the South in the American Civil War, see Mill to Fawcett 6 March 1862 (*Mill-Taylor Collection*, vol. LVII, f. 23). The sentence we have quoted in the text above is in Mill to Cairnes, 30 October 1864 (*Mill-Taylor Collection*, vol. LV, f 57 verso).

37   G.J. Stigler, 'The Nature and Role of Originality in Scientific
      Progress' in *Essays*, 9. In Sir A. Grant, ed., *Recess Studies*
      (1870), F. Jenkin used surely for the first time in Great Britain
      'the graphic method of curves' to illustrate Thornton's strictures
      on the law of demand and supply.

38   J.S. Mill, 'Thornton on Labour and its Claims,' in *Fortnightly
      Review* (1 May 1869). Reprinted in *Coll. Works*, V, to which
      page references given in the text apply. Mill had wished to
      publish the review in the *Edinburgh*, but must have found his
      opinions too much at variance with those of Reeves, its editor.
      See letters of Reeves to Mill in the *Mill-Taylor Collection*, Box
      of Additional Material (M 409).

39   See E.S. Beesly, 'Trades' Unions,' in *Westminster Review*,
      October 1861, 513 ff.

40   As Mill's review enhanced the importance of the footnote
      beyond what the author had seen in it, in the second edition
      Thornton conceded it the honour of the main text, still without
      understanding Mill's reasons for rejecting the short-run version.
      See *On Labour* [1869] 84-85, and [1870], 82-88.

41   The passage is to be found in H. Fawcett's *The Economic
      Position of the British Labourer* (1865), 120.

42   Taussig has criticized Thornton for presenting the wages fund
      doctrine in terms of a money fund, because such a presentation
      could give rise to the idea that, accordingly, the only obstacle to
      trade union activity affecting the general level of wages is the
      limitation of the monetary supply. Thornton surely did not
      think of the consequences of conceiving the fund in money
      terms, as he would take it for granted that Britain was on the
      gold standard and hence that money supply could not be
      managed at will. In fact, *pace* Taussig, the wages fund doctrine
      did *not* rule out the possibility of improvements in workers' real
      wages through inflation.

43   See Thornton, *On Labour* [1870], 88.

44   In this letter he alluded to the limitations on wage increases
      through foreign competition: the consequent fall in profits, he
      said 'might doubtless send capital to other countries, but we
      must recollect that the movement for higher wages and shorter

working hours is common to all the industrious nations.' (Mill to Fawcett, 1 January 1866, Elliot ed., *Letters*, II, 52). Thus he did not advance the Senior argument that productivity in the export industries determines the limits of wage increase. Unfortunately he took a course which implied that differences in wage levels between countries are due to differences in the bargaining power of the trade unions, which is both historically and analytically false.

45   The rejection of the yearly period of production lies for me at the origin of the 'recantation.' In a recent article, 'The Role of Fixed Technical Coefficients in the Evolution of the Wages Fund Controversy,' *Oxford Economic Papers*, NS, XX, 3 (November 1968), 320-341, Mr S. Hollander gives a different explanation, which, though plausible, seems to me less in accordance with the texts. Mr. Hollander starts from the idea, quite plausible in itself, that since Mill came to hold that in the short run wages could increase at the expense of profits, then he must have conceived demand for labour to be a zero elasticity function (drawn vertically to the X ordinate). This is not true; Marshall may have done so, but not Mill, who had no clear idea of the elasticity of the demand for labour in the short run (in the long run he held it to be a unit elasticity curve). Mill's demand for labour may have been zero elastic, but for a very short span, and not beyond the point when current profits had all been swallowed by wages. Mr Hollander then proceeds to say that a zero-elastic demand for labour can only happen in a model where production coefficients are fixed and there is no substitutability at all between capital and labour. We have seen that Mill thought the combination of capital and labour to be technically determined, but it is doubtful that he realized the implications of this (though Cairnes may have done). He surely did not, as Mr Hollander asserts, 'recant' the wages fund doctrine because he realized that a net increase in accumulation would mean a different wages fund according to the technical coefficients in the various industries at the time; that is to say, because he saw that the wages fund was not predetermined, but a residual of the process of accumulation. Cf. note 48 below.

46   Thornton asserted that if the 'bucket' theory were true, 'wages must be and have been nearly stationary. . . all variations in their rate being mere oscillations. . . what they were then they must have been a hundred years before, or for that matter indeed, at the time of the Conquest.' (259). The anonymous

writer in the *Quarterly* rather asserted that a high rate of profits produced high wages, and that wage increases at the expense of profits proved short-lived.

47   Thornton, *On Labour*, Book III, ch. IV.

48   Mill was quite unaware of the effects of a general rise in wages when different capital-labour ratios in the several industries were allowed into the model. See Hicks, *Theory of Wages*, ch. IX, sec. 3.

49   'The *Times* joins in the chorus, notwithstanding Mr. Courtney, who I do hope has no hand in the matter,' Mill told Cairnes, 4 October 1872, *Mill-Taylor Collection*, LV, ff. 189, v, 190 r. A search through the leaders of *The Times* for the few months previous to the letter reveals no such attitude. The only leader written by Courtney on Wages and Prices (*The Times*, 22 August 1872 attributed to Courtney in 'Courtney Collection' (LSE), vol. XX) is quite unexceptionable.

50   J. Stirling, 'J.S. Mill on Trade Unions' in Sir A. Grant ed., *Recess Studies* (1870), 313. Professor Sir Arnold Plant called my attention to this passage; he agreed with Stirling's conclusions as to Mill's softheartedness.

51   Cf [1848] and [1871] in *Coll. Works*, III, 930.

52   *Coll. Works*, III, 933.

53   *Coll. Works*, V, 666.

Chapter 6   Laissez-faire

1   Mill to Cairnes, 15-IX-1870, 'Mill-Taylor Collection,' LV, 171, criticizing Bastiat. Pointed out to me by Mr. P. Jackson.

2   J. Bartlet Brebner, '*Laissez-faire* in Nineteenth Century Britain,' *The Tasks of Economic History*, VIII (1948). In a letter to Cairnes on 22 April 1872 Mill wrote: 'One gets accustomed to strange things, but to find myself held up as an apostle of Centralisation was indeed something unexpected.'

3   Cf. E. Lipson, *Planned Economy or Free Enterprise: the Lessons of History* (1944). See the table of contents: IV, 2,

'The Trend towards *Laissez-faire* (1660-1880)' and IV, 3, 'The Reaction from *Laissez-faire* (1800-1918)'.

4   [J.S. Mill] leader on the Poor Law in *The Sun*, 12 May 1834.

5   It must be admitted, however, that the Reformed Parliament was very unruly. Cf. Young, *Portrait of an Age*, 31.

6   [J.S. Mill] 'Municipal Institutions,' in the *Examiner*, 11 August 1833, 497-9.

7   [J.S. Mill] 'The Employment of Children in Manufactories,' in the *Examiner*, 29 January 1832, 67-8.

8   See the *Examiner*, 26 February 1832, 131.

9   Mill's *Autobiography*, W. Cl., 137.

10   Iris Mueller quotes this passage in *The Influence of French Thought on J.S. Mill*, 70. Cf. the following entry in Henry Cole's diary: 'Nov. 12, 1831. Walked home with John Mill. That no general principles of government can be formed suitable to all ages. That the present system of Government was like that of a man who should fence round his field and leave the corn to sow itself & the ground to be tilled by itself.' See Anna J. Mill, 'Some Notes on Mill's Early Friendship with Henry Cole,' *The Mill News Letter*, IV, 1 (Spring, 1969) 6.

11   The idea of negative or destructive principles and positive or constructive ones was typically Saint-Simonian. The principle of *laissez-faire*, once it had completed its work of destroying harmful economic institutions, would disappear, yielding to a period of construction.

12   Carlyle to Mill, 22-II-33, Mill to Carlyle, 11-12-IV-33, in *Letters of Thomas Carlyle to J.S. Mill, etc.* by Alexander Carlyle, and Mill, *Coll. Works*, XII, 152.

13   Tocqueville, 'Voyages en Angleterre. . .,' in *Oeuvres*, V (2), 53 (26 May 1835), René Mayer edition.

14   'Municipal Institutions' in the *Examiner*, 11 August 1833.

15   The *Edinburgh Review* (1840), 57. Cf. J.H. Burns, in 'J.S. Mill

and Democracy,' *Political Studies*, V, 2 and 3 (1957), 174.

16   [John Austin], 'Centralization,' in *Edinburgh Review* (1847), 221-258.

17   See the text in *Coll. Works*, XIII, 712. It is my interpretation that the phrase *axiomata media* here used by Mill refers to such economic rules as *laissez faire*. Perhaps one day the letter of Austin to which Mill was replying, will be found and settle the question.

18   Mill made too handsome an acknowledgement to Comte for the idea of appending a section on 'the generalia or first principles of the various arts' in any exposition of a body of practical rules (*Logic* [1st ed.] II, 620). Cf. Comte, *Cours de philosophie positive* (1839-1842) [4th edition by Littré, 1877], I, 54.

19   The point was made by A.L. Harris in his book *Economics and Social Reform* (1958).

20   Page references at the end of quotations from the *Principles* are to vol. III of the *Coll. Works*.

21   [N.W. Senior], 'Mill, The Principles of Political Economy,' in the *Edinburgh Review*, LXXXVIII (October 1848), 331-2. Source of attribution, Marian Bowley, *Senior*, 345.

22   Cf. Hayek, *The Constitution of Liberty*, 159, 455, n20.

23   See Chapter viii of Book V of Mill's *Principles*, 'Of the Ordinary Functions of Goverment, Considered as to Their Economical Effects.'

24   Mill, *Principles*, V, ix. One of the necessary functions of the State, the control of the quantity of money, was discussed by him in the Political Economy Club. See the diaries of J.L. Prevost, entry for the 3 April 1845, in *Proceedings of the Political Economy Club*, VI (London, 1921) 292.

25   See W.J. Baumol, *Welfare Economics and the Theory of the State* (1952), 149-152.

26   Mill reminded the interventionists proposing optional activities

that all direct interferences of the government cost money, which has to be collected through taxes, that is, coercively. On the other hand, in his chapter on the consequences of the tendency of profits to a minimum in civilized countries *(Principles*, IV, v), Mill deduced from his analysis that it weakens in an advanced country 'the force of the economical argument against the expenditure of public money for really valuable, even though industrially unproductive, purposes, if for any great object of justice or philanthropic policy, such as the industrial regeneration of Ireland, or a comprehensive measure of colonisation or of public education, it were proposed to raise a large sum by way of loan, politicians need not demur to the abstraction of so much capital, as tending to dry up the permanent sources of the country's wealth, and diminish the fund which supplies the subsistence of the labouring population' (748).

27   Cf. Mill, *On Liberty* (Everyman ed.), 164-5.

28   By neo-liberals I mean the group of economists associated with the Vienna school, the Chicago school, or the German Review *Ordo*.

29   Cf. J. Bentham, 'Defence of a Maximum,'*Economic Writings*, Stark, ed., vol. III, 258.

30   Robbins, *Theory of Economic Policy*, 16. See also Hla Myint, *Theories of Welfare Economics* (1948) ch. IV.

31   Adam Smith, *Wealth of Nations* [II, iii], vol. I, p. 321 (Cannan edition).

32   Adam Smith, *Wealth of Nations* [II, iii], vol. I, p. 323 (Cannan). Bentham criticized this view of Adam Smith's in his *Defence of Usury*.

33   See T.S. Ashton, 'The Treatment of Capitalism by Historians,' Hayek ed., *Capitalism and the Historians* (1954), 47.

34   Mill included five more cases in this category of policies based on erroneous theories. The first was protectionism. The second the attempt to lower the price of food by legal regulation, either in times of inflation or in times of shortage. The third case was the establishing of monopolies. The fourth was the case of the

Combination Laws. The fifth was impediments to the freedom of opinion. In all of them one could make reflections analogous to those concerning Usury Laws.

35   This point is emphasized by Robbins in *Politics and Economics* (1963), 33, 'Freedom and Order.' Mill felt no doubts about what kind of government suited a backward country. In a letter of 21 December 1837 to Professor Nichol, Mill wrote: 'There is much to be said about Ireland. I myself have always been for a good stout Despotism — for governing Ireland like India. But it cannot be done. The spirit of Democracy has got too much head there, too prematurely' (J.S. Mill, *Coll. Works*, XII, 365).

36   Mill was already thinking of these questions of the defects of the market in 1845. On 3 April 1845, the question 'Government Direction of Private Industry,' proposed by him, was discussed at the Political Economy Club. J.L. Prevost records the occasion in his Diary, *Proceedings of the Political Economy Club*, VI (1921), 291-2.

37   *Coll. Works, V,* 732.

38   In *The Economist* of 3 April 1847 we read: 'Were education left untouched by the State, its own beauties and inherent advantages are so great that the people would be as naturally attracted to it as they are to high wages... We advocate *laissez-faire* in education, therefore, as, in trade' (391, *in principio*). Reference in Scott Gordon, 'The London Economist and laissez-faire,' in *Journal of Political Economy*, LXIII, 6 (December 1955). See, however, the number for 10 December 1864, where that Review takes up a stand similar to Mill's: 'Only those who are themselves the most cultivated know the value of this sort of culture.'

39   There was however some relation between the limitation of working hours of women and children, and those of adult male workers: cotton mills had to close for all workers when women and children went home in obedience to the new Factory Act, at least until a judicial decision permitted the relay system expressly forbidden in the Act. See Cole, G.D.H. and Postgate, R.W., *The Common People* (1938), 308, and Sir L. Woodward, *The Age of Reform, 1815-1870* (The Oxford History of England, 1962), 154-5. For protection of the adult, cf. Woodward, *ibid,* 612.

40 See *Proceedings of the Political Economy Club*, VI, Diary of J.L. Prevost, 3 April 1845.

41 [J.S. Mill] Review of the 'Report on the Sanitary Condition of the Labouring Population of Great Britain,' in the *Examiner*, 20 August 1842, 530-1. For further details see my article, 'John Stuart Mill and *laissez-faire:* London Water,' in *Economica*, XXXIII, 129 (February, 1966), 76.

42 Mill to James Henderson, 22 August 1868, Elliot, ed., *The Letters of John Stuart Mill*, II, 120. For an account of the whole incident, see S.E. Finer's book, *The Life and Times of Sir Edwin Chadwick*, 498.

43 The economist Torrens had proposed years before, in 1834, that the government should intervene to solve this problem. See Robbins, *Torrens*, 250, n.3.

44 *The Economist*, 28 April 1865, attacking the proposal to grant a 24 hour copyright for newspaper articles, asserted: 'As it is with newspapers, so it is with books, so it is with inventions; the priority of publication or use, if diligently and properly employed, is all that an author or an inventor can require to realise all the pecuniary reward due to his labours.' (Reference in S. Gordon, 'The London Economist and Laissez-Faire'). *The Economist's* position may not have been as illjudged as it seems to be on first sight: there are many proposals at the present time to reduce the term for which an invention can be patented, since patents are an important cause of the imperfection of the market and the creation of cartels.

45 See Cairnes's commentaries in Appendix H, *Coll. Works*, III, 1046-7.

46 Cf. Joan Robinson, *Economic Philosophy* (1963), 143.

47 J.S. Mill, 'Posthumous "Chapters on Socialism" ' in *Coll. Works*, V, 730-1.

48 Mill composed the *Principles* in a little more than a year and a half. *Autobiography*, W. Cl, 199.

49 See W.J. Baumol, *Welfare Economics and the Theory of the State*, 140 ff.

50   P. 15 of the pamphlet, *Public Agency versus Trading Companies. The Economical and Administrative Principles of Water Supply for the Metropolis.* . . (London, 1851). There is a fuller account of this incident and its implications in my article 'John Stuart Mill and *laissez-faire*: London Water,' 71-83.

51   A sentiment scarcely shared by Chadwick, a bureaucrat in the Prussian style, as Finer calls him; see *Chadwick*, book X, epilogue, 'Bureaucracy and Democracy.'

52   When in Parliament, it was Mill who introduced for the first time a Bill for the establishment of a London County Council. See *Autobiography*, W. Cl., 243.

53   'Chadwick Papers,' University College Library, London. Quoted by permission of the Librarian, Mr Scott.

54   Hayek, ed., *J.S. Mill and Harriet Taylor. Their Correspondence and Subsequent Marriage*, 200. The other quotations in the text are taken from the same page or the two following.

55   *British Parliamentary Papers*, 1854-55, XX, 92-98.

56   See J.S. Mill, *Considerations on Representative Government* (London, 1861), ch. xiv. The references in the text are to the Everyman edition of *Utilitarianism, Liberty and Representative Government*.

57   The system was only fully applied to the Indian Civil Service. (*Repr. Govt.* 343). There was a mistaken idea that candidates had for a long time been selected for the East India Company on the competitive examination system. Admission through competitive examinations was introduced by the Company precisely in 1854.

58   Oliver MacDonagh, 'The 19th Century Revolution in Government,' *The Historical Journal*, I (1958).

59   [J.S. Mill], 'Centralization,' in *Edinburgh Review*, CXV (April 1862) 323-356.

60   See J.S. Mill, *On Representative Government*, end of chapter IV (Everyman edition), 226-7. Karl Marx in his admirable pamphlet

Le 18 Brumaire de Louis Napoléon Bonaparte (1852), besides noting the importance of the small peasants among the Emperor's supporters, passes some very severe judgements on the centralization of the French administrative machine.

61   Everyman edition, 168.

62   However, Mill would have exempted savings from all taxation, so that his proposal of a proportional income tax meant in effect a progressive tax on expenditure. See Lord Robbins's Introduction, *Coll. Works*, IV, xxv.

63   Luis Angel Rojo, 'Libertad y organización económica,' in *Tiempo de España*, num. 1 ('Libertad y organización,' Madrid 1963), 150-8.

Chapter 7   Socialism

1   Sidney Olivier, 'J.S. Mill and Socialism,' in *Today* NS, II(1884), 490-504.

Schumpeter, *History of Economic Analysis* (1954), 531-3.

Margaret Cole, *Makers of the Labour Movement* (1948),126: 'His thought was leading him steadily and directly towards socialism.'

K. Marx, *Capital*, 'Preface' to the second edition, 19.

Leslie Stephen, *The English Utilitarians*, III, *John Stuart Mill* (1900), 230.

Robbins, *Theory of Economic Policy* (1952), 142 ff.

2   Quoted by E.H. Carr in *What is History?* (Pelican 1964), 152.

3   G.D.H. Cole, *A History of Socialist Thought*, I, *The Forerunners 1789-1850* (1953), 86.

4   John Rae, *Contemporary Socialism* (1884),1 ff., especially 3-4.

5   An excellent comment on this whole aspect of socialism is Professor J. Talmon's book, *Political Messianism* (1960).

6   Only the Babouvists and the Blanquists were in favour of revolution during this period. But few people noticed the existence of these groups. See Cole, *History of Socialist Thought*, I, 164.

7   See Lecture IV in Lord Robbins's *Theory of Economic Policy*, esp. 112.

8   Never put into practice on a national scale, he said, except in the Empire of the Incas, 'not likely to be erected into a type for modern aspirations' ([1848] *Coll. Works*, III, Appendix A, 975, [II, i, 3]).

9   [1848], *Coll. Works*, III, 980 [II,i, 3].

10   See Mill, 'On the Definition and Method of Political Economy,' *Coll. Works*, IV, 319-20 and 321-2.

11   [1848], *Coll. Works*, III, 979-80, [II, i, 3].

12   He did note the fact that 'all persons are not equally fit for all labour; and the same quantity of labour is an unequal burden on the weak and the strong,' ([1848], *Coll. Works*, III, 977 [II, i, 3]).

13   [1848], *Coll. Works*, II, 982, note a-a, and 987 [II, i 5]. No paragraph in the first edition.

14   Elie Halévy, 'English Public Opinion and the French Revolutions of the Nineteenth Century,' in A. Colville and H. Temperley, *Studies in French History* (London 1935), 56-7.

15   *Coll. Works*, XIII, 732.

16   *Coll. Works*, XIII, 733-4.

17   Mill to J.P. Nichol, 30 September 1848, *Coll. Works*, XIII, 739.

18   [J.S. Mill], 'The French Revolution of 1848, and its Assailants,' in *Westminster Review*, LI (April, 1849). (Also in *Diss. and Disc.*, II, 335-410). The pagination in the text refers to the *Westminster*. Cf. Hayek, ed., *J.S. Mill and H. Taylor*, 141.

19   Mill accepted the disclaimer of Louis Blanc and other socialist leaders from any responsibility for the fighting in June 1848. See Mill's strong words in his letter to J.P. Nichol, 30 September 1848, *Coll. Works*, XIII, 740, and J.S. Mill, 'Déclaration du citoyen André Jules Lechevalier...' in the *Spectator*, XXII (8 December 1849), 1165.

20 N.W. Senior, 'Abstinence Concluded,' in *Course of Lectures Delivered at the University of Oxford in the years 1848-9*, 56-7. Seen in Robbins, *Theory of Economic Policy*, 141.

21 Hayek, ed., *J.S. Mill and H. Taylor*, 134-148. Extracts to be found in Appendix G of *Principles, Coll. Works*, III, 1026 ff.

22 [1849], *Coll. Works*, III, 978 [II, i, 3].

23 [1849] *ibid*. And the assertion of the sentence preceding the suppressed passage is applied in this 2nd edition only to Owenism instead of to socialism in general.

24 J.S. Mill to Harriet Taylor, 21 February 1849, *Coll. Works*, III, 1029.

25 Mill to Harriet, 19 February 1849, *Coll. Works*, III, 1028.

26 The article, signed Ion, is 'Some Consequences Reconsidered' in the section 'On Associative Progress,' *The Leader*, 27 July 1850, p. 416.

27 D. [J.S. Mill], letter to *The Leader*, 'Constraints of Communism,' in the issue of the 3 August 1850, p. 447. Letter dated 1 August 1850.

28 See *Coll. Works*, III, Appendix A, 978, note e, note f-f, note h-h, apart from what has been commented on in the text. In the chapter 'On the Probable Futurity of the Labouring Classes' another significant change may be noted: see *Coll. Works*, III, 764, note k-k [IV, vii, 2].

29 Schumpeter, *History of Economic Analysis*, 456, note 11.

30 The size of the share of the national income going to the distributive sector was greatly resented in the nineteenth century presumably because this was not thought productive.

31 Edmund Wilson, *To the Finland Station* (first edition 1940) (Fontana paperback), 93.

32 Mill to Carlyle, 25 November 1833, *Coll. Works*, XII, 193. Seen in Pankhurst, *The St. Simonians, Mill and Carlyle*, 98-99.

33   *Coll. Works*, III, 1031.

34   Mill to Harriet, 21 March 1849, *Coll. Works*, III, 1030.

35   Mill to Harriet, 31 March 1849, *Coll. Works*, III, 1031-32.

36   See, for example, Ch. Fourier, *Oeuvres Complètes*, V, 217 ff.

37   Mill's posthumous 'Chapters on Socialism,' in *Fortnightly Review*, *Coll. Works*, V, 748 note.

38   Mill to Harriet, 19 February 1849, *Coll. Works*, III, 1028.

39   See Hayek ed., *J.S. Mill and Harriet Taylor*, 300, note 44.

40   [J.S. Mill] review in *Westminster* (October 1851), of *Political Economy* by F.W.Newman (a brother of the Cardinal).*Coll. Works* V, 439-57. See also Mill to John Jay, about November 1848, *Coll. Works*, XIII, 740-1.

41   Cf. *Marx and Engels on Malthus*, ed. D.L. Meek and R.L. Meek (1953), 109.

42   Cf. [1852], *Coll. Works*, II, 205, with [1848 and 1849], *Coll. Works*, III, 976.

43   These words of [1852], *Coll. Works* II, 207, are taken from the closing paragraphs of the chapter on Property in the first and second editions. See [1848 and 1849], *Coll. Works*, III, 986.

44   Compare the way this point is worded in the third edition, [1852], *Coll. Works*, II, 209, with [1848 and 1849] *Coll. Works*, III, 979, lines 20-25.

45   Two passages were removed in the third edition (apart from the beginning of sect. 4): those that are not contained in brackets in *Coll. Works*, III, 981 and beginning of 982 [1849, II, i, 4].

46   In the third edition, the passages not in brackets in *Coll. Works*, III, 982-985 [1849, II, i, 5] were also removed.

47   Schumpeter, *History of Economic Analysis*, 532.

48   Robbins, *Theory of Economic Policy*, 167.

49   Cf. Professor Stillinger's 'Introduction' to *Early Draft*, pp. 5-11,
      and Stillinger, 'The Text of John Stuart Mill's *Autobiography*,'
      in *Bulletin of the John Rylands Library*, XLIII (1960-1), 223.

50   Cf. *Early Draft*, 173-4, with World Classics edition, 197-8.

51   J.S. Mill, Posthumous 'Chapters on Socialism,' in *Fortnightly*,
      also in *Coll. Works*, V, 703-53. The page numbers in the text
      refer to the latter.

52   Cf. Link, *English Theories of Economic Fluctuations*, 168-9.

53   Mill showed great esteem for Blanc. Cf. Hayek, ed., *J.S. Mill and
      Harriet Taylor*, 141, *Coll. Works*, XIII, 740; and Packe, *The Life
      of John Stuart Mill*, 430.

54   Cf. Schumpeter's *History of Economic Analysis*, 646.

55   Mill to Sterling, 20-22 October, 1831, *Coll. Works*, XII, 78.

56   Cf. St John Packe, *J.S. Mill*, 103, with *Coll. Works*, XII, 83-4.

57   See Mill to Gustave d'Eichthal, 21 May 1871, referring to the
      antisocialist economist Wolowsky. (*Correspondance avec G.
      d'E.*, 233). Also Helen Taylor to Kate Amberley, 5 October
      1871 (*Amberley Papers*, II, 414). Finally, Mill to Dupont White,
      6 December 1871 (Elliot, II, 319-20).

58   Mill to Georges Brandes, 4 March 1872 (Elliot, *Letters*, II, 334).

59   Transl. from Baron de Lavelèye, *Lettres inédites de Stuart Mill*,
      (1885), 23.

60   On the differences between Mill's 'Land Tenure Reform
      Association' and Marx's 'Land and Labour League,' see G.D.H.
      Cole, *The History of Socialist Thought*, II, 382-3 and Land
      Tenure Reform Association, *Report of the Inaugural Public
      Meeting... Mr. John Stuart Mill in the Chair*, 5-6.

61   A. Marshall, *Industry and Trade*, p. vii, quoted in Mrs Joan
      Robinson's *Economic Philosophy* (1962), 55.

62   In the final version, the phrase: 'which represent a more

advanced opinion' is substituted for the last six words. Compare *Early Draft*, 174, with World Classics Edition, 199.

63   See Mill, *Autobiography* (W. Cl.), 195-6, and *Early Draft* (ed. by J. Stillinger), 172-3. Mill says: 'We were *now* much less democrats' [my italics].

64   Baron Macaulay, 'The People's Charter,' *Complete Writings*, IX, 312. Louis Reybaud, *Economistes modernes* (reprinted from the *Revue des deux mondes*, 1 April 1855), Paris, 1862.

65   Lord Robbins, 'Introduction' to *Coll. Works*, IV, xl. The proofs of this introduction were kindly lent to me by Lord Robbins.

Chapter 8   The Future of Society

1   Mill, *Autobiography*, W. Cl., 208. It is doubtful that, as Mill asserts, he took the contrast between a paternalist and an individualist conception of society 'from the lips of his wife,' unless he did so in 1844. It has been said that Harriet contributed to Mill's intellectual work by giving him back what he had told her, and this might be one instance of it.

2   Mill to MacVey Napier, 9 November 1844, in *Coll. Works*, XIII, 643-4.

3   [J.S. Mill], 'The Claims of Labour,' in the *Edinburgh Review* (April, 1845), also in *Coll. Works*, IV, 374.

4   John Locke, 'Second Treatise of Civil Government,' Paragraph 27, in *Two Treatises on Government*, ed. by T.I. Cook (New York, 1947), 134.

5   J.S. Mill, unfinished speech at the Co-operation Society (1825). Cf. above, chapter 3, note 14 and text. Also *Principles, Coll. Works*, II, 215 [II, ii, 1].

6   J.S. Mill, unfinished speech at the Co-operation Society.

7   An interesting attempt to reconstruct the principle of private property on a Utilitarian basis, without reference to the labour theory of property, may be found in Professor F. von Hayek's *The Constitution of Liberty* (1960).

8   In accordance with general practice, Utilitarian considerations also entered another part of his argument on the right of property, namely the discussion of the reasons in favour of prescription; *Coll. Works*, II, 217 [II, ii, 2].

9   *A contrario*, see Mill to C.E. Norton, 26 June 1870: 'I do not, indeed, quite agree with your friend, Mr. Wright, when, in the passage quoted and concurred in by you, he seems to say that, from the utilitarian point of view, the right of private ownership is founded *solely* on the motives it affords to the increase of public wealth; because independently of those motives, the feeling of security of possession and enjoyment, which could not (in the state of advancement mankind have yet reached) be had without private ownership, is of the very greatest importance as an element of human happiness' (*Proceedings of the Massachusetts Historical Society*, L, 24, 1917). On the distinction between short-run and long-run Utilitarianism, see F.A. Hayek, *The Constitution of Liberty*, 159, and note 20 to chapter IX of that book.

10   [1848] *Coll. Works*, II, 223 and note b-b [II, ii, 4]. In the third edition the last clause was amended to read thus: 'The power of bequest may be so exercised as to conflict with the permanent interests of the human race' (*Ibid*).

11   After the doctrinal battle against the intangibility of endowments had been won, however, he turned against excessive control of 'excentric' legacies. *Coll. Works*, IV, 193-222, and V, 620ff.

12   Should it be decided not to fix an absolute maximum on the amount to be inherited, Mill would have agreed to steeply graduated death duties, according to his evidence before the 1852 and 1861 Parliamentary Committees on personal income taxation. Regarding this latter tax, apart from accepting that a minimum should be exempt, he favoured the exemption of savings, which meant that his income tax was a progressive, not proportional, tax on income. See n.6.62. Also Robbins's commentary in the section 'Income and Property Taxation' in his 'Introduction' to *Coll. Works*, volume IV, xxiv-xxv.

13   In the third edition [1852] the passage quoted in the text above reads: 'wealth which could no longer be employed in over-enriching a few. . .'. See also *Principles*, V, ix, where he returns to the subject of inheritance.

14   A. Bain, *J.S. Mill* (1882), 89. The main reviews of the *Principles* made no important mention of the said proposals. Hodgskin, in his article in the *Economist* of 27 May 1848, was silent on the question. So were Senior (*Edinburgh*, October 1848) and Bagehot (*Prospective Revue*, 1848). Grote, in the *Spectator* for 13 May, 1848, p. 469, made a short allusion to Mill's discussion of inheritance laws, dismissing Mill's alternative proposals to a French type system.

       The only discussion of any importance of Mill's views on inheritance seems to have been that of the follower of Marx, J.G. Eccarius, in 'A Working Man's Refutation of Some Points of Political Economy; endorsed and advocated by J.S. Mill, Esq., M.P.' in *The Commonwealth* [London], from 10 November 1866 to 31 March 1867, afterwards published in Germany under the title *Eines Arbeiters Widerlegung des nationalö cönomischen Lehren J.S. Mills* (Berlin, 1869). In his twelfth article, he shows strong disappointment that Mill should wish to make the property system work better by means of the limitation of succession, when in his opinion it should be completely overhauled.

15   John Locke, 'Second Treatise of Civil Government,' paragraph 50, *Two Treatises of Government*, ed. by T.I. Cook (1947), 145.

16   Thiers, *De la Propriété*, 122-3, 126-7, 58, 79.

17   See articles listed in J.S. Mill, *Bibliography of the Published Writings of* −, McMimm and others, eds. (Evanston, 1945), 60-68. Sometime later, the popular party in Ireland proposed to Mill that he should stand for Parliament representing a rural Irish county, 'in consequence,' he says, 'of my opinions on the Irish Land Question' (*Autobiography*, W. Cl., 237).

18   Mill presented the 'dynamic', 'historical', or 'Comtian' method for the first time in his *System of Logic* (1843), but its importance there is also over-estimated beyond its true significance in Mill's methodological thought. Cf. O. Kubitz, *The Development of Mill's Logic* (1932).

19   Below this minimum capitalists would refuse to accumulate more than was necessary to replace existing capital. Such a minimum would be lower in advanced countries.

20   Contrary to Mill's opinion, it seems that it is precisely in a stationary state that the gains of some must be at the expense of' others; only in a progressive state is it the case that gains and losses are relative, not absolute. See, however, that very Millian book, *The Costs of Economic Growth*, by E.J. Mishan (1967).

21   Cf. Frank Knight, 'The Ricardian Theory of Production and Distribution,' *On the History and Method of Economics* (Chicago, 1956), esp. 37-9, and note 2.

22   Cf., however, 'Civilization' (*Westminster Review* [1836], also *Diss. and Disc.*, I, 160 ff.), an attempt to distinguish the bad from the good effects of the progress of the country on its inhabitants.

23   But see note 1 above.

24   J.E. Cairnes, 'His Work in Political Economy,' in *J.S. Mill: Notices of his Life and Works. . . reprinted from the Examiner* (London, 1837), 49-50.

25   *Autobiography*, W.Cl., 207, note. See appendix II of *J.S. Mill and Harriet Taylor: their Correspondence, etc.*, F. Hayek, ed., 275-279: 'An Early Essay by Harriet Taylor.'

26   Mill claimed that the article on the 'Enfranchisement of Women,' *Westminster Review* (July 1851) was in fact written by his wife, he himself acting as little more than an amanuensis and editor (*Diss. and Disc.*, II, 411-412).

27   James Fitzjames Stephen, *Liberty, Equality, Fraternity* (1873), 206.

28   In his article 'The Sugar Refinery Bill and the Slave Trade,' in the *Examiner* 18 September 1831, 594-5, Mill made a strong plea that effective measures be taken to stop slave trade from Africa; but he argued that slave traffic among West Indian islands be permitted, so that the planters of impoverished islands could recoup some of their losses by selling their slaves in the more fertile ones. Perhaps, as Professor J. Robson suggested to me, the planters' point of view had been put to Mill by his friend Sterling, who was at that time managing a plantation in St Vincent. Or perhaps he simply partook in the relatively cooler attitude of the Radicals to the question of

emancipating the slaves, described by E. Halévy in his *History of the English People*, III, 84-5.

29   In his letters to his American correspondents, Mill explained the change of convictions in England, by the fact that the anti-slavery feeling had not been exercised on any great object for the length of a generation; by the dislike of the upper classes of England for the brashness of the North American Democracy; and finally by the great ignorance of American questions, which made them believe that the North was bent upon a war of conquest, and that the South was fighting for its independence.

30   [T. Carlyle], 'Occasional Discourse on the Negro Question,' in *Fraser's Magazine*, XL (December 1849), 670-679; reprinted in an enlarged form as a pamphlet, under Carlyle's name, with the title, *Occasional Discourse on the Nigger Question* (1853). And D. [J.S. Mill], Letter on 'The Negro Question,' in *Fraser's Magazine*, XLI (January 1850), 25-31. It is clear from the letter that Mill knew the identity of the author.

31   [J.S. Mill], 'The Contest in America,' in *Fraser's Magazine*, LXV (February 1862). Also in *Diss. and Disc.*, III.

32   See *Letters*, H. Elliot, ed., I, 263, 268-9, 276-81, 300-2, 303-4; and II, 31-2.

33   The Mill-Cairnes correspondence is full of the American War in those years. See the late Mrs A. Weinberg's *J.E. Cairnes and the American Civil War* (1970).

34   *Coll. Works*, III, 766 [IV, vii, 4]. The words in brackets in the text were added in 1849 after the 1848 Revolution had taken place in France.

35   J.S. Mill, *On Representative Government*, chap. VII (Everyman ed., 256).

36   Mill to E. Herford, 22 January 1850, *Letters,* H. Elliot ed., I, 153.

37   Mill, *Autobiography*, W. Cl., 263. He also defended the extension of the franchise in 1848, when Hume's Reform Bill was being debated; see his unsigned leaders in the *Daily News*, 8

July 1848, 19 July 1848, 25 July 1848, especially the second, where the advantages of a large working class representation in Parliament are put forward. Professor Burns called my attention to the fact that Mill favoured *universal* suffrage, though coupled with plural voting.

38   [1848] IV, vii, 4. This passage was omitted from the 1852 edition and all later editions (see *Coll. Works*, III, 766-7), presumably because of the words it contained against competition, since in this third edition he wanted 'to disconnect the co-operative cause from the exaggerated or altogether mistaken declamations against competition, so largely indulged in by its supporters.' (Preface to the 3rd ed.) It is also possible that the reason may have been a desire to expunge references to unavoidable hostility between employers and employed.

39   Here Mill was perhaps unwittingly exaggerating the opposition of interests between the capitalists and the wage earners; it is not in the interests of employers to pay as low wages as they can, but to have as low costs as possible. Mill himself remarked this elsewhere (*Coll. Works*, II, 413, [II, xv, 7]).

40   Cf. Carlyle, *Past and Present* (1843), 198 and *passim*.

41   J. Saville, 'The Christian Socialists of 1848' in *Democracy and the Labour Movement* (1954), edited by J. Saville, 149 ff.

42   [J.S. Mill], 'The Claims of Labour,' in *Edinburgh Review* (April 1845), reprinted in *Coll. Works*, IV, 363-89.

43   Mill, *Letters*, H. Elliot, ed., I, 172-3.

44   *The Co-operator* [Manchester], no. 52 (June 1864), 5-6.

45   J.S. Mill to Harriet Taylor, 4 February 1854; *J.S. Mill and Harriet Taylor*, F. Hayek ed., 202.

46   See J. Stillinger's 'Introduction' to *The Early Draft of John Stuart Mill's Autobiography* (1961), 5-11.

47   See J. Hamburger, *Intellectuals in Politics: John Stuart Mill and the Philosophic Radicals* (Yale, 1965), 267.

48   A.V. Dicey, *Law and Opinion*, 424. Accounts of Mill's

parliamentary career are to be found in his *Autobiography* and in Packe's somewhat romanticized biography. The complete list of Mill's interventions in Parliament was made available to me by Professor Robson.

49   *Autobiography*, W. C1., 247. The obituary article in *The Times* is mentioned in Appendix II.

50   Cf. p. 254.

51   The explanation for this most often put forward consists in pointing out that he did not foresee the steady advance in technology that has taken place since his time. Cf. J.J. Spengler, 'Mill and Economic Development,' in B.F. Hoselitz, ed., *Theories of Economic Growth* (1960).

52   Neither of them foresaw the leading role nationalism was destined to play.

53   See K. Marx, *Oeuvres*, I (La Pléyade), édition établie par Maximilien Rubel: *Adresse Inaugurale et Statuts de l'Association Internationale des Travailleurs* (1864). The original text was published in English but I do not have it at hand. Marx had been entrusted with the drafting of it.

54   See J. Vanek, 'Decentralization under Workers' Management: A Theoretical Appraisal,' *American Economic Review*, LIX, 5 (December 1969), 1006-1014, and the literature there mentioned.

55   Alfred Marshall, 'The Future of the Working Classes' reprinted in *Memorials of Alfred Marshall*, ed. by A.C. Pigou (London 1925).

56   E. Wilson, *To the Finland Station* (1st. ed., 1940) (Fontana paperback) 486-7.

Chapter 9   Conclusion   Where Mill Failed and Where He Succeeded

1   Hugh Dalton, *Some Aspects of the Inequality of Incomes in Modern Communities* (London, 1920, 2nd. ed., 1925), 69.

2   Mill in conversation with Lavelèye, in 1873. E.de Lavelèye, *Lettres inédites de John Stuart Mill* (1885), 23.

3   Mill to Cairnes, 5 December 1871, *Mill-Taylor Collection*, vol. LV, item 84, ff. 179v-180r. Cairnes had told him on 23 October 1871: 'You will probably have got from Jevons a copy of his volume on "The Theory of Political Economy" and I shall much like to hear what you think of it. My own impressions are not favourable, though I think there is a good deal of utility in the book. His theory of value appears to me to resolve itself, if not into an identical proposition, into a perfectly barren generalization; and I own I have no faith in the development of economic doctrines by mathematics. What you have said on the subject of nomenclature in the second vol. of your Logic seems to me decisive upon this point.' *Mill-Taylor Collection* (copy), vol. LVI A, item 61, ff. 353-4.

4   Mill in conversation with Lavelèye, *ibid.*

5   Mill to Professor C.D.H. Rau of Heidelberg, 20 March 1852, *Letters*, H. Elliot ed., I, 170.

Appendix II   The Diabolical Handbills

1   Quoted by Field, *Essays on Population* (1931), p.107. Little can be added to Field's account of the whole incident in that book. See also N.E. Himes: 'J.S. Mill and Robert Owen in English Neo-Malthusianism,' in *Quarterly Journal of Economics*, XLII (1942), 627-40, and 'J.S. Mill's Attitude towards Neo-Malthusianism,' in *Economic Journal, Economic History Suppt.*, 4 (1929), 457-84.

2   According to Falconer however, in *Note upon a Paper* (1845) (a printed leaflet that we shall comment on later), the incident occurred before July 1822, but it was to Falconer's interest to set the date earlier in order to exonerate Roebuck completely from any charge of taking part in the adventure and it is my belief that his memory failed him. Also I have been unable to find any reference around the summer of 1823 in the Press, or even the records of the Magistrates Courts which might contain some reference to the affair. But in favour of the date chosen in the text, one can find in volume 68 of the 'Place Papers' in the British Museum that there are two letters from a Mrs Fildes to Carlile, the agitator (not to be confused with Carlyle, the writer), of 7 July 1823, enclosing one of the diabolical handbills; her second letter, of the 7 September 1823, states that she had received the diabolical handbills six weeks earlier. Cf. Field *Essays on Population*, 79.

3   Printed copies of these handbills are to be found among the
        papers of Francis Place in the British Museum. Rough drafts of
        the second and third handbill are corrected in the latter's
        handwriting, according to Field in *Essays on Population*, p.108.
        Moreover the substance of the handbills fits in with what we
        know of Place's thought. Field believes that he knows who the
        author was, someone totally unknown.
                For some time they were attributed to Robert Owen,
        especially because of an anonymous letter in the *Black Dwarf*
        which asserted that it was Owen who had brought details of the
        method from France. But it must be pointed out that this letter
        was almost certainly written by Place himself (Field, *op.cit.*,
        p.99) and does not say that Owen had written the handbills,
        only that he had brought the idea from France. Owen denied
        the imputation of authorship of the handbills years later in a
        letter to the *Morning Chronicle* of 8 October 1827. (See N.E.
        Himes, 'The Place of J.S. Mill and Robert Owen in the History
        of English Neo-Malthusianism,' in *Quarterly Journal of
        Economics*, XLII (August 1928), 639.) As we shall see further
        on, in Mill's time it was believed that the writings circulated
        were *Every Woman's Book; or What is Love? containing most
        important instructions for the prudent regulation of the
        Principle of Love, and the number of a family*. I have seen the
        1833 edition. The author was known to be R. Carlile. But it
        does not seem very likely that Mill circulated it, in view of the
        points mentioned in this note and the date of the first
        publication of *What is Love?*: Himes reports that it appeared
        under the title 'What is Love?' in the *Republican* of 5 May
        1825. It was not published as an independent pamphlet and
        with the title we have given above, until February 1826.

4   *Black Dwarf*, XI, 19 [5 November, 1823], 660.

5   See also 'Francis Place Collection', British Museum, 68, folios
        115-7.

6   Cf. *The Early Letters of J.S. Mill, 1812-1848*, Mineka ed., *Coll.
        Works*, XIII, 367.

7   Hayward published two works that I have been unable to see,
        the first lost through bombing during the war: *On the Origin
        and History of the Benchers of the Inns of Court* (London,
        1848), and *The Ballot for Benchers, by a Templar* (printed

privately and anonymously in London, 1848). Charles Neate, another person involved in the quarrel of 1832 between Roebuck and Hayward, published *Remarks on a Late Decision of the Judges as Visitors of the Inns of Court* (London, 1848; lost in the bombing of the British Museum).

8   Preserved at the Middle Temple library.

9   [Abraham Hayward], *Letter to Stopford Augustus Brooke* [n.d.]. It is to be found in the library of the Athenaeum Club in London, and was kindly shown to me by the librarian, Miss Walker.

   The translation of the quotation heading the letter is as follows: Wagner: 'I have often heard a comedian boast that he could teach a parson.' Faust: 'Yes, when the parson is a comedian, which happens all too often.'

10   M. St. J. Packe, *J.S. Mill*, 72, footnote.

Bibliography

This list includes essentially all articles mentioned in the text, except that the writings mentioned in the Preface are not noted here. Some very few unmentioned documents are included, as being interesting and not widely known. Square brackets are used for writers who published anonymously or under pseudonym, or for information added by the author.

1 J. S. MILL

1.1 Bibliographies

Amano, Keitaro: *A John Stuart Mill Bibliography*, Osaka, 1956.

Mill, J.S.: *Bibliography of the Published Writings of—*, ed. by N. McMimm, Hainds, McNabb and McCrimmon, Evanston, Ill., 1945.

Bibliography in *The Mill News Letter*, n° 1 ff., Toronto, 1965-.

1.2 Manuscripts

Mill, J.S.: 'Closing Speech on the Co-operative System,' 1825. [Seen in Prof. J.M. Robson's typescript.] [Repr. under wrong title and with pages misplaced, in *Archiv für Sozialwissenschaft und Sozialpolitik*, 62 (1929), 225-39, 466-7.]

Mill, J.S.: 'Intended Speech at the Co-operation Society, never delivered,' 1825, MS Connecticut College for Women, previously unpublished. [Seen in Prof. J.M. Robson's typescript.]

'The Mill-Taylor Collection,' Library of the London School of Economics, especially: LV Mill to Cairnes, LVI Cairnes to Mill (Copies), LVII Mill to Fawcett, Box of Additional Material.

Mill, J.S.: Letter from J.S. Mill to Harriet Taylor, 7 February 1854, 'Yale University Collection of J.S. Mill's Letters.' [Seen in Prof. J.M. Robson's typescript.]

1.3 Letters

Mill, J.S.: *Lettres inédites de Stuart Mill*, ed. by Lavelèye, E., Baron de —, Brussels-Paris, 1885.

Mill, J.S.: 'Unpublished Letters from J.S. Mill to Professor Nichol,' ed. by Knight, *Fortnightly Review*, N.S., LXI (1897), 660-78.

Mill, J.S.: *Correspondance inédite avec Gustave d'Eichthal, 1828-42, 1864-71*, Prologue and translation by E. d'Eichthal, Paris, 1898.

Mill, J.S.: *Lettres inédites de J.S. Mill à A. Comte, publiées avec les réponses de Comte et une introduction*, par L. Lévy-Bruhl, Paris 1889.

Mill, J.S.: *The Letters of* –, ed. with an introduction by H.S.R. Elliot, London, 1910.

Mill, J.S.: 'Letters of John Stuart Mill to Charles Eliot Norton,' in *Proceedings of the Massachusetts Historical Society*, 50 (1917), 11-25.

Mill, J.S. and Taylor, Harriet: Letters of –, in F.A. von Hayek, *John Stuart Mill and Harriet Taylor: Their Friendship and Subsequent Marriage*, Chicago, 1951.

Mill, J.S.: *The Earlier Letters of* –, *1812 to 1848*, ed. by F.E. Mineka [Vols. XII and XIII of J.S. Mill's *Collected Works*], Toronto and London, 1963.

Mill, J.S.: Letters to McVeigh Napier, in *Selection from the Correspondence of McVeigh Napier*, ed. by M. Napier, London, 1879.

1.4 Collections of Mill's work (in order of publication)

Mill, J.S.: *Essays on Some Unsettled Questions of Political Economy*, London, 1844.

Mill, J.S.: *Dissertations and Discussions; Political, Philosophical, and Historical*, 4 vols., London, 1859-75.

Mill, J.S.: *Utilitarianism, Liberty, and Representative Government*, Everyman, London, 1910.

Mill, J.S.: *Collected Works of John Stuart Mill*, general editor F.E.L. Priestley; associate editor J.M. Robson, Toronto and London, University of Toronto Press, Routledge and Kegan Paul. [To date there have been published: vols. II and III, *Principles of Political Economy*, ed. J.M. Robson, 1965; vols. IV and V, *Essays on Economics and Society*, ed. J.M. Robson, 1967; vols. XII and XIII, *The Earlier Letters of John Stuart Mill, 1812-1848*, ed. Francis E. Mineka, 1963; vol. X, *Essays on Ethics, Religion and Society*, textual ed. J.M. Robson, 1969.]

1.5 Articles, speeches and books published in his lifetime (in order of publication)

1823-4

[Mill, J.S.]: [Four letters on the need to limit population in] *The Black Dwarf*, London 27 November 1823, 10 December 1823, 7 January 1824, 25 February 1824. [In the Bodleian Library, Oxford.]

1825

[Mill, J.S.]: 'The Quarterly Review on Political Economy,' *Westminster Review*, January, 1825, 213-32. [Repr. in *Coll. Works*, IV]

[Mill, J.S.]: 'The Corn Laws,' *Westminster Review*, April, 1825, 394-420. [Repr. in *Coll. Works*, IV]

1826

[Mill, J.S.]: 'The Silk Trade,' *Westminster Review*, January, 1826, 136-49. [Repr. in *Coll. Works*, IV]

[Mill, J.S.]: 'Paper Currency and Commercial Distress,' *Parliamentary Review, Session of 1826*, 630-62. [Repr. in *Coll. Works*, IV]

1827

[Mill, J.S.]: 'The New Corn Law,' *Westminster Review*, January, 1827, 169-86 [Repr. in *Coll. Works*, IV]

1828

[Mill, J.S.]: 'Trade with India,' *Parliamentary Review for the Session of 1826-7*, vol. II, 1828.

[Mill, J.S.]: 'Intercourse Between the United States and the British Colonies in the West Indies,' *Parliamentary Review for the Session of 1826-7*, vol. II, 1828.

1831

A.B. [Mill, J.S.]: 'The Spirit of the Age,' *The Examiner*, London 6 January – 29 May 1831. [Repr. by F.A. Hayek, Chicago, 1942.]

[Mill, J.S.]: 'The Emigration Bill' [Lord Howick's], *The Examiner*, 27 February 1831, 130-31.

[Mill, J.S.]: 'The Sugar Refinery Bill and the Slave Trade,' *The Examiner*, 18 September 1831, 594-5.

1832

[Mill, J.S.]: 'The Employment of Children in Manufactories,' *The Examiner*, 29 January 1832, 67-8.

[Mill, J.S.]: [a paragraph in reply to a letter on the subject of the employment of women in factories], *The Examiner*, 26 February 1832, 131.

[Mill, J.S.]: [a paragraph in reply to a correspondent on 'Landlords Claims'], *The Examiner*, 6 May 1832, 295.

1833

[Mill, J.S.]: 'Of, the Right and Wrong of State Interference with Corporation and Church Property,' *The Jurist*, III, February, 1833. [Repr. in *Dissertations and Discussions*, I, 1 ff.]

[Mill, J.S.]: 'Municipal Institutions,' *The Examiner,* 11 August 1833, 496-7.

A.B. [Mill, J.S.]: 'The Corporation Bill,' *The Examiner,* 20 October 1833, 559-60.

[Mill, J.S.]: 'The Currency Juggle,' *Tait's Edinburgh Magazine,* II, January, 1833, 461-7. [Repr. in *Diss. and Disc.* also in *Coll. Works,* IV.]

[Mill, J.S.]: 'Appendix (B), Remarks on Bentham's Philosophy,' in E.L. Bulwer, *England and the English,* London, 1833. [Repr. *Coll. Works,* X, App. C, 499-502]

[Mill, J.S.?]: 'Appendix (C), A Few Observations on Mr Mill,' in E.L. Bulwer, *England and the English,* London, 1833.

1834

[Mill, J.S.]: 'Notes on Newspapers. 12 February. Attendance in the House,' *Monthly Repository,* N.S. VIII, 1834, 167-9.

[Mill, J.S.]: 'Notes on the Newspapers. 18 April. The Proposed Reform of the Poor Laws,' *Monthly Repository,* N.S., VIII, 1834, 360-4.

[Mill, J.S.]: 'Notes on Newspapers. 15 March. The Trades' Unions,' *Monthly Repository,* N.S., VIII, 1834, 246-8.

A. [Mill, J.S.]: 'Notes on the Newspapers. 19 April. Government by Brute Force,' *Monthly Repository,* N.S., VIII, 1834, 364-8.

A. [Mill, J.S.]: 'Notes on the Newspapers. 1 May. The Press and the Trades' Unions,' *Monthly Repository,* N.S., VIII, 1834, 435-7.

[Mill, J.S.]: [Leading article on Mr Walter's pamphlet against the Poor Law Amendment Bill], *Morning Chronicle,* 12 May 1834, p.2.

[Mill, J.S.]: [First leader, on the Poor Law Amendment Bill], *The Sun,* 12 May 1834, p.2.

A. [Mill, J.S.]: 'On Miss Martineau's Summary of Political Economy,' *Monthly Repository,* N.S., VIII, 1834, 318-22. [Repr. in *Coll. Works,* IV.]

A. [Mill, J.S.]: 'Notes on Newspaper. 6 June. Business in the House of Commons,' *Monthly Repository,* N.S., VIII, 1834, 523-5.

[Mill, J.S.]: 'The New Colony' I and II, *The Examiner,* 29 June 1834, 403, and *ibid.,* 6 July 1834, 419.

[Mill, J.S.]: '[A review of E.G. Wakefield's book] *The New British Province in South Australia...',* *The Examiner,* 20 July 1834, 453-4.

A. [Mill, J.S.]: 'Notes on Newspapers. 23 July. Lord Brougham's

Speech on the Poor Law Amendment Bill,' *Monthly Repository*. N.S., VIII, 1834, 596-7.

A.B. [Mill, J.S.]: 'The New Australian Colony,' *Morning Chronicle*, 23 October 1834, p.3.

1835

A. [Mill, J.S.]: 'De Tocqueville on Democracy in America,' *London Review*, II, 3, October 1835, 85-129.

1836

[Mill, J.S.]: 'Civilization — Signs of the Times,' *London and Westminster Review* [henceforth, *Westminster Rev.*], January, 1846, 1-28. [Repr. in *Diss. and Disc.* I, 160-205.]

[Mill, J.S.]: 'On the Definition of Political Economy; and on the Method of Philosophical Investigation in that Science,' *Westminster Review* (October 1836), 1-29. [Repr. as 'On the Definition of Political Economy; and on the Method of Investigation Proper to it,' in *Essays on Some Unsettled Questions of Political Economy* (1844). Also in *Coll. Works*, IV.]

1837

[Mill, J.S.]: '[A review of E.G. Wakefield's book] *Popular Politics*,' *The Examiner*, 29 January 1837, 70-1.

[Mill, J.S.]: [An unheaded leading article on H.G. Ward's Bill on the sale of lands in the colonies], *The True Sun*, 22 February 1837, p.3.

1838

[Mill, J.S.]: 'Lord Durham and the Canadians,' *Westminster Rev.*, XXX, January, 1838, 1ff.

[Mill, J.S.]: 'Bentham,' *Westminster Review*, XXXI, April, 1838, 1-44. [Repr. in *Diss. and Disc.*, and *Coll Works*, X, 75-115]

1839

A. [Mill, J.S.]: 'Reorganization of the Reform Party,' *Westminster Rev.*, XXXII, April, 1839, 475-508.

1840

[Mill, J.S.]: 'Coleridge,' *Westminster Rev.*, XXXIII, March, 1840, 257-302. [Repr. in *Diss. and Disc.* and *Coll. Works*, X, 117-63.]

[Mill, J.S.]: 'Democracy in America' [a review of Tocqueville's book], *Edinburgh Review*, LXXII, October, 1840, 1-47. [Repr. in *Diss. and Disc.* II, 1 ff.]

1841

[Mill, J.S.] [at least in part]: 'Kensington. The following is the

Petition Agreed to at a Meeting Held at Kensington on Tuesday Evening,' *Morning Chronicle,* 17 June 1841: [Repr. in *Coll. Works,* V, Appendix B, 761-3.]

1842

[Mill, J.S.]: [Review of the] 'Report of the Sanitary Condition of the Labouring Population of Great Britain,' *The Examiner,* 20 August 1842, 530-1. [In his *Bibliog.,* 54, Mill says he wrote 'the greater part' of it.]

1843

Mill, J.S.: *A System of Logic, Ratiocinative and Inductive,* 1st edition, London, 1843.

1844

Mill, J.S.: 'Of the Laws of Interchange Between Nations: and the Distribution of the Gains of Commerce among the Countries of the Commercial World' [written around 1829, but not published until 1844 with the other] *Essays on Some Unsettled Questions of Political Economy,* London, 1844. [Repr. in *Coll. Works,* IV, 232-261.]

Mill, J.S.: 'The Influence of Consumption upon Production' [written around 1829], *Essays on Some Unsettled Questions.* [Repr. in *Coll. Works,* IV, 262-79.]

Mill, J.S.: 'On Profits, and Interest' [written around 1829], *Essays on Some Unsettled Questions.* [Repr. in *Coll. Works,* IV, 290-308.]

Mill, J.S.: *Essays on Some Unsettled Questions of Political Economy,* London, 1844.

[Mill, J.S.]: 'The Currency Question,' *Westminster Rev.,* June, 1844, 579-98. [Repr. in *Coll. Works.,* IV, 341-61.]

1845

[Mill, J.S.]: 'The Claims of Labour,' *Edinburgh Review,* LXXXI, April, 1845, 498-525. [Repr. in *Diss. and Disc.,* II. Also in *Coll. Works,* V, 363-89.]

1846-7

[Mill, J.S.]: [Review of] 'Duveyrier's Political Views of French Affairs,' *Edinburgh Review,* LXXXIII, April, 1846, 453-74.

[Mill, J.S.]: [47 leading articles on Irish problems in] *Morning Chronicle,* 5 October 1846 — 7 April 1847.

1848

[Mill, J.S.]: [A First Leader on the Reform debate on Joseph Hume's Motion], *Daily News,* 8 July 1848, p.3.

[Mill, J.S.] :: [A First Leader on Reform, dealing with the advantages of having a commensurate working class representation in Parliament], *Daily News,* 19 July 1848.

[Mill, J.S.] : [A Leading Article on the Equalisation of Electoral Districts and against Sgt. Talfourd's Speech], *Daily News,* 25 July 1848, pp 2-3.

Mill, J.S.: *The Principles of Political Economy with Some of Their Applications to Social Philosophy* [1st edition], London, 1848. [2nd ed., London 1849; 3rd. ed., 1852; 4th ed., 1857; 5th ed., 1862; 6th ed., 1865; 7th ed., 1871; ed. by Ashley, 1909; Vols. II and III of *Coll. Works,* ed. by J.M. Robson, Toronto, 1964.]

1849

[Mill, J.S.] : 'The French Revolution of 1848, and its Assailants,' *Westminster Review,* LI, April, 1849, 1-47. [Repr. in *Diss. and Disc.,* II, 335-410.]

[Mill, J.S.] : 'Déclaration du citoyen André Jules Lechevalier...', *The Spectator,* XXII, 8 December 1849, 1165.

1850

D. [Mill, J.S.] : [A letter on] 'The Negro Question,' *Fraser's Magazine,* 41, January, 1850, 25-31.

Mill, J.S.: [Examination of —, in the] *Report of the Select Committee on Investments for the Savings of the Middle and Working Classes,* 'Minutes of Evidence' in *B.P.P.,* 1850, XIX, pp. 253-66, 'J.S. Mill, Esq., examined.' [Repr. in *Coll. Works,* V, 405-29.]

D. [Mill, J.S.] : 'Constraints of Communism' [a letter dated 1 August 1850, in] *The Leader,* 3 August 1850, 447.

1851

[Mill, J.S.] : '[Review of F. Newman's] *Lectures on Political Economy,' Westminster Rev.,* October, 1851, 81-101. [Repr. in *Coll. Works,* V, 439-57.]

Mill, J.S.: [Letter in] *Public Agency v. Trading Companies. The Economical and Administrative Principles of Water-Supply for the Metropolis. Correspondence between J.S. Mill, Esq., Author of 'Principles of Political Economy,' and the Metropolitan Sanitary Association on the Proper Agency for Regulating the Water-Supply for the Metropolis, as a Question of Economical and Administrative Principle,* London [1851].

1855

Mill, J.S.: 'Mr John Stuart Mill,' in 'Papers Relating to the Reorganization of the Civil Service,' *British Parliamentary Papers,* 1854-55, XX, 94-100.

1859

Mill, J.S.: *On Liberty,* London, 1859. [Repr. in *Utilitarianism, Liberty, and Representative Government,* Everyman, London, 1910.]

Mill, J.S.: *Dissertations and Discussions; Political, Philosophical and Historical,* 4 vols., London, 1859-75 [2 vols., 1859; 3 vols., 1867; 4 vols., 1875].

1861

Mill, J.S.: [An Essay in Five Chapters entitled] 'Utilitarianism,' *Fraser's Magazine,* LXIV, October, November, December 1861. [Reprinted as a book in 1863, also repr. in *Utilitarianism, Liberty, and Representative Government* and *Coll. Works,* X, 203-59.]

1862

[Mill, J.S.]: 'The Contest in America,' *Fraser's Magazine,* LXV, 386, February, 1862, 258-68. [Also in *Diss. and Disc.,* III, 179-205.]

[Mill, J.S.]: 'Centralization,' *Edinburgh Review,* CXV, April, 1862, 323-58 [mainly a review of Dupont-White's book of that title].

[Mill, J.S.]: 'The Slave Power,' *Westminster Rev.,* October, 1862, 489-510. [A review of J.E. Cairnes's book of that title.]

1864

Mill, J.S.: [Mill's Speech to the London Co-operation Society], *The Co-operator* [Manchester] 52, June, 1864, 5-6.

1865

Mill, J.S.: 'Auguste Comte and Positivism,' *Westminster Rev.,* April and June, 1865. [Repr. as a book, London, 1865. Also *Coll. Works,* X, 261-367.]

1867

Mill, J.S.: *Speech of John Stuart Mill, M.P., on the Admission of Women to the Electoral Franchise, Spoken in the House of Commons, May 20th, 1867,* London, 1867.

1868

Mill, J.S.: *England and Ireland,* London, 1868.

1869

Mill, J.S.: 'Endowments,' *Fortnightly Review,* N.S., V, April, 1869, 377-90. [Repr. in *Diss. and Disc.,* IV. Also in *Coll. Works,* V.]

Mill, J.S.: 'Thornton on Labour and its Claims,' *Fortnightly Review*, V, May, 1869, 505-18, 680-700. [Repr. in *Diss. and Disc.*, IV. Also in *Coll. Works.*, V, 631-68.]

Mill, J.S.: *The Subjection of Women*, London, 1869.

1871

Mill, J.S.: 'Explanatory Statement, [Appended to] *Programme of the Land Tenure Reform Association*, London, 1871. [Repr. in *Diss. and Disc.*, IV. Also *Coll. Works*, V, 687-95.]

Mill, J.S.: [Presidential Address to the Land Tenure Reform Association, in] *Report of the Inaugural Meeting of the Land Tenure Reform Association. Monday, 15 May 1871, Mr J.S. Mill in the Chair.* [Repr. in *Diss. and Disc.*, IV, 251-65.]

1873

Mill, J.S.: 'Advice to Land Reformers,' and 'Should Public Bodies be Required to Sell their Land?' *The Examiner*, 4 January 1873, pp.1-2, and 11 January 1873, pp.29-30. [Repr. in *Diss. and Disc.*, IV, 266-77, under the title 'Advice to Land Reformers,' incomplete.]

Mill, J.S.: 'The Right of Property in Land,' *The Examiner*, 19 July 1873. [Repr. as a pamphlet by the 'Land Tenure Reform Association,' also in *Diss. and Disc.*, IV, 288-302.]

1.6 Articles, speeches and books published posthumously (in order of publication)

Mill, J.S.: *Autobiography*, London, 1873.

Mill, J.S.: *Three Essays on Religion: Nature, the Utility of Religion and Theism*, London, 1874. [Repr. *Coll. Works*, X, 369-489.]

Mill, J.S.: '[Posthumous] Chapters on Socialism,' *Fortnightly Review*, N.S., XXV, 1879, 217-37, 373-82, 513-30. [Repr. in *Coll. Works*, V, 703-53.]

Mill, J.S.: 'Two Speeches on Population' [1825], ed. H. Laski, *Journal of Adult Education*, IV, 1 October, 1929, 38-61.

Mill, J.S.: 'Further Reply... on Population' [in fact, the 'Closing Speech' in the debate on the Owenite system] [1825], in *Archiv fur Sozialwissenschaft und Sozialpolitik*, 62 (1929), 225-39 and 466-67. [MS: Connecticut College for Women.]

Mill, J.S.: *The Spirit of the Age*, ed., by F.A. Hayek, Chicago, 1942.

Mill, J.S.: *The Early Draft of John Stuart Mill's Autobiography*, ed. by J. Stillinger, Urbana, 1961.

1.7 Works of editing, selection and translation

Mill, J.S. (editor): Bentham, Jeremy, *The Rationale of Judicial Evidence*, London, 1827.

Mills, J.S. (editor): Mill, James, *Analysis of the Phenomena of the Human Mind,* 2nd edition, London, 1869.

Mill, J.S. (trans.): *Four Dialogues of Plato.* Translated by J.S. Mill ['Protagoras,' 'Phaedro,' 'Gorgias,' 'The Apology of Socrates,' first published in *Monthly Repository*], ed. by Ruth Borchardt, London, 1946. [Another five translations have remained unpublished: 'Charmides,' 'Eutyphron,' 'Laches,' 'Lysis,' and 'Parmenides.']

2 OTHER WRITERS

2.1 Manuscripts

Cairnes, John Elliot: Letters to Mill (copies) 'Mill-Taylor Collection', vol. LVI, A.

Cairnes, J.E.: [Notes to the 5th edition of J.S. Mill's *Principles* (1862). Used by Mill in the preparation of the 6th edition (1865)], 'Mill-Taylor Collection,' vol, LVI, B.

Courtney, Leonard: 'Notebook containing a list of leaders, and other articles, written for the Times by Leonard Courtney, and payment therefore, 1864-1880,' 'Courtney Collection,' XX, Library of the London School of Economics.

The 'Francis Place Collection' of the British Museum. [Guardbooks, 'Printed Books Department'; manuscripts, especially letters, in 'Manuscript Department'.]

Place, Francis: 'Narrative of the Proceedings to Procure the Repeal of the Laws against Combinations of Workmen, Emigration of Artizans [and] Exportation of Machinery; 1810-1825.' British Museum, Add. MSS. 27.798.

Webb, S. and B.: [Manuscript sources relating to the Amalgamated Society of Engineers], Vol. A, XVI, item 2. 'Past History' [an abstract of Burnett, 'A Model Trade Society', in *Newcastle Weekly Chronicle,* 3 July 1875], 'Trade Union Collection,' at the London School of Economics.

Webb, S. and B.: 'Senior, Nassau *and* Tomlison. The practical results of the existing law and existing habits of combinations,' Vol. A.I, Item 3: 'Typescript extract from the manuscript report to the Home Office in 1830.' 'Trade Union Collection,' at the London School of Economics.

2.2 Letters (published)

Carlyle, Thomas: *Letters of − to John Stuart Mill, John Sterling, and Robert Browning,* edited by A. Carlyle, London, 1923.

Comte, Auguste: *Lettres d'Auguste Comte a John Stuart Mill, 1841-1846,* Paris, 1877.

Comte, A.: *Lettres inédites de J.S. Mill à A. Comte...* Paris, 1889.

2.3 Books, Articles and other Publications

Anon.: *Character, Object and Effects of Trades' Unions, with Some Remarks on the Law Concerning Them,* London, 1834.

Anon. [Hayward; Abraham?]: *Report of the Proceedings before the Judges, as Visitors of the Inns of Court, on the Appeal of A. Hayward, Esq., Q.C.,* London, 1848. [Middle Temple Library, London.]

Anon: *To the Married of Both Sexes* [1823?]. [A leaflet kept in vol. 61 of the 'Francis Place Papers,' in the British Museum.]

Anon.: *To the Married of Both Sexes in Genteel Life* [1823?]. [Vol. 61 of the 'Francis Place Papers'.]

Anon.: *To the Married of Both Sexes of the Working People* [1823?]. [Vol. 61 of the 'Francis Place Papers'.]

Archibald, G.C.: 'The State of Economic Science,' *British Journal for the Philosophy of Science,* X, 37, May, 1959.

Ashley, W.J.: 'Introduction' to J.S. Mill, *The Principles of Political Economy,* London, 1909.

Ashton, T.S.: 'The Treatment of Capitalism by Historians,' in F. Hayek, ed., *Capitalism and the Historian,* 33-63, London, 1954.

[Austin, J.]: 'Centralization', *Edinburgh Review,* LXXXV, April 1847, 221-58.

Austin, J.: *The Province of Jurisprudence Determined,* London, 1832. [Published together with 'The Uses of the Study of Jurisprudence,' with an introduction by H.A.L. Hart, London, 1954.]

Bagehot, Walter: *Lombard Street,* London, 1873.

Bagehot, W.: *The English Constitution* [1867], London, 1963.

Bagehot, W.: *The Postulates of English Political Economy* [Introd. by Alfred Marshall], London, 1885.

[Bagehot, W.] 'Principles of Political Economy,' *The Prospective Review,* IV, 16, 1848, 460-502.

Bain, Alexander: *James Mill, a Biography,* London, 1882.

Bain, A.: *John Stuart Mill, A criticism; with personal recollections,* London, 1882.

Baumol, W.J.: *Economic Dynamics. An Introduction,* New York, 1954.

Baumol, W.J.: *Welfare Economics and the Theory of the State*, London, 1952.

Beer, M.: *A History of British Socialism*, London, 1940 [1st ed., 1919-20].

Beesly, E.S.: 'Circulars of the Executive Council of the Amalgamated Society', *The Operative* (London), 29 November 1851.

[Beesly, E.S.]: 'Trades' Unions,' *Westminster Rev.*, October, 1861, 510-42.

[Bentham, Jeremy]: *Constitutional Code; for the Use of all Nations and all Governments professing Liberal Opinions*, Vol. I, London, 1830. [This work only appeared in its complete form in *Works*, ed. by J. Bowring, IX, 1-662.]

Bentham, J.: 'Defence of a Maximum containing... Hints respecting the Selection of Radical Remedies against Dearth and Scarcity' [1801]. [MS. first published in *Jeremy Bentham's Economic Writings*, W. Stark ed., III, 247-302.]

[Bentham, J.]: *Defence of Usury; Shewing the Impolicy of the Present Legal Restraints on the Terms of Pecuniary Bargains in a Series of Letters to a Friend to which is added a letter to Adam Smith, Esq., LL.D. on the Discouragements opposed by the above Restraint to the Progress of Inventive Industry* [London], 1787. [Later published under his name, and then reprinted in *Jeremy Bentham's Economic Writings*, ed. W. Stark, 121-207.]

Bentham, J.: *Economic Writings*, a critical edition based on his printed works and unprinted manuscripts, ed. W. Stark, 3 vols., London, 1952-4.

[Bentham, J.]: *Emancipate your Colonies! addressed to the National Convention of France, Anno 1793. Shewing the uselessness and mischievousness of distant dependencies to an European State*, London, 1830. [This is the second edition of *J.B. to the National Convention of France*, London, 1793. Repr. in *Works*, ed. J. Bowring, 407-18.]

[Bentham, J.]: *A Fragment on Government; being an examination of what is delivered, on the subject of Government in General in the Introduction to Sir William Blackstone's Commentaries*, London, 1776. [Repr. in *Works*, ed. J. Bowring, I, 221-95.]

Bentham, J.: 'Manual of Political Economy' [1793-95]. [MS. edited in *Jeremy Bentham's Economic Writings*, ed. W. Stark, I, 219-73.]

Bentham, J.: 'Method and Leading Features of an INSTITUTE OF POLITICAL ECONOMY (Including Finance) considered not only as a Science but as an Art,' [1801-4]. [MS. ed. W. Stark in *J. Bentham's Economic Writings*, III, 303-80.]

[Bentham, J.]: *An Introduction to the Principles of Morals and Legislation*, printed in the year 1780 and now first published, London 1798. [Republished later under his name. Also in *Works*, ed. by J. Bowring, I, 1 ff.]

[Bentham, J.]: *Panopticon; or the Inspection House: containing the idea of a new principle of construction applicable to any sort of establishment in which persons of any description are to be kept under inspection; and in particular to Penitentiary-houses, Prisons, Houses of Industry, Work-houses, Poor Houses, Manufactories, Madhouses, Lazarettos, Hospitals, and Schools... written in the year 1787*, London, 1791. [Bentham dealt with the subject in other publications.]

Bentham, J.: *The Rationale of Judicial Evidence*, ed. J.S. Mill, 5 vols., London, 1827.

Bentham, J.: *Supply without Burden; or Escheat vice Taxation: being a Proposal for a Saving in Taxes by an Extension of the Law of Escheat: including Strictures on the Taxes on Collateral Succession, comprized in the Budget of the 7th December 1795*, London, 1795. [Repr. in *J. Bentham's Economic Writings*, W. Stark, I, 279-367.]

Bentham, J.: *Traités de Législation Civile et Pénale. Précédés de Principes généraux de Législation, et d'une Vue d'un Corps complet de Droit: terminés par un Essai sur influence des Tems et des Lieux relativement aux Lois. Par Mr. Jérémie Bentham, jurisconsulte anglois. Publiés en François par Et. Dumont, de Genève, d'après les Manuscrits confiés par l'Auteur. A Paris... An X.= MDCÇCII* [2nd. ed. 1820.]

Bentham, J.: *The Works of —*, published under the superintendance of his executor, J. Bowring, 11 vols., Edinburgh, 1839-43.

Berlin, I.: *Two Concepts of Liberty*, Oxford, 1958.

Bernstein, E.: *Evolutionary Socialism*, trans. into English by Edith C. Harvey, London, 1909. [German ed., 1899.]

Blake, William: *Observations on the Effects Produced by the Expenditure of the Government during the Restriction of Cash Payments*, London, 1823.

Blanc, Louis: *L'organisation du travail*, Paris, 1839.

Blaug, Mark: *Economic Theory in Retrospect*, Homewood, Illinois, 1962. [2nd ed., 1968.]

Blaug, M.: *Ricardian Economics. A historical study*, New Haven, 1958.

Block, M.: *Les progres de la science économique depuis Adam Smith. Révision des doctrines économiques*, Paris, 1890.

Bottomore, T.B.: *Elites and Society*, London, 1964.

Bowley, Marian: *Nassau Senior and Classical Economics*, London, 1937.

Bradlaugh, Ch.: *Elements of Social Science* [London?, 1870?]

Brebner, J. Bartlet: 'Laissez Faire and State Intervention in Nineteenth Century Britain,' *The Tasks of Economic History* (Suppt. VIII to the *Journal of Economic History*, (1948) 59-73.]

[Bullion Report[: *Report, together with Minutes of Evidence and Accounts, from the Select Committee appointed [by the House of Commons] to inquire into the cause of the High Price of Gold Bullion... 1810.*

Bulwer, Edward Lytton: *England and the English*, London, 1833.

Bunge, N.K.: 'J.S. Mill envisagé comme économiste,' [1868] *Esquisse de Litterature politico-economique* [1st Russian ed. 1895], Basle, 1898.

Burns, J.H.: 'J.S. Mill and Democracy, 1829-1861,' *Political Studies*, V, 2 and 3, June and October 1957, 158-75 and 281-94.

Cabet, Etienne. *Voyage en Icarie, roman philosophique et social* 2nd ed. Paris, 1842.

Cairnes, J.E.: 'His Work in Political Economy,' in *J.S. Mill: Notice of his Life and Work... Reprinted from the Examiner*, 47-52, London, 1873.

Cairnes, J.E.: *Some Leading Principles of Political Economy newly expounded*, London, 1874.

Cannan, E.: *A History of the Theories of Production and Distribution in English Political Economy from 1776 to 1848* [1898], 3rd ed. London, 1953.

Caritat, Marie (Marquis de Condorcet): *Esquisse d'un tableau historique des progrès de l'esprit humain*, Paris, 1794.

[Carlile, R.]: 'What is Love?' *The Republican*, 5 May 1825. [Corrected and enlarged and published as a pamphlet in February 1826, under the title: *Every Woman's Book; or, What is Love? Containing most important instructions for the prudent regulation of the Principle of Love, and the number of a family*. The copy I have used is dated 1838: 'London. Printed and Published by A. Carlile, Water Lane, Fleet St.']

Carlyle, Thomas: *Letters of – to John Stuart Mill, John Sterling, and Robert Browning,* ed. A. Carlyle, London, 1923.

[Carlyle, T.] : 'Occasional Discourse on the Negro Question,' *Fraser's Magazine,* XL, December, 1849, 670-9. [Reprinted, with some additions, in book form, London, 1853.]

Carlyle, T.: *Past and Present,* London, 1843.

Carr, E.H.: *What is History?* [1961], Pelican Books, London, 1964.

[Chadwick, E.] : The Poor Law Commission, *Report on the Sanitary Condition of the Labouring Population of Great Britain,* London, 1842.

Christie, W.D.: *J.S. Mill and Mr Abraham Hayward, Q.C.; a Reply about Mill to a Letter to the Rev. Stopford Brooke, privately circulated and actually published. By –,* London, 1873.

Cole, G.D.H.: *A History of Socialist Thought,* Vol. I. *The Forerunners 1789-1850,* London, 1953; Vol. II: *Marxism and Anarchism, 1850-1890,* London, 1954.

Cole, G.D.H. and Postgate, R.W.: *The Common People, 1746-1938,* London, 1938.

Cole, Margaret (née Postgate): *Makers of the Labour Movement,* London, 1948.

Colville, A. and Temperley, H. (eds.): *Studies in Anglo-French History* [article by E. Halévy, 'English Public Opinion and the French Revolutions of the Nineteenth Century'], Cambridge, 1935.

Comte, A.: *Lettres inédites de J.S. Mill à A. Comte, publiées avec les réponses de Comte et une introduction,* par L. Lévy-Bruhl, Paris, 1889.

Comte, A.: *Cours de Philosophie Positive.* [1830-42]. 4th ed. by E. Littré, Paris, 1877.

Comte, A.: *Système de politique positive* [In collaboration with Saint-Simon], Paris, 1824.

Corry, B.A.: *Money, Saving, and Investment in English Economics, 1800-1850,* New York, 1962.

Cossa, L.: *Introduzione allo studio dell'economia politica* [1876], 3rd ed., Milan 1892. Translated by W.S. Jevons as *Guide to the Study of Political Economy...* [with a preface by Jevons], London, 1880.

[Crombie, A.] : *The Strike, or a Dialogue between Andrew Plowman and John Treadle,* London, 1834.

Crossman, R.H.S.: Introduction to Bagehot, *The English Constitution,* London, 1963.

Dalton, H.: *Some Aspects of the Inequality of Incomes in Modern Communities*, London, 1920.

Dicey, A.V.: *Lectures on the Relation between Law and Public Opinion in England during the Nineteenth Century*, London-New York, 1905.

Dunning, T.J.: *Trades' Unions and Strikes, their Philosophy and Intention*, London, 1860. [2nd ed., revised, London, 1873.]

Eccarius, J.G.: 'A Working Man's Refutation of Some Points of Political Economy, endorsed and advocated by J.S. Mill, Esq., M.P.', *The Commonwealth* (London), 10 November 1866 to 31 March 1867. [Repr. under the title *Eines Arbeiters Widerlegung der national-ökonomischen Lehren J.S. Mills*, Berlin, 1869.]

Economist, The: 'Midsummer Sermon. Group attitudes to work in industrial societies can be quite irrational,' 20 June 1964, p.1324.

Economist, The: 'Newspaper Copyright,' 28 April 1855, pp.448-9.

Economist, The: 'Regulation of the Supply of Water,' 19 January 1850, pp.61-2.

Economist, The: 'Shall the State Educate the People?' 3 April 1847, pp.379-81 [by T. Hodgskin].

F.Y.E. [Edgeworth, F.Y.] : 'John Stuart Mill,' *Palgrave's Dictionary of Political Economy*, ed. by H.G. Higgs, London, 1923.

Ely, R.T.: *The Past and Present of Political Economy*, Baltimore, 1884.

Examiner, The: 'Sentimental Socialism,' 28 January 1854, p.51.

Examiner, The: 'The Socialist Conference at the Society of Arts,' 4 February 1854, p.68.

Examiner, The (ed. H.R. Fox-Bourne): *J.S. Mill: Notices of his Life and Works. Together with two papers written by him on the Land Question*. Reprinted from –, London, 1873.

Falconer, Th.: *Note upon a Paper Circulated by Abraham Hayward, Esq., of the Inner Temple, one of Her Majesty's Counsel* [London], 14 July 1845.

Fawcett, H.: *The Economic Position of the British Labourer*, Cambridge, 1865.

Fawcett, H.: 'Strikes: their Tendencies and Remedies,' *Westminster Rev.*, N.S., XVIII, July, 1860, 297 ff.

Feuer, L.S.: 'J.S. Mill and Marxian Socialism', *Journal of the History of Ideas*, X, April, 1949, 297-303.

Field, J.A.: 'The Early Propagandist Movement in English

Population Theory,' in *Essays on Population*, Chicago, Ill., 1931.

Finer, S.E.: *The Life and Times of Sir Edwin Chadwick*, London, 1952.

Fourier, F.C.M.: *Oeuvres Complètes*, 6 vols., Paris, 2nd. ed., 1841-5.

Froude, J.A.: *Thomas Carlyle: A History of his life in London, 1834-1881*, London, 1884.

Gide, C. and Rist, C.: *A History of Economic Doctrines*, [Paris, 1908] London, 1961. [Translation, London, 1915.]

Godwin, William: *An Enquiry Concerning Political Justice and its influence on general virtues and happiness*, London, 1793 [2nd ed. 1796.]

Gonnard, R.: *Histoire des doctrines économiques*, 4th ed., Paris, 1943.

Gordon, S.: 'The London Economist and the High Tide of Laissez Faire,' *Journal of Political Economy*, LXIII, 6, December, 1955, 461-88.

Grampp, W.D.: *The Manchester School of Economics*, London, 1960.

Grant, Sir, A. (ed.): *Recess Studies* [containing J. Stirling's 'J.S. Mill on Trade Unions'], Edinburgh, 1870.

[Grote, George]: 'J.S. Mill's Principles of Political Economy,' *The Spectator*, 13 May 1848, 467-9.

Halévy, E.: 'English Public Opinion and the French Revolutions of the 19th Century,' in *Studies in Anglo-French History*, ed. by A. Colville and H. Temperley, 51-60, Cambridge, 1935.

Halévy, E.: *L'ère des tyrannies: études sur le socialisme et la guerre*, Paris, 1938.

Halévy, E.: *The Growth of Philosophic Radicalism* [1st French ed., 1901-4], trans. Mary Morris [with a bibliography by C.W. Everett], 2nd ed., London, 1952.

Halévy, E.: *A History of the English People in the Nineteenth Century* [1st French ed., 1913-32], trans. E.I. Watkin and D.A. Barker, London, revised 1949-52.

Halévy, E.: *Thomas Hodgskin, 1781-1869* [1st French ed. 1903], London, 1956.

Hamburger, J.: *James Mill and the Art of Revolution*, New Haven and London, 1963.

Hamburger, J.: *Intellectuals in Politics. John Stuart Mill and the Philosophic Radicals*, New Haven and London, 1965.

[Handloom Weavers Report]: *Report of the Commission on the Distress of the Handloom Weavers, British Parliamentary*

Papers, 1841, X. [Mainly by N.W. Senior.]

Harris, A.L.: *Economics and Social Reform,* New York, 1958.

Harris, A.L.: 'J.S. Mill on Monopoly and Socialism,' *Journal of Political Economy,* LXVII, December, 1959, 604-11.

Harrison, Frederic: [Letter on the builders' strike in] *The Daily News,* 1 August 1861, p.3, cols. 4-6.

Oedipus [Haslam?] : *The Marriage Problem* [Dublin?] , 1867.

Hayek, F.A.: *The Constitution of Liberty,* London, 1960.

Hayek, F.A. (ed.): *John Stuart Mill and Harriet Taylor, Their friendship and subsequent marriage,* Chicago, 1951.

[Hayward, A.] : *The Ballot for Benchers, by a Templar* [Printed privately in] London, 1848.

The author of 'John Stuart Mill' in the 'Times' [Hayward, Abraham] : *Letter to Stopford Augustus Brooke* [London, 1873].

Hayward, A.: *On the Origin and History of the Benchers of the Inns of Court,* London, 1848.

Hicks, J.R.: *The Theory of Wages,* 2nd Edition, London, 1963.

Himes, N.E.: 'The Birth Control Handbills of 1823,' *The Lancet,* 6 August 1927, 313.

Himes, N.E.: 'J.S. Mill's attitude towards Neo-Malthusianism,' *Economic Journal, Economic History Suppt.* No. 4, 1929, 457-84.

Himes, N.E.: 'The Place of J.S. Mill and R. Owen in the History of English Neo-Malthusianism,' *Quarterly Journal of Economics,* XLII, 3, August, 1929, 627-40.

[Hodgskin, Thomas] : 'Literature. The Principles of Political Economy,' *The Economist,* 27 May 1848, 603-4.

[Hodgskin, T.] : 'Shall the State Educate The People?' in *The Economist,* 3 April 1847, p.379-81.

Hollander, S.: 'The Role of Fixed Technical Coefficients in the Evolution of the Wages Fund Controversy, *Oxford Economic Papers,* NS., XX, 3, August 1968, 320-41.

Holyoake, G.I.: *J.S. Mill as some of the Working Classes Knew Him... An answer to a letter circulated by 'The author of the article in "The Times" on Mr Mill's death,'* London, 1873.

Humboldt, Carl Wilhelm von —: *The Sphere and Duties of Government* [1st ed. in German, 1851], trans. J. Cailhard, London, 1854.

Hutchison, T.W.: *A Review of Economic Doctrines 1870-1929,* Oxford, 1953.

Ingram, J.K.: *A History of Political Economy*, Edinburgh, 1888.

Ion [Pseudonym]: 'Some Consequences Reconsidered,' *The Leader*, 27 July 1850, p.416.

Jevons, W.S.: *The Theory of Political Economy*, London, 1871.

Johnson, H.G.: 'Demand for Commodities is *not* Demand for Labour,' in *Economic Journal*, LIX, 236, December, 1949, 531-6.

Keynes, J.M.: *The End of Laissez-Faire*, London, 1936.

Kinloch, T.F.: *Six English Economists*, London, 1928.

Knight, F.: 'The Ricardian Theory of Production and Distribution,' [1935], *On the History and Methods of Economics. Selected Essays*, 37-88, Chicago, 1956.

Kubitz, O.A.: *The Development of J.S. Mill's System of Logic*, Univ. of Illinois, 1932. [Illinois Studies in the Social Science, vol. 18, no 1, ii.]

Land Tenure Reform Association: *Programme. With an Explanatory Statement by J.S. Mill*, London, 1871.

Land Tenure Reform Association: *Report of the Inaugural Public Meeting of the –, Monday, 15 May, 1871. Mr J.S. Mill in the Chair*, London, 1871.

Lavelèye, E. (Baron de): *Lettres inédites de John Stuart Mill... (Extract from the Revue de Belgique)*, Brussels-Paris, 1885.

Lekachman, R.K.: *History of Economic Ideas*, New York, 1959.

Levi, A.W.: 'The Mental Crisis of John Stuart Mill' in *Psychoanalytic Rev.*, XXXII, January 1945, 86-101.

Link, R.C.: *English Theories of Economic Fluctuations, 1815-1848*, New York, 1959.

Lipson, E.: *A Planned Economy or Free Enterprise. The lessons of History*, London, 1944.

Locke, John: 'Second Treatise of Civil Government,' in *Two Treatises of Government* [1690], ed. by T.I. Cooke, New York, 1947.

Longe, F.D.: *A Critical Examination of Mr. George's 'Progress and Poverty' and Mr Mill's Theory of Wages*, London, 1883.

Longfield, M.: *Lectures on Political Economy*, Dublin, 1834.

Lowenthal, Esther: *The Ricardian Socialists*, New York, 1911.

Macaulay, T.B.: 'The People's Charter,' *The Works of Lord –, complete*, VIII, London, 1879.

[Macaulay, T.B.]: 'Mr [James] Mill's Essay on Government,' *Edinburgh Review*, XLIX, March, 1829, 159-89. [Repr. vol. I of *Miscellaneous Writings,* London, 1880.]

McCleary, G.F.: *The Malthusian Population Theory,* London, 1953.

[McCulloch, J.R.] : 'Combination Laws – Restraints on Emigration,' *Edinburgh Review,* XXXIX, Jan., 1824, 315-45.

J.R.M.C. [McCulloch, J.R.] : *An Essay on the Circumstances which Determine the Rate of Wages, and the Condition of the Labouring Classes,* Edinburgh, 1826. [Rev. ed. of 1824 article.]

[McCulloch, J.R.] : 'Taxation,' *Supplement to the Encyclopaedia Britannica,* Edinburgh, 1824.

McDonagh, Oliver: 'The Nineteenth Century Revolution in Government,' *Historical Journal,* I, 1, 1958, 52-67.

Mack, Mary P.: *Jeremy Bentham, an Odyssey of Ideas. 1748-1792,* London, 1962.

Mallet, J.L.: 'Diaries,' in Political Economy Club, *Proceedings,* VI, London, 1921.

[Malthus, T.R.] : *An Essay on the Principle of Population as it affects the Future Improvement of Society, with Remarks on the Speculations of Mr Godwin, M. Condorcet, and other Writers,* London, 1798.

Malthus, T.R.: *An Essay on the Principle of Population, or a View of its Past and Present Effects on Human Happiness, with an Inquiry into our Prospects respecting the Future Removal or Mitigation of the Evils which it occasions,* London, 1803.

[Malthus, T.R.] : 'Political Economy' [a review of the article 'Political Economy,' *Supplement to the Encyclopaedia Britannica,* 1824, by J.R. McCulloch], *Quarterly Review,* XXX, January 1824, 297-334.

Malthus, T.R.: *Principles of Political Economy considered with a view to their Practical Application,* London, 1820.

Markham, F.M.H.: 'Introduction' to: H., Comte de Saint-Simon, *Selected Writings,* Oxford, 1952.

Marshall, Alfred: 'The Future of the Working Classes' [Read to the Cambridge Reform Club in 1873]. *Memorials of Alfred Marshall,* ed. by A.C. Pigou, London, 1925.

Marshall, A.: *Industry and Trade,* London, 1919.

Marshall, A.: *Principles of Economics* [1st ed. 1890], 8th ed. London, 1920.

Marshall, T.H.: Lectures on the Extension of Citizenship, London, *Citizenship and Social Class and Other Essays,* London, 1950.

Martineau, Harriet: *Illustrations of Political Economy,* London, 1832-4, Vol. III, *A Manchester Strike* (1832).

Martineau, Harriet: *The Turn-out: or, Patience the Best Policy,* London, 1829.

Marx, Karl: *Address and Provisional Rules of the Working Men's International Association.* (1864) Repr. in Karl Marx, *Selected Works... Prepared by the Marx-Engels-Lenin Institute, Moscow,* vol. II, London, 1942.

Marx. K.: *Capital, a Critique of Political Economy,* vol. I, *The Progress of Capitalist Production,* 2nd ed. of the English trans. Chicago, 1915.

Marx, K.: *Le dix-huit Brumaire de Louis Napoléon Bonaparte* [1852], Lille, 1891.

Marx, K.: '3ème partie: de Ricardo a l'économie vulgaire,' *Histoire des doctrines économiques, Oeuvres complètes,* trans. J. Molitor, Paris, 1924-5.

Marx, K. and Engels, F.: *Manifesto of the Communist Party* [1848], trans. Samuel Moore, 1888, Moscow, n.d.

Marx, K. and Engels, F.: *Marx and Engels on Malthus,* eds. D.L. and R.L. Meek, London, 1953.

Meek, R.L.: 'The Decline of Ricardian Economics in England,' *Economics and Ideology and other Essays,* London, 1967.

Mill, Anna J.: 'Some Notes on Mill's Early Friendship with Henry Cole,' *Mill News Letter,* IV, 1 (Spring 1969), 6.

Mill, James.: *Analysis of the Phenomena of the Human Mind. [1829] A new edition with notes... by Alexander Bain, Andrew Findlater, and George Grote. Edited... by J.S. Mill,* London, 1869.

[Mill, James]: [Articles on] 'Banks of Savings,' 'Beggars,' 'Benefit Societies,' 'Colonies,' 'Government,' [etc.] *Supplement to the... Encyclopaedia Britannica,* Edinburgh, 1824.

P.Q. [Mill, James]: 'The Church and its Reform,' *London Review,* I, 2, April-July, 1835, 257-95.

Mill, James: *Commerce Defended. An answer to the arguments by which Mr Spence, Mr Cobbett, and others have attempted to prove that commerce is not a source of national wealth,* London, 1808.

Mill, James: *Elements of Political Economy,* London, 1821. [2nd ed., London, 1824; 3rd ed., London, 1826.]

Mill, James: *Essays on 1. Government. 2. Jurisprudence. 3. Liberty of the Press. 4. Prisons and Prison Discipline. 5. Colonies. 6. Law of Nations. 7. Education... Reprinted... from the Supplement to the Encyclopaedia Britannica* [1828.]

Mill, James: *History of British India*, London, 1817.

Mishan, E.J.: *The Costs of Economic Growth*, London, 1967.

[Moore, Th.]: 'Ode to the Goddess Ceres,' and 'Ode to the Sublime Porte,' in *Odes upon Cash, Corn, Catholics, and other matters*, London, 1828. [Reprints of satirical poems that appeared in the *Times*.]

Morley, John: *The Life of W.E. Gladstone*, London-New York, 1903.

Mueller, Iris: *John Stuart Mill and French Thought*, Urbana, Ill., 1965.

Myint, Hla: *Theories of Welfare Economics*, London, 1948.

Myrdal, G.: *The Political Element in the Development of Economic Theory*, trans. from the German by Paul Streeten, London, 1963.

Napier, MacVey: *Selections from the Correspondence of... MacVey Napier* [ed. M. Napier], London, 1879.

Neate, Charles: *Remarks on a Late Decision of the Judges as Visitors of the Inns of Court*, London, 1848 [lost in British Museum bombing.]

Nesbitt, G.: *Benthamite Reviewing. The First Twelve Years of the Westminster Review (1824-1836)*, New York, 1934.

Newman, F.W.: *Lectures on Political Economy*, London, 1851.

[Northcote, Stafford and Trevelyan, Charles]: 'The Organization of the Permanent Civil Service,' *British Parliamentary Papers*, 23 November 1853. [1854, XXVII, 1.]

O'Brien, D.P.: *J.R. McCulloch*, London, 1970.

Olivier, S.: 'J.S. Mill and Socialism,' *Today*, N.S., II, 1884, 490-504.

Operative, The: 'Circulars of the Executive Council of the Amalgamated Society of Engineers,' 29 November, 1851, 173-5.

Packe, M.St.J.: *The Life of John Stuart Mill*, London, 1954.

Palgrave's Dictionary of Political Economy, ed. by H. Higgs [1894-9], London, 1923.

Pankhurst, R.: *The St. Simonians, Mill, and Carlyle*, London, 1957.

Pigou, A.C.: 'Mill and the Wages Fund,' in *Economic Journal*, LIX, 234, June, 1949, 171-80.

Pigou, A.C.: *The Policy of Land Taxation*, London. 1909.

Pike, D.: *Paradise of Dissent. South Australia, 1829-1857*, London-Adelaide, 1957.

[Place, Francis?]: 'The Distress of the Mass of the People. Causes and Remedies,' *The Black Dwarf,* XI, 21, 19 November, 1823.

Place, Francis: *Illustrations and Proofs of the Principle of Population: including an examination of the proposed remedies of Mr Malthus* [1822], ed. N.E. Himes, London, 1930.

Popper, K.R.: *The Logic of Scientific Discovery,* London, 1959.

Popper, K.R.: *The Poverty of Historicism,* London, 1957.

Prevost, J.L.: 'Diaries,' *Proceedings of the Political Economy Club,* VI, London, 1921.

Rae, John: *Contemporary Socialism,* London, 1884.

Rambaud, J.: *Histoire des doctrines économiques,* Paris, 1899.

Ratzlaff, C.S.: 'Economic Control in the Nineteenth Century,' *Planned Society,* ed. Findlay Mackenzie, New York, 1937.

Report of the Proceedings before the Judges as Visitors of the Inns of Court, on the Appeal of A. Hayward, Esq., Q.C. London, 1848. [To be found at the Middle Temple Library, London.]

'Report from the Select Committee on Investments for the Savings of the Middle and Working Classes,' *British Parliamentary Papers,* 1850 (508), XIX, 169.

'Report from the Select Committee appointed to inquire into the cause of the high price of Gold Bullion, and to take into consideration the State of the Circulating Medium, and of the Exchange between Great Britain and Foreign parts', *British Parliamentary Papers,* 1810 (349), III, 1.

'Report from the [Royal] Commission... for Inquiring into the Condition of the Unemployed Handloom Weavers in the United Kingdom', *British Parliamentary Papers,* 1841 (296), X, 273.

Reybaud, Louis: *Economistes modernes... J.S. Mill, [etc.]* [Repr. from the *Revue des deux Mondes,* 1 April 1855], Paris, 1862.

Ricardo, D.: *An Essay on the Influence of a Low Price of Corn on the Profits of Stock* [1815], *Works,* IV.

Ricardo, D.: *Plan for the Establishment of a National Bank.* [1823], *Works,* IV.

Ricardo, D.: *On the Principles of Political Economy and Taxation,* [1st ed., 1817; 2nd ed. 1819; 3rd ed., 1821]. *Works,* I.

Ricardo, D.: *On Protection to Agriculture* [1822], *Works,* IV.

Ricardo, D.: *The Works and Correspondence of David Ricardo,* ed. by P. Sraffa in collaboration with Maurice Dobb, 10 vols., London, 1951-5.

Robbins, Lionel: *The Economist in the Twentieth Century and other Lectures in Political Economy*, London, 1954.

Robbins, Lionel: *Politics and Economics*, London, 1963.

Robbins, Lionel: *Robert Torrens and the Evolution of Classical Economics*, London, 1958.

Robbins, Lionel: *The Theory of Economic Policy in English Classical Political Economy*, London, 1952.

Robinson, Joan: *Economic Philosophy*, London, 1963.

Robson, J.M.: *The Improvement of Mankind. The Social and Political Thought of John Stuart Mill*, London, 1968.

Rogin, Leo: *The Meaning and Validity of Economic Theory. A Historical Approach*, New York, 1956.

Rojo, L.A.: 'Libertad y organización económica,' *Tiempo de España*, num. 1, *Libertad y Organización*, Madrid, 1963.

Roll, Erich: *A History of Economic Thought*, 3rd ed., London, 1954.

Russell, B. and Russell, P., eds.: *The Amberley Papers*, London, 1937.

Saint-Simon, Henry, Comte de:– *Selected Writings*, ed. F.M.H. Markham, Oxford, 1952.

Samuelson, P.A.: 'Economists and the History of Ideas,' in *American Economic Review*, LII, 1, March, 1962, 1-18.

Saville, J.: 'The Christian Socialists of 1848,' *Democracy and the Labour Movement*, ed. J. Saville, 149 ff., London, 1954.

Say, J.B.: *Traité d'économie politique: ou simple exposition de la manière dont se forment, se distribuent, et se consomment les richesses*, Paris, Year XI [1803].

Sayers, R.S.: 'Ricardo's Views on Monetary Questions' [1953], *Papers in English Monetary History*, ed. Ashton, T.S., London, 1964.

Schapiro, J.S.: 'J.S. Mill, Pioneer of Democratic Liberalism in England,' *Journal of the History of Ideas*, IV, 1943, 127-60.

Schapiro, J.S.: 'Comment,' in *Journal of the History of Ideas*, X, 1949, 303-4.

Schumpeter, J.A.: *History of Economic Analysis*, London, 1954.

Schwartz, Pedro: 'John Stuart Mill and Laissez Faire: London Water,' *Economica*, N.S., XXXIII, 129, February, 1966, 71-83.

Senior, N.W.: *Course of Lectures Delivered at the University of Oxford in the Years 1848-1849*.

Senior, N.W.: *Industrial Efficiency and Social Economy*, ed. S. Levy, London, 1929.

Senior, N.W.: 'An Introductory Lecture on Political Economy...' [London, 1827], *Selected Writings on Economics by Nassau W. Senior,* New York [A.M. Kelly], 1966.

Senior, N.W.: 'Mill, The Principles of Political Economy,' *Edinburgh Review,* LXXXVIII, October, 1848, 293-339.

Senior, N.W.: *Three Lectures on the Cost of Obtaining Money,* London, 1830.

Senior, N.W. [chief editor]: 'Report of the Commission on the Distress of the Handloom Weavers,' *British Parliamentary Papers,* 1841, X.

Shonfield, A.: *Modern Capitalism, The Changing Balance of Public and Private Power,* London, 1965.

Smellie, K.B.: *A Hundred Years of English Government,* 2nd ed. London, 1950.

Smith, A.: *The Wealth of Nations,* ed. by E. Cannan, London, 1904.

Spengler, J.J.: 'J.S. Mill on Economic Development,' in *Theories of Economic Growth,* ed. B.F. Hoselitz, Glencoe, Ill., 1960.

W.A. Sr. [Spooner, Rev. W.A.] : 'Wages Fund,' *Palgrave's Dictionary of Political Economy* [1899], ed. H. Higgs, London, 1926.

Sraffa, Piero: Editorial comments on Ricardo's *Works and Correspondence.*

Stamp, C.G.: 'The Incidence of Increment Duties,' in *Economic Journal,* XXIII, June, 1913, 194-205.

Stephen, James Fitzjames: *Liberty, Equality, Fraternity,* London, 1873.

Stephen, Leslie: *The English Utilitarians,* Vol. III, *John Stuart Mill,* London, 1900.

Stephen, L. (ed.): *The Dictionary of National Biography,* London, 1885.

Stigler, G.J.: 'The Nature and Role of Originality in Scientific Progress' [1955], *Essays in the History of Economics,* Chicago, 1965.

Stigler, G.J.: 'The Ricardian Theory of Value and Distribution' [1952], *Essays in the History of Economics,* Chicago, 1965.

Stigler, G.J.: 'Ricardo and the 93 Per Cent Labor Theory of Value' [1958], *Essays in the History of Economics,* Chicago, 1965.

Stillinger, J.: 'Introduction' to the *Early Draft of John Stuart Mill's Autobiography,* Urbana, 1961.

Stillinger, J.: 'The Text of J.S. Mill's Autobiography,' in *Bulletin of the John Ryland Library,* XLIII, 1, 1960, 220-42.

Stirling, J.: 'J.S. Mill on Trade Unions,' in *Recess Studies*, ed. Sir A. Grant, Edinburgh, 1870.

Talmon, J.L.: *Political Messianism: the Romantic Phase*, London, 1960.

Taussig, F.W.: *Wages and Capital. An Examination of the Wages Fund Doctrine*, New York, 1896.

Tawney, R.: *Equality* [1931], London, 1952.

Thiers, L.A.: *De la Propriété*, Paris, 1848.

Thompson, Thomas Perronet: *A Catechism on the Corn Laws: with a List of Fallacies and the Answers*, London [2nd ed.] , 1827.

Thornton, Henry: *An Enquiry into the Nature and Effects of the Credit of Great Britain*, London, 1802.

Thornton, W.T.: 'His Career at India House,' *J.S. Mill. Notices of His Life and Works... reprinted from the Examiner*, London, 1873.

Thornton, W.T.: *On Labour: its wrongful claims and rightful dues: its actual present and possible future*, London, 1869. [Reprints articles from the *Fortnightly Review* from May to December, 1867.]

Thornton, W.T.: *Over Population and its Remedy: or an enquiry into the extent and causes of the distress prevailing among the labouring classes*, London, 1846.

Thornton, W.T.: *Plea for Peasant Prorietors: with the outlines of a plan for their establishment in Ireland*, London, 1848.

Tocqueville, A., Comte Clérel de: *Oeuvres, papiers, et correspondances*, ed. J.P. Mayer, Paris, 1951.

Torrens, R.: 'A Paper on the Means of Reducing the Poors Rates and of Affording Effectual and Permanent Relief to the Labouring Classes,' *The Pamphleteer*, X, 1817, 509-28.

Torrens, R.: *On Wages and Combinations*, London, 1834.

Torrens, R.: *Reply to the Objections of the Westminster Review to the Government Plan for the Regulation of the Currency*, London, 1844.

Tucker, G.S.L.: *Progress and Profits in British Economic Thought. 1650-1850*, Cambridge, 1960.

Tufnell, E.C.: *Character, Object and Effects of Trades' Unions: with Some Remarks on the Law concerning them*, London, 1834.

Viner, J.: 'Adam Smith and Laissez Faire'; chapter V of *Adam Smith 1776-1926; Lectures to Commemorate the Sesquicentennial of the Publication of the Wealth of Nations*, by J.M. Clark and others, Chicago, 1928.

Viner, J.: 'Bentham and J.S. Mill: the Utilitarian Background,' in *American Economic Review,* XXXIX, 2, March 1949, 360-82.

Viner, J.: *Studies in the Theory of International Trade,* London, 1937.

Wakefield, E.G.: *England and America,* London, 1833.

Wakefield, E.G.: *A Letter from Sydney and other Writings on Colonization,* [1834], London and Toronto, 1929.

Wallas, Graham: *Human Nature in Politics,* London, 1908.

Wallas, G.: *The Life of Francis Place,* London, 1898.

Webb, S.: 'Historic,' in *Fabian Essays,* ed. by Bernard Shaw, London, 1889.

Webb, S. and Webb, B.: *English Local Government,* containing *English Poor Law History,* Part II, *The Last Hundred Years,* London-New York, 1929.

Webb, S. and Webb, B.: *The History of Trade Unionism* [1920], London, 1950.

Wellesley Index to Victorian Periodicals, 1824-1900, ed. W.E. Houghton, Toronto, 1966.

Willey, B.: *Nineteenth Century Studies. Coleridge to Matthew Arnold,* London, 1949.

Wilson, E.: *To the Finland Station,* London, 1941.

Winch, D.N.: 'Classical Economics and the Case for Colonization,' *Economica,* N.S., XXX, 120 (November 1963).

Wooler, John: [Three leaders on the population question], *The Black Dwarf,* 4 December 1823, 31 December 1823, 4 February 1824. [In the Bodleian Library, Oxford.]

Young, Allyn: 'Increasing Returns and Economic Progress,' in *Economic Journal,* XXXVIII, December, 1928, 525-42.

Young, G.M.: *Victorian England, Portrait of an Age,* 2nd ed., Oxford, 1953.

Young, G.M., ed.: *Victorian Years,* Oxford Univ. Press., 1934.

Index of Persons

There is no entry under the heading 'John Stuart Mill.' since he is covered by the subject index. Reference to the notes are not to pages, but to number of note and chapter (in brackets).

Subject Index

This index covers concepts related to J.S. Mill only. There are no entries under the titles of his works. References to the notes are not to pages, but to number of note and chapter (in brackets).